Contemporary Authors

Bibliographical Series

American Poets

ISSN 0887-3070

Contemporary

Authors

Bibliographical Series

American Poets

Ronald Baughman
University of South Carolina
Editor

volume 2

A Bruccoli Clark Book
GALE RESEARCH COMPANY
BOOK TOWER
DETROIT, MICHIGAN 48226

Editorial Directors

Matthew J. Bruccoli

Richard Layman

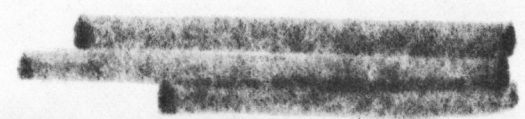

To

Charles and Mildred Smith

Judith Smith Baughman

and

Elizabeth Baughman

Contents

Plan of the Work

Contemporary Authors Bibliographical Series (CABS) is a survey of writings by and about the most important writers since World War II in the United States and abroad. *CABS* is a new key to finding and evaluating information on the lives and writings of those authors who have attracted significant critical attention.

Purpose

Designed as a companion to the long-established *Contemporary Authors* bio-bibliographical series, *CABS* is dedicated to helping students, researchers, and librarians keep pace with the already massive and constantly growing body of literary scholarship that is available for modern authors of recognized stature. While this proliferation of literary criticism has provided a rich resource, it has also presented a perplexing problem: in the face of so much material, how does one efficiently find the required information, and how does one differentiate the good from the bad?

The purpose of *CABS* is to provide a guide to the best critical studies about major writers: to identify the uses and limitations of individual critiques, and to assist the user with the study of important writers' works.

Scope

CABS will include American as well as foreign authors, in volumes arranged by genre and nationality. Some of the subjects to be covered in the series include contemporary American dramatists, contemporary British poets, and contemporary American short story writers, to cite only a selection. While there will be a concentration of volumes on American and English writers, the scope of *CABS* is world literature, and volumes are also planned on contemporary European, South American, Asian, and African writers.

Format

Each volume of *CABS* provides primary and secondary bibliographies as well as an analytical bibliographical essay for approximately ten major writers. *CABS* entries consist of three parts:

1. A primary bibliography that lists works written by the author, divided for ease of use into:

   —Books and Pamphlets

   —Selected Other: translations, books edited by the subject of the entry, other material in books in which the subject had some role short of full authorship, and important short works that appeared in periodicals, all separated by rubrics.

   —Editions, Collections

2. A secondary bibliography that lists works about the author, divided into:

   —Bibliographies and Checklists

   —Biographies

   —Interviews

   —Critical Studies, subdivided into:

       Books

       Collections of Essays

       Special Journals and Newsletters

       Articles and Book Sections

3. An analytical bibliographical essay in which the merits and the deficiencies of major critical and scholarly works are thoroughly discussed. This essay is divided into categories corresponding to those in the secondary bibliography.

Although every effort has been made to achieve consistency in the shaping of the checklists and essays included in this volume, each entry necessarily reflects the output of an author and his or her critics. Thus, if a writer has not published notebooks or translations, these rubrics or subrubrics are omitted from the primary checklist; similarly, if there is no biography or collection of essays on the author, these headings do not appear in the secondary checklist or in the essay.

CABS also contains a Critic Index, citing critics discussed in the bibliographical essays. For the convenience of researchers, this index will cumulate in all volumes after the first. Beginning with Volume 2, *CABS* will also include a cumulative Author Index, listing all the authors presented in the series.

Compilation Methods

Each *CABS* entry is written by an authority on his subject. The entries are reviewed by the volume editor—who is a specialist in the field—and the accuracy of the bibliographical details is verified at the Bruccoli Clark editorial center. Each bibliographical entry is checked whenever possible against the actual publication cited in order to avoid repeating errors in other printed bibliographies. Full citations are provided for each item to facilitate location and the use of interlibrary loans.

Unlike other study guides which are limited to a small selection of writers from earlier eras or which specialize in studies of individual authors, *CABS* is unique in providing comprehensive bibliographical information for the full spectrum of major modern authors. *CABS* is a map to the published critical appraisals of our most studied contemporary writers. It tells students and researchers what is available, and it advises them where they will find the information they seek about a writer and his works.

The publisher and the editors are pleased to provide researchers with this basic and essential service.

Preface

This volume provides a guide to works by and about eleven major poets: John Berryman, Elizabeth Bishop, James Dickey, Robert Hayden, Randall Jarrell, Robert Lowell, Howard Nemerov, Charles Olson, Theodore Roethke, Anne Sexton, and Richard Wilbur. Besides attracting extensive critical attention, the works of these writers illustrate the diversity of thought and technique in American poetry since World War II. Some of the authors included in this volume clearly belong to distinct schools of contemporary poetry, while others have pursued their own aesthetic concerns independent of literary main currents. All continue to exert considerable influence on American poetry today.

Often labeled confessional poets, Robert Lowell, John Berryman, and Anne Sexton have attracted much biographical as well as critical commentary. Chronicling the development of Lowell's reputation, Steven Gould Axelrod assesses the eighteen books on the poet that have appeared since 1962 and carefully charts the reactions presented in essays and reviews of each of Lowell's collections. Sonya Jones's entry on Berryman reflects critics' often complex views—admiring and disparaging—of the "desperate life" reflected in the poet's best work. Similarly, Diana Hume George traces the evolution in Sexton's critical reception from early ambivalent (if not overtly hostile) responses to later more balanced evaluations, often achieved through feminist readings.

Showing that Elizabeth Bishop has often been treated as a modern romantic and as a disciple of Marianne Moore, Barbara Page focuses upon critical responses to Bishop's handling of imaginative interior landscapes and documents the poet's often uncertain relationship with her feminist readers. Fred M. Fetrow, who regards Robert Hayden as a seminal figure in the growing black aesthetic movement, laments the relatively small amount of commentary on this poet's works but suggests areas for future scholarly inquiry. On the other hand, confronted by a mass of critical material on Charles Olson, Alan Golding classifies the various assessments of this complex poet/aesthetic theorist, thereby making his work and the commentary it has inspired more accessible to the general reader.

Two poets who have often been regarded as more classically formal than most of their contemporaries are Richard Wilbur and Howard Nemerov. Bruce Michelson analyzes the alternately denigrating and highly complimentary assessments of Wilbur's poetry, while also delineating his roles as translator and dramatist. Through their checklist and essay, Deborah S. Murphy and Gloria Young suggest the variety of critical responses evoked by Nemerov's multiple voices that range from the satirically comic to the deeply meditative and philosophical.

Tracing responses to Randall Jarrell's poetry, translations, criticism, and novel, Sister Bernetta Quinn draws upon her long career as a Jarrell scholar to identify central issues that have dominated the commentary on the writer's life and work. Ronald Baughman's entry on James Dickey provides an overview of the critical approaches to this poet-critic-novelist and then moves to the separate issues, themes, and technical studies that recur in the secondary material on Dickey. Treating the reception of Theodore Roethke, James R. McLeod and Judith A. Sylte identify studies focusing upon psychoanalytic theory, poetic technique, thematic currents, and philosophical or artistic influences.

Though they have had a formidable task, the authors of these entries have successfully provided order to the vast amount of critical commentary on each poet. This volume demonstrates how excellent poets attract excellent critics who increase readers' understanding of the artists' accomplishments. The scholars who have contributed to this volume are recognized authorities on their subjects, and I am honored to be associated with them.

I am indebted to Judith Smith Baughman for her careful line-editing, her constant questioning, and her unfailing support. She immeasureably improved this volume.

—Ronald Baughman
College of Applied Professional Sciences
University of South Carolina

Acknowledgments

This book was produced by Bruccoli Clark, Inc. The in-house editor was Jefferson Matthew Brook.

Art supervisor is Patricia M. Flanagan. Copyediting supervisor is Patricia Coate. Production coordinator is Kimberly Casey. Supervisor of Typography is Laura Ingram. The production staff includes Rowena Betts, Kathleen M. Flanagan, Joyce Fowler, Ellen Hassell, Pamela Haynes, Judith K. Ingle, Beatrice McClain, Judith McCray, Mary Scott Sims, Joycelyn R. Smith, James Adam Sutton, and Lucia Tarbox. Jean W. Ross is permissions editor.

Walter W. Ross and Rhonda Marshall did the library research with the assistance of the staff at the Thomas Cooper Library of the University of South Carolina: Lynn Barron, Daniel Boice, Connie Crider, Kathy Edman, Michael Freeman, Gary Geer, David L. Haggard, Jens Holley, Marcia Martin, Dana Rabon, Jean Rhyne, Jan Squire, and Ellen Tillett.

Contemporary Authors

Bibliographical Series

American Poets

John Berryman

(1914-1972)

Sonya Jones
Allegheny College

PRIMARY BIBLIOGRAPHY

Books

Twenty Poems. In *Five Young American Poets,* ed. John Ciardi. Norfolk, Conn.: New Directions, 1940. Poems.

Poems. Norfolk, Conn.: New Directions, 1942. Poems.

The Dispossessed. New York: Sloane, 1948. Poems.

Stephen Crane. New York: Sloane/London: Methuen, 1950. Biography.

Homage to Mistress Bradstreet. New York: Farrar, Straus & Cudahy, 1956.

Homage to Mistress Bradstreet And Other Poems. London: Faber & Faber, 1959; New York: Farrar, Straus & Giroux, 1968. Poems.

The Arts of Reading, by Berryman, Ralph Ross, and Allen Tate. New York: Crowell, 1960. Essays.

77 Dream Songs. New York: Farrar, Straus & Giroux/London: Faber & Faber, 1964. Poems.

Berryman's Sonnets. New York: Farrar, Straus & Giroux, 1967; London: Faber & Faber, 1968. Poems.

Short Poems. New York: Farrar, Straus & Giroux, 1967. Poems.

His Toy, His Dream, His Rest: 308 Dream Songs. New York: Farrar, Straus & Giroux, 1968; London: Faber & Faber, 1969. Poems.

The Dream Songs. New York: Farrar, Straus & Giroux, 1969. Poems.

Love & Fame. New York: Farrar, Straus & Giroux, 1970; London: Faber & Faber, 1971. Poems.

Delusions, Etc. New York: Farrar, Straus & Giroux/London: Faber & Faber, 1972. Poems.

Recovery. New York: Farrar, Straus & Giroux/London: Faber & Faber, 1973. Novel.

The Freedom of the Poet. New York: Farrar, Straus & Giroux, 1976; London: Faber & Faber, 1977. Essays.

Henry's Fate & Other Poems 1967-1972. New York: Farrar, Straus & Giroux, 1977; London: Faber & Faber, 1977. Poems.

Selected Poems

"Dream Songs," *Times Literary Supplement,* 14 Feb. 1975, p. 161.

"Posthumous Dream Songs," *New Yorker,* 19 May 1975, p. 44.

"Six Dream Songs," *Harper's,* 250 (June 1975), 68-69.

"Two Poems," *Atlantic Monthly,* 236 (Nov. 1975), 68-69.

"Posthumous Dream Song," *New Yorker,* 5 July 1976, p. 30.

Selected Essays

"The Ritual of W. B. Yeats," *Columbia Review,* 17 (May-June 1936), 26-32.

"F. Scott Fitzgerald," *Kenyon Review,* 8 (Winter 1946), 103-112.

"Lowell, Thomas, & C.," *Partisan Review,* 14 (Jan.-Feb. 1947), 73-85.

"Young Poets Dead," *Sewanee Review,* 55 (July-Sept. 1947), 504-514.

"Waiting for the End, Boys," *Partisan Review,* 15 (Feb. 1948), 254-267.

"Poetry of Ezra Pound," *Partisan Review,* 16 (Apr. 1949), 377-394.

Lewis, Matthew Gregory. *The Monk,* ed. Louis F. Peck, introduction by Berryman. New York: Grove Press, 1952, 11-28.

"Shakespeare at Thirty," *Hudson Review,* 6 (Summer 1953), 175-203.

"From the Middle and Senior Generations," *American Scholar,* 28 (Summer 1959), 384-390.

"Symposium on Robert Lowell's 'Skunk Hour.' " In *New World Writing 21,* ed. Stewart Richardson and Corlies M. Smith. New York: Lippincott, 1963, 148-155. Reprinted as "Despondency and Madness" in *The Contemporary Poet as Artist and Critic,* ed. Anthony Ostroff. Boston: Little, Brown, 1964.

Dreiser, Theodore. *The Titan,* afterword by Berryman. New York: New American Library, 1965, 503-511.

"One Answer to a Question," *Shenandoah,* 17 (Autumn 1965), 67-76. Reprinted as "Changes" in *Poets on Poetry,* ed. Howard Nemerov. New York: Basic Books, 1966.

"Stephen Crane, *The Red Badge of Courage.*" In *The American Novel: From James Fenimore Cooper to William Faulkner,* ed. Wallace Stegner. New York: Basic Books, 1965, 86-96.

"Three and a Half Years at Columbia." In *University on the Heights,* ed. Wesley First. New York: Doubleday, 1969, 51-60.

Edited Book

Nashe, Thomas. *The Unfortunate Traveller; or, The Life of Jack Wilton,*
ed. with an introduction and note by Berryman. New York:
Putnam's, 1960.

Recordings

John Berryman. Library of Congress, 13 Feb. 1948.
John Berryman. Library of Congress, 1951.
John Berryman. Library of Congress, 24 Feb. 1958.
National Poetry Festival. Library of Congress, 22-24 Oct. 1962.

Collection

Selected Poems 1938-1968. London: Faber & Faber, 1972. Poems.

SECONDARY BIBLIOGRAPHY

Bibliographies and Checklists

Arpin, Gary Q. *John Berryman: A Reference Guide.* Boston: G. K. Hall,
1976. Secondary.
Kelly, Richard J. *John Berryman: A Checklist.* Metuchen, N.J.: Scarecrow
Press, 1972. Primary and secondary.
Kelly and Ernest C. Stefanik, Jr. "John Berryman: A Supplemental
Checklist—Part I," *John Berryman Studies,* 1 (Apr. 1975), 25-35.
Primary and secondary.
_____. "John Berryman: A Supplemental Checklist—Part II,"
John Berryman Studies, 1 (July 1975), 23-31. Primary and sec-
ondary.
_____. "John Berryman: A Supplemental Checklist—Part III,"
John Berryman Studies, 2 (Winter 1976), 48-50. Primary and sec-
ondary.
Stefanik, Ernest C., Jr. *John Berryman: A Descriptive Bibliography.* Pitts-
burgh: University of Pittsburgh Press, 1974. Primary.
_____. *"John Berryman: A Descriptive Bibliography:* Addenda," *John
Berryman Studies,* 2 (Winter 1976), 38-47. Primary.

_____. "A John Berryman Checklist," *Bulletin of Bibliography*, 31 (Jan.-Mar. 1974), 1-4, 28. Primary.

Biographies: Books

Haffenden, John. *The Life of John Berryman*. Boston: Routledge & Kegan Paul, 1982.
Simpson, Eileen. *Poets In Their Youth: A Memoir*. New York: Random House, 1982.

Biographies: Major Articles and Book Sections

Aiken, Conrad. "A Letter," *Harvard Advocate*, 103 (Spring 1969), 23.
"All we fall down & die . . . ," *Minnesota Daily*, 10 Jan. 1972, p. 3.
Alvarez, A. *The Savage God: A Study of Suicide*. New York: Random House, 1972.
Barza, Steven. "About John Berryman," *Colorado Quarterly*, 26 (Autumn 1977), 51-72.
Bellow, Saul. "John Berryman, Friend," *New York Times Book Review*, 27 May 1973, pp. 1-2. Reprinted as foreword to Berryman, *Recovery*.
Bishop, Elizabeth. "Thank You Note," *Harvard Advocate*, 103 (Spring 1969), 21.
"Catholic Rites Set for Berryman," *Minneapolis Star*, 10 Jan. 1972, p. 9B.
Ciardi, John. "A Eulogy for John Berryman," *Saturday Review*, 10 May 1972, p. 48.
Close, Roy M. "Death Was a Recurring Theme in Life Work of Poet Berryman," *Minneapolis Star*, 8 Jan. 1972, p. 15A.
Cook, Bruce. "Berryman, 1914-1972: 'I Am Headed West Also,' " *National Observer*, 22 Jan. 1972, p. 21.
Cott, Jonathan. "Theodore Roethke and John Berryman; Two Dream Poets." In *On Contemporary Literature*, ed. Richard Kostelanetz. New York: Avon, 1964, 520-531.
Dodsworth, Martin. "John Berryman: An Introduction." In his *The Survival of Poetry*. London: Faber & Faber, 1970, 100-132.
Engle, Monroe. "An Educational Incident," *Harvard Advocate*, 103 (Spring 1969), 18.
Haffenden, John. "Drink as Disease: John Berryman," *Partisan Review*, 44, no. 4 (1977), 565-583. Reprinted in his *The Life of John Berryman*.

Howard, Jane. "Whiskey and Ink, Whiskey and Ink," *Life,* 21 July 1967, pp. 67-76.

Hyde, Lewis. "Alcohol & Poetry: John Berryman and the Booze Talking," *American Poetry Review,* 4 (July-Aug. 1975), 7-12.

"John Berryman, Poet, Is Dead; Won the Pulitzer Prize in 1965," *New York Times,* 8 Jan. 1972, p. 33.

Lask, Thomas. "Five Poet Friends Honor Berryman," *New York Times,* 11 May 1972, p. 23.

_____. "Sought Own True Voice," *New York Times,* 8 Jan. 1972, p. 33.

Lowell, Robert. "For John Berryman," *New York Review of Books,* 6 Apr. 1972, pp. 3-4.

_____. "John Berryman," *Harvard Advocate,* 103 (Spring 1969), 17.

Meredith, William. "In Loving Memory of the Late Author of the Dream Songs," *Saturday Review,* 20 May 1972, p. 48.

"Poet Berryman Killed in Plunge From Bridge," *Minneapolis Tribune,* 8 Jan. 1972, pp. 1A, 3A.

"Poet Berryman Leaps to Death," *Saint Paul Dispatch,* 7 Jan. 1972, pp. 1, 2.

Rosenthal, M. L. "Other Confessional Poets." In his *The New Poets: American and British Poetry Since World War II.* New York: Oxford University Press, 1967, 118-130.

"*77 Dream Songs* Wins Pulitzer Prize," *Minnesota Daily,* 4 May 1965, p. 1.

Van Doren, Mark. *Autobiography.* New York: Harcourt, Brace, 1958, 211-213.

_____. "John Berryman," *Harvard Advocate,* 103 (Spring 1969), 17.

Wasserstrom, William. "Cagey John: Berryman as Medicine Man," *Centennial Review,* 12 (Summer 1968), 334-354.

Berryman in Fiction

Simpson, Eileen. *The Maze.* New York: Simon & Schuster, 1975. Novel based on Berryman's life.

Selected Interviews

Berg, Martin. "A Truly Gentle Man Tightens and Paces: An Interview with John Berryman," *Minnesota Daily*, 20 Jan. 1970, pp. 9, 10, 14, 15, 17.

"Berryman Gets $10,000 Award," *Minneapolis Tribune*, 17 Nov. 1967, p. 1.

Haas, Joseph. "Who Killed Henry Pussycat? I did, says John Berryman, With love & a poem, & for freedom o," *Chicago Daily News*, 6 Feb. 1971, pp. 4-5.

Heyen, William. "John Berryman: A Memoir and an Interview," *Ohio Review*, 15 (Winter 1974), 46-65.

Kostelanetz, Richard. "Conversation with Berryman," *Massachusetts Review*, 11 (Spring 1970), 340-347.

Lundegaard, Bob. "Song of a Poet: John Berryman," *Minneapolis Sunday Tribune*, 27 June 1965, pp. 1-2E.

McClelland, David, et al. "An Interview with John Berryman," *Harvard Advocate*, 103 (Spring 1969), 4-9.

Meras, Phyllis. "John Berryman on Today's Literature," *Providence Sunday Journal*, 26 May 1963, p. 20W.

"Poetry Once Was Nonsense to Berryman," *Minneapolis Tribune*, 6 Jan. 1969, p. 22.

"Pulitzer Prize Once a 'Nothing' to Him; Now Berryman's Happy to Accept," *Minneapolis Star*, 4 May 1965, p. 18D.

Sisson, Jonathan. "My Whiskers Fly: An Interview with John Berryman," *Ivory Tower*, 14 (3 Oct. 1966), 14-18, 34-35.

Stitt, Peter. "The Art of Poetry: John Berryman 1914-72," *Paris Review*, 14 (Winter 1972), 177-207.

Strudwick, Dorothy. "Homage to Mr. Berryman," *Minnesota Daily*, 5 Nov. 1956, pp. 6, 16.

" 'U' Professor Awarded Pulitzer Poetry Prize," *Minneapolis Tribune*, 4 May 1965, p. 1.

Watson, Catherine. "Berryman Ends Poem of 13 Years," *Minneapolis Tribune*, 12 May 1968, p. 1E.

Critical Studies: Books

Arpin, Gary Q. *The Poetry of John Berryman*. Port Washington, N.Y.: Kennikat Press, 1978.

Bloom, James D. *The Stock of Available Reality: R. P. Blackmur and John Berryman*. Lewisburg, Pa.: Bucknell University Press, 1984.

Conarroe, Joel. *John Berryman: An Introduction to the Poetry.* New York: Columbia University Press, 1977.

Haffenden, John. *John Berryman: A Critical Commentary.* New York: New York University Press, 1980.

Linebarger, J. M. *John Berryman.* New York: Twayne, 1974.

Martz, William J. *John Berryman.* Minneapolis: University of Minnesota Pamphlets On American Writers, no. 85, 1969.

Critical Studies: Special Journal

John Berryman Studies (University of Minnesota, Minneapolis, Minn.). 1975- .

Critical Studies: Major Articles and Book Sections

Aaron, Daniel. Review of *Stephen Crane, Hudson Review,* 4 (Autumn 1951), 471-473.

Abercrombie, Ralph. "American Story-Teller," *Spectator,* 29 June 1951, p. 870.

Aiken, Conrad. "Poetry: What Direction?," *New Republic,* 12 May 1941, pp. 670-671.

Alvarez, A. "Berryman's Nunc Dimittis," *Observer,* 4 May 1969, p. 30.

_____. "Bottom Drawer," *Observer,* 5 May 1968, p. 26.

_____. "I don't think I will sing any more," *New York Times Book Review,* 25 June 1972, pp. 1, 12, 14.

_____. "The Joker in the Pack," *Observer,* 22 Nov. 1964, p. 27.

_____. "Poetry and Poverty," *Observer,* 10 May 1959, p. 24.

Ames, Carol. "The Form and the Language of John Berryman's *Recovery,*" *Notes on Modern American Literature,* 4 (Winter 1979), Item 4.

Andrews, Lyman. "Dream Worlds," *London Times,* 1 June 1969, p. 54.

Armstrong, Robert. "Unchartered Territories," *Poetry Review,* 50 (July-Sept. 1959), 175-176.

Arpin, Gary Q. " 'I Am Their Musick': Lamentations and *The Dream Songs,*" *John Berryman Studies,* 1 (Jan. 1975), 1-6.

Atlas, James. "The Dream Songs: To Terrify and Comfort," *Poetry,* 115 (Oct. 1969), 43-46.

"Badge of Courage," *Times Literary Supplement,* 8 June 1951, p. 356.

Barbera, Jack V. "Scrupulosity and the First Step: Berryman's *Recovery,*" *Notes on Modern American Literature,* 4 (Winter 1979), Item 2.

Beach, Joseph Warren. "Five Makers of American Fiction," *Yale Review*, new series, 40 (Summer 1951), 744-751. Review of *Stephen Crane*.

Bewley, Marius. "Poetry Chronicle," *Hudson Review*, 20 (Autumn 1967), 500-504.

Bland, Peter. "Poetry," *London Magazine*, new series, 8 (Aug. 1968), 97-99.

Blum, Morgan. "Berryman as Biographer, Stephen Crane as Poet," *Poetry*, 78 (Aug. 1951), 298-307. Review of *Stephen Crane*.

Bly, Robert. "A Garage Sale of Berryman's Poetry," *Minneapolis Tribune*, 13 Dec. 1970, pp. 10E-11E.

Bogan, Louise. "Verse," *New Yorker*, 7 Nov. 1964, pp. 242-243.

_____. "Verse," *New Yorker*, 30 Mar. 1968, pp. 136-137.

Bornhauser, Fred. "Poetry By the Poem," *Virginia Quarterly Review*, 41 (Winter 1965), 146-152. Review of *77 Dream Songs*.

Brinnin, John Malcolm. "The Last Minstrel," *New York Times Book Review*, 23 Aug. 1964, p. 5. Review of *77 Dream Songs*.

Browne, Michael Dennis. "Henry Fermenting: Debts to the Dream Songs," *Ohio Review*, 15 (Winter 1974), 75-87.

Brownjohn, Alan. "Henry Himself," *New Statesman*, 30 May 1969, p. 776.

Burford, William. "Majesty and Trash," *Southwest Review*, 36 (Summer 1951), xii-xv.

Burns, Gerald. "U.S. Poetry 1967—The Books That Matter," *Southwest Review*, 53 (Winter 1968), 101-106.

Butscher, Edward. "John Berryman: In Memorial Perspective," *Georgia Review*, 27 (Winter 1973), 518-525.

Carruth, Hayden. "Declining Occasions," *Poetry*, 112 (May 1968), 119-121.

_____. "Love, Art and Money," *Nation*, 2 Nov. 1970, pp. 437-438.

Ciardi, John. "The Researched Mistress," *Saturday Review*, 23 Mar. 1957, pp. 36-37.

Clarke, Clorinda. Review of *Stephen Crane*, *Catholic World*, 173 (May 1951), 158-159.

Clemons, Walter. "Man on a Tightrope," *Newsweek*, 1 May 1972, pp. 113-114.

Close, Roy M. "Berryman's Last Poems Reflect His Relationship with Subjects," *Minneapolis Star*, 11 May 1972, p. 5B.

"Congested Funeral: Berryman's New Dream Songs," *Times Literary Supplement*, 26 June 1969, p. 680.

Connelly, Kenneth. "Henry Pussycat, He Come Home Good," *Yale Review*, new series, 58 (Spring 1969), 419-427.

Conrad, Sherman. "Poetry as a Jackdaw's Nest," *Poetry*, 58 (May 1941), 90-96.

Cournos, John. Review of *Stephen Crane, Commonweal*, 12 Jan. 1951, pp. 356-357.

Curran, Mary Doyle. "Poems Public and Private," *Massachusetts Review*, 6 (Winter-Spring 1965), 414-415.

Daiches, David. "Wit, Sense and Poetry," *New York Herald Tribune Weekly Book Review*, 21 Nov. 1948, p. 22.

Dale, Peter. "Three Poets: Can Belief and Form Come in Bags of Tricks?," *Saturday Review*, 8 July 1972, pp. 57-58.

Daniel, Robert. "A Glimpse of the Future," *Sewanee Review*, 49 (Oct.-Dec. 1941), 553-561.

Davis, Douglas M. "Poets are Finding New Room to Stretch Out," *National Observer*, 9 Sept. 1969, p. 4B.

Davis, Robert Gorham. "The Fascinating Mr. Stephen Crane," *New York Times Book Review*, 10 Dec. 1950, p. 4. Review of *Stephen Crane*.

Davison, Peter. "Madness in the New Poetry," *Atlantic Monthly*, 215 (Jan. 1965), 90-93.

Deutsch, Babette. "Poets—Timely and Timeless," *New Republic*, 29 Mar. 1943, pp. 420-421.

_____. "The Younger Generation," *New York Herald Tribune Books*, 12 Jan. 1941, p. 13.

Dickey, James. "Orientations," *American Scholar*, 34 (Autumn 1965), 646-658. Reprinted in his *Babel to Byzantium*. New York: Farrar, Straus & Giroux, 1968.

Dickey, William. "A Place in the Country," *Hudson Review*, 22 (Summer 1969), 360-362.

Dodsworth, Martin. "Agonistes," *Listener*, 9 May 1968, p. 612.

_____. "Henry's Hobble," *Listener*, 22 May 1969, p. 731.

Donoghue, Denis. "Berryman's Long Dream," *Art International*, 20 Mar. 1969, pp. 61-64.

Duffy, Martha. "The Last Prayers," *Time*, 1 May 1972, p. 81.

Eberhart, Richard. "Song of the Nerves," *Poetry*, 73 (Oct. 1948), 43-45.

Eckman, Frederick. "Moody's Ode: The Collapse of the Heroic," *University of Texas Studies in English*, 36 (1957), 80-92.

Elliott, George P. "Poetry Chronicle," *Hudson Review*, 17 (Autumn 1964), 451-464.

Evans, Arthur, and Catherine Evans. "Pieter Bruegel and John Berryman: Two Winter Landscapes," *Texas Studies in Literature and Language,* 5 (Autumn 1963), 310-318.

Feldman, B. Review of *Berryman's Sonnets, Denver Quarterly,* 2 (Spring 1967), 168-169.

Finney, Kathe Davis. "Berryman's Baby Talk: 'Nuffin Welf,' " *Notes in Modern American Literature,* 4 (Winter 1979), Item 1.

Fitts, Dudley. "Deep in the Unfriendly City," *New York Times Book Review,* 20 June 1948, p. 4. Review of *The Dispossessed.*

Fitzgerald, Robert. "The Dream Songs," *Harvard Advocate,* 103 (Spring 1969), 24.

_____. "Notes on American Poetry After 1945," *American Review,* 1 (Autumn 1960), 127-135.

_____. "Poetry and Perfection," *Sewanee Review,* 56 (Aug. 1948), 685-697.

Flanagan, John T. Review of *Stephen Crane, American Literature,* 23 (Jan. 1952), 510-511.

Flint, R. W. "A Romantic on Early New England," *New Republic,* 27 May 1957, p. 28.

Fraser, G. S. "I, They, We," *New Statesman,* 2 May 1959, pp. 614-615.

_____. "The Magicians," *Partisan Review,* 38 (Winter 1971-1972), 469-478.

_____. "A Pride of Poets," *Partisan Review,* 35 (Summer 1968), 467-475.

Frye, Northrup. "Books of the Month: Poetry," *Canadian Forum,* 22 (Oct. 1942), 220.

Furbank, P. N. "New Poetry," *Listener,* 10 Dec. 1964, p. 949.

Fussell, Paul, Jr. "A Poetic Trip Through Puberty and Beyond," *Los Angeles Times Book Review,* 28 Feb. 1971, p. 8.

Galler, David. "Four Poets," *Sewanee Review,* 69 (Winter 1961), 168-174.

Garrigue, Jean. "Language Noble, Witty and Wild," *New Leader,* 15 Feb. 1965, p. 24.

_____. "Rapidly Shifting States of Mind," *New Leader,* 2 Dec. 1968, pp. 13-14.

Gelpi, Albert. "Homage to Berryman's *Homage,*" *Harvard Advocate,* 103 (Spring 1969), 14-17.

Gilman, Milton. "Berryman and the Sonnets," *Chelsea,* 22/23 (June 1968), 158-167.

Glauber, Robert H. "The Poet's Intention," *Prairie Schooner,* 39 (Fall 1965), 276-280.

Goldman, Michael. "Berryman: Without Impudence and Vanity," *Nation*, 24 Feb. 1969, pp. 245-246.

Gordon, Ambrose. Review of *Homage to Mistress Bradstreet, Yale Review*, new series, 46 (Dec. 1956), 298-300.

Grant, Damian. "Centre Court," *Tablet*, 6 July 1968, p. 673.

_____. "Late Excellence," *Tablet*, 16 Aug. 1969, p. 812.

Greene, Graham. "The Badge of Courage," *New Statesman & Nation*, 2 June 1951, pp. 627-628.

Griffin, Howard. "The Cold Heart, The Cold City," *Voices*, 136 (Winter 1949), 52-53.

Gullans, Charles. "Edgar Bowers' *The Astronomers*, And Other Verse," *Southern Review*, new series, 2 (Jan. 1966), 196-197.

Hamilton, Ian. "John Berryman," *London Magazine*, new series, 4 (Feb. 1965), 93-100.

Havinghurst, Walter. "Book Accurately Surveys Stephen Crane's Career," *Chicago Sunday Tribune Book Week*, 4 Feb. 1951, p. 5.

Hayman, Ronald. "On Recent Poetry," *Encounter*, 34 (Feb. 1970), 86-87.

Heffernan, Michael. "John Berryman: The Poetics of Martyrdom," *American Poetry Review*, 13 (Mar./Apr. 1984), 7-12.

Heyen, William. "Fourteen Poets: A Chronicle," *Southern Review*, new series, 6 (Spring 1970), 546-547.

Holder, Alan. "Anne Bradstreet Resurrected," *Concerning Poetry*, 2 (Spring 1969), 11-18.

Hollis, C. Carroll. "Stephen Crane," *America*, 17 Feb. 1951, p. 591.

Holmes, John. "Speaking in Verse," *New York Times Book Review*, 30 Sept. 1956, p. 18.

Honig, Edwin. "Berryman's Achievement," *Cambridge Review*, 30 May 1969, pp. 377-378.

Howes, Victor. "More Dream Songs," *Christian Science Monitor*, 5 Dec. 1968, p. 24.

_____. "On Meeting Mr. John Berryman, Poet," *Christian Science Monitor*, 18 Feb. 1971, p. 5.

Hughes, Riley. Review of *Stephen Crane, Thought*, 27 (Summer 1952), 307.

Jackson, Bruce. "Berryman's Chaplinesque," *Minnesota Review*, 5 (Jan.-Apr. 1965), 90-94.

Jaffe, Daniel. "A Shared Language in the Poet's Tongue," *Saturday Review*, 3 Apr. 1971, pp. 31-33, 46.

Jarrell, Randall. "Verse Chronicle," *Nation*, 17 July 1948, pp. 80-81.

John, Godfrey. "Old Words find New Relationships," *Christian Science Monitor*, 30 July 1964, p. 5.

Johnson, Carol. "John Berryman and Mistress Bradstreet: A Relation of Reason," *Essays in Criticism* (Oxford), 14 (Oct. 1964), 388-396.

_____. "John Berryman: The Dream Songs," *Harvard Advocate*, 103 (Spring 1969), 23-25.

Jones, Claude E. "Stephen Crane," *Nineteenth Century Fiction*, 6 (June 1951), 74-76.

Jones, Frank. "Skilled Workers," *Nation*, 17 Apr. 1943, pp. 569-570.

Kavanagh, P. J. "A Giving Man," *Guardian*, 8 May 1969, p. 9.

Kelly, Richard. "The Berryman Manuscripts," *John Berryman Studies*, 2 (Winter 1976), 29-33.

Kermode, Frank. "Talent and More," *Spectator*, 1 May 1959, p. 628.

Kessler, Jascha. "The Caged Sybil," *Saturday Review*, 14 Dec. 1968, pp. 34-35.

Kunitz, Stanley. "No Middle Flight," *Poetry*, 90 (July 1957), 244-249.

Lask, Thomas. "Both In and Out of His Time," *New York Times*, 13 Aug. 1968, p. 37.

Lieberman, Laurence. "The Expansional Poet: A Return to Personality," *Yale Review*, 57 (Winter 1968), 258-271.

Linebarger, J. M. "A Commentary on *Berryman's Sonnets*," *John Berryman Studies*, 1 (Jan. 1975), 13-24.

Lowell, Robert. "The Poetry of John Berryman," *New York Review of Books*, 28 May 1964, pp. 3-4 [vol. 2].

"Man in Search of a Hero," *Time*, 25 Dec. 1950, pp. 58-59.

Markfield, Wallace. "Stephen Crane: Cynic and Cavalier," *New Leader*, 34 (15 Jan. 1951), 21-22.

Martz, Louis L. "Recent Poetry: The Elegiac Mode," *Yale Review*, 54 (Winter 1965), 285-298.

Mazzaro, Jerome. "False Confessions," *Shenandoah*, 22 (Winter 1971), 86-88.

Mazzocco, Robert. "Harlequin in Hell," *New York Review of Books*, 29 June 1967, pp. 12-16 [vol. 8].

Meredith, William. "A Bright Surviving Actual Scene: Berryman's 'Sonnets,' " *Harvard Advocate*, 103 (Spring 1969), 19-22.

_____. "Henry Tasting All the Secret Bits of Life: Berryman's Dream Songs," *Contemporary Literature*, 6 (Winter-Spring 1965), 27-33.

_____. "Love's Progress," *New York Times Book Review*, 7 May 1967, p. 8.

Meyer, Gerard Previn. "Vigorous Swimmer in the Poetic Stream,"

Saturday Review of Literature, 10 July 1948, p. 21.

Mills, Ralph J., Jr. " . . . and a critical estimate of his unique poetic talents," *Showcase/Chicago Sun-Times,* 21 May 1972, p. 2.

_____. "Inward Agony and Wonder," *Chicago Sun-Times Book Week,* 3 Nov. 1968, p. 10.

Molesworth, Charles. "Full Count," *Nation,* 23 Feb. 1970, pp. 217-219.

Montague, John. "American Pegasus," *Studies: An Irish Quarterly Review,* 48 (Summer 1959), 183-191.

_____. "I Survive You," *Guardian,* 26 Apr. 1968, p. 7.

Morse, Samuel French. "Twelve Poets," *Virginia Quarterly Review,* 44 (Summer 1968), 507-512.

Neill, Edward. "Ambivalence of Berryman: An Interim Report," *Critical Quarterly,* 16 (Autumn 1974), 267-276.

Nims, John Frederick. "Homage in Measure to Mr. Berryman," *Prairie Schooner,* 32 (Spring 1958), 1-7.

North, Michael. "The Public Monument and Public Poetry: Stevens, Berryman, and Lowell," *Contemporary Literature,* 21 (Spring 1980), 267-285.

Oberg, Arthur. "John Berryman: The Dream Songs and the Horror of Unlove," *University of Windsor Review,* 6 (Fall 1970), 10-11.

O'Hara, J. D. "Berryman's Everyman," *Chicago Tribune Book World,* 7 Dec. 1969, pp. 6-7.

Parker, Derek. "Hats Off—A Genius," *Poetry Review,* 60 (Autumn 1969), 211.

Pearson, Gabriel. "John Berryman—Poet as Medium," *Review* (Oxford), no. 15 (Apr. 1965), 3-17.

Peden, William. Review of *Homage to Mistress Bradstreet, New Mexico Quarterly,* 26 (Autumn 1956), 289-291.

Pikoulis, John. "John Berryman's 'Elegy for Alun Lewis,' " *American Literature,* 56 (Mar. 1984), 100-101.

Pinsker, Sanford. "John Berryman and Robert Lowell: The Middle Generation, Reconsidered," *Literary Review,* 27 (Winter 1984), 252-261.

"Poetry: Combatting Society With Surrealism," *Time,* 24 Jan. 1969, p. 72.

Porterfield, Jo R. "The Melding of a Man: Berryman, Henry, and the Ornery Mr. Bones," *Southwest Review,* 58 (Winter 1973), 30-46.

Press, John. "Five Poets," *Punch,* 30 Dec. 1964, p. 1010.

Pritchard, William H. "Love and Fame," *New York Times Book Review,* 24 Jan. 1971, pp. 5, 25.

Ramsey, Paul. "In Exasperation and Gratitude," *Sewanee Review,* 74 (Autumn 1966), 936-938.

Rich, Adrienne. "Mr. Bones, He Lives," *Nation,* 25 May 1964, pp. 538, 540.

Ricks, Christopher. "Desperate Hours," *New Statesman,* 15 Jan. 1965, p. 79.

_____. "Recent American Poetry," *Massachusetts Review,* 11 (Spring 1970), 313-338.

Rosenthal, M. L. "The Couch and Poetic Insight," *Reporter,* 25 Mar. 1965, pp. 53-54.

Schendler, Sylvan. "Berryman's Dream," *Indian Journal of American Studies,* 3 (June 1973), 91-96.

Schulman, Grace. "Poets and Sonneteers," *Shenandoah,* 19 (Spring 1968), 73-76.

Scott, Winfield Townley. "The Dry Reaction," *Poetry,* 58 (May 1941), 86-90.

_____. "Mistress Bradstreet and the Long Poem," *Poetry Broadside,* 1 (Spring 1957), 5-13.

Seidel, Frederick. "Berryman's Dream Songs," *Poetry,* 105 (Jan. 1965), 257-259.

Sergeant, Howard. "Poetry Review," *English,* 15 (Spring 1965), 154.

Seymour-Smith, Martin. "Bones Dreams On," *Spectator,* 9 May 1969, pp. 622-623.

Shapiro, Alan. " 'A living to fail': The Case of John Berryman," *Tri-Quarterly,* no. 58 (Fall 1983), 114-125.

Shapiro, Karl. "Major Poets of the Ex-English Language," *Washington Post Book World,* 26 Jan. 1969, p. 4.

Sheehan, Donald. "Varieties of Technique: Seven Recent Books of American Poetry," *Contemporary Literature,* 10 (Spring 1969), 287-291.

Simons, John L. "Henry on Bogie: Reality and Romance in 'Dream Song No. 9' and *High Sierra," Literature Film Quarterly,* 5 (Summer 1977), 269-272.

Slavitt, David R. "Deep Soundings and Surface Noises," *New York Herald Tribune Book Week,* 10 May 1964, p. 14.

Smith, Ray. "Poetry in Motion: Berryman's 'Toy' Presents Dialogue of Self and Soul," *Minneapolis Star,* 26 Nov. 1968, p. 2B.

Smith, William Jay. "Pockets of Thought," *Harper's,* 229 (Aug. 1964), 100-102.

Spiller, Robert E. "Great Stylist," *Saturday Review of Literature,* 27 Jan. 1951, p. 11.

Stanford, Derek. "For Other than Poets," *Time and Tide,* 29 Aug. 1959, pp. 936-937.

Stepanchev, Stephen. "For an Excellent Lady," *New Leader,* 22 May 1967, pp. 26-28.

Stillman, Clara Gruening. "Stephen Crane, That Long Neglected Genius of Imaginative Realism," *New York Herald Tribune Book Review,* 17 Dec. 1950, p. 5.

Stitt, Peter A. "Berryman's Vein Profound," *Minnesota Review,* 7, no. 4 (1967), 356-359.

_____. "John Berryman: The Dispossessed Poet," *Ohio Review,* 15 (Winter 1974), 66-74.

_____. "John, Henry, & Mr. Bones," *Ivory Tower,* 1 June 1964, p. 37.

Stone, Edward. Review of *Stephen Crane, South Atlantic Quarterly,* 50 (July 1951), 440-441.

Strachan, Pearl. "The World of Poetry," *Christian Science Monitor,* 3 Oct. 1942, p. 10.

Swallow, Alan. "Some Current Poetry," *New Mexico Quarterly Review,* 18 (Winter 1948), 460.

Symons, Julian. "New Poetry," *Punch,* 19 June 1968, p. 902.

Tate, Allen. "The Last Omnibus," *Partisan Review,* 8 (May-June 1941), 243-244.

Thompson, John. "An Alphabet of Poets," *New York Review of Books,* 1 Aug. 1968, pp. 33-36.

Thwaite, Anthony. "Guts, Brains, Nerves," *New Statesman,* 17 May 1968, p. 659.

Toler, Sister Colette. "Strength and Tenderness," *Spirit,* 35 (Nov. 1968), 149-150.

Toynbee, Philip. "Berryman's Songs," *Encounter,* 24 (Mar. 1965), 76-78.

Tube, Henry. "Henry's Youth," *Spectator,* 26 Apr. 1968, pp. 566-567.

Tulip, James. "The American Dream of John Berryman," *Poetry Australia,* no. 31 (Dec. 1969), 45-48.

Turco, Lewis. "Of Laureates and Lovers," *Saturday Review,* 14 Oct. 1967, p. 31.

Updike, John. "Notes," *New Yorker,* 26 Jan. 1957, pp. 28-29.

Vendler, Helen. "Malevolent Flippancy," *New Republic,* 11 Nov. 1981, pp. 33-36.

_____. "Savage, Rueful, Irrepressible Henry," *New York Times Book Review,* 3 Nov. 1968, pp. 1, 58-59.

Vonalt, Larry P. "Berryman's *The Dream Songs*," *Sewanee Review*, 79 (Summer 1971), 464-469.

Wallace, Ronald. "John Berryman: Me, Wag." In his *God Be With the Clown*. Columbia: University of Missouri Press, 1984, 171-201.

Walsh, Malachy. "John Berryman: A Novel Interpretation," *Viewpoint*, 10 (Spring 1969), 5-21.

Wanning, Andrews. "A Portrait of Stephen Crane," *Partisan Review*, 18 (May-June 1951), 358-361.

Warner, Anne B. "Berryman's Elegies: One Approach to *The Dream Songs*," *John Berryman Studies*, 2 (Summer 1976), 5-22.

Weber, Brom. "Two American Men of Letters," *Western Review*, 16 (Summer 1952), 239-334.

Weiser, David. "*Berryman's Sonnets:* In and Out of the Tradition," *American Literature*, 55 (Oct. 1983), 388-404.

Weiss, Neil. "The Grace and the Hysteria," *New Leader*, 3 July 1948, p. 10.

White, Elizabeth Wade. Review of *Homage to Mistress Bradstreet*, *New England Quarterly*, 29 (Dec. 1956), 545-548.

Wiggin, Maurice. "Boredom Becomes Exhilaration," *London Times*, 3 Jan. 1965, p. 33.

Williams, Oscar. "Five Young American Poets," *Living Age*, 359 (Jan. 1941), 496-498.

Wilson, Edmund. "Stephen Crane—Hannah Whitall Smith," *New Yorker*, 6 Jan. 1951, pp. 77-85.

Wilson, Patrick. "The Ironic Title of Berryman's *Love and Fame*," *Notes on Contemporary Literature*, 5 (Sept. 1975), 10-12.

Winters, Yvor. "Three Poets," *Hudson Review*, 1 (Autumn 1948), 402-406.

Woods, John. "Five Poets," *Shenandoah*, 16 (Spring 1965), 85-91.

Zabel, Morton D. "Hero and Victim," *Nation*, 24 Feb. 1951, pp. 187-188.

"Zoo-Maze: The World in Vaudeville," *Times Literary Supplement*, 15 Apr. 1965, p. 292.

BIBLIOGRAPHICAL ESSAY

Bibliographies and Checklists

Richard J. Kelly's *John Berryman: A Checklist* (1972), the first bibliography on Berryman, lists both primary and secondary material through mid-1972; Ernest C. Stefanik, Jr.'s *John Berryman: A Descriptive Bibliography* (1974), the only full, descriptive bibliography of primary material published through 1973, provides facsimiles of title pages for Berryman's works published in America and England and includes privately printed "Dream Songs" that first appeared in limited editions. Following their book-length studies, Kelly and Stefanik joined forces to update their works. Issues of *John Berryman Studies* for April 1975, July 1975, and Winter 1976 contain primary and secondary supplements to their earlier bibliographies. *John Berryman: A Reference Guide* (1976) by Gary Q. Arpin completes many of the secondary entries first cited by Kelly, but Arpin's book also contains an annotation for each entry, an aid which is especially helpful to scholars working in specialized areas. While Kelly's book is useful primarily for generalists, Stefanik's and Arpin's books, respectively, are the best sources for primary and secondary listings. Clearly, however, an annotated guide to secondary material appearing since 1976 would be useful to students of Berryman.

Biographies: Books

John Haffenden's *The Life of John Berryman* (1982) is the only book-length scholarly biography of Berryman to date, and it should be considered along with Eileen Simpson's *Poets In Their Youth: A Memoir* (1982) to give a multifaceted perspective on Berryman as poet and person. Whereas Haffenden is strong on details and documents, Simpson offers a moving account of her first husband's life within the context of his generation of American poets.

The story of Berryman's boyhood in Oklahoma, his family's move to Tampa, Florida, during the real estate boom of the 1920s, and the suicide of his father, John Allyn Smith, on 26 June 1926, had already been covered by Joel Conarroe in *John Berryman: An Introduction to the Poetry* (1977) and by J. M. Linebarger in *John Berryman* (1974) (see Critical Studies: Books). But having access to key papers and people, Haffenden is able to offer a fuller view of Berryman's father's suicide and to touch on the poet's love-hate relationship with his mother, Martha. Whereas Haffenden hesitates to analyze fully Berryman's mother, Simpson boldly profiles a woman given to telling shifting versions of Smith's suicide. Simpson thoroughly explores the antagonism between Berryman and his mother and its possible psychological damage.

Among the strengths of Haffenden's biography are the chapters on the later years when Berryman was in and out of hospitals to attempt recovery from alcoholism. His underlying thesis that Berryman's was a sensibility that "construed affliction as creative stimulant" is persuasive. Furthermore, Haffenden includes a large number of previously unpublished Berryman notes and letters, many of which are housed at the University of Minnesota. *The Life of John Berryman* is, in fact, a careful and exacting piece of scholarship. What it lacks primarily is life—a shortcoming which Simpson's highly readable memoir overcomes.

Published three years after Berryman's suicidal leap from a Minneapolis bridge, Eileen Simpson's roman à clef, *The Maze* (1975), also offers insights into Berryman, especially into the poet in search of his own voice. Cast as Benjamin Bold, heavily imbibing poet, Berryman is pictured as a "high stepping horse" whose energies are frequently overpowering. *The Maze* is a compelling, well-written novel, but it should not be read as factual account. Like *Poets In Their Youth*, it is most valuable in providing a sense of who Berryman was, emotionally and psychologically, and of the high price he paid for his art.

Biographies: Major Articles and Book Sections

The Savage God: A Study of Suicide (1972) by A. Alvarez is necessary reading for an understanding of Berryman. By juxtaposing Berryman with Ernest Hemingway and Sylvia Plath, among others, Alvarez shows how children of suicides frequently reenact a suicidal parent's death. That Berryman was haunted by his father's suicide is indisputable, and Alvarez convincingly sets forth a Freudian explanation as to why his obsession led ultimately to his own suicide.

For insiders' views of Berryman, coupled with appreciation for his poetic achievements, two articles are indispensable: Saul Bellow's "John Berryman, Friend" (1973) and Robert Lowell's "For John Berryman" (1972). Both articles were published in the wake of their subject's death; both understand, as Bellow writes, that Berryman had no resources left: "the cycle of reform and relapse had become a bad joke that could not continue."

William Meredith's "In Loving Memory of the Late Author of the Dream Songs" (1972) is also important for anyone interested in Berryman biography. Of particular interest is Meredith's account of time spent with Berryman at a symposium at Goddard College in Vermont. Carrying with him a three-month badge of abstinence from Alcoholics Anonymous, Berryman spoke of "the idiot temptation to live a Christian life." At this point, he felt he had conquered his alcoholism. Also interesting is Meredith's discussion of Berryman's metaphors, which sometimes derive their power from comparisons between things that "merely look alike," the critic declares.

Jane Howard ("Whiskey and Ink, Whiskey and Ink," 1967) and Lewis Hyde ("Alcohol & Poetry: John Berryman and the Booze Talking," 1975) both have published significant articles about Berryman's life. Howard's portrait of Berryman in *Life*, with color photographs, captures what Saul Bellow in his 1973 tribute called the "electrifying intensity" of Berryman's personality as well as his tendency—explored in greater depth by Lewis Hyde—to confuse personal honesty with self-aggrandizement. By 1967 Berryman was in serious trouble with alcohol, and his alcoholism, Howard shows, was fueled by an inability to handle fame. Hyde's article, which appeared three years after Berryman's death, is the only work published to date that deals primarily with symptoms of alcoholism in Berryman's work. The critic sometimes undercuts his own questions with restrictive answers from Alcoholics Anonymous, but generally, his discussion of the disease in Berryman's life and in *The Dream Songs* is persuasive.

Selected Interviews

John Berryman lived a desperate life, and it is nowhere captured more compellingly than in William Heyen's "John Berryman: A Memoir and an Interview" (1974). Heyen's memoir grew out of his bewildering attempts to get the poet to Brockport, New York, for a reading and a television interview. A few sentences from Heyen characterize Berryman's visit: "For two days, 48 sleepless hours, I wondered about his heart, miraculous machine: kept him going through fifty-six years, his chain-smoking, alcoholism, insomnia, rages and crying jags and a memory that would not let the dead die." Heyen's essay ends on a note that reflects the feelings of many people for whom Berryman's "suicide deepened every question" asked about poetry: "I loved/love him, and cherish him, and will always count it among the privileges of my life that I met him. But I realize, also, that I am often afraid of him, that the bad angels also hovered around him, that the God he turned to at the end did not rescue this rare man from his despair. Unless, and I will keep trying to find out, this is exactly what happened."

Of equal importance to Heyen's essay is the last interview that Berryman granted; published in the *Paris Review* for Winter 1972, the conversation took place in October 1970 at St. Mary's Hospital, Minneapolis. Talking with Peter Stitt about his poetry and about his religious conversion, Berryman reiterated his feeling that intense suffering is necessary to the making of great art. Several sections from Stitt's interview merit attention, but one paragraph of Berryman's conversation is crucial to an understanding of his poetic process: "Certain great artists can make out without it, Titian and others, but mostly you need ordeal. My idea is this: the man is extremely lucky who is presented with the worst possible ordeal which will not actually kill him. At that point, he's in business. Beethoven's deafness, Goya's deafness, Milton's blindness, that kind of thing. . . . I hope to be nearly crucified."

Though less notable than Heyen's or Stitt's for its memorable quotations, David McClelland's 1969 *Harvard Advocate* interview with Berryman is important for the light it sheds on the genesis of "huffy Henry," persona of *The Dream Songs*. In this interview, Berryman acknowledges his artistic debt to the French poet Arthur Rimbaud.

Critical Studies: Books

For the generalist, William J. Martz's 1969 University of Minnesota Pamphlet, *John Berryman,* and J. M. Linebarger's 1974 Twayne book, *John Berryman,* are reliable guides through a poetic world once described by Robert Lowell as "a great Pierrot's universe, more tearful and funny than one can easily bear." Both works are good introductions, though because of its 1969 publication date, Martz's pioneering pamphlet does not treat Berryman's poetry after *The Dream Songs*.

Martz dwells largely on two issues in Berryman's work: first, the "problem of style"; and second, Berryman's primary poetic attempt to reflect how it feels to be a sensitive individual in a threatening world. Early reviewers, according to Martz, showed great consistency in recognizing what Dudley Fitts in a 1948 *New York Times Book Review* article called discrepancies between "craft and art" and what Randall Jarrell in the same year identified as Berryman's problem with "subject and style." Berryman's basic weakness as a young poet was not so much a need for stylistic development as it was for discovery of "how" and "to what" style was best applied. The early Berryman had to turn from "straining for effect at the price of poem quality," and turn he did with *Homage to Mistress Bradstreet,* Martz contends. Berryman before *Homage* writes in a style that is ultimately dramatic, but he tends to be a "speaker" of individual poems and does not become a developed character, says Martz. He creates a sufficient number of poems to establish "the fact of his talent," but his work is marred by "vagueness, obscurity, and failure to project a clear dramatic situation." With *Homage,* the early Berryman becomes at age forty the later Berryman who writes in a style, or styles, directed toward dramatic immediacy, the critic shows.

While there is, according to Martz, a "striking contrast" in the early and later styles of John Berryman, his poetic subject remains fairly constant. "What he cares about," Martz writes of *The Dispossessed,* "is our common humanity and its survival in the face of possible threats. He cares about caring." Similarly, because of the "tenderness of the speaker," *Homage to Mistress Bradstreet* "immediately defines itself as a poem of personal caring." In technique, Martz declares, *77 Dream Songs* is an extension or variant of *Homage,* moving from a "relatively ordered consciousness, Anne's, to a relatively disordered consciousness, Henry's." As the *Dream Songs* progress, they become increasingly and plainly autobiographical. Still, Berryman's subject is, the critic reiterates, "how it feels" to be "John Berryman struggling with his own life, with the whole problem, human, spiritual, call it what you will, of his own identity." In the final analysis, according to Martz, Morgan Blum's summary judgment, in the August 1951 *Poetry,* of Berryman's *Stephen Crane* has "the force of an epithet": "Flawed but distinguished."

While Linebarger agrees with Martz's charge that Berryman's early poems are sometimes trite, he thinks that Martz has done *Stephen Crane* a disservice by quoting Blum's comment about Berryman's "inability to reduce his insights to reasoned discourse." Blum was referring to only one chapter of the Crane biography, Linebarger argues; furthermore, he contends, "to conclude, as Martz does, that Berryman's poetry generally is 'sloppy in craft' is absurd. Throughout his career Berryman was considered a 'poet's poet,' an epithet reserved for writers of superb technical control."

Surveying Berryman's life and career in his first chapter, Linebarger loosely divides Berryman's poetic output into four periods. The early period begins with "Twenty Poems" (1940) and ends with

The Dispossessed (1948). While Linebarger agrees with Martz that *Homage to Mistress Bradstreet* belongs to a "transitional period when Berryman had escaped the influence of Yeats and Auden and had found voices of his own," he places less weight on the poem as a pivotal one than does Martz. Written in 1947, *Berryman's Sonnets* also belong to this transitional period, for according to Linebarger, they helped Berryman to overcome "his reticence about self." The third period begins in 1955 when Berryman began to write *The Dream Songs,* and in his fourth chapter, Linebarger examines characteristic subjects of the songs: sociopolitical concerns, the nature of art and poetry, religion, love, psychological disorder, and the overwhelming sense of loss that dominates Berryman's poetry from early to late. *Love & Fame* (1970), *Delusions, Etc.* (1972), and *Recovery* (1973) belong to the fourth period which is, Linebarger writes, "comparatively direct, explicit, and obviously autobiographical."

According to Linebarger, Berryman solved the "problem of style" in *The Dispossessed* where mixed levels of diction and wrenched syntax appear as imperfect forerunners of the techniques used in *Homage* and *The Dream Songs.* But two problems remained: how to express personality and how to manage form. The *Sonnets* represent a step beyond *The Dispossessed* in their presentation of "deep, personal emotion," but in *Homage* Berryman "seems to have been writing more in literary rebellion" against T. S. Eliot and "The Waste Land" than in self-expression. These two problems were not resolved concurrently, Linebarger argues, until Berryman began writing *The Dream Songs.*

In response to Martz's statement that *The Dream Songs* "lacks plot, either traditional or associative," Linebarger quotes Berryman: "Those are fighting words. It has plot. Its plot is the personality of Henry as he moves on in the world." While Linebarger appears to remain mildly skeptical of Berryman's view that the "poetic personality behind a long poem is a sufficient organizing and unifying device," he does Berryman the service of exploring the poem on his own terms. He looks at Henry's persistent conflict with academia, at his recurring delusions, at his anxiety and guilt and "plights & gripes" with an objective eye. Ultimately, he concludes, "if any single feeling dominates *The Dream Songs,* it is the same sense of loss that hovered over the early poems, the *Sonnets,* and *Homage.*" Berryman's reputation as an important poet was established with *The Dream Songs,* according to Linebarger, but their achievement rests more with style than with character. Qualifying a remark by Allen Tate that they "cannot be imitated," Linebarger writes: "Berryman made a style his own, and no one can imitate it without the source becoming immediately apparent." This section of Linebarger's book is his most compelling—possibly because he regards *The Dream Songs* as "the most important poetry published in America during the 1960s."

For Linebarger, the fourth period of Berryman's career did not enhance his reputation either as a poet or writer of fiction. Too many passages in *Love & Fame* suffer from the "weakness of much of the confessional poetry of our time: the descent into embarrassing self-revelation," and the 102 poems of *Delusions, Etc.* are "unremarkable," the critic believes. Berryman's uncompleted novel *Recovery* seems to Linebarger "unsalvageable as a work of art." His discussion of Berryman's late poetry is Linebarger's weakest—undoubtedly because these "embarrassing" and "unremarkable" poems could not measure up to their forerunners.

Like Linebarger's book, Joel Conarroe's *John Berryman: An Introduction to the Poetry* (1977) and Gary Q. Arpin's *The Poetry of John Berryman* (1978) are chronological surveys. Both see Berryman's achievement in his creation of a comic, fractured, and unnerving language that corresponds to the sense of loss at the heart of his work. Their sense of audience, however, is very different. As John Unterecker writes in his "Foreword" to Conarroe's *Berryman,* "The combination of Berryman and Conarroe is so heady as to turn every reader into an instant collaborator." However, Arpin's book is helpful primarily to professors of American and comparative literature.

Conarroe begins to fulfill Unterecker's promise when, echoing Ralph Waldo Emerson's famous line, his opening sentence proclaims that Berryman "could never be charged with the sort of foolish consistency that is alleged to be the sign of a small mind." And talking about Berryman's birthday under the sign of Scorpio, the astrological sign that contributes to the imagery of the *Sonnets,* Conarroe continues: "Born three days earlier he would have been an even-handed Libra, and we would be without the more daring and passionate of his poems. Or so would say those who put their faith in celestial bodies. Picasso was also born on October 25." Conarroe's casual style no doubt contributes to the reader's willing collaboration, but the critic's honesty is equally arresting. He admits early on to a preference for *The Dream Songs,* saying outright that some of Berryman's "bloodless" early work "seems to have been composed by a well-programmed computer." His account of how Berryman composed the songs—"the songs are built with pieces of the poet"—reads like a good novel: "Sitting all night in his green chair, puffing on Tareytons and drinking either bourbon or coffee, Berryman brought forth songs the way a tree produces leaves, in the process scattering pages, and ashes, all over the rug."

For Conarroe, Berryman's poetry begins with his life. As the critic sees it, Berryman's intentions are clearly therapeutic: "his interest is mainly in rescuing himself from himself." If Conarroe sometimes loses sight of the distinction between Berryman and his imaginative re-creations, he resists at every turn the temptation to lord criticism over art. He has written the most sensitive and sensible book on John Berryman to date, even describing *Recovery* as a "strong and moving" book that might be better read as a journal than as fiction.

Ultimately, Conarroe stays closer to Berryman's insistence that "poetry is composed by actual human beings" than does Arpin. For Arpin, Berryman's major thematic concern is the relationship between the poet and his culture. Accordingly, he situates Berryman within the Symbolist tradition, and his book is valuable for its exploration of Henry as *poète maudit* who finds it "increasingly difficult to find anything that makes the suffering worthwhile." Both Arpin's discussion of Berryman's work in Freudian terms and his suggestion that Freud's *Civilization and Its Discontents* provides a useful gloss on some of Berryman's early work are interesting and accurate.

Arpin appears to prefer the union of lyric and narrative in *Homage to Mistress Bradstreet* to the technique used in *The Dream Songs,* which was "too available to the daily events of Berryman's life, perhaps." But his preference by no means prevents him from interesting speculation about Berryman's poetic precedents. His discussion of French poet Tristan Corbière's possible influence on Berryman's mature style is one such example. Although Arpin's work is obviously learned, occasionally his insistence on technical terms produces baffling juxtapositions. To say that "the anapest and iamb-trochee combinations" of a particular song "buffet the reader about" is to tread dangerously close to a mixed metaphor.

While all four critical works previous to John Haffenden's *John Berryman: A Critical Commentary* (1980) open doors into their subject's poetic world, it is Haffenden's book in which one finds the fullest and most satisfactory interpretation. Not only is this work praiseworthy for its sensitive readings of the poetry from *Homage to Mistress Bradstreet* to *Delusions, Etc.,* but Haffenden amplifies his text by including unpublished notes Berryman made while in the process of writing his poems. The critic reveals, for instance, that the "demon lover" of

"Dream Song 351" is an allusion to Adrienne Rich's poem by the same name; Berryman's first draft manuscript is written on the back of a copy of Rich's poems. Haffenden identifies, too, the "horrible saints" from whom the poet flinches in "Vespers" (*Delusions, Etc.*) since a draft manuscript names them as Dan Berrigan and Simone Weil. The critic also provides composition dates for many of the *Dream Songs*—useful information since they were not published in the order in which they were written. Songs originally planned for certain books were moved around, Haffenden declares, according to Berryman's "woolly sense of demarcation."

If one comes away from Haffenden's biography, *The Life of John Berryman*, with certain reservations, one comes back again and again to his *Critical Commentary* with gratitude. Not least among its many strengths is the critic's discussion of the epic models Berryman had in mind for *The Dream Songs*. They included Dante's *Divine Comedy*, Archbishop Philip Carrington's explication of the liturgical structure of the *Bible*, the categories set forth by Joseph Campbell in *The Hero with a Thousand Faces*, and Homer's *Iliad*. In the final analysis, Haffenden argues wisely: "*The Dream Songs* needs to be judged in terms less of received generic categories than of its own identity."

Critical Studies: Special Journal

John Berryman Studies (*JBS*), published at the University of Minnesota, is an invaluable critical resource for scholars concerned with Berryman. In the pages of *JBS*, which first appeared in January 1975, critics update primary and secondary bibliographies, grapple with Henry's identity, re-read Berryman's early poems and sonnets, and explore the intricacies of Berryman's poetic method and style.

The appearance of updated primary and secondary checklists in *John Berryman Studies* has already been noted. Three essays are characteristic of other work appearing in the journal. "Berryman's Elegies: One Approach to *The Dream Songs*" (Summer 1976) is by Anne B. Warner, whose unpublished dissertation (Emory University, 1979) explores literary tradition and psychoanalytic technique in *The Dream Songs*. In her *JBS* article Warner treats the *Dream Songs* written to Delmore Schwartz and others who were part of Berryman's generation—a generation, according to Henry, whom God "wrecked." Warner's essay offers a sensitive explication of those *Dream Songs* that Berryman once called "one solid block of agony." J. M. Linebarger's "A Commentary on *Berryman's Sonnets*" (January 1975) treats Berryman's experiments with the sonnet form. These early sonnets, begun during the summer of 1947, foreshadow Berryman's structural innovations in *The Dream Songs,* Linebarger says. Also worthy of attention is Gary Q. Arpin's " 'I Am Their Musick': Lamentations and *The Dream Songs"* (January 1975). Berryman was widely read in theology, and here Arpin traces Biblical references to "Lamentations." In light of critical controversy about Berryman's religious conversion, it is refreshing to read a critic who takes the theological dimensions of Berryman's work seriously. Too often interest in the meaning of religion in his life obscures his expert use of it as a poetic resource.

As is true with most specialized journals, the essays published in *JBS* should prove most helpful to readers who have background knowledge about contemporary American poetry and the poetry of John Berryman. Although the essays are by no means inaccessible, they offer greatest resonance to those who approach them after having done preliminary investigation into primary and secondary materials.

Critical Studies: Major Articles and Book Sections

"John Berryman has made a creepy, scorching book, and something more. Through a device too integral to seem devised, he manages private history without self-photography, public utterance without platform manners." So begins what Berryman himself considered to be the single most important article published about *The Dream Songs,* because the writer understood the poem for what he tried to make it: Adrienne Rich's "Mr. Bones, He Lives" (1964). Rich explains why many critics have seen *The Dream Songs* with its complex figure Henry as Berryman's major achievement:

> He is in a position to use—and does—any conceivable tone of voice and manner to needle, wheedle, singe, disarm and scarify the reader. . . . the dialect of blackface Henry, with its half sly, half bitter self-deprecations, merges into a kind of Berryman middle-style after the abrupt "Come away, Mr. Bones," and moves into a language belonging to the same poetic nerve centers as the beginning of "Hyperion" and the late poems of [William Carlos] Williams—in other words, a diction which a few poets earn a few times in their lives.

Several critical articles have addressed the diction of *The Dream Songs,* and at least two should be read for what they add to Rich's explanation. In addition to "needling" and "wheedling," Berryman used baby talk to disarm readers into sympathizing with the "plights & gripes" of Henry. In her 1979 *Notes in Modern American Literature* essay Kathe Davis Finney explores his use of infantile inflections such as "nuffin welf " in ten of the *Dream Songs*. Baby talk combined with an invocation of archaic language can create a poetic diction that Jean Garrigue describes as "Language Noble, Witty and Wild." Her article in the 15 February 1965 *New Leader* indeed touches the nerve centers of Berryman's diction.

Not all critics have found Berryman to be the "Great Stylist" headlined in the 27 January 1951 *Saturday Review of Literature* with Robert E. Spiller's byline. Some, in fact, see his poetry as more "creepy" than "scorching." Next to Rich's analysis of the "steely thread of strength running through the dislocation and ruin," perhaps no other article has had more impact than Hayden Carruth's 1970 *Nation* article, "Love, Art and Money." Carruth finds Berryman's *Love & Fame* intolerable in its "self-contradiction, special pleading, vagueness," and "splotchy muddlement of crude desires." The critic seizes the occasion of reviewing *Love & Fame* to proclaim: "The time has come, surely, to say that Berryman's poetry is usually interesting and sometimes witty but almost never moving, and that in spite of its scope and magnitude it lacks the importance that has been ascribed to it in recent years by many critics, editors and readers." Patrick Wilson, however, in his September 1975 *Notes on Contemporary Literature* essay, debates Carruth's appraisal. Wilson sees irony in *Love & Fame*'s title and in its text.

Certainly, from the time when critics like Robert Fitzgerald did not hesitate to apply the epithet "classic" to *Homage to Mistress Bradstreet* (see Fitzgerald's 1960 "Notes on American Poetry After 1945"), Berryman's poetry has been both praised and denounced. While Ronald Wallace in his Berryman chapter in *God Be With the Clown* (1984) finds much to appreciate in the self-deprecating humor of *The Dream Songs*, Helen Vendler complains in the 11 November 1981 *New Republic* about his "malevolent flippancy." While in his Winter 1968 *Yale Review* article Laurence Lieberman sees as "endless, inexhaustible, always unpredictable" Berryman's possibilities for movement between the "bizarre melodrama of a loser-in-love" and the "hallucinatory dreamworld of his inner life," M. L. Rosenthal writes in the 25 March 1965 *Reporter* that the first 77 *Dream Songs* offer "no real justification intrinsically for further development." That Berryman's work has generated both critical accolades and diatribes is understandable. His poetry lived and flourished in the layers of his personality (see Lieberman's article cited above for a distinction between "confessional poetry" and "expansional poetry"), and his personality was by no means simple or at all times agreeable. His poetry, like his personality, was erratic; he, like his persona Henry, was in Adrienne Rich's words "fiendishly intelligent." To borrow William Burford's prophetic title, employed for a *Southwest Review* essay published before *The Dream Songs* began to appear, Berryman ended his poetic career with a body of work that is both "Majesty and Trash."

Yet some of the most interesting critical essays about Berryman's work refrain from either praise or damnation, their authors preferring to examine questions about poetic form and aesthetics. David Weiser, for example, examines Berryman's poetic forms in ways that are immensely helpful. In his *"Berryman's Sonnets:* In and Out of the Tradition" (1983) Weiser says that the sonnets actually employ a theory of invention that prevailed in the Renaissance. According to Weiser, when Berryman "echoes Shakespeare we are more impressed by deviations from the source than by fidelity to it." Weiser also declares that Berryman's language combines American slang with Elizabethan euphony. The form of his *Sonnets* is not Shakespearean, however, but Petrarchan; that is, the inner lines of each quatrain make one rhyme and the outer lines another, the critic shows. Self-criticism, as Weiser notes, is an integral part of the Petrarchan mode. But Berryman did not write his early sonnets merely as a formal exercise. While his decision to revive an apparently outmoded structure with all its conventions "implies a firm belief in the continuity of literary culture," his contrast of old conceits with "something definite"—his aching arm, for instance—shows his "radical departure from tradition," Weiser contends.

Ultimately, in Weiser's view, Berryman wrote sonnets "to explore, however inconclusively, a theme that would concern him throughout his career"—love. Yet, as the critic reveals, love was not for Berryman the transcendent force that Renaissance poets had glorified; rather, "an illicit love affair brought out his awareness of an underlying conflict between inner impulses and outer norms." As Weiser rightly asserts, for Renaissance poets the clash had been internal, between a poet's own powers of reason and his passion. For Berryman, and for other American writers, it was "another version of the conflict between the individual and society." Weiser is correct in his argument that love is a theme that concerned Berryman throughout his career, from the *Sonnets* through *The Dream Songs* to

Love & Fame. Plenty of evidence suggests, however, that the underlying conflict prompted by desire was internal (self versus self) as well
as representative of an individual poet at odds with his society.

For readers interested in aesthetic influences, two essays explore
the visual arts. The first, "Pieter Bruegel and John Berryman: Two
Winter Landscapes" (1963), explores Berryman's translation of Bruegel's painting into poetry. Arthur and Catherine Evans, a comparative
literature specialist and an art historian respectively, demonstrate successfully the vital link between the arts as inspirations for the creative
imagination. Not only do they argue convincingly that one can enter
Bruegel's painting by entering Berryman's poem but their essay is a
model of interdisciplinary criticism. The second essay, John L. Simons's "Henry on Bogie: Reality and Romance in 'Dream Song No.
9' and *High Sierra*" (1977), argues that the Bogart film explains much
of "Dream Song No. 9." This particular *Dream Song* is among the most
difficult to understand, but reading in the last stanza that "Bogart's
duds/truck back to Wardrobe," one sees with Simons's help that "horrible Henry, foaming" has simply gone to the movies and, by imaginative extension, become part of the plot.

While critics generally have tended to admire Berryman's craft,
his virtuosity, and his daring, they have been disturbed by what Lieberman called in his 1968 essay the poet's "over-fixation on self-
gloom," the tone of which is frequently a "superarticulate mental wail."
And they have been concerned, both sympathetically and unsym-
pathetically, about his "trumped-up self-preenings" within the context
of his generation of American poets. James Atlas comments, for example, about *His Toy, His Dream, His Rest* in the October 1969 issue
of *Poetry:*

> Randall Jarrell was struck by a car as he walked along some
> isolated road; Delmore Schwartz died alone in a Broadway hotel;
> and Sylvia Plath committed suicide: all in all, the legacy of poets
> in America since World War II is a disturbing one; it terrifies, it
> deadens, it gives us little comfort. At best a poetry of eloquent
> exhaustion, our voice at worst has been wrenched from a language
> of disorder and disease. Nervous, autistic, and ill-at-ease, we have
> surrendered ourselves to the possibilities at hand and refused to
> emerge from the forms of virtuosity.

Worried about the predicament of poet as "invalid," Atlas goes on to say that the brilliance of *The Dream Songs* is "symphonic." They "stun the language into fury."

Similarly, in his "Madness in the New Poetry" (1965), Peter Davison sees in *The Dream Songs* "as much to admire as to be vexed at." He dislikes the "lack of order, the perversity, the self-pity" with "righteous impatience," but he finds Berryman's handling of the three six-line stanzas "fluid, fascinating, never routine, never rhythmically sloppy." Davison also notes that "order, decision, wisdom, beauty are not often to be found, for the search here is for the self and for the selves within the self." It could be argued, Davison writes, that this search is "not a proper task for poetry," but it is, nonetheless, one that Berryman pursues in a spirit of "unquenchable subjectivity"— the weakness of *The Dream Songs*. Davison has "no wish to play down the relevance of madness and poetry," but in his opinion, "the poet as poet bears responsibility for the excellence and wholeness of his poem more than for his self's wholeness, no matter how mad he happens to be."

In his approach to Berryman, Davison differs on this point with Lieberman, who sets "expansional poetry" in opposition to T. S. Eliot's theory of impersonality. According to Lieberman, "fidelity to the human being—to the uniqueness of personality behind the poem—is primary; perfection of the art, secondary" to expansional poets, including Berryman. Both Davison and Lieberman are convincing, and each, within the context of his argument, is right. When asked in an interview how he felt about the tag "confessional poetry," the lesser form of Lieberman's two poetic returns to personality, Berryman responded, "with rage and contempt." But in *The Freedom of the Poet*, Berryman staunchly opposed Eliot's notion that personality ought to be extinguished in poetry. He admonished critics who are not themselves writers of poetry to remember that poems are written by actual human beings: "When Shakespeare wrote 'Two loves I have,' reader, he was not kidding."

The most influential articles about Berryman were written by critics who are themselves poets—Adrienne Rich and Hayden Carruth. This is not to say that Berryman was a "poet's poet" or that poets are necessarily better equipped to judge a colleague's work than are scholars. Rather, it is intended, by way of conclusion, to point to a third essay that is remarkable for its level-headedness and solid judgment—"No Middle Flight" by poet and critic Stanley Kunitz. Writing in a 1957 *Poetry* article, before Berryman and his Henry had entered the literary world, Kunitz declined to attach "classic" to *Hom-*

age to Mistress Bradstreet, as had Robert Fitzgerald in his 1960 essay. He also hesitated to call it "a very big achievement," as did Robert Lowell in his *New York Review of Books* article (1964). Yet "few modern poets can even approximate his [Berryman's] command of the stanzaic structure," Kunitz wrote. *Bradstreet* is "impressive in its ambition and virtuosity," but "the flaws are real for me." For Kunitz, the ambitiousness of Berryman's *Homage to Mistress Bradstreet* resides not so much in its material and style as in the poet's intention "to relate himself to the American past through the discovery of a viable myth, and to create for his vehicle a grand and exalted language, a language of transfiguration." Berryman's intention recalls that of Hart Crane in *The Bridge,* Kunitz declares.

After at least half-a-dozen readings, Kunitz says that he retains his first impression of the poem's failings. Its very ambitiousness works against it: "the scaffolding of the poem is too frail to bear the weight imposed upon it. . . . The display of so much exacerbated sensibility, psychic torment, religious ecstasy seems to be intermittently in excess of what the secular occasion requires; the feelings persist in belonging to the poet instead of becoming the property of the poem." In this last point, Kunitz echoes Davison's insistence that the poet's first responsibility is to the wholeness of the poem itself. And throughout his essay, Kunitz in many ways foreshadows the mixed tone of Berryman criticism to date: the poet is a superb craftsman, but he is "tempted to inflate what he cannot subjugate."

Writing about *Homage to Mistress Bradstreet,* Kunitz offers at least two observations that can and have been made about the whole of John Berryman's work. First, his poetry "seethes with an almost terrifying activity." Secondly, his failures are "worth more than most successes," for they demonstrate that "Berryman is now entitled to rank among our most gifted poets."

Elizabeth Bishop

(1911-1979)

Barbara Page
Vassar College

PRIMARY BIBLIOGRAPHY

Books

North & South. Boston: Houghton Mifflin, 1946. Poems.

Poems: North & South—A Cold Spring. Boston: Houghton Mifflin, 1955. Abridged as *Poems*. London: Chatto & Windus, 1956. Poems.

Brazil, by Bishop and the editors of *Life*. New York: Time, 1962; London: Sunday Times, 1963. Text for pictorial history.

Questions of Travel. New York: Farrar, Straus & Giroux, 1965. Poems, one story.

Selected Poems. London: Chatto & Windus, 1967. Poems.

The Ballad of the Burglar of Babylon. New York: Farrar, Straus & Giroux, 1968. Poem.

The Complete Poems. New York: Farrar, Straus & Giroux, 1969; London: Chatto & Windus, 1970. Poems.

Geography III. New York: Farrar, Straus & Giroux, 1976. Poems, one translation.

The Complete Poems, 1927-1979. New York: Farrar, Straus & Giroux, 1983. Poems.

The Collected Prose, edited with an introduction by Robert Giroux. New York: Farrar, Straus & Giroux, 1984. Essays, stories.

Selected Essay

"Influences," *American Poetry Review*, 14 (Jan./Feb. 1985), 11-16. Adapted from 13 Dec. 1977 speech.

Translations

Brant, Alice (Dayrell). *The Diary of "Helena Morley,"* translated and edited with an introduction by Bishop. New York: Farrar, Straus & Cudahy, 1957; London: Gollancz, 1958.

"Three Stories by Clarice Lispector," translated by Bishop, *Kenyon Review,* 26 (Summer 1964), 500-511.

Edited Book

An Anthology of Twentieth-Century Brazilian Poetry, edited with an introduction by Bishop and Emanuel Brasil. Middletown, Conn.: Wesleyan University Press, 1972.

Miscellaneous

Mindlin, Henrique E. *Modern Architecture in Brazil.* New York: Reinhold, 1956. Uncredited contribution by Bishop.

SECONDARY BIBLIOGRAPHY

Bibliographies

MacMahon, Candace W. *Elizabeth Bishop: A Bibliography, 1927-1979.* Charlottesville: University Press of Virginia, 1980. Primary and secondary.

Schwartz, Lloyd. "Bibliography, 1933-81." Collected in *Elizabeth Bishop and Her Art,* ed. Schwartz and Sybil P. Estess, 331-341. Primary and secondary. See Collection of Essays.

Wyllie, Diana E. *Elizabeth Bishop and Howard Nemerov: A Reference Guide.* Boston: G. K. Hall, 1983. Primary and secondary.

Biographies: Major Articles and Book Sections

Brown, Ashley. "Elizabeth Bishop: In Memoriam," *Southern Review,* 16 (Apr. 1980), 257-259.

_____. "Elizabeth Bishop in Brazil," *Southern Review,* 13 (Oct. 1977), 688-704. Collected in Schwartz and Estess. See Collection of Essays.

Giroux, Robert. Introduction to *Elizabeth Bishop: The Collected Prose.* New York: Farrar, Straus & Giroux, 1984, vii-xxii.

Merrill, James. "Elizabeth Bishop (1911-1979)," *New York Review of Books*, 6 Dec. 1979, p. 6. Collected in Schwartz and Estess.

Nash, Mildred J. "Elizabeth Bishop's Library: A Reminiscence," *Massachusetts Review*, 24 (Summer 1983), 433-437.

Schwartz, Lloyd. "Elizabeth Bishop, 1911-1979," *Boston Phoenix*, 16 Oct. 1979, p. 12. Collected in Schwartz and Estess. See Collection of Essays.

Stevenson, Anne. "Letters from Elizabeth Bishop," *Times Literary Supplement*, 7 Mar. 1980, pp. 261-262.

Wehr, Wesley. "Elizabeth Bishop: Conversations and Class Notes," *Antioch Review*, 39 (Summer 1981), 319-328.

Selected Interviews

Brown, Ashley. "An Interview with Elizabeth Bishop," *Shenandoah*, 17 (Winter 1966), 3-19. Collected in Schwartz and Estess. See Collection of Essays.

Spires, Elizabeth. "An Afternoon with Elizabeth Bishop," *Vassar Quarterly*, 75 (Winter 1979), 4-9. Expanded and republished as "The Art of Poetry XXVII: Elizabeth Bishop," *Paris Review*, 23 (Summer 1981), 56-83.

Starbuck, George. " 'The Work!' A Conversation with Elizabeth Bishop," *Ploughshares*, 3, nos. 3 & 4 (1977), 11-29. Collected in Schwartz and Estess. See Collection of Essays.

Critical Studies: Book

Stevenson, Anne. *Elizabeth Bishop.* New York: Twayne, 1966.

Critical Studies: Collection of Essays

Schwartz, Lloyd, and Sybil P. Estess, eds. *Elizabeth Bishop and Her Art.* Ann Arbor: University of Michigan Press, 1983.

Critical Studies: Special Issues of Journals

"Elizabeth Bishop: A Symposium," *Field*, no. 31 (Fall 1984).

Ivask, Ivar, ed. "Homage to Elizabeth Bishop, Our 1976 Laureate," *World Literature Today*, 51 (Winter 1977).

Critical Studies: Major Articles and Book Sections

Alvarez, A. "Imagism and Poetesses," *Kenyon Review,* 19 (Spring 1957), 321-326. Review of *Poems: North & South—A Cold Spring.*

Ashbery, John. "Second Presentation of Elizabeth Bishop," *World Literature Today,* 51 (Winter 1977), 8, 10-11.

_____. "Throughout Is This Quality of Thingness," *New York Times Book Review,* 1 June 1969, pp. 8, 25. Review of *Complete Poems.* Collected as *"The Complete Poems"* in Schwartz and Estess.

Bidart, Frank. "On Elizabeth Bishop," *World Literature Today,* 51 (Winter 1977), 19. Collected in Schwartz and Estess.

Blasing, Mutlu K. " '*Mont d'Espoir* or *Mount Despair;'* The Re-verses of Elizabeth Bishop," *Contemporary Literature,* 25 (Fall 1984), 341-353.

Bloom, Harold. "*Geography III* by Elizabeth Bishop," *New Republic,* 176 (5 Feb. 1977), 29-30. Review.

Bogan, Louise. "Verse," *New Yorker,* 22 (5 Oct. 1946), 121-123. Review of *North & South.* Republished as "Elizabeth Bishop" in *A Poet's Alphabet: Reflections on the Literary Art and Vocation,* ed. Robert Phelps and Ruth Limmer. New York: McGraw-Hill, 1970, 219-220. Collected as "On *North & South*" in Schwartz and Estess.

Bromwich, David. "Elizabeth Bishop's Dream-Houses," *Raritan,* 4 (Summer 1984), 77-94.

_____. "Morality and Invention in a Single Thought," *New York Times Book Review,* 27 Feb. 1983, pp. 7, 30-31. Review of *Complete Poems, 1927-1979.* Collected in Schwartz and Estess.

Corn, Alfred. Review of *Geography III, Georgia Review,* 31 (Summer 1977), 533-537.

Costello, Bonnie. "The Complete Elizabeth Bishop," *Poetry,* 142 (July 1983), 231-242. Review of *Complete Poems, 1927-1979.*

_____. "The Fine Art of Remembrance," *Partisan Review,* 52 (Spring 1985), 153-157. Review of *Collected Prose.*

_____. "The Impersonal and the Interrogative in the Poetry of Elizabeth Bishop." Collected in Schwartz and Estess, 109-132.

_____. "Marianne Moore and Elizabeth Bishop: Friendship and Influence," *Twentieth Century Literature,* 30 (Summer/Fall 1984), 130-149.

_____. "Vision and Mastery in Elizabeth Bishop," *Twentieth Century Literature,* 28 (Winter 1982), 351-370.

Dodsworth, Martin. "Unamerican Editions," *Times Literary Supplement,* 23 Nov. 1967, p. 1106. Review of *Selected Poems.*

Dubie, Norman. "So a Goldfinch!," *Seneca Review,* 9 (May 1978), 104-113. Review of *Geography III.*

Eberhart, Richard. "With Images of Actuality," *New York Times Book Review,* 17 July 1955, p. 4. Review of *Poems: North & South—A Cold Spring.*

Edelman, Lee. "The Geography of Gender: 'The Waiting Room,' " *Contemporary Literature,* 26 (Summer 1985), 179-196.

Ehrenpreis, Irvin. "Loitering between Dream and Experience," *Times Literary Supplement,* 22 Jan. 1971, p. 92. Review of *Complete Poems.*

Elkins, Mary J. "Elizabeth Bishop and the Act of Seeing," *South Atlantic Review,* 48 (Nov. 1983), 43-57.

Estess, Sybil P. "Elizabeth Bishop: The Delicate Art of Map Making," *Southern Review,* 13 (Oct. 1977), 705-727. Abridged and collected as "Description and Imagination in Elizabeth Bishop's 'The Map' " in Schwartz and Estess.

_____. "Shelters for 'What is Within': Meditation and Epiphany in the Poetry of Elizabeth Bishop," *Modern Poetry Studies,* 8 (Spring 1977), 50-60.

_____. "Toward the Interior: Epiphany in 'Cape Breton' as Representative Poem," *World Literature Today,* 51 (Winter 1977), 49-52.

Fowlie, Wallace. "Poetry of Silence," *Commonweal,* 65 (15 Feb. 1957), 514-516.

Frankenberg, Lloyd. "Elizabeth Bishop." In his *Pleasure Dome.* Boston: Houghton Mifflin, 1949, 331-338.

Fraser, G. S. "Potential for Variety," *New Statesman,* 53 (5 Jan. 1957), 22-23.

_____. "Some Younger American Poets," *Commentary,* 23 (May 1957), 461.

Goldensohn, Lorrie. "Elizabeth Bishop's Originality," *American Poetry Review,* 7 (Mar./Apr. 1978), 18-22.

Gordon, Jan B. "Days and Distances: The Cartographic Imagination of Elizabeth Bishop," *Salmagundi,* no. 22-23 (Spring/Summer 1973), 294-305. Republished in *Contemporary Poetry in America,* ed. Robert Boyers. New York: Schocken, 1974.

Hall, Donald. Review of *Poems: North & South—A Cold Spring, New England Quarterly,* 29 (June 1956), 250-252.

Hamilton, Ian. "Women's-Eye Views," *Observer,* 31 Dec. 1967, p. 20. Review of *Selected Poems.* Republished in his *Poetry Chronicle.* London: Faber & Faber, 1973, 160-162.

Handa, Carolyn. "Elizabeth Bishop and Women's Poetry," *South At-*

lantic Quarterly, 82 (Summer 1983), 269-281.

Hardwick, Elizabeth. "The Perfectionist," *New Republic,* 19 Mar. 1984, pp. 32-35.

Hecht, Anthony. "Awful but Cheerful," *Times Literary Supplement,* 26 Aug. 1977, p. 1024. Review of *Geography III.*

Hochman, Sandra. "Some of America's Most Natural Resources," *Book Week,* 20 Feb. 1966, p. 4. Review of *Questions of Travel.*

Hollander, John. "Questions of Geography," *Parnassus,* 5 (Spring/ Summer 1977), 359-366. Review of *Geography III.* Collected as "Elizabeth Bishop's Mappings of Life" in Schwartz and Estess.

Hopkins, Crale D. "Inspiration as Theme: Art and Nature in the Poetry of Elizabeth Bishop," *Arizona Quarterly,* 32 (Autumn 1976), 197-212.

Howard, Richard. "Comment." In his *Preferences.* New York: Viking Press, 1974, 31. Collected in Schwartz and Estess.

James, Clive. "Everything's Rainbow," *Review,* 25 (Spring 1971), 51-57. Republished in his *First Reactions: Critical Essays 1968-1979.* New York: Alfred A. Knopf, 1980, 45-52.

Jarrell, Randall. "Fifty Years of American Poetry," *Prairie Schooner,* 37 (Spring 1963), 21. Republished in his *The Third Book of Criticism.* New York: Farrar, Straus & Giroux, 1969, 325. Collected in Schwartz and Estess.

_____. "The Poet and His Public," *Partisan Review,* 13 (Sept./Oct. 1946), 491, 498-500. Republished in his *Poetry and the Age.* New York: Knopf, 1953, 223, 234-235. Collected as "On *North & South*" in Schwartz and Estess.

Kalstone, David. "All Eye," *Partisan Review,* 37 (Spring 1970), 310-315. Review of *Complete Poems.*

_____. "Conjuring with Nature: Some Twentieth-Century Readings of Pastoral." In *Twentieth-Century Literature in Retrospect,* ed. Reuben A. Brower. Harvard English Studies, 2. Cambridge, Mass.: Harvard University Press, 1971, 247-268.

_____. "Elizabeth Bishop: Questions of Memory, Questions of Travel." In his *Five Temperaments: Elizabeth Bishop, Robert Lowell, James Merrill, Adrienne Rich, John Ashbery.* New York: Oxford University Press, 1977, 12-40. Collected in Schwartz and Estess.

_____. "Prodigal Years: Elizabeth Bishop and Robert Lowell, 1947-49," *Grand Street,* 4 (Summer 1985), 170-193.

_____. "Questions of Memory—New Poems by Elizabeth Bishop," *Ploughshares,* 2, no. 4 (1974-1975), 173-181.

_____. "Trial Balances: Elizabeth Bishop and Marianne Moore," *Grand Street*, 3 (Autumn 1983), 115-135.

Keller, Lynn. "Words Worth a Thousand Postcards: The Bishop/ Moore Correspondence," *American Literature*, 55 (Oct. 1983), 405-429.

Keller, and Cristanne Miller. "Emily Dickinson, Elizabeth Bishop, and the Rewards of Indirection," *New England Quarterly*, 57 (Dec. 1984), 533-553.

Laurans, Penelope. " 'Old Correspondences': Prosodic Transformations in Elizabeth Bishop." Collected in Schwartz and Estess, 75-95.

Lehman, David. " 'In Prison': A Paradox Regained." Collected in Schwartz and Estess, 61-74.

Leithauser, Brad. "The 'complete' Elizabeth Bishop," *New Criterion*, 1 (Mar. 1983), 36-42. Review of *Complete Poems, 1927-1979*.

Lowell, Robert. "Thomas, Bishop, and Williams," *Sewanee Review*, 55 (Summer 1947), 496-500. Review of *North & South*. Collected in Schwartz and Estess.

McClatchy, J. D. "The Other Bishop," *Canto*, 1 (Winter 1977), 165-174. Review of *Geography III*.

McFarland, Ronald E. "Some Observations on Elizabeth Bishop's 'The Fish,' " *Arizona Quarterly*, 38 (Winter 1982), 365-376.

McNally, Nancy L. "Elizabeth Bishop: The Discipline of Description," *Twentieth Century Literature*, 11 (Jan. 1966), 189-201.

Mazzaro, Jerome. "Elizabeth Bishop and the Poetics of Impediment," *Salmagundi*, no. 27 (Summer/Fall 1974), 118-144. Revised as "The Poetics of Impediment: Elizabeth Bishop" in his *Postmodern American Poetry*. Urbana: University of Illinois Press, 1980, 166-198.

_____. "Elizabeth Bishop's Particulars," *World Literature Today*, 51 (Winter 1977), 46-49.

_____. "The Recent Poems of Elizabeth Bishop," *South Carolina Review*, 10 (Nov. 1977), 99-115.

Meredith, William. "Invitation to Miss Elizabeth Bishop." Collected in Schwartz and Estess, 216-218.

Mills, Ralph J., Jr. "Elizabeth Bishop." In his *Contemporary American Poetry*. New York: Random House, 1965, 72-83.

Mizener, Arthur. "New Verse," *Furioso*, 2 (Spring 1947), 72-75. Review of *North & South*. Collected in Schwartz and Estess.

Moore, Marianne. "Archaically New." In *Trial Balances: An Anthology of New Poetry,* ed. Ann Winslow. New York: Macmillan, 1935, 82-83. Collected in Schwartz and Estess.

_____. "Imagination in Action," *Poetry,* 94 (July 1959), 247-249. Review of *The Diary of "Helena Morley." * Republished as "Senhora Helena" in her *A Marianne Moore Reader.* New York: Viking, 1961, 226-229. Collected in Schwartz and Estess.

_____. "A Modest Expert," *Nation,* 163 (28 Sept. 1946), 354. Review of *North & South.* Collected in Schwartz and Estess.

Moore, Richard. "Elizabeth Bishop: 'The Fish,' " *Boston University Studies in English,* 2 (Winter 1956/1957), 251-259.

Mortimer, Penelope. "Elizabeth Bishop's Prose," *World Literature Today,* 51 (Winter 1977), 17-18.

Moss, Howard. "All Praise," *Kenyon Review,* 28 (Mar. 1966), 255-262. Review of *Questions of Travel.* Republished in his *Writing against Time.* New York: Morrow, 1969, 136-147.

_____. "The Canada-Brazil Connection," *World Literature Today,* 51 (Winter 1977), 29-33. Republished in his *Whatever is Moving.* Boston & Toronto: Little, Brown, 1981, 38-53.

_____. "The Long Voyage Home," *New Yorker,* 60 (1 Apr. 1985), 104-112. Review of *Collected Prose.*

_____. "The Poet's Voice," *New Yorker,* 53 (13 Feb. 1978), 122-124. Review of *Five Temperaments: Elizabeth Bishop, Robert Lowell, James Merrill, Adrienne Rich, John Ashbery,* by David Kalstone. New York: Oxford University Press, 1977.

Motion, Andrew. "Elizabeth Bishop," The 1984 Chatterton Lecture. Proceedings of the British Academy, 70. London: Oxford University Press. Forthcoming.

Mullen, Richard. "Elizabeth Bishop's Surrealist Inheritance," *American Literature,* 54 (Mar. 1982), 63-80.

Nemerov, Howard. "The Poems of Elizabeth Bishop," *Poetry,* 87 (Dec. 1955), 179-182. Review of *Poems: North & South—A Cold Spring.*

Newman, Anne R. "Elizabeth Bishop's 'Roosters.' " In *A Book of Rereadings in Recent American Poetry,* ed. Greg Kuzma. Lincoln, Neb.: Pebble and The Best Cellar Press, 1979, 171-183.

_____. "Elizabeth Bishop's 'Songs for a Colored Singer,' " *World Literature Today,* 51 (Winter 1977), 37-40.

Page, Barbara. "Shifting Islands: Elizabeth Bishop's Manuscripts," *Shenandoah,* 33, no. 1 (1981-1982), 51-62.

Paz, Octavio. "Elizabeth Bishop, or the Power of Reticence," *World Literature Today,* 51 (Winter 1977), 15-16. Collected in Schwartz and Estess.

Perloff, Marjorie. "Elizabeth Bishop: The Course of a Particular," *Modern Poetry Studies,* 8 (Winter 1977), 177-192.

Pinsky, Robert. "The Idiom of a Self; Elizabeth Bishop and Words- worth," *American Poetry Review,* 9 (Jan./Feb. 1980), 6-8. Collected in Schwartz and Estess.

_____. "Poetry and the World," *Antaeus,* nos. 40/41 (Winter- Spring 1981), 481-487.

_____. *The Situation of Poetry: Contemporary Poetry and Its Traditions.* Princeton: Princeton University Press, 1976, 75-77, 162.

Procopiow, Norma. "Survival Kit: The Poetry of Elizabeth Bishop," *Centennial Review,* 25 (Winter 1981), 1-19.

Quebec, Ruth. "Water, Windows, and Birds: Image-Theme Patterns in Elizabeth Bishop's *Questions of Travel,*" *Modern Poetry Studies,* 10 (Spring 1980), 68-82.

Rich, Adrienne. "The Eye of the Outsider: The Poetry of Elizabeth Bishop," *Boston Review,* 8 (Apr. 1983), 15-17. Review of *The Complete Poems, 1927-1979.*

Rosenthal, M. L. *The Modern Poets: A Critical Introduction.* New York: Oxford University Press, 1960, 253-255, 261.

Ryan, Michael. "A Dark Gray Flame," *New England Review and Bread Loaf Quarterly,* 6, no. 4 (1984), 518-529.

Schwartz, Lloyd. "The Mechanical Horse and the Indian Princess: Two Poems from *North & South,*" *World Literature Today,* 51 (Winter 1977), 41-44.

_____. "One Art: The Poetry of Elizabeth Bishop, 1971-76," *Ploughshares,* 3, nos. 3 & 4 (1977), 30-52. Collected in Schwartz and Estess.

Scott, Nathan A., Jr. "Elizabeth Bishop: Poet without Myth," *Virginia Quarterly Review,* 60 (Spring 1984), 255-275.

Shapiro, David. "On a Villanelle by Elizabeth Bishop," *Iowa Review,* 10 (Winter 1979), 77-81.

Sheehan, Donald. "The Silver Sensibility: Five Recent Books of Amer- ican Poetry," *Contemporary Literature,* 12 (Winter 1971), 106-110. Review of *Complete Poems.*

Shore, Jane. "Elizabeth Bishop: The Art of Changing Your Mind," *Ploughshares,* 5, no. 1 (1979), 178-191.

Slater, Candace. "Brazil in the Poetry of Elizabeth Bishop," *World Literature Today,* 51 (Winter 1977), 33-36.

Smith, William Jay. "New Books of Poems," *Harper's,* 233 (Aug. 1966), 89-90. Review of *Questions of Travel.*

Southworth, James G. "The Poetry of Elizabeth Bishop," *College English*, 20 (Feb. 1959), 213-217.

Spiegelman, Willard. "Elizabeth Bishop's 'Natural Heroism,' " *Centennial Review*, 22 (Winter 1978), 28-44. Collected in Schwartz and Estess.

_____. "Landscape and Knowledge: The Poetry of Elizabeth Bishop," *Modern Poetry Studies*, 6 (Winter 1975), 203-224.

Stepanchev, Stephen. "Elizabeth Bishop." In his *American Poetry Since 1945: A Critical Survey*. New York: Harper & Row, 1965, 69-79.

Tomlinson, Charles. "Elizabeth Bishop's New Book," *Shenandoah*, 17 (Winter 1966), 88-91. Review of *Questions of Travel*.

Van Dyne, Susan R. "Double Monologues: Voices in American Women's Poetry," *Massachusetts Review*, 23 (Autumn 1982), 461-485.

Vendler, Helen. *"An Anthology of Twentieth-Century Brazilian Poetry,"* *New York Times Book Review*, 7 Jan. 1973, pp. 4, 12, 14, 16, 18. Review.

_____. "Domestication, Domesticity and the Otherworldly," *World Literature Today*, 51 (Winter 1977), 23-28. Republished in her *Part of Nature, Part of Us: Modern American Poets*. Cambridge, Mass.: Harvard University Press, 1980, 97-110. Collected in Schwartz and Estess.

_____. "Recent Poetry: 8 Poets," *Yale Review*, 66 (Spring 1977), 417-420. Review of *Geography III*.

Wallace, Patricia B. "The Wildness of Elizabeth Bishop," *Sewanee Review*, 43 (Winter 1985), 95-115.

Wallace-Crabbe, Chris. "Matters of Style: Judith Wright and Elizabeth Bishop," *Westerly*, 23 (Mar. 1978), 53-57.

Wegs, Joyce M. "Poets in Bedlam: Sexton's Use of Bishop's 'Visits to St. Elizabeth's' in 'Ringing the Bells,' " *Concerning Poetry*, 15, no. 1 (1982), 37-47.

Wilbur, Richard. "Elizabeth Bishop: A Memorial Tribute Read at the American Academy of Arts & Letters, 7 December 1979," *Ploughshares*, 6 (Fall 1980), 10-14. Collected in Schwartz and Estess.

Williams, Oscar. "North but South," *New Republic*, 115 (21 Oct. 1946), 525. Review of *North & South*. Collected in Schwartz and Estess.

Williamson, Alan. *"A Cold Spring:* The Poet of Feeling." Collected in Schwartz and Estess, 96-108.

Wood, Michael. "R.S.V.P.," *New York Review of Books*, 9 June 1977, pp. 29-30. Review of *Geography III*.

BIBLIOGRAPHICAL ESSAY

Bibliographies

The three most important bibliographies of Elizabeth Bishop's work all include primary and secondary material and overlap to some degree, but serve complementary purposes. Candace W. MacMahon's *Elizabeth Bishop: A Bibliography, 1927-1979* (1980) is the essential work for libraries and other collectors of Bishop's published writings. The largest part of the book consists of a chronologically listed description of Bishop's separate and collected publications, together with information about each work (such as the size and date of a printing), quotations from correspondence between Bishop and her publishers, and textual variants. Other sections list translations of Bishop's work into foreign languages, recordings, musical settings, anthologies containing her work, interviews, and published letters or excerpts from letters. Secondary material includes books wholly or partially about Bishop, reviews, obituaries, poems about or dedicated to her, and a selection—by no means comprehensive—of critical articles. The unpublished poems listed in an appendix have since been printed in *The Complete Poems, 1927-1979*. In preparing her bibliography, MacMahon had the help of Bishop herself, who also supplied a brief foreword. The book is quite accurate and thorough, especially in its treatment of primary sources, and is indispensable to anyone concerned with the history of Bishop's publications.

Lloyd Schwartz's "Bibliography, 1933-81," which is printed at the end of *Elizabeth Bishop and Her Art* (1983), edited by Schwartz and Sybil P. Estess, offers a compact checklist of Bishop's collected and uncollected work (including fugitive writings, such as dust jacket blurbs Bishop wrote for other authors), interviews, and a selection of secondary material. His listing of articles and reviews treating Bishop is more extensive than MacMahon's but omits some items she includes. For purposes of bibliographical citation, Schwartz's listings are incomplete (page numbers are omitted, for instance), but his format is handy, and the articles and reviews have been winnowed to reflect his judgment of the most significant writings about Bishop up to 1981.

Like Schwartz's bibliography, Diana E. Wyllie's *Elizabeth Bishop and Howard Nemerov: A Reference Guide* (1983) covers material appearing through 1980 and therefore does not record the publication of *The Complete Poems, 1927-1979*, *The Collected Prose*, or the steady stream of new writing about Bishop prompted by her rising reputation after her death. Wyllie's *Guide*, introduced by a brief history of Bishop's career, presents an annotated, strictly chronological checklist in two parts: writings by and writings about Bishop. Listing secondary material chronologically gives a clear impression of the development of critical opinion about Bishop's work, yet different kinds of material are lumped together: MacMahon's book-length bibliography, for example, will be found among the articles, reviews, and other shorter writings also published in 1980. Although Wyllie's *Guide* aims at comprehensiveness, her annotations are often brief. However, her book is useful, especially to persons studying Bishop for the first time or to those seeking a year-by-year survey of the criticism.

Biographies: Major Articles and Book Sections

At present there is no full-scale biography of Bishop, although information about her life and career can be found in Anne Stevenson's critical book, *Elizabeth Bishop* (1966), in interviews conducted by Ashley Brown, George Starbuck, and Elizabeth Spires, and in other sources, some of which have been reprinted in Schwartz and Estess's collection, *Elizabeth Bishop and Her Art*. Stevenson's "Letters from Elizabeth Bishop" (1980) includes passages from a correspondence begun when the critic was writing her book about Bishop. Memorial tributes, such as those by Ashley Brown ("Elizabeth Bishop In Memoriam"), James Merrill ("Elizabeth Bishop [1911-1979]"), and Lloyd Schwartz ("Elizabeth Bishop, 1911-1979"), offer intimate glimpses of Bishop by friends and fellow poets; recollections by Mildred J. Nash ("Elizabeth Bishop's Library: A Reminiscence") and Wesley Wehr ("Elizabeth Bishop: Conversations and Class Notes") give a sense of how she appeared to two of her former students. Some of the works discussed in Critical Studies: Major Articles and Book Sections also include biographical matter. The most important of these articles, all of which were published in the 1980s, are David Kalstone's "Prodigal Years: Elizabeth Bishop and Robert Lowell, 1947-49" and "Trial Balances: Elizabeth Bishop and Marianne Moore," Lynn Keller's "Words Worth a Thousand Postcards: The Bishop/Moore Correspondence," and Bonnie Costello's "Marianne Moore and Elizabeth Bishop: Friendship and Influence." Personal reminiscences and biographical information may also be found in other reviews, obituaries, and articles; Candace Slater's "Brazil in the Poetry of Elizabeth Bishop" (1977), for instance, gives some of her social and political conditions as they affected Bishop during her residence in that country, and Elizabeth Hardwick, in "The

Perfectionist" (1984), recalls encounters with Bishop in Brazil and elsewhere. For an overview of Bishop's life and career, one may consult any of three recent biographies in standard reference works: John Unterecker's in *American Writers, A Collection of Literary Biographies,* edited by Leonard Unger (New York: Scribners, 1974); Ashley Brown's in the *Dictionary of Literary Biography 5: American Poets Since World War II, Part 1,* edited by Donald J. Greiner (Detroit, Mich.: Bruccoli Clark/Gale Research, 1980); and Sybil P. Estess's in *American Women Writers,* edited by Lina Mainiero (New York: Ungar, 1979). Of these, Unterecker's offers the fullest discussion of Bishop's life, work, and critical reputation. Another, more personal sketch of her life, especially as it relates to her prose writings, is found in the introduction to the *Collected Prose,* by Robert Giroux, Bishop's publisher and friend of many years. Work in progress of biographical interest includes an oral history being prepared by Peter Brazeau, a volume similar in format to his study of Wallace Stevens, *Parts of a World* (New York: Random House, 1983); a selection of Bishop's letters, being edited by David Kalstone; and Kalstone's forthcoming book on Bishop, Robert Lowell, and Randall Jarrell.

Selected Interviews

Of the three most informative interviews, the one conducted for the Winter 1966 *Shenandoah* by Bishop's friend Ashley Brown in her home near Petrópolis in Brazil is the most relaxed. In all three, however, despite Bishop's well known aversion to self-disclosure and her distrust of talk about art or life, she reveals a good deal about her personal history, education, and friendships with other artists; about her tastes, standards, and methods as a writer; and about her writing of particular poems. In the interview with Brown, Bishop offers the most systematic version of her intellectual biography: her early reading of fairy tales; her discovery of Gerard Manley Hopkins and the modern poets; her literary friendships at Vassar with Mary McCarthy and others; her fascination with George Herbert among the Metaphysical poets; and her defense of T. S. Eliot's high modernism against the fashion of the 1930s for "political thinking" in poetry, her need to resist writing like W. H. Auden. She also discusses the large presence of Wallace Stevens when she began to publish, her early interest in surrealism and continuing interest in popular lyrics, her affection for the philosopher John Dewey, and, above all, her long, cherished friendships with Marianne Moore and Robert Lowell. Neither Moore nor Lowell is ever far from her mind, at least during these interviews: Lowell, her closest affinity, and Moore, a slightly daunting, beloved artistic and moral conscience. In all three interviews, Bishop distinguishes between her active interest in social and political issues and her objection to propaganda and didacticism in art. Talking with Brown, Bishop offers a telling statement about what she saw as a shift in poetic psychology in the modern period—the attempt "to dramatize the mind in action rather than in repose"—that strongly affected her own practice. The other distinctive feature of the Brown interview arises from the interest of each in Brazilian culture. Bishop explains how modern poetry in the Portuguese language of Brazil differs from that in English and describes herself as "a completely American poet" who has been influenced by her residence in Brazil. Brown's interview and his biographical essay "Elizabeth Bishop in Brazil" provide a vivid picture of the writer's life in South America.

George Starbuck's " 'The Work!' A Conversation with Elizabeth Bishop" (1977), conducted after her return to the United States, opens with recollections of her years in Brazil and her interest in its history, her dissatisfaction with changes made by the editors at Time-Life in her book *Brazil,* and her learning to translate from the Portuguese while working on *The Diary of "Helena Morley."* Bishop touches on the subject of literary influences and describes how she met Marianne Moore and Robert Lowell. Of particular interest in this interview are comments Bishop makes about the backgrounds of two early poems ("Large Bad Picture" and "Roosters") and of several works from her then just published *Geography III* ("The Moose," "Crusoe in England," and "In the Waiting Room"). These remarks underscore Bishop's habit of drawing on real experience and her strict conscience about matters of fact, but also give some idea of how her imagination acts on her material: a rereading of *Robinson Crusoe,* for example, makes her want to "re-see" his life by omitting the moralistic Christianity. When Starbuck mentions that the "Roosters," which Bishop wrote with World War II in mind, had recently come to sound like a feminist tract, Bishop thoughtfully reflects on being a woman poet and on the politics of feminism. She explains that her objection to appearing in anthologies of poetry by women stems from her feminine principles against separating the sexes. The subject of feminism also draws autobiographical comments of unusual candor: first, that the young women of her college generation were so accustomed to being "put down" that they quickly learned to adopt a tough, ironic attitude, and second, that if she had been a man she might have written more.

In the 1979 *Vassar Quarterly* interview conducted by Elizabeth Spires at Bishop's apartment on Lewis Wharf in Boston, Bishop again touches on the subject of feminism and her objection to being played off as "old-fashioned" against explicitly political women poets. The principal focus of the interview, however, is on her view of herself as an artist. Once again she reviews her personal history and travels, tells engaging anecdotes (notably one about how news of her having won a Pulitzer Prize was received by neighbors in her remote mountain village in Brazil), and describes how her poems "The Moose" and "One Art" and her story "In the Village" got written. Discussing the importance of childhood memories ("You are fearfully observant then"), Bishop describes some vivid recollections of her very early years but remarks that she has tried to avoid making a cult of writing about childhood. Spires elicits anecdotes about Bishop's "romantic" adolescence and college years and about her ambitions to be a composer, a painter, a doctor—but never by conscious decision a poet. Confessing that she has suffered all her life from being shy, Bishop describes her embarrassment at poetry readings and her reluctance to teach writing classes. In this interview Bishop gives the most complete account of her habits of composition, the slow gestation of most of her poems and the unfinished work, and her particular interest in the visual arts.

Critical Studies: Book

The only book-length study of Bishop is Anne Stevenson's *Elizabeth Bishop,* written in 1966 but still useful in many respects, and, though a slender volume, surprisingly ambitious in its effort to relate Bishop's career to broad currents of thought in art, philosophy, and science during the first half of the twentieth century. Most of the book is interpretive rather than biographical, but it includes a chronology and a sketch of Bishop's family history and the circumstances of her life to 1965, noting especially the exceptionally painful losses and dislocations of her early childhood: her father's death and her mother's insanity; her removal from the affectionate care of her maternal grandparents in Nova Scotia to her father's family in Worcester, Massachusetts, and then to an aunt in Boston; and the serious attacks of asthma and other illnesses that kept her from regular school attendance. Stevenson finds Bishop rare among contemporary writers in preserving a "distinctively childlike vision with regard to human tragedy"; she says that though the poet has never developed her observations into an explicit philosophy or core of belief, she implicitly conveys a view of nature as "the apersonal, amoral condition of life" that makes no concessions to the aspirations and desires of human beings.

In her early poems of dream and fantasy, Bishop describes subconscious experience without trying to explain it or to imitate it. Stevenson finds such poems both intriguing and unsatisfactory: because the irrational remains unexplained, these works evade interpretation and raise doubts that human beings can ever understand anything absolutely, even the commonest occurrences. Stevenson points out that although most of the poems in Bishop's first book, *North & South*, are connected with her travels, they are not travel poems but instead are about her sense of place, literally the visible surfaces of things and their shifting relationships. Stevenson attributes the purity and resonance of the images in the early works to Bishop's absorption in the world of things rather than in self-analysis and finds the work of her midlife, during her residence in Brazil, less intensely visual but freer in the expression of emotion. Stevenson's conjecture that in her youth Bishop "*knew* less about the world and therefore could *see* more of it" sets up an opposition between seeing and knowing; yet in nearly all of Bishop's work, sight is the means to knowledge. Bravely (but mistakenly) Stevenson predicts that Bishop's work would develop toward a poetry of intellectual abstraction, in keeping with her interest in abstract painting. In fact, her late poems continue in the direction of the greater emotional candor that Stevenson discovers in the middle period while they also circle back to memories rooted in childhood and experiences of her personal life.

Bishop has been obsessed, says Stevenson, with the problem of reality, because she is drawn equally toward the imaginative world of dreams and the everyday world of practicality and common sense. The critic contends that art relieves the tension and reconciles the two worlds by bringing them together momentarily "into a sustained and even mystical but never unbelievable whole." In this context, Stevenson introduces the much quoted "Darwin" letter, a statement she elicited from Bishop and that many critics have regarded as the poet's best explanation of her method as an artist and her way of approaching reality. In technique, Stevenson finds Bishop modern in her preoccupation with direct description of the physical world and her tendency to avoid statements of abstract ideas, thus obliging the reader to concentrate on the mental process of perception; but the critic sees her subject as traditional in that the underlying meaning of her poems is rational. In a puzzlingly weak reading of Bishop's "At the Fishhouses," a poem many critics have considered one of her best, Stevenson takes note of the admirable rhythm and sound qualities of the descriptive passages, then speculates that the poet was not aware of using alliteration or other such devices but "heard what she wrote with an ear more sensitive than knowledge"—an underestimation of Bishop's meticulous and highly conscious craftsmanship. Stevenson further judges the simile to which the poem rises (the sea "is like what we imagine knowledge to be . . .") a failure because Bishop departs from her usual practice in presenting an abstract idea directly, so that "At the Fishhouses" becomes "merely a well-trained poem by a good poet." This statement is an instance of the critic being trapped by her preconceived theory of what poetry should be.

Stevenson observes that Bishop, like Wallace Stevens, "puts great emphasis on the organizing power of the imagination" but that she does not hold her perception to "the measure of abstract ideas." In her poems, however, she raises questions of knowledge also raised by modern philosophers and scientists, notably Ludwig Wittgenstein and Werner Heisenberg. Because Bishop does not lack moral certainty but is troubled by "a profound sense of human ignorance," Stevenson finds her in some ways more modern than the great modernist poets T. S. Eliot and Ezra Pound because "she is always true to her sense of ignorance." Her triumph as an artist, Stevenson declares, is that while in mood she comes close to despair, her poems remain under the control of form, wit, and irony and become "an opportunity for elegance."

Critical Studies: Collection of Essays

Elizabeth Bishop and Her Art (1983), edited by Lloyd Schwartz and Sybil P. Estess, offers a rich assembly of material by and about the poet. It is divided into three parts: a group of critical essays (four of them printed here for the first time); a collection of reviews, introductions, and comments, mostly by other poets, about Bishop's work and her life; and a selection—"In Her Own Words"—of Bishop's occasional prose, interviews, and excerpts from essays and reviews. In a provocative foreword, Harold Bloom places Bishop in a tradition that begins with Ralph Waldo Emerson, includes Emily Dickinson, and culminates with Robert Frost, Wallace Stevens, and Marianne Moore; Bloom also places Bishop with William Wordsworth and contrasts their "poetry of deep subjectivity" to the confessional poetry of

Samuel Taylor Coleridge and many of Bishop's contemporaries. Although some of its material is fragmentary, the collection provides a useful directory to sources (where, for instance, Bishop remarked of the confessional poets, "You just wish they'd keep some of these things to themselves," or where Lowell praised Bishop for having "gotten a world, not just a way of writing"). The volume may serve as an introduction to the poet's career but is more useful to those who already know something of her work and literary relationships. The editors' purpose is to show that after enduring years of "misconception, effusion, or condescension," Bishop has finally come to be recognized as a major voice in modern poetry. Because the critical essays included here presuppose some familiarity with critical commonplaces about Bishop—her preoccupation with geography and travel, and her descriptive technique, formal control, understatement, and detachment, for example—they may give a beginner the feeling of having entered a room in the middle of a conversation. For this reason, one might be well advised to read *Elizabeth Bishop and Her Art* from back to front: from Bishop's own words, to the commentaries of other poets, to the important critical essays.

Among these essays, David Kalstone's "Elizabeth Bishop: Questions of Memory, Questions of Travel," reprinted from his book *Five Temperaments* (1977), has properly been placed first, as it traces threads of continuity and marks stages of development through Bishop's whole career. Kalstone examines the elusiveness of form and tone in the early poems: an exuberance in "Florida," for example, that leaves the total structure open to question; the concentrated attention to landscapes that seems at first to exclude the observer; the patient conjuring in "At the Fishhouses" that finally rises to a vision; the exploration of the limits of description in "The Sandpiper," where "every detail is a boundary, not a Blakean microcosm"; and the precarious possession of disappearing or run-down worlds by patient description or domesticating comparisons. Kalstone finds in Bishop's story "In the Village" a gloss on her tendency to seek out landscapes that dwarf or exclude human beings: as the mother, going mad, utters a scream, "the child vanishes literally, and metaphorically as well, in that moment of awakening and awareness of inexplicable adult pain." In *Questions of Travel*, Kalstone says, Bishop's exploration of the landscapes of Brazil suggests how questioning can lead "through the looking glass of natural history" into a symbolic "interior." Bishop examines the world closely, Kalstone argues, because she does not view the human presence in it "as totally real." In *Geography III*, the critic shows, Bishop recalls her earlier works and provides new treatments of them. "In the Waiting Room" invites an autobiographical reading and recalls "In the Village"; "Poem" echoes the earlier "Large Bad Picture," as both concern paintings by Bishop's great-uncle; and "The Moose" returns to the Nova Scotia poems, while "Crusoe in England" looks back to travels in the Southern hemisphere, raising "questions *after* travel." In these works—and especially in "The End of March" and "One Art"—Bishop seems more explicit about naming lost or slender connections as her subject. A new note has entered, however, Kalstone believes: a surprised pleasure "at the power over loss and change which memory has given her writing." In his analysis Kalstone neatly links two elements in *Geography III* that may initially seem at odds: the return to the past and the new self-possession.

Helen Vendler's essay "Domestication, Domesticity and the Otherworldly" (first printed in *World Literature Today*, 1977, and reprinted in her book *Part of Nature, Part of Us,* 1980) examines what she describes as a continuing vibration in Bishop's work "between two frequencies—the domestic and the strange." In her poems of travel, however, "it is not only the exotic that is strange and not only the local that is domestic," Vendler says, for Bishop finds something inscrutable at the heart of the domestic scene. The ultimate threat to the "conjoined intimacy" of the domestic is death, and, conversely, the "definition of life" in Bishop's poems entails "the conversion of the strange to the familial, of the unexplored to the knowable, of the alien to the beloved." Vendler offers persuasive readings of Bishop's poems that should dispel any lingering assumption that her work consists of static observations: in "Poem," for example, which begins with the speaker looking at a small landscape painting, "a strange terrain becomes first recognizable, then familiar, and then beloved." But finally the reader is released from an induced intimacy through a "dismantling," a renewed realization of loss, which in "One Art" takes the extreme form of "disaster." In Bishop's poems, Vendler distinguishes the domestication of the land from the achievement of domesticity, which becomes possible only through the stirring of the affections. Yet, the critic believes, Bishop takes a step beyond domesticity to "the contemplation of the sublimity of the nonhuman world." In "The Moose" the conjoined intimacy of the travelers on the bus is interrupted by the appearance of an animal, to which they respond with joy. Reading Bishop as a modern heir to the Romantic tradition, Vendler argues that in the pure presence of the moose—of that which is perpetually strange and mysterious—the poet gains assurance of "the inexhaustibility of being." Knowledge that "the earth's being is larger than our human enclosures" thus gives "a joy more strange than the familiar blessings of the world made human."

Robert Pinsky's "The Idiom of a Self; Elizabeth Bishop and Wordsworth" (reprinted from the January/February 1980 *American Poetry Review*) avoids discussion of Romanticism as such. He instead uses lines from the *Prelude* about the "mutual domination" of acts of Nature and of "higher minds" (which do not simply feel but also create mutations of outward appearances) to get at what he regards as Bishop's great subject: the contest or "trade-agreement" between the single human soul and the world of artifacts or other people. Pinsky examines Bishop's idiom because it is through language—articulating, mapping, and, especially, defining what she is *not*—that the poet restores herself against the immensity of the world. In "The Waiting Room," a poem about a crisis in the growth of a mind, what the child discovers is not a genial kinship with the world but how "unlikely" her situation is. Contrary to those who have praised Bishop, sometimes faintly, for her loving eye toward the physical world, Pinsky finds a mind "as embattled or resistant as it is loving." He thereby sees this poet as a Wordsworthian "higher mind" at work in the world of things and people: through "perfected plain English" she names, places, and masters—if only momentarily—the terrain. In her poems, it is by persistent attention that Bishop achieves, in Pinsky's view, "freedom of identity"—that is, the power to distinguish between "what one learns and what one is."

In yet another essay linking Bishop with Wordsworth, Willard Spiegelman, in "Elizabeth Bishop's 'Natural Heroism' " (1978), argues that Bishop goes beyond the efforts of Wordsworth and his Romantic heirs to democratize language and poetic subjects, because she replaces "traditional ideas of bravery with a blend of domestic and imaginative strengths." Although he considers Bishop's antimartial "Roosters" atypical, he believes that she often indirectly attacks military formulas and grapples with received values. In "Manuelzinho," a poem that has seemed to some readers disturbingly patronizing, Spiegelman sees instead an "ambivalent and tricky" reversal of roles between patron and tenant-farmer in the speaker's plea at the end for forgiveness. In such relationships, Bishop's "natural"—that is, common or universal—heroism exceeds that of Wordsworth, who demanded epiphanies of otherworldly visitors, whereas Bishop seeks only mutual support, the critic declares. In Bishop's "The Fish" Spiegelman sees a paradigm for much of her work: first a traditional heroic conflict is intimated, then undercut; next comes a "mild revelation"; finally, a "positive re-action" proves the speaker's new-style heroism. The speaker's victory is not the conquest of an enemy, but "the embracing, subsuming, and internalizing of him" by an act of love. This reading is plausible for "The Fish" but provides a questionable pattern for most of her work.

Two essays in this collection examine the relation between isolation and the imagination in Bishop's work. In an original essay, " 'In Prison': A Paradox Regained," David Lehman views Bishop's early story as a paradoxical quest for freedom of the imagination through an escape into "the unadorned cell of consciousness." Lehman finds in the story an anticipation of themes in mature poems such as "The End of March." Lloyd Schwartz's 1977 interpretation of *Geography III*, "One Art: The Poetry of Elizabeth Bishop, 1971-76," defines, as his title indicates, Bishop's constant need to readjust her readers' vision of the world. Like Kalstone, Schwartz sees increased candor in the late poems but also suggests that the early works are more deeply felt and less objective than most critics have supposed. In "The End of March," Schwartz argues, Bishop does not just return to a longing for the Romantic isolation of the story "In Prison" but corrects this longing when the speaker turns away from the boarded up house on the beach as "perfect!—But impossible."

In "The Impersonal and the Interrogative in the Poetry of Elizabeth Bishop," an original essay concerned with Bishop's search for a "home," Bonnie Costello argues that the impersonal voice in Bishop's poems results not from self-denial but rather from questioning of the self through a questioning of the world and human knowledge of it. Because "home"—one's relation to other times, places, and things— is uncertain, the seeker is obliged to question his world and himself; but paradoxically these questions, by pointing to what one can never directly see or get to, give structure to experience and self-awareness. In many of her poems, Costello contends, Bishop uses both the impersonality of her narration and distancing masks to shield the reader from the disorientation she depicts; but in *Geography III,* in the "Elizabeth" of "In the Waiting Room" and in "Crusoe in England" and "The Moose," the masks come dangerously close to identification with the poet herself. By this point, though, Bishop is able to assert a strong ordering presence, Costello says, so that, while she does not falsify her situation—of trauma, dislocation, or dream—readers are not disoriented but are instead guided through a change of consciousness by the interrogative mode. Because Bishop finds the self always changing as the world changes, she remains elusive and reticent, while her questions point to "the very form of our identity," Costello argues.

Critical Studies: Special Issues of Journals

The publication of *Geography III* and the selection of Bishop as the first North American to receive the *Books Abroad*/Neustadt International Prize for Literature, in 1976, marked a turning point in her critical reputation—a general public acknowledgment of her place among the best poets of her generation. In the next year *Books Abroad*, newly renamed *World Literature Today*, published its "Homage to Elizabeth Bishop," comprising tributes and a group of essays about various aspects of her work. In his "Second Presentation of Elizabeth Bishop," John Ashbery praises her as a "writer's writer's writer," whose work inspires intense loyalty in authors of every sort. For Ashbery, Bishop's great subject is the "continually renewed sense of discovering the strangeness, the unreality of our reality at the very moment of becoming conscious of it *as* reality." In her brief "Laureate's Words of Acceptance," Bishop likens herself to the sandpiper of her poem, "Just running along the edges of different countries and continents, 'looking for something.' " Octavio Paz, whom Bishop had translated, offers an eloquent tribute in his "Elizabeth Bishop, or the Power of Reticence." In highly metaphorical language, Paz describes "the color, the temperature, the tone, the quality" of her voice. Like Ashbery, he finds that in her poetry "things waver between what they are and being something distinct from what they are," and observes that this uncertainty is manifested sometimes in humor, other times in metaphor, but is resolved in imaginative leaps by which things are transformed through poetic acts having "the lightness of a game and the gravity of a decision." Her poems have the perfection of living forms, not of theorems, and thus have the integrity of objects made of words that both speak and know when to keep silent, Paz says; in contrast to poets who have allowed ideology and confession to make them garrulous, Bishop gains power from the pauses and silences between her words. In his remarks, "On Elizabeth Bishop," Frank Bidart lays emphasis on "the pain and tremendous struggle" beneath the perfection of her poems, noting the eyes of Bishop's "Giant Toad," which "bulge and hurt," and her "Giant Snail," who can move only with the greatest effort of will. In her work, the world "seems almost to *demand* that someone observe, describe, bear it," Bidart declares.

Two essays in this *World Literature Today* offer highly focused readings of particular poems. In "The Mechanical Horse and the Indian Princess: Two Poems from *North & South*," Lloyd Schwartz contrasts dramatically different poems—"Cirque d'Hiver," set in Paris, and "Florida," Bishop's initial exploration of the tropics. The first is an Apollonian poem "about restraint, necessity," whereas the second is Dionysian, "about hysteria, tantrums, ferocity, 'strong tidal currents,' " Schwartz states. In his close reading of these poems, the critic shows that although "Florida" is a corollary and corrective to "Cirque d'Hiver," in both poems Bishop explores the condition of being trapped in one's own existence. Sybil Estess's "Toward the Interior: Epiphany in 'Cape Breton' as Representative Poem" is an account of how the careful description in that poem gives rise to meditation leading to the achievement of a new consciousness, a recomposition of the poet's mind. Less successful is Estess's attempt to find in Bishop a version of James Joyce's notion of epiphany; her qualified comparison of Joyce and Bishop points to differences more important than the resemblances between them. In "Cape Breton," Bishop's epiphany is that both the idyllic, unhurried natural world and the mechanical devices that disturb it—the observable external objects and the hidden interior—continue in an inevitable cycle of flux, Estess contends.

In "Elizabeth Bishop's Particulars," Jerome Mazzaro describes how as a young writer he first read Bishop's poems, and how over time his understanding of her changed. From the start, Mazzaro gained instruction from the "properties" of her work, meaning not only her exactly observed subject matter but also her flexible prosodic structures. At first struck by Bishop's "direct sensuous apprehension of life," he gradually became aware of a movement in her poems from sensitive memory to reflection, and from simple to complex thinking. Her late poems, however, still develop by particulars, so that "the poem's awarenesses" are defined by their source in experience rather than "any overriding theory of art," Mazzaro declares. Bishop has opened the formal elements of poetry "to new possibilities for seeing and tracking life," challenging restrictions placed on vision by tradition and theories of art. Less radical than Berryman and Lowell, who made their language personal and inimitable, Bishop "purifies the language we all use" and therefore can be more profitably imitated, this critic says.

For Howard Moss, in "The Canada-Brazil Connection," geography tells only part of the story. What Bishop connects in her work are the normal and the odd, the homely and the fantastic, and the domestic *in* the exotic. Bishop's imagination is stirred by new places or by old ones seen from a new viewpoint, but more than a change of view is implied in her "transference" to another world: "Where other poets change coats, Bishop sheds skins," Moss notes. In each new poem, he says, we are led to a "widening of perception in general. Who else would have connected a sandpiper and William Blake? Or Baudelaire and marimba music?" By precise description, Bishop exposes differences where conformity, even banality, had been assumed. Her particulars test reality but also test—and prove—the truthfulness of the poet, "putting both the viewer and the viewed on the scale." Despite Bishop's clarity of vision, Moss says, a division deeper than geographical polarities complicates her perception and creates an electric undercurrent in her poetry: "reserve at war with the congenial," judgment with acceptance. The seeming casualness of Bishop's poems is belied by their concentration; they reject alternatives yet explore profound emotions. In her poems, "restraint" does not imply diminution or self-enclosure but "elegance and withheld power," Moss concludes.

In 1984, *Field,* a journal of contemporary poetry and poetics, devoted part of one issue to a symposium on Bishop, a fulfillment of "the simple wish to honor her poetic canon." Eight poets are included, and each has selected a single poem for comment. For the most part, the commentaries are short, informal, and idiosyncratic, though two writers pursue a theme: David Walker on the "ordinary" in "Filling Station" and Sherod Santos on Bishop's "patience" in "The End of March." In a somewhat more formal analysis, Elizabeth Spires reads "At the Fishhouses" as a meditation on the problem of " 'netting' or knowing anything with any degree of certainty in a physically everchanging world." In "Some Notes on 'One Art,' " J. D. McClatchy, in the most ambitious of these commentaries, argues that Bishop chooses the villanelle because the intractable strictness of its form permits the articulation of a grief barely under control. The *Field* symposium mostly returns to familiar themes among Bishop's critics but attests to her continuing appeal for this generation of poets.

Critical Studies: Major Articles and Book Sections

In 1935 Marianne Moore effectively introduced Bishop to the public in "Archaically New," the older poet's comments accompanying a small selection of early Bishop poems printed in the anthology *Trial Balances.* Bishop had been published before, but Moore's praise of her "rational considering quality," her "oblique, intent way of work-ing," and her originality in technique announced a line of succession by defining Bishop's art in terms of Moore's own achievements as a high modernist poet. When Bishop's first book, *North & South*, was published in 1946, Moore's review hailed "A Modest Expert," who was "spectacular in being unspectacular." At the same time, Bishop was taken up by the poets of her own generation who would dominate critical opinion: Randall Jarrell declared, in "The Poet and His Public," that "all her poems have written underneath, *I have seen it*"; Robert Lowell, in "Thomas, Bishop, and Williams," found in her "unrhetorical, cool, and beautifully thought out poems" something eluding description, and also identified two opposing factors—a weary, stoically persisting motion and "a terminus, rest, sleep, fulfill-ment or death." Both Jarrell and Lowell, in common with other re-viewers, called attention to Moore as a model for or influence on Bishop's first book. Much of the subsequent critical analysis of Bishop's work has been an elaboration of or reaction to the terms laid down by these poets and has weighed also the presence of Moore and Lowell in Bishop's career. Because she published infrequently and avoided literary circles, and because there remained something elusive (as Lowell was the first to observe) about her much admired craft, she was not identified with any particular school of poetry but in successive decades has continued to be taken up for praise and discriminating comment by poets: in the 1950s, by Richard Eberhart, Howard Nem-erov, and, in England, G. S. Fraser; in the 1960s, by Howard Moss, James Merrill, and John Ashbery; and from the 1970s on, as her reputation grew, by a widening range of poets, some having little in common but admiration for her work.

Bishop has had her detractors, as well (although neglect rather than denigration has done her more harm). Oscar Williams, in his 1946 *New Republic* review of *North & South*, found her overeducated in the fashionable style of Auden and Wallace Stevens, while Stephen Stepanchev, in *American Poetry Since 1945: A Critical Survey* (1965), failed to find a unifying design in her descriptive details. Among her English critics, Bishop's reception has been mixed. She was faulted by Ian Hamilton, in his December 1967 assessment of *Selected Poems*, for the coolness and excessive control of the early poems, and by Charles Tomlinson, in his review of *Questions of Travel*, for giving "resolutely minor answers" to big questions. Since her death in 1979, Bishop's reputation has risen steadily among American readers; re-viewing *Complete Poems, 1927-1979* in the *New York Times Book Review*,

David Bromwich wrote that among the poets of her generation "Elizabeth Bishop alone now seems secure beyond the disputation of schools or the sway of period loyalties." In England, Andrew Motion presented his 1984 Chatterton Lecture, an extensive examination of her work, as an "introduction" to Bishop—who, the critic contends, has been overshadowed by her contemporaries Lowell and Berryman and whose neglect may have resulted from the suggestion that her poems were excessively refined. Motion observes, however, that because of a shift in taste during the 1980s, Bishop has influenced a new generation of English poets interested in pictorial language and ingenuity in the use of metaphor, to whom her eye, wit, and feeling especially appeal.

Several of the earliest extended discussions of Bishop's poems center on her meticulous descriptive technique. Nancy L. McNally, in "Elizabeth Bishop: The Discipline of Description" (1966), sees Bishop's poetic intentions as different from those of Moore, but follows the familiar line back to Moore in describing Bishop as "an impersonal but highly perceptive observer." McNally asserts that Bishop avoids moralizing in favor of "vision"—that is, clear seeing—and allows descriptive details, rather than theme or symbol, to "form the framework of her poems." In her 1973 *Salmagundi* article, "Days and Distances: The Cartographic Imagination of Elizabeth Bishop," Jan B. Gordon generalizes Bishop's interest in topography to a method, then complains that it reduces life to a "flat objectivity," just as Bishop reduces complex poetic issues to technical questions. In Gordon's judgment, "We see no possibility of a therapeutic progression in a world so relativized that 'North's as near as West' precisely because hers is at best a two-dimensional craft." In 1974, Jerome Mazzaro, in his "Elizabeth Bishop and the Poetics of Impediment," offers a counterargument to such critics as Stepanchev and Gordon, who find Bishop's poems lacking in design or direction, and to McNally and others who find her impersonal. By "impediment," Mazzaro (borrowing a suggestion from John Crowe Ransom) means a density of detail that asserts the value of what is being described. Bishop's poems do not progress toward a definite goal because she sees her situation in life, not just her attitude toward it, as relative, Mazzaro declares; abandoning preconceived superstructures of thought, she amasses detail into significant form, giving to the reader "the only durability that she has discovered"—the poem.

In her essay "Elizabeth Bishop: The Delicate Art of Map Making" (1977), Sybil P. Estess, invoking Wallace Stevens, agrees that "Bishop's map reveals the interpenetration of imagination and reality." But whereas Mazzaro suggests that time and necessity create the contours of the "impediments" Bishop shaped into poems of experience, Estess argues that the imagination does not violate "things as they are"— Bishop's images are not arbitrary—but that imagination also "illuminates the particular contours of any reality." Discussing Bishop's "Sandpiper," Estess distinguishes the Blakean visionary search for ultimate illumination (which Bishop rejects) from acts of contemplation ("re-finding the things of this world") and of meditation (seeking "understanding, sometimes even transcendence"). The illumination of particulars by seeing them in a new way is what Estess calls "epiphany." (See the comments above on Estess's "Toward the Interior: Epiphany in 'Cape Breton' as Representative Poem.") Marjorie Perloff, like Mazzaro and Estess, disputes critics who accuse Bishop of being "too impersonal, too detached, too unwilling to go beyond surfaces and expose her inner feelings." In her "Elizabeth Bishop: The Course of a Particular" (1977), she analyzes Bishop's story "In the Village" to show that the sights and sounds the child so eagerly takes in do not really detach her from the situation of her mother's breakdown, but instead allow her "to exorcise pain that would otherwise be unbearable" and to discipline herself so that it no longer hurts. Although otherwise close to Mazzaro in her reading of Bishop, Perloff finds the "ecological" lyrics—such as "Map" and the "Bight"—"that treat the particular as numinous rather than as representative" more successful than poems such as "Roosters," "Weed," and "The Fish," which Mazzaro prefers for their psychological and symbolic values. Perloff concludes that Bishop's sparsely peopled landscapes are nonetheless "expressive of a very personal vision" and of a commitment of herself to the world.

In an early essay, "Conjuring with Nature: Some Twentieth-Century Readings of Pastoral" (1971), David Kalstone places Bishop with Frost and Stevens as poets whose relation to nature is not that of companionable song but of exploration. Bishop, labeled by this critic a modern pastoral artist, takes uncertainty of vision for granted, but by an "absolute submission to the scene she describes" finds a way "to reclaim the nature from which her speakers are excluded." Kalstone offers a careful reading of the language in "At the Fishhouses," a scene "almost without a spectator," in which the fisherman, a Wordsworthian solitary, "is faded into the scene"; the critic thus shows that it is by imagining the encircling powers of nature that the poet "wins some power over them." Following Kalstone's lead, Willard Spiegelman, in "Landscape and Knowledge: The Poetry of Elizabeth Bishop" (1975), argues that she is "an epistemological poet in the tradition of William Wordsworth and S. T. Coleridge." Spiegelman discovers in "At the Fishhouses" and other poems of nature the formula for the Romantic lyric: "a dramatic encounter with a scene or an individual" leading to a moral decision "or to the acceptance of the boundaries of self and world." (See also Spiegelman's "Elizabeth Bishop's 'Natural Heroism,' " 1978, Helen Vendler's "Domestication, Domesticity and the Otherworldly," 1977, and Robert Pinsky's "The Idiom of a Self; Elizabeth Bishop and Wordsworth," 1980.) Examining the poems of *Geography III,* J. D. McClatchy, in "The Other Bishop" (1977), borrowing words from "At the Fishhouses," argues that Bishop has too often been read as a poet "absolutely clear," whereas she has revealed herself as a poet "cold dark deep." He suggests that Randall Jarrell's "The Other Frost" offers as much illumination of Bishop as it does of its actual subject, Robert Frost, since the two poets are equally "obsessed with the vain, bleak effort to domesticate the world." In *Geography III,* despite the topological title, Bishop's concern is not with spatial but with temporal relations, with history, memory, fixation, and with "overdetermined context or undermining agent," McClatchy declares.

David Bromwich, in "Elizabeth Bishop's Dream-Houses" (1984), also attempts to redirect critical opinion away from praise of her accuracy and charm, and especially away from Lowell's "misreading of Bishop as a voice of resonant sincerity." Bromwich argues that "Bishop's work offers resistance to any surmise about the personality of the author" because the poems have been furnished with "eccentric details or gestures" that protect them from appropriation by the reader. The critic describes Bishop in martial terms, as an artist whose "weapons in art as in life" suggest reserves of personal strength. Like Frost and Stevens, Bishop (at the end of "The Monument") invokes "the power of metaphor to shape a life," and she gains authority by "active displacements of perspective," he contends; moreover, in Bishop sexuality is elusive because it has been allegorized, allegory being a safeguard of the soul's integrity. Bromwich finds in her geographical poems "a figure of the soul's encounter with fate," in which a dream of freedom "is interpreted as a helpless revolt against the conditions of experience." Bromwich's argument, though perhaps overstated, offers a bracing counter to the sometimes patronizing view of Bishop as merely a well-mannered sensitive observer.

For Bonnie Costello, in "Vision and Mastery in Elizabeth Bishop"

(1982), Jarrell's claim that Bishop's poems have written beneath them *"I have seen it"* sounds too much like a "Romantic absolute invested in the physical world." Instead, Costello believes, Bishop "is more likely to write 'I have seen it leaving,' for mutability is her theme." In the poet's works, Costello finds a cycle of feeling that begins with a dismantling or pushing back of some comprehensive vision and leads to darkness or something impenetrable from which emerges a "compensatory glimpse" of a mundane figure or image. This process does not produce, as some critics have called it, an "epiphany," an image of permanence; it provides, instead, a source of momentary satisfaction, the critic declares. Costello, like Bromwich, finds manipulations of perspective in Bishop's poems and argues that they function to disrupt the feeling of mastery one gains by viewing a landscape from a fixed vantage point. While Bishop described herself as a Wordsworthian nature poet, Costello places her with Keats and Stevens, in "the line of reticent chameleon poets." Bishop is not, however, autumnal like Keats, nor elegiac like Stevens: "She does not descend into darkness but returns to 'all the untidy activity,' 'awful but cheerful,' " Costello writes. Barbara Page's study of Bishop's rough drafts, "Shifting Islands: Elizabeth Bishop's Manuscripts" (1981-1982), draws a parallel between her habits of revision in writing poems and the subject of revision or reconsideration treated in the poems. In Bishop's tribute to Lowell, "North Haven," mutability is not associated with death but with the vitality of the imagination; the sadness of Lowell's death is that he can no longer change himself or revise his words, Page declares. In "Santarém," Bishop works her drafts away from a confrontation between opposing choices (life/death, right/wrong, male/female) toward a resolution in the act of remembering that reconciles mind and sense in a "dazzling dialectic." This is a process, which in "Questions of Travel" allows the poet to dream her dream and have it too, Page argues. In "Elizabeth Bishop: The Art of Changing Your Mind" (1979), Jane Shore examines Bishop's verbal habit of changing her metaphors mid-poem. At times the poet seems ambivalent toward her image, but on closer inspection the reader detects, in a second point of view, "a contradictory, often perverse, subtext," Shore says. In her metaphors (the taximeter as a "moral owl" is an exemplary case), Bishop brings together images that not only contrast with but ominously undercut one another, and by shifting metaphors within the poem, "she lets us hold the two, often conflicting, views of the same things at the same time." Bishop's handling of metaphor offers a paradigm, Shore believes, for the conflicts in "Santarém":

"ferrying back and forth between the two halves of the metaphor," Bishop makes her readers change their minds by showing them something one way, then another, while creating a new world in the "fusions of metaphor."

Michael Ryan's 1984 essay, "A Dark Gray Flame," examines the question of tone in Bishop's work and her success in writing vernacular poems free from the "ceremoniously 'poetic.' " Returning to remarks made by Marianne Moore in 1944 (in "Precision and Feeling") and to Howard Moss in his praise of Bishop's "exactitude of detail," Ryan describes her passion for the discovery of similarity amid dissimilarity, which both "makes something wonderful out of something ordinary" and transmutes it by introducing the life of the describer into the thing described without the mediation of a "comprehensive philosophy." (Howard Moss has shown how the particularity of Bishop's description also leads readers to question the actuality of sameness among similar things. See his "The Canada-Brazil Connection" discussed in another part of this essay.) The "strangeness" of Bishop's poems derives from her "turning" them, often by a change in rhythm, so that she can begin with an "absolute naturalness of tone" and still enact the transmutation of elements that transforms the language from prose to poetry. This effect is achieved without mystification; in contrast to the works of the Symbolists, "the mystery in Bishop's poetry depends on clarity, the transparent surface of words," Ryan argues.

In "Elizabeth Bishop's Surrealist Inheritance" (1982) Richard Mullen locates some of the mystery in Bishop's poetry in "her preoccupation with dreams, sleep, and the borders between sleeping and waking." His essay traces Bishop's early interest in the surrealist doctrines of German painter Max Ernst and others but is most useful in noting ways in which her work differs from that of the surrealists. Where the surrealists render objects enigmatic by dissociating them from their expected surroundings, Bishop links disparate things by a process of "ingenious association." An exponent of idiomatic American speech, she rejects the surrealists' deliberate violations of syntax, just as she avoids the grotesque distortings of dream images of the paintings of Salvador Dali or the poems of André Breton; instead, Mullen declares, she prefers "to investigate natural displacements," the "always-more-successful surrealism of everyday life," as she put it.

Like Michael Ryan, Lorrie Goldensohn, in "Elizabeth Bishop's Originality" (1978), is concerned with how Bishop, as a descriptive artist, achieves her distinctive tone; it is one that is accomplished primarily, the critic believes, through leaps of incongruity and dislocations that Goldensohn identifies as a form of zeugma, the linking of opposed or discordant elements. Pointing out the many instances, especially in the earlier poems, of miniaturization, she argues that in these distortions of perspective, "the issue is control by imaginative power": the powers of the conceiver grow "proportionately large as the landscape shrinks." At the heart of Bishop's adjustments of perspective in poems like "Florida," Goldensohn finds a "dual exhilaration and depression" and the mind of "a natural dialectician working both sides of the street." In Bishop's reticence, the critic sees a strategic understatement, a refusal of the Romantic egotistical sublime, and a preference for "the traditional masks of the unidentified observer-narrator or the dramatized speaker." In the later poems, however, Goldensohn discovers "mutations of focus": as Bishop more and more adopts the perspective of a child, "space contracts, objects enlarge." The art of *Geography III*, which is domestic and pastoral, gives readers that "little of our earthly trust," which for Bishop is all humans have; but, in Goldensohn's view, it is a "little" that achieves closure and completeness when seen with the "enlarging powers of attention."

Two speculative essays raise the question of whether the shifts in perspective that many critics have noticed in Bishop's work are not characteristic of the poetry of women in general. In "Double Monologues: Voices in American Women's Poetry" (1982), Susan R. Van Dyne argues that a "doubleness of perspective or tone" is the single distinguishing feature in the poetry of American women, who have been obliged to stand "beside themselves," abandoning "an assertive, imposing presence" for "an obliquely positioned, yet wonderfully encompassing eye." Often, the most powerful implications of poems composed under these conditions are discharged in silence and entrusted to innuendo, Van Dyne suggests. This technique can work to good effect, as in Bishop's "Poem"; recalling a childhood scene, she takes up a Wordsworthian subject without "succumbing to the temptation of egocentricity implied in the Romantic or post-Romantic vision" and achieves an emotional clarity in exploring "the resonances of her childlike voice alongside her characteristic reserve and self-irony." In "Emily Dickinson, Elizabeth Bishop, and the Rewards of Indirection" (1984), Lynn Keller and Cristanne Miller also see poetic gains through the restraints imposed on the voices of women. Observing that in common conversation women are less directive than men and are more likely to use questions to deflect attention from themselves to another person or to the topic, Keller and Miller examine the techniques of indirection in literary tradition and in women's speech that Dickinson and Bishop have used to "hide strength while exercising it," to reveal intense personal concerns, and to subvert the direct statement of the poem with socially disruptive perspectives. The critics' most arresting analysis is of Bishop's "Brazil, January 1, 1502," which offers a contrast to David Bromwich's discussion in "Elizabeth Bishop's Dream-Houses" (discussed above). In this poem, according to Keller and Miller, "Bishop suggests a pattern of action for the woman poet" by identifying with the predicament of the native women of Brazil, who, repeating their calls, retreat into the tapestry of the wilderness. Nature is thus both self-renewing and permanent—"embroidered"—and both conceals and includes the women who retreat into it. As a woman poet and the maker of the tapestry of nature in the poem, Bishop implicitly identifies herself with a lasting creation. She consequently both calls attention to herself as a visual artist and creator of an indestructible work and effaces herself "from the surface of a poem ostensibly about the conquest of Brazil," Keller and Miller declare. (See also Adrienne Rich's "The Eye of the Outsider," 1983, a review of *The Complete Poems, 1927-1979,* in which she reads Bishop "as part of a female and lesbian tradition rather than simply as one of the few and 'exceptional' women admitted to the male canon.")

The remarkable friendship between Bishop and Moore has been examined from different angles in three essays, published within a year's time. Lynn Keller's "Words Worth a Thousand Postcards: The Bishop/Moore Correspondence" (1983) describes the letters between the two poets and traces the stages of their relationship principally in regard to the growth of Bishop's career. Keller divides what she calls the apprenticeship period into two parts: the first extending from their meeting in 1934, while Bishop was still in college, until the fall of 1936, when Moore began introducing Bishop to the literary scene; and the second encompassing that period when Moore took an active part in offering Bishop advice and criticism of her work. During these years, Moore's interest became increasingly "possessive and controlling," Keller says, while Bishop slowly gained self-confidence, until, in the fall of 1940, she decisively refused Moore's intrusive revisions of "Roosters." Although their friendship endured until Moore's death and she continued to offer Bishop both public and private encouragement, thereafter their literary relationship changed. Bishop rarely sent Moore unpublished poems since the younger poet realized that, despite certain sympathies of taste and outlook, the two writers were very different.

Bonnie Costello, who also provides a history of this relationship in "Marianne Moore and Elizabeth Bishop: Friendship and Influence" (1984), draws a series of incisive and illuminating contrasts between the personal and poetic character of Moore, "the Protestant poet of manners and morals," and Bishop, "the skeptic poet of mysteries." Costello asserts that the mentor and her protegée formed a partnership of complementary rather than mutual interests—between the gentlewoman, who "looks after the good and the beautiful," and the seeker, who "looks after the true." Costello quotes at length from Moore's proprietary letter correcting "Roosters" and from Bishop's reply—which, incidentally, offers an important commentary on one of her best poems—to show how clearly their interests and aesthetic standards diverged. Moore cherished "neatness of finish" and a cerebral, civilized manner, while for Bishop, "the language of poetry is justified by its faithfulness to the texture of experience." In Costello's view, Bishop learned from Moore the lesson of restraint. This lesson served her well as her "moral inquiry" led her toward the expression of a "tragic rather than exemplary beauty," unanchored by the kind of fixed moral base from which Moore's poems proceed but instead moving toward the moral condition of uncertainty and mystery, loss, temporality, memory, and desire. Costello notes, however, that Moore and Bishop together revived the art of personification, scorned by many modernists; for them, "personification was as much a way of getting outside the limits of the human perspective as of imposing a human point of view." The "armored Moore" (in Lowell's words) and the dreamy, "disarmed traveler" lived very different lives; yet Bishop found in Moore "a source of stability, vigorous enchantment, optimism, and dedication to craft," while Moore found in Bishop "a source of vicarious adventure and mystery" and an admirable example of personal and artistic courage, Costello concludes.

In "Trial Balances: Elizabeth Bishop and Marianne Moore" (1983), David Kalstone, pursuing his interest in biography and art, offers the most vivid picture of Bishop and Moore in their long relationship, from Bishop's first reading Moore's poetry in college—"it immediately opened up my eyes to the possibility of the subject-matter I could use"—to the memoir of Moore that Bishop left unfinished at her death (now published as "Efforts of Affection" in *The Collected Prose*). Kalstone's essay views Bishop as a necessary traveler owing to the early loss of her parents and home, a traveler who felt like something of a "truant" beside Moore in her life of "domestic economy," and who found in the older woman "both a model and a point of departure, an authority against which she could explore, even indulge, her more anarchic impulses." In the early years of their friendship, Bishop seemed little interested in Moore's connection to the modernist poets but was attracted by her old-fashioned manners and mannerisms—like those of her relatives in Nova Scotia—as well as "her forthright notions about writing and style." Moore's influence, or example (Kalstone finds her exact role in Bishop's emergence as a poet mysterious), helped Bishop find her vocation: "Bishop was a keen observer before she met Moore; learning that this could be a way of life identified with a way of writing was another matter." Only gradually did the "truant" Bishop discover that her traveler's observations were a poetic strength "rather than a dereliction or a self-indulgence." In gradually finding how to allow urgent feeling to appear and reorder her sensibilities so that she might "place" her childhood, Bishop learned to trust indirection and deflected her energies from narrative to description. Differing from Keller in his estimate of Bishop's "apprenticeship," Kalstone notes that Bishop had already struck out on an independent course when she met Moore. But he contends that the example of Moore's poems, which "locate an intellectual or emotional impulse, a center of energy," helped Bishop dispel her narrative ambitions "in favor of description and observation" of the kind that permitted her to write poems like "At the Fishhouses," "Cape Breton," and "Over 2,000 Illustrations and a Complete Concordance."

In his "Prodigal Years: Elizabeth Bishop and Robert Lowell, 1947-49" (1985), Kalstone turns to the other crucial literary friendship in Bishop's life. Between Bishop and Lowell there was no question of apprenticeship; but while Lowell was at home in "the grit of the postwar-poetry world," Bishop "fell easily into the role of amateur and outsider," and Lowell took the place Moore had filled before. Both Moore and Lowell were industrious and directorial, both pressed Bishop's career forward, and against both she played out "private dramas of disobedience which seemed to nourish the discomfited poems she was writing," Kalstone asserts. Following trips to Nova Scotia and Cape Breton in the late 1940s, Bishop wrote "At the Fishhouses" and other major landscape poems as "attempts to naturalize her homelessness." (Missing from them, Kalstone observes, is "the remembered recuperative power of village life," which appears in the stories she was able to write only later, after she settled in Brazil.) Bishop was reading Lowell and had images from his poems in her mind. At the core of Kalstone's essay is his persuasive reading of the autobiographical element in her poem "The Prodigal," which, he believes, reveals what she owed to Lowell's poems and "to their shared darker moods." In this poem Bishop sorted out the questions of influence and of the tensions between her life in Key West and her memories of Nova Scotia. Lowell was influential at this moment because "he had given her a way of talking about her own instability and had implicitly challenged her to do so." Kalstone's use of biography to locate a source of Bishop's strength as a descriptive artist and as a poet of indirection illuminates the haunting humanity in her poems. His readings point the way to fresh understanding of Bishop's life and art.

James Dickey

(1923-)

Ronald Baughman
University of South Carolina

PRIMARY BIBLIOGRAPHY

Books

Into the Stone and Other Poems, in *Poets of Today VII,* edited by John Hall Wheelock. New York: Scribners, 1960. Poems.

Drowning with Others. Middletown, Conn.: Wesleyan University Press, 1962. Poems.

Helmets. Middletown, Conn.: Wesleyan University Press, 1964; London: Longmans, 1964. Poems.

The Suspect in Poetry. Madison, Minn.: Sixties Press, 1964. Essays.

Buckdancer's Choice. Middletown, Conn.: Wesleyan University Press, 1965. Poems.

Poems 1957-1967. Middletown, Conn.: Wesleyan University Press, 1967; London: Rapp & Carroll, 1967. Poems.

Spinning the Crystal Ball. Washington, D. C.: Library of Congress, 1967. Essay.

Babel to Byzantium: Poets and Poetry Now. New York: Farrar, Straus & Giroux, 1968. Reprinted with new afterword. New York: Ecco Press, 1981. Essays.

Metaphor as Pure Adventure. Washington, D. C.: Library of Congress, 1968. Essay.

Deliverance. Boston: Houghton Mifflin, 1970; London: Hamish Hamilton, 1970. Novel.

The Eye-Beaters, Blood, Victory, Madness, Buckhead and Mercy. Garden City, N. Y.: Doubleday, 1970; London: Hamish Hamilton, 1971. Poems.

Self-Interviews, recorded and edited by Barbara and James Reiss. Garden City, N.Y.: Doubleday, 1970. Essays.

Jericho: The South Beheld, text by Dickey and paintings by Hubert Shuptrine. Birmingham, Ala.: Oxmoor House, 1974. Essays.

The Zodiac. Garden City, N.Y.: Doubleday, 1976; London: Hamish Hamilton, 1976. Bloomfield Hills, Mich. & Columbia, S.C.: Bruccoli Clark, 1976—Limited edition of 61 numbered and signed copies, each of which contains one page of the revised working draft of the poem. Poem.

God's Image, text by Dickey and etchings by Marvin Hayes. Birmingham, Ala.: Oxmoor House, 1977. Essays.

Tucky the Hunter. New York: Crown, 1978; London: Macmillan, 1979. Children's poem.

The Strength of Fields. Garden City, N.Y.: Doubleday, 1979. Poems and translations.

Puella. Garden City, N.Y.: Doubleday, 1982. Poems.

Night Hurdling: Poems, Essays, Conversations, Commencements, and Afterwords. Columbia, S.C. & Bloomfield Hills, Mich.: Bruccoli Clark, 1983.

Selected Letters

Bartlett, Lee, and Hugh Witemeyer. "Ezra Pound and James Dickey: A Correspondence and a Kinship," *Paideuma,* 2 (Fall 1982), 290-312. Letters between Pound and Dickey, with commentary by Bartlett and Witemeyer.

Journal

Sorties. Garden City, N.Y.: Doubleday, 1971. Journal and essays.

Selected Prose

"Small Visitors from a Timeless Place: The South as One Poet Has Known It," *Playboy,* 21 (Oct. 1974), 152-154, 220-221.

"Notes for Works in Progress." In *Pages: The World of Books, Writers, and Writing,* ed. Matthew J. Bruccoli and C. E. Frazer Clark, Jr. Detroit: Gale Research, 1976, 9-19.

"Frantic to Overtake Himself," *New York Times Book Review,* 18 Sept. 1977, pp. 7, 44. Review of *Jack: A Biography of Jack London* by Andrew Sinclair.

"Compassionate Classicist," *New York Times Book Review,* 10 Dec. 1978, pp. 14, 56-57. Review of *This Blessed Earth* and *Afternoon: Amaganset Beach* by John Hall Wheelock.

Eberhart, Richard. *Of Poetry and Poets,* foreword by Dickey. Urbana: University of Illinois Press, 1979, ix-xii.
Twain, Mark. *The Adventures of Tom Sawyer and Adventures of Huckleberry Finn,* introduction—"Boys of the River-God"—by Dickey. New York: New American Library, 1979, v-x.
"Selling His Soul to the Devil by Day . . . and Buying it Back by Night," *T.V. Guide,* 14 July 1979, pp. 18-20.
Wyrick, Charles L., Jr. *Oystering: A Way of Life,* foreword by Dickey. Charleston, S.C.: Carolina Art Association, 1983 [1].

Selected Story

"Cahill Is Blind," *Esquire,* 85 (Feb. 1976), 67-69, 139-144.

Translation

Yevtushenko, Yevgeny. *Stolen Apples,* 12 poems adapted by Dickey. Garden City, N.Y.: Doubleday, 1971.

Screenplays

Deliverance. Warner Bros., 1972. Carbondale & Edwardsville: Southern Illinois University Press, 1982.
Call of the Wild. Charles Fries, 1976.

Documentary Films

A Poetry Experience on Film: Lord, Let Me Die But Not Die Out. Chicago: Encyclopaedia Britannica, 1970. About Dickey.
One-Third of a Nation: The Depression in the South. South Carolina Educational Television, 1982. Dickey narrates.

Recordings

The Poems of James Dickey (1957-1967). Spoken Arts, SA 984.
The Spoken Arts: Treasury of 100 Modern American Poets, vol. 15, SA 1054.
James Dickey Reading His Poetry. Caedmon, 1971—TC 1333.

Editions and Collections

Poems. Melbourne, Australia: Sun Books, 1968. Poems.

Lieberman, Laurence. *The Achievement of James Dickey: A Comprehensive Selection of His Poems with a Critical Introduction*. Glenview, Ill.: Scott, Foresman, 1968. Poems.

The Early Motion: Drowning with Others and Helmets. Middletown, Conn.: Wesleyan University Press, 1981. Poems.

Falling, May Day Sermon, and Other Poems. Middletown, Conn.: Wesleyan University Press, 1981. Poems.

The Central Motion: Poems 1968-1979. Middletown, Conn.: Wesleyan University Press, 1983. Poems.

SECONDARY BIBLIOGRAPHY

Bibliographies and Checklists

Ashley, Franklin B. *James Dickey: A Checklist*. Columbia, S.C. & Detroit: Bruccoli Clark/Gale Research, 1972. Primary.

Covel, Robert C. "Bibliography," *James Dickey Newsletter*, 1 (Fall 1984), 15-27. Primary and secondary.

_____. "Bibliography," *James Dickey Newsletter*, 2 (Fall 1985), 21-30. Primary and secondary.

Elledge, Jim. *James Dickey: A Bibliography, 1947-1974*. Metuchen, N.J. & London: Scarecrow Press, 1979. Primary and secondary.

_____. "James Dickey: A Supplementary Bibliography, 1975-1980: Part I," *Bulletin of Bibliography*, 38 (Apr.-June 1981), 92-100, 104. Primary and secondary.

_____. "James Dickey: A Supplementary Bibliography, 1975-1980: Part II," *Bulletin of Bibliography*, 38 (July-Sept. 1981), 150-155. Secondary.

Glancy, Eileen K. *James Dickey: The Critic as Poet: An Annotated Bibliography with an Introductory Essay*. Troy, N.Y.: Whitson, 1971. Primary and secondary.

Hill, Robert W. "James Dickey: A Checklist." Collected in *James Dickey: The Expansive Imagination*, ed. Richard J. Calhoun, 215-228. Secondary. See Critical Studies: Collections of Essays.

Vannatta, Dennis. "James Dickey: A Checklist of Secondary Sources." Collected in *The Imagination as Glory: The Poetry of James Dickey*, ed. Bruce Weigl and T. R. Hummer, 174-195. Secondary. See Critical Studies: Collections of Essays.

Wright, Stuart T. *James Dickey: A Bibliography of His Books, Pamphlets, and Broadsides*. Dallas, Tex.: Pressworks, 1982. Primary.

Selected Interviews

Arnett, David L. "An Interview with James Dickey," *Contemporary Literature*, 16 (Summer 1975), 286-300.

Ashley, Franklin B. "James Dickey: The Art of Poetry," *Paris Review*, 17 (Spring 1976), 52-88. Reprinted in *Writers at Work*, ed. George Plimpton. New York: Viking, 1981, 199-229.

Barnwell, W. C. "James Dickey on Yeats: An Interview," *Southern Review*, 13 (Spring 1977), 311-316.

Bruccoli, Matthew J. "James Dickey." In *Conversations with Writers: Volume I*. Detroit: Bruccoli Clark/Gale Research, 1977, 24-45.

Cassidy, Jerry. "What the Poetry Editor of *Esquire* Is Like: Interview with James Dickey," *Writer's Digest*, 54 (Oct. 1974), 16-20.

Davis, Will, et al. "James Dickey: An Interview." Collected in *James Dickey: Splintered Sunlight*, ed. Patricia De La Fuente, 6-23. See Critical Studies: Collections of Essays.

Graham, John. "James Dickey." In *The Writer's Voice: Conversations with Contemporary Writers*, ed. George Garrett. New York: William Morrow, 1973, 228-247.

Greiner, Donald J. " 'That Plain-Speaking Guy': A Conversation with James Dickey on Robert Frost." In *Robert Frost: Centennial Essays*, compiled by the Committee on the Frost Centennial. Jackson: University Press of Mississippi, 1974, 51-59.

Heyen, William, and Peter Marchant. "A Conversation with James Dickey," *Southern Review*, new series, 9 (Winter 1973), 135-156. Reprinted as "In Louisiana" in *Night Hurdling*.

Kizer, Carolyn, and James Boatwright. "A Conversation with James Dickey," *Shenandoah*, 18 (Autumn 1966), 3-28. Collected in *James Dickey: The Expansive Imagination*, ed. Richard J. Calhoun. See Critical Studies: Collections of Essays. Reprinted as "In Virginia" in *Night Hurdling*.

Moyers, Bill. *A Conversation with James Dickey*. New York: Educational Broadcasting Corporation, 1976. Mimeographed transcription of Dickey's appearance on *Bill Moyers' Journal*, 25 Jan. 1976. Reprinted as "Conversation on a Dock" in *Night Hurdling*.

Norman, Geoffrey. "*Playboy* Interview: James Dickey," *Playboy*, 20 (Nov. 1973), 81-82, 86, 89, 92, 94, 212-216.

Packard, William. "Craft Interview with James Dickey," *New York*

Quarterly, no. 10 (Spring 1972), 16-35. Reprinted in *The Craft of Poetry: Interviews from* The New York Quarterly," ed. Packard. Garden City, N.Y.: Doubleday, 1974. Reprinted as "In New York" in *Night Hurdling.*

Page, William. "River City Interview with James Dickey," *Memphis State Review,* 5 (Fall 1984), 30-39.

Critical Studies: Books

Baughman, Ronald. *Understanding James Dickey.* Columbia: University of South Carolina Press, 1985.

Bowers, Neal. *James Dickey: The Poet as Pitchman.* Columbia: University of Missouri Press, 1985.

Calhoun, Richard J., and Robert W. Hill. *James Dickey.* Boston: Twayne, 1983.

Critical Studies: Collections of Essays

Calhoun, Richard J., ed. *James Dickey: The Expansive Imagination: A Collection of Critical Essays.* De Land, Fla.: Everett/Edwards, 1973.

De La Fuente, Patricia, ed. *James Dickey: Splintered Sunlight: Interview, Essays, and Bibliography.* "Living Authors Series" Number 2. Edinburg, Tex.: Pan American University, 1979.

Weigl, Bruce, and T. R. Hummer, eds. *The Imagination as Glory: The Poetry of James Dickey.* Urbana & Chicago: University of Illinois Press, 1984.

Critical Studies: Newsletter

James Dickey Newsletter, ed. Joyce M. Pair. Dunwoody, Ga.: DeKalb Community College, Fall 1984- .

Critical Studies: Special Issue of Journal

South Carolina Review, 10 (Apr. 1978).

Critical Studies: Major Articles and Book Sections

Adams, Percy. "The Epic Tradition and the Novel," *Southern Review,* new series, 9 (Spring 1973), 300-310.

Armour, Robert. "*Deliverance.* Four Variations on the American

Adam," *Literature/Film Quarterly*, 1 (July 1973), 280-285.

Barshay, Robert. "Machismo in *Deliverance*," *Teaching English in the Two-Year College*, 1, no. 3 (1975), 169-173.

Baughman, Ronald. "James Dickey's *The Eye-Beaters:* 'An Agonizing New Life,' " *South Carolina Review*, 10 (Apr. 1978), 81-88.

_____. "James Dickey's War Poetry: 'A Saved, Shaken Life,' " *South Carolina Review*, 15 (Spring 1983), 38-48.

Beaton, James F. "Dickey Down the River." In *The Modern American Novel and the Movies*, ed. Gerald Peary and Roger Shatzkin. New York: Ungar, 1978, 293-306.

Beidler, Peter G. " 'The Pride of Thine Heart Hath Deceived Thee': Narrative Distortion in Dickey's *Deliverance*," *South Carolina Review*, 5 (Dec. 1972), 29-40.

Bennet, Ross. " 'The Firebombing': A Reappraisal," *American Literature*, 52 (Nov. 1980), 430-448.

_____. "Orion with Green Eyes: James Dickey's Poems of Hunting," *Essays in Literature*, 2 (Aug. 1974), 28-47.

Berke, Roberta. "The American Blue Toad Swallows a Spanish Fly." In her *Bounds Out of Bounds: A Compass for Recent American and British Poetry*. New York: Oxford University Press, 1981, 107-128.

Berry, David C. "Harmony with the Dead: James Dickey's Descent into the Underworld," *Southern Quarterly*, 12 (Apr. 1974), 233-244. Collected in Weigl and Hummer.

Berry, Wendell. "James Dickey's New Book," *Poetry*, 105 (Nov. 1964), 130-131. Review of *Helmets*.

Bledsoe, Jerry. "What Will Save Us From Boredom?," *Esquire*, 80 (Dec. 1973), 227-233. Review of the movie *Deliverance*.

Bloom, Harold. "James Dickey: From 'The Other' through *The Early Motion*," *Southern Review*, 21 (Winter 1985), 63-78.

Bly, Robert. *"Buckdancer's Choice,"* *Sixties*, no. 9 (Spring 1967), 70-79. (Listed in the table of contents as "The Collapse of James Dickey.") Review-essay.

_____. "Prose vs. Poetry," *Choice*, no. 2 (1962), 65-80. Review of *Drowning with Others*.

_____. [as "Crunk"]. "The Work of James Dickey," *Sixties*, no. 7 (Winter 1964), 41-57.

Bobbitt, Joan. "Unnatural Order in the Poetry of James Dickey," *Concerning Poetry*, 11 (Spring 1978), 39-44.

Bowers-Hill, Jane. " 'With Eyes Far More than Human': Dickey's Misunderstood Monster," *James Dickey Newsletter*, 1 (Fall 1984), 2-8.

Bowers-Martin, Jane. *"Jericho* and *God's Images*: The Old Dickey Theme." Collected in Weigl and Hummer, 143-151.

Buck, Carol. "The 'Poetry Thing' with James Dickey," *Poetry Australia,* 21 (Apr. 1968), 4-6.

Burnshaw, Stanley. "James Dickey," *Agenda,* 14-15 (Winter-Spring 1977), 120-124. Review of *The Zodiac.*

Calhoun, Richard J. "After a Long Silence: James Dickey as South Carolina Writer," *South Carolina Review,* 9 (Nov. 1976), 12-20.

_____. " 'His Reason Argues with His Invention': James Dickey's *Self-Interviews* and *The Eye-Beaters," South Carolina Review,* 3 (June 1971), 9-16. Collected in Calhoun.

_____. "Whatever Happened to the Poet-Critic?," *Southern Literary Journal,* 1 (Autumn 1968), 75-88. Collected in Calhoun.

Carnes, Bruce. "Deliverance in James Dickey's 'On the Coosawattee' and *Deliverance," Notes on Contemporary Literature,* 7 (Mar. 1977), 2-4.

Carroll, Paul. "James Dickey as Critic," *Chicago Review,* 20 (Nov. 1968), 82-87. Review of *Babel to Byzantium.*

_____. "The Smell of Blood in Paradise." In his *The Poem in Its Skin.* Chicago: Follett, 1968, 43-49.

Cassill, R. V. "The Most Dangerous Game of the Poet James Dickey," *South Carolina Review,* 10 (Apr. 1978), 7-11.

Clausen, Christopher. "Grecian Thoughts in Home Fields: Reflections on Southern Poetry," *Georgia Review,* 32 (Summer 1978), 283-305.

Corrington, John William. "James Dickey's Poems: 1957-1967: A Personal Appraisal," *Georgia Review,* 22 (Spring 1968), 12-23.

Covel, Robert. "The Metaphysics of Experience: James Dickey's 'The Scarred Girl,' " *James Dickey Newsletter,* 1 (Spring 1985), 24-30.

Davis, Charles E. "The Wilderness Revisited: Irony in James Dickey's *Deliverance," Studies in American Fiction,* 4 (Autumn 1976), 223-230.

Davison, Peter. "The Difficulties of Being Major: The Poetry of Robert Lowell and James Dickey," *Atlantic Monthly,* 220 (Oct. 1967), 116-121. Revised and collected as "The Great Grassy World from Both Sides: The Poetry of Robert Lowell and James Dickey" in Calhoun.

DeMott, Benjamin. "The 'More Life' School and James Dickey," *Saturday Review,* 28 Mar. 1970, pp. 25-26, 38.

Dempsy, Michael. *"Deliverance*/Boorman: Dickey in the Woods," *Cinema,* 8 (Spring 1973), 10-17.

Dickey, William. "Talking About What's Read," *Hudson Review*, 18 (Winter 1965-1966), 613-617. Review of *The Suspect in Poetry*.

_____. "The Thing Itself," *Hudson Review*, 19 (Spring 1966), 146-155. Review of *Buckdancer's Choice*.

Donald, David Herbert. "Promised Land or Paradise Lost: The South Beheld," *Georgia Review*, 29 (Spring 1975), 184-187.

Donoghue, Denis. "The Good Old Complex Fate," *Hudson Review*, 17 (Summer 1964), 267-277.

Doughtie, Edward. "Art and Nature in *Deliverance*," *Southwest Review*, 64 (Spring 1979), 167-180.

Edwards, C. Hines, Jr. "Dickey's *Deliverance*: The Owl and the Eye," *Critique: Studies in Modern Fiction*, 15, no. 2 (1973), 95-101.

Evans, Oliver. "University Influence on Poetry," *Prairie Schooner*, 35 (Summer 1961), 179-180. Review of *Poets of Today VII*.

Eyster, Warren. "The Regional Novels," *Sewanee Review*, 79 (Summer 1971), 469-474.

Flint, R. W. "Poetry Chronicle," *Partisan Review*, 29 (Spring 1962), 290-294. Review of *Drowning with Others*.

Friedman, Norman. "The Wesleyan Poets, II: The Formal Poets, 2," *Chicago Review*, 19 (Jan. 1966), 55-72.

Galler, David. "Versions of Accident," *Kenyon Review*, 26 (Summer 1964), 581-584. Review of *Helmets*.

Goldstein, Laurence. " 'The End of All Our Exploring': The Moon Landing and Modern Poetry," *Michigan Quarterly Review*, 18 (Spring 1979), 192-217.

Gregor, Arthur. "James Dickey, American Romantic: An Appreciation." Collected in Calhoun, 77-80.

Greiner, Donald J. "The Harmony of Bestiality in James Dickey's *Deliverance*," *South Carolina Review*, 5 (Dec. 1972), 43-49.

Guillory, Daniel L. "Myth and Meaning in James Dickey's *Deliverance*," *College Literature*, 3 (1976), 56-62.

_____. "Water Magic in the Poetry of James Dickey," *English Language Notes*, 8 (Dec. 1970), 131-137.

Guttenberg, Barnett. "The Pattern of Redemption in Dickey's *Deliverance*," *Critique: Studies in Modern Fiction*, 18, no. 3 (1977), 83-91.

Haule, James M. " 'The Thing Itself Is in That': Closure In The Poetry of James Dickey." Collected in De La Fuente, 31-44.

Hill, Robert W. "Editorial," *South Carolina Review*, 10 (Apr. 1978), 3-4.

_____. "James Dickey: Comic Poet." Collected in Calhoun, 143-155.

Hinz, Evelyn J. "Contemporary North American Literary Primitivism: *Deliverance* and *Surfacing.*" In *Hemispheric Perspectives on the United States: Papers for the New World Conference,* ed. Joseph S. Tulchin. Westport, Conn.: Greenwood Press, 1975, 150-171.

Hollahan, Eugene. "An Anxiety of Influence Overcome: Dickey's *Puella* and Hopkins' The Wreck of the 'Deutschland,' " *James Dickey Newsletter,* 1 (Spring 1985), 2-12.

Holley, Linda Tarte. "Design and Focus in James Dickey's *Deliverance,*" *South Carolina Review,* 10 (Apr. 1978), 90-98.

Howard, Richard. "On James Dickey," *Partisan Review,* 33 (Summer 1966), 414-428, 479-486. Reprinted as "James Dickey: 'We Never Can Really Tell Whether Nature Condemns Us or Loves Us' " in *Alone with America: Essays in the Art of Poetry in the United States Since 1950,* ed. Howard. New York: Atheneum, 1969.

Italia, Paul G. "Love and Lust in James Dickey's *Deliverance,*" *Modern Fiction Studies,* 21 (Summer 1975), 203-213.

Jameson, Frederic. "The Great American Hunter, or, Ideological Content in the Novel," *College English,* 34 (Nov. 1972), 180-197.

Jolly, John. "Drew Ballinger as 'Sacrificial God' in James Dickey's Deliverance," *South Carolina Review,* 17 (Spring 1985), 102-107.

Jones, Betty Ann. "*Jericho*: The Marketing Story." In *Pages: The World of Books, Writers and Writing,* ed. Matthew J. Bruccoli. Detroit: Gale Research, 1976, vol. 1, 248-253.

Kael, Pauline. "After Innocence," *New Yorker,* 1 Oct. 1973, pp. 113-118. Review of the movie *Deliverance.*

Korges, James. "James Dickey and Other Good Poets," *Minnesota Review,* 3 (Summer 1963), 473-491.

Kostelanetz, Richard. "Flyswatter and Gadfly," *Shenandoah,* 16 (Spring 1965), 92-95. Review of *The Suspect in Poetry.* Collected in Calhoun.

Kunz, Don. "Learning the Hard Way in James Dickey's *Deliverance,*" *Western American Literature,* 12 (Feb. 1978), 289-301.

Landress, Thomas. "Traditionalist Criticism and the Poetry of James Dickey," *Occasional Review,* 3 (Summer 1975), 5-26.

Leibowitz, Herbert. "The Moiling of Secret Forces: *The Eye-Beaters, Blood, Victory, Madness, Buckhead and Mercy,*" *New York Times Book Review,* 8 Nov. 1970, pp. 20, 22. Collected in Weigl and Hummer.

Lennox, John. "Dark Journeys: *Kamoursaka* and *Deliverance,*" *Essays on Canadian Writing,* 12 (1978), 84-104.

Lensing, George. "James Dickey and the Movements of Imagination." Collected in Calhoun, 157-175.

_____. "The Neo-Romanticism of James Dickey," *South Carolina Review*, 10 (Apr. 1978), 20-32.

Libby, Anthony. "Fire and Light, Four Poets to the End and Beyond," *Iowa Review*, 4 (Spring 1973), 111-126.

Lieberman, Laurence. "The Expansional Poet: A Return to Personality," *Yale Review*, 57 (Winter 1968), 258-271. Review of *Poems 1957-1967*. Reprinted as "John Berryman, William Stafford, and James Dickey. The Expansional Poet: A Return to Personality" in his *Unassigned Frequencies: American Poetry in Review, 1964-77*. Urbana, Chicago & London: University of Illinois Press, 1977.

_____. "James Dickey: The Deepening of Being." In his *The Achievement of James Dickey: A Comprehensive Selection of His Poems with a Critical Introduction*, 1-21. Reprinted in his *Unassigned Frequencies: American Poetry in Review, 1964-77*. Collected in Weigl and Hummer.

_____. "Notes on James Dickey's Style," *Far Point*, 2 (Spring-Summer 1968), 57-63. Collected in Calhoun. Reprinted in Leiberman, *Unassigned Frequencies: American Poetry in Review, 1964-77*.

_____. "The Worldly Mystic," *Hudson Review*, 20 (Autumn 1967), 513-520. Collected in Calhoun. Reprinted as "James Dickey: The Worldly Mystic" in Leiberman, *Unassigned Frequencies: American Poetry in Review, 1964-77*.

Lindborg, Henry J. "James Dickey's *Deliverance*: The Ritual of Art," *Southern Literary Journal*, 6 (Spring 1974), 83-90.

Longen, Eugene M. "Dickey's *Deliverance*: Sex and the Great Outdoors," *Southern Literary Journal*, 9 (Spring 1977), 137-149.

Love, Glen A. "Ecology in America," *Colorado Quarterly*, 21 (Autumn 1972), 175-185.

McGinnis, Wayne D. "Mysticism in the Poetry of James Dickey," *New Laurel Review*, 5, nos. 1-2 (1975), 5-10.

Marin, Daniel B. "James Dickey's *Deliverance*: Darkness Visible," *South Carolina Review*, 3 (Nov. 1970), 49-59. Collected in Calhoun.

Markos, Donald W. "Art and Immediacy: James Dickey's *Deliverance*," *Southern Review*, new series, 7 (Summer 1971), 947-953.

Martz, William J. "A Note on Meaningless Being in 'Cherrylog Road.' " Collected in Calhoun, 81-83.

Mason, Kenneth C. "A Book to Relish," *Prairie Schooner*, 54 (Winter 1980-1981), 107-108. Review of *The Strength of Fields*.

Meredith, William. "James Dickey's Poems," *Partisan Review*, 32 (Summer 1965), 456-457. Review of *Helmets*.

Metz, Violette. "The Blessed Beasts and Children: An Examination of Imagery in James Dickey's *Poems 1957-1967*." Collected in De La Fuente, 45-55.

Mills, Ralph J., Jr. *Creation's Very Self: On the Personal Element in Recent American Poetry*. Fort Worth: Texas Christian University Press, 1969, 3-4, 9, 14, 18-19.

_____. "The Poetry of James Dickey," *Triquarterly*, 11 (Winter 1968), 231-242. Collected in Weigl and Hummer.

Mizejewski, Linda. "Shamanism toward Confessionalism: James Dickey, Poet," *Georgia Review*, 32 (Summer 1978), 409-419. Collected in Weigl and Hummer.

Monk, Donald. "Colour Symbolism in James Dickey's *Deliverance*," *Journal of American Studies*, 11 (Aug. 1977), 261-279.

Nemerov, Howard. "Poems of Darkness and a Specialized Light," *Sewanee Review*, 71 (Jan.-Mar. 1963), 99-104. Review of *Drowning with Others*. Collected in Weigl and Hummer.

Niflis, N. Michael. "A Specialized Kind of Fantasy: James Dickey on the Razor's Edge," *Southwest Review*, 57 (Autumn 1972), 311-317. Collected in Weigl and Hummer.

Norman, Geoffrey. "The Stuff of Poetry," *Playboy*, 18 (May 1971), 148-149, 230, 232, 236, 238, 240, 242.

Oates, Joyce Carol. "Out of Stone, Into Flesh: The Imagination of James Dickey," *Modern Poetry Studies*, 5 (Autumn 1974), 97-144. Reprinted in her *New Heaven, New Earth: The Visionary Experience in Literature*. New York: Vanguard, 1974. Collected in Weigl and Hummer.

O'Neil, Paul. "The Unlikeliest Poet," *Life*, 61 (22 July 1966), 68-70, 72-74, 77-79.

Patrick, Richard. "Heroic *Deliverance*," *Novel*, 4 (Winter 1971), 190-192.

Peters, Robert. "The Phenomenon of James Dickey, Currently," *Western Humanities Review*, 34 (Spring 1980), 159-166. Review of *The Strength of Fields*.

Pierce, Constance. "Dickey's 'Adultery': A Ritual of Renewal," *Concerning Poetry*, 9, no. 2 (1976), 67-69.

Ramsey, Paul. "James Dickey: Meter and Structure." Collected in Calhoun, 177-194.

Rose, Maxine S. "On Being Born Again: James Dickey's 'May Day Sermon to the Women of Gilmer County, Georgia, by a Woman

Preacher Leaving the Baptist Church,' " *Research Studies*, 46 (Dec. 1978), 254-258.

Samuels, Charles Thomas. "How Not to Film a Novel," *American Scholar*, 42 (Winter 1972-1973), 148-150, 152, 154. Review of the movie *Deliverance*.

_____. "What Hath Dickey Delivered?," *New Republic*, 162 (18 Apr. 1970), 23-26. Review of *Deliverance*.

Seale, Jan. "Narrative Technique in James Dickey's 'May Day Sermon.' " Collected in De La Fuente, 24-30.

Silverstein, Norman. "James Dickey's Muscular Eschatology," *Salmagundi*, nos. 22-23 (Spring-Summer 1973), 258-268.

Simon, John. "More Brass than Enduring," *Hudson Review*, 15 (Aug. 1962), 455-468. Review of *Drowning with Others*.

Skinner, Izora. "A Fun Poem by James Dickey." Collected in De La Fuente, 56-58.

Sloan, Thomas O. "The Open Poem Is a Now Poem: Dickey's May Day Sermon." In *Literature as Revolt and Revolt as Literature: Three Studies in the Rhetoric of Non-Oratorical Forms*. Minneapolis: Proceedings of the Fourth Annual University of Minnesota Spring Symposium in Speech Communication, 1970, 17-31. Collected in Calhoun.

Smith, Dave. "The Strength of James Dickey," *Poetry*, 137 (Mar. 1981), 349-358. Collected in Weigl and Hummer. Reprinted in Smith, *Local Assays: On Contemporary American Poetry*. Urbana & Chicago: University of Illinois Press, 1985.

Smith, Mack. "James Dickey's Varieties of Creation: The Voices of Narrative," *James Dickey Newsletter*, 1 (Spring 1985), 18-22.

Smith, Raymond. "The Poetic Faith of James Dickey," *Modern Poetry Studies*, 2, no. 1 (1972), 259-272.

Spears, Monroe K. *Dionysus and the City: Modernism in Twentieth-Century Poetry*. London, Oxford & New York: Oxford University Press, 1970, 13n, 250, 252-260, 269.

Stephenson, Shelby. " 'Mystic-Double Tongue'—James Dickey's Constant Song," *James Dickey Newsletter*, 1 (Spring 1985), 15-17.

Stephenson, William. "Deliverance from What?," *Georgia Review*, 28 (Spring 1974), 114-120.

Strange, William C. "To Dream, to Remember: James Dickey's *Buckdancer's Choice*," *Northwest Review*, 7 (Fall-Winter 1965-1966), 33-42.

Strong, Paul. "James Dickey's Arrow of Deliverance," *South Carolina Review*, 11 (Nov. 1978), 108-116.

Sullivan, Rosemary. *"Surfacing* and *Deliverance,"* *Canadian Literature*, 67 (Winter 1976), 6-20.

Taylor, Chet. "A Look into the Heart of Darkness: A View of *Deliverance."* Collected in De La Fuente, 59-64.

Van Ness, A. Gordon, III. "Steering to the Morning Land: The Poet as Redeemer in Dickey's *The Zodiac," James Dickey Newsletter*, 2 (Fall 1985), 2-10.

Wagner, Linda. *"Deliverance:* Initiation and Possibility," *South Carolina Review*, 10 (Apr. 1978), 49-55.

Weatherby, H. L. "The Way of Exchange in James Dickey's Poetry," *Sewanee Review*, 74 (July-Sept. 1966), 669-680. Collected in Calhoun and in Weigl and Hummer.

Willson, Robert F., Jr. *"Deliverance* from Novel to Film: Where Is Our Hero?," *Literature/Film Quarterly*, 2 (Winter 1974), 52, 54-55, 57-58.

Winchell, Mark Royden. "The River Within: Primitivism in James Dickey's *Deliverance," West Virginia University Philological Papers*, 23 (Jan. 1977), 106-114.

Yardley, Jonathan. "More of Superpoet," *New Republic*, 163 (5 Dec. 1970), 26-27. Review of *Self-Interviews*.

BIBLIOGRAPHICAL ESSAY

Bibliographies and Checklists

Jim Elledge's *James Dickey: A Bibliography, 1947-1974* (1979), together with his two-part supplement for 1975-1980 in consecutive 1981 issues of the *Bulletin of Bibliography*, provides the most reliable and complete primary and secondary listings of Dickey material through 1980. Substantially annotated, Elledge's bibliographies also supply reprint information for both the poet's and his critics' works. The 1979 volume presents 554 primary and 668 secondary entries; the supplementary list contains 242 primary and 112 secondary items.

As he explains in the preface to his volume, part of Elledge's purpose in compiling his work is "to correct errors and confusing entries" appearing in two previous bibliographical studies: Eileen K. Glancy's *James Dickey: The Critic as Poet: An Annotated Bibliography with an Introductory Essay* (1971) and Franklin B. Ashley's *James Dickey: A Checklist* (1972). Glancy's book, which lists primary items published between 1951 and 1970 and secondary items published between 1960 and 1970, provides information on where individual Dickey works are collected and reprinted; it also offers brief annotations of critical essays and reviews treating his poetry collections and *Deliverance*. Ashley's checklist of primary material records printings of Dickey's books and pamphlets through 1971 and notes first appearances of his shorter works in periodicals and in books other than his own. The first section of his checklist has been superseded by Stuart T. Wright's *James Dickey: A Bibliography of His Books, Pamphlets, and Broadsides* (1982), a descriptive list of American and English printings of Dickey's books and other separately bound publications through June 1982.

Both of the collections of essays on Dickey that have appeared to date include useful checklists. In *James Dickey: The Expansive Imagination: A Collection of Critical Essays* (1973), Robert W. Hill provides a brief but noteworthy primary and secondary list of material appearing between April 1969 and early 1973, a list designed to supplement Glancy's work. For *The Imagination as Glory: The Poetry of James Dickey* (1984), Dennis Vannatta assembles an outstanding checklist of secondary sources. His bibliography is particularly useful since it records within its thirteen pages 312 significant discussions of Dickey's works.

The most up-to-date primary and secondary checklists to appear are those compiled by Robert C. Covel for the *James Dickey Newsletter* (Fall 1984, Fall 1985). Concentrating on the period from 1975 to the present, he cites Dickey appearances and such secondary material as reviews, articles, chapters of books, brief mention, and dissertations. Covel also notes earlier items that have not appeared in previous bibliographies. Since the checklist will be a continuing feature of the newsletter, this source may prove the most important means of keeping current with Dickey's publications as well as with the growing body of secondary material treating his work.

Biographies

Although no full-length biography has been written about Dickey, information about his life appears in all three of the critical books published to date and in standard reference book entries. However, the most rewarding source of biographical material is his own work. The essays, interviews, journal, and reviews collected in *Self-Interviews, Sorties, Babel to Byzantium*, and *Night Hurdling* are often highly autobiographical. Furthermore, Dickey is a voluminous letter-writer, and when the correspondence and other papers housed at the University of South Carolina's South Caroliniana Library, at the library of Washington University in St. Louis, and at the Library of

Congress are eventually published—or at least mined by scholars—they should yield much additional information on his life.

Selected Interviews

Dickey has granted many interviews, the best of which yield valuable information about his life and art. Through these conversations the poet reveals his wide knowledge of literature, for he often comments upon English-language and non-English-language writers from almost every literary age. In addition, he frequently explores his own ideas, influences, and techniques through these discussions. Affable and often humorous, Dickey may, on occasion, test the gullibility of his interviewer; and because he has been asked certain questions again and again, some of his answers assume the character of set pieces. Yet these conversations—and his own book *Self-Interviews*—provide an excellent portrait of the man and his work.

An important early interview is Carolyn Kizer and James Boatwright's "A Conversation with James Dickey" (1966). Kizer, who introduces and then repeatedly refers to the "virility cult" so often associated with Dickey, inquires whether he has consciously cultivated an overtly masculine image. Acknowledging his impatience with the portrait of the poet as a rarefied, misunderstood being who publicly indulges his private agonies, Dickey rejects the notion that he has striven to create Hemingwayesque persona. Later in this interview, however, his comments may tend to advance rather than negate Kizer's assumptions: "Somebody (I think it was Yeats maybe) said that a man running at full speed has neither a brain nor a heart. I'm trying to get into the psychological state of the man running at full speed and see what he does have. . . . My work is almost entirely physical rather than intellectual or mental." The poet also notes that a career as a teacher of young writers seems vital to his generation of artists but that an academic environment can at times impose restrictions on one's life. Dickey discusses as well writers who have been part of his literary heritage, especially Theodore Roethke. The Kizer-Boatwright interview is particularly important because the assumptions made, questions asked, and answers given are so frequently returned to in subsequent discussion.

In "A Conversation with James Dickey," an interview conducted by William Heyen and Peter Marchant in late 1970 and published in 1973, Dickey reads and comments on three poems: "The Performance," which allows him to elaborate on his World War II night bombing missions; "The Heaven of Animals," which calls forth his views on the correct relationship between man and nature, especially within the predator-prey engagement; and "Sled Burial, Dream Ceremony," which elicits his discussions of death, the "ultimate strange place" most alien to man. "Sled Burial, Dream Ceremony" also prompts Dickey to define his conception of the balance between creativity and technique: "The true creative act is to conceive, first, a thing, and then to find your way through the process of administration of formal techniques to making that strange vision live." Declaring that death has been a prominent force in his work and his life, Dickey sees in *Deliverance* a possible counter to death, for the confrontations that occur in the novel illustrate "the energizing of certain capacities in men which ordinarily do not have a chance to surface."

Another important discussion published in 1973 is Geoffrey Norman's "*Playboy* Interview: James Dickey." After adroitly deflecting questions about his taste in cars and clothing, Dickey focuses upon his view of nature, the significance of war to his life and career, and the high incidence of alcoholism and suicide among creative people. He voices his attraction to Herman Melville's conception of unknown forces hidden beneath nature's peaceful surface—"an apparently serene surface which masks some hidden horror, some unknown universal evil." Dickey explains how recurrent figures in his poetry, the shark and the snake, represent this "hidden horror": they are the antitheses of the seemingly ordered world of man and therefore inspire in him terror and awe. The poet also declares that his Army Air Force experience caused him to think of himself primarily as a survivor and consequently to identify with those who are "enthusiasts." Such writers as Malcolm Lowry, who risked public censure for his alcoholism in order to pursue intensity in his art and life, dangerously tread the boundaries separating sanity and insanity, life and death, Dickey says. And sometimes the creative man, like Lowry, destroys himself. Yet Dickey prefers these enthusiasts for experience and art to the "rather bloodless notions of poetry" and life espoused by such figures as T. S. Eliot.

On 25 January 1976 the television program *Bill Moyers' Journal* broadcast a conversation between Moyers and Dickey taped at Dickey's home in Columbia, South Carolina. Much of their discussion centers around their shared regional heritage. Dickey says that although he does not wish to be identified solely as a Southern writer, he feels fortunate to have been born a Southerner because people in the South value highly man's relationship with the landscape. Furthermore, because of their frequent rural isolation, Southerners crave human conversation, which in turn creates a special ability to tell and to write elaborate stories. They are also burdened with the historical reality of having lost a war, which places them in the tradition of major characters in the *Iliad*. These historical/cultural influences, Dickey believes, help explain why so many great American writers come from the South. Yet while acknowledging his Southern roots Dickey more emphatically identifies himself as "a creature of World War II" since his "most formative years were taken up with waging war against an enemy, not one face of whom I had ever seen." The war shaped his values, he asserts, giving him an abhorrence of moderation and instead instilling him with a drive for living as an enthusiast and an excessive.

More clearly intended for a literary audience is Franklin B. Ashley's 1976 *Paris Review* interview, "James Dickey: The Art of Poetry," reprinted in George Plimpton's *Writers at Work* (1981). Beginning with questions about Dickey's education and his careers in advertising and teaching, Ashley then pursues the writer's roles as poet and critic. The interviewer mentions the frequent charge that Dickey has been a "rough" reviewer, to which the poet replies: "I don't believe that a reviewer or a critic can really criticize well unless he can praise well. I always liked that about Randall Jarrell. He praised well. . . . James Agee praises well. You've got to be able to like the right things to be enabled to dislike the wrong things. People misconstrue John Simon. He *does* praise well. He doesn't find much to praise, but he praises well. John Simon hates so much so vehemently because he likes so little so strongly." To illustrate his own likes and dislikes, Dickey offers his assessments of various contemporary writers: he applauds William Stafford for his direct, seemingly simple language that says something significant and Theodore Roethke for his power to move readers into their own sensibilities; Dickey also repeats his well-known attacks on Sylvia Plath and Robert Lowell for what he considers their self-indulgence in personal failing. Ashley also once again raises the question of whether Dickey promotes a "virility cult," especially in *Deliverance*. Contrasting his own characters to Ernest Hemingway's bullfighters and boxers—"Their *business* is violence"—the writer denies that his four suburbanites are inherently brutal figures: "*Deliverance* is really a novel about how decent men kill, and the fact that they get away with it raises a lot of questions about staying within the law—whether decent people have the right to go outside the law when they're encountering human monsters."

Matthew J. Bruccoli's 4 March 1977 discussion, published in *Conversations with Writers: Volume I*, treats both Dickey's process of composition and his educational-occupational-publishing history. This interview is particularly notable for its establishing of concrete facts. It places and dates the writer's work experience in advertising agencies and his terms as poet-in-residence at various colleges and universities; it also clarifies the sources, dates, and places of composition of certain of his individual works, especially early ones. The interview concludes with a fine discussion of *Alnilam,* Dickey's novel-in-progress, a discussion which focuses on a thematic division between mind and body in the work.

Three interviews report Dickey's responses to single writers or works. In Donald J. Greiner's " 'That Plain-Speaking Guy': A Conversation with James Dickey on Robert Frost," conducted for a 1974 Frost centennial volume, Dickey indicates that beginning writers can learn from Frost's "plainness and . . . colloquialism of . . . language," from his ability to say "the most amazing things without seeming to raise his voice." On the other hand, the contemporary poet maintains that Frost did not learn painter Pablo Picasso's great lesson: "never be trapped in a single style." Of all Frost's poems, Dickey most likes "Acquainted with the Night" and "After Apple-Picking."

In W. C. Barnwell's "James Dickey on Yeats: An Interview" (1977), Dickey announces that he especially admires William Butler Yeats's "authentically non-logical way of reasoning. I mean Yeats will say something like, if Aquarius does not stand at the end of Leo, how can the archer send an arrow through the heart of Sagittarius?" Such transcendence of ordinary rational processes clearly parallels Dickey's own elevation of imagination over reason. But he also disapproves of Yeats's fondness for closed forms in poetry, his belief that a work "should end like the click of a closed box." Borrowing William James's phrase, Dickey declares that he strives in his own "open" poetry for the "fluidity and flux and flow of human experience." Asked to name the five most influential poets of any language in the twentieth century, he ranks Yeats and Eliot as the most significant poets in English; Federico García Lorca in Spanish; Paul Valéry in French; and Rainer Maria Rilke in German. Of all the twentieth-century poets, Dickey labels Yeats "*the* great" master.

Although it touches briefly on some of the early poems, David L. Arnett's "An Interview with James Dickey" (1975) concentrates on *Deliverance.* In this discussion Dickey provides background information about real people who served as models for his novel's major characters and describes an actual canoe trip he had once made down a wild river: "That was an horrendous trip! I mean, that trip down the Coosawattee through the fir forest and those other places was the grimmest physical experience I'd had since I was in the service." When Arnett suggests that protagonist Ed Gentry is a Christ figure, particularly because of the wounds in his side and the palm of his hands suffered when he falls from a tree, Dickey discounts this interpretation. Instead he points out that Ed's fall attempts to capture the "wonderful action writing" that appears in "Milton's voyage of Satan through Chaos, which is the best thing in *Paradise Lost.* . . . he [Satan] goes through Chaos, in which there's nothing to grab hold of, and things sink away under him, and he flounders and just tries to make it any way he can. That was what I was thinking about then. But the wound in the side I got more or less from the Council of Archery hunting accidents—about people falling on their arrows and what that would feel like and what would it do to you to see an arrow come through your own flesh and that sort of thing."

These interviews provide the reader of Dickey with a variety of insights into the writer's composition practices, his assessments of other writers, his aspirations for his own art, and his life and character. The discussions effectively capture the intensity, the expansiveness, and the learning of the man and writer.

Critical Studies: Books

Surprisingly, no book-length study of Dickey's works appeared before 1983. In that year, Richard J. Calhoun and Robert W. Hill published their Twayne volume, *James Dickey.* Calhoun and Hill provide an intelligent and helpful overview of his poetry, novel, and nonfiction prose. They identify the writer as a "modern romantic" whose "major source of energy and knowledge" is the natural world, since nature grants man a vision of life and death.

Providing explications of major poems in *Into the Stone, Drowning with Others, Helmets,* and *Buckdancer's Choice,* the first four chapters define themes and techniques that both continue and evolve in Dickey's later works. These four chapters seem more detailed and persuasive than the final four. Calhoun and Hill note that the poems in *Falling,* the last section of *Poems 1957-1967,* feature protagonists who, like figures in the earlier works, attempt to connect with the Other, to encompass all experience; yet, the critics contend, the technique used—the long, loose line—may undercut the earlier lyrical impulse and produce daring, even dangerous effects: "At times ridiculous, bombastic, and prolix, Dickey's long-line works demand the reader's indulgence. Such letting go yields treasures unimagined by safe and managerial minds."

Although the major focus of their book is on the poetry, Calhoun and Hill's chapters on the novel *Deliverance* and Dickey's nonfiction prose also supply valuable insights. The authors see in *Deliverance* the familiar Dickey theme that immersion in primitive nature both re-generates and endangers contemporary suburban man. They regard the writer's critical views as "important contributions to Dickey's own vision of a freer, personal, but still carefully postmodern poetry." Calhoun and Hill's discussion may too heavily emphasize the poet's concern with nature, when in fact it is only one of many important subjects for his art. Nonetheless, their commentary proves interesting and instructive.

Neal Bowers, a generally respected commentator on American poetry, has written a perplexing book that creates as many questions about his intentions as it provides answers about Dickey's work. In *James Dickey: The Poet as Pitchman* (1985) Bowers contends that Dickey's popularity as a poet and novelist is the result of carefully orchestrated self promotion, the elements of which are borrowed from techniques he mastered during his earlier career as a successful advertising ex-ecutive and copywriter. Bowers asserts that Dickey is a pitchman for himself, for his poetry, and for God. Although the critic insists that the term *pitchman* is not intended to be pejorative, he does not per-suade, for he constantly suggests that all activities related to market-ing—to commercial endeavors in general—are tainted: "unlike the typical salesman" is a representative Bowers phrase. Furthermore, his supporting evidence for his thesis is often quite shaky; for example, he cites Dickey's statement that he knew *Deliverance* would be a "win-ner" to prove that he creates as much for the marketplace as for noncommercial artistic reasons.

If Bowers had limited his discussion to this kind of assessment only, one could dismiss his book as mere ax-grinding or worse. But he balances his caustic evaluations of Dickey's motives with astute assessments of the poetry; and his suggestion that Dickey moves from promoting himself to promoting his poetry to promoting his vision of God is interesting. Moreover, Bowers takes pains to assure the reader that Dickey's activities as a "pitchman" have improved the lot of other poets, as well as his own—by boosting the fees paid for poetry readings, for example. Yet questions about Bowers's own motives in offering this analysis tend to undercut the effectiveness of his book.

Another 1985 study of Dickey's works is Ronald Baughman's *Understanding James Dickey,* one of the first volumes in the University of South Carolina Press's "Understanding Contemporary American Literature" series. Baughman's book, intended as a reader's companion to Dickey's poetry and prose, finds its central thesis in the writer's statement in *Sorties,* "More and more I see myself as the poet of *survival.*" As a survivor Dickey must, Baughman declares, address the question of his own possible guilt in relationship to those who populate his world. The critic sees in the Dickey canon a progression from self-laceration to sustained questioning to final renewal, a pattern supported by Robert Jay Lifton's 1973 study of combat survivors, *Home from the War.* Within this framework, Baughman examines such central Dickey topics as war, family, society, love, and nature, and he defines the writer's important symbols and his technical development. Offering a chronologically arranged treatment of the poetry collections and *Deliverance* and concluding with a chapter on Dickey's criticism, the book also provides close explications of the most significant of Dickey's individual poems.

Critical Studies: Collections of Essays

The earliest collection of criticism on Dickey, *James Dickey: The Expansive Imagination: A Collection of Critical Essays* (1973), edited by Richard J. Calhoun, contains some highly important discussions, many of which are treated in greater detail in the Major Articles and Book Sections part of this essay. Among the articles the collection reprints are Peter Davison's "The Great Grassy World from Both Sides: The Poetry of Robert Lowell and James Dickey," a revision of his *Atlantic Monthly* essay "The Difficulties of Being Major: The Poetry of Robert Lowell and James Dickey"; H. L. Weatherby's seminal analysis "The Way of Exchange in James Dickey's Poetry"; and Laurence Lieberman's influential study "The Worldly Mystic." One of the earliest of the interviews, "A Conversation with James Dickey" by Kizer and Boatwright, is also collected here, as are such fine essays on individual works as Thomas O. Sloan's "The Open Poem Is a Now Poem: Dickey's May Day Sermon," William J. Martz's "A Note on Meaningless Being in 'Cherrylog Road,'" and Daniel B. Marin's "James Dickey's *Deliverance*: Darkness Visible." In addition to his checklist updating Glancy's bibliography, Robert W. Hill contributes "James Dickey: Comic Poet," while articles by George Lensing ("James Dickey and the Movements of Imagination"), Arthur Gregor ("James Dickey, American Romantic: An Appreciation"), Paul Ramsay ("James Dickey: Meter and Structure"), and Lieberman ("Notes on James Dickey's Style") focus on influences or technique. Calhoun himself provides two essays, one of them being his fine appraisal of Dickey as critic—"Whatever Happened to the Poet-Critic?"—which is paired with Richard Kostelanetz's "Flyswatter and Gadfly," an important early review-essay on Dickey's critical writings in *The Suspect in Poetry*. All in all *The Expansive Imagination* offers a sampling of excellent commentary on a variety of Dickey works, themes, and techniques.

Editor Patricia De La Fuente's *James Dickey: Splintered Sunlight* (1979), which contains five original essays, an interview, and a brief secondary checklist for 1975-1978, is the product of a James Dickey conference held at Pan American University in Edinburg, Texas, during March 1979. The essays, first delivered as lectures at the conference, include Jan Seale's discussion of narrative technique in "May Day Sermon," Violette Metz's analysis of imagery in *Poems 1957-1967*, James M. Haule's identification of devices of closure in the poetry in general, Izora Skinner's consideration of the children's poem *Tucky the Hunter*, and Chet Taylor's treatment of the heart-of-darkness motif in *Deliverance*. Although these essays are somewhat uneven in quality, they are all lively. The pamphlet concludes with a collection of student responses to the poet's campus visit, their often quite perceptive views of what he has called his "barnstorming for poetry."

The Imagination as Glory: The Poetry of James Dickey (1984), edited by Bruce Weigl and T. R. Hummer, collects twelve essays and reviews (several of them discussed under Major Articles and Book Sections), the fine Vannatta secondary checklist (treated above), and two essays by Dickey himself—"The Imagination as Glory" and "The Energized Man." The volume presents, in its editors' words, "a history of critical response to Dickey's poetry" and "the most important and at the same time the most characteristic statements within the body of Dickey's criticism." Included in this collection are Joyce Carol Oates's "Out of Stone, into Flesh: The Imagination of James Dickey," a remarkable interpretation of the poet's major themes; Ralph J. Mills, Jr.'s "The Poetry of James Dickey"; and, of course, Weatherby's "The Way of Exchange in James Dickey's Poetry." Weigl and Hummer have taken care to include, alongside essays of high praise, assessments that define apparent failures in the writer's work; Mills's commentary is a case in point, as are Herbert Leibowitz's "The Moiling of Secret Forces," a review of *The Eye-Beaters;* Jane Bowers-Martin's "*Jericho* and *God's Im-*

ages: The Old Dickey Theme"; and Linda Mizejewski's "Shamanism toward Confessionalism: James Dickey, Poet," a lament for the writer's apparent lack of control in *The Zodiac*. This collection is the most comprehensive gathering of critical essays, since it draws its material from almost twenty-five years of commentary on Dickey's work.

Critical Studies: Newsletter

The *James Dickey Newsletter*, which publishes two issues each year, initially appeared in the fall of 1984. Edited by Joyce M. Pair, who has assembled a distinguished editorial board as well as an excellent advising/contributing editorial staff, the newsletter has already provided substantial contributions to the study of Dickey's work. Its first issue, for example, included critical essays, poems by writers other than Dickey, a brief remembrance by Dickey's high-school track coach, reviews, and the first Covel checklist, to be updated in subsequent fall issues. A reviewer for *Choice* gave the *James Dickey Newsletter* a strongly favorable appraisal that concluded with the line, "Recommended for all collections of modern American literature."

Critical Studies: Special Issue of Journal

The *South Carolina Review*, 10 (April 1978) is the only special issue of a journal to date devoted to Dickey. Beginning with Robert W. Hill's "Editorial" that catalogues comments praising and damning Dickey's works and that thereby reflects the strong judgments elicited by his canon, the issue includes five essays on Dickey's poetry or *Deliverance:* George Lensing's "The Neo-Romanticism of James Dickey," a discussion of the contemporary poet's aesthetic differences with T. S. Eliot; Linda Wagner's "*Deliverance:* Initiation and Possibility," a view that the novel features an initiation-through-wilderness process similar to that found in Mark Twain's *Adventures of Huckleberry Finn;* Linda Tarte Holley's "Design and Focus in James Dickey's *Deliverance*," a demonstration of how protagonist Ed Gentry's developing creative imagination saves his life in the wilderness and afterwards; Ronald Baughman's "James Dickey's *The Eye-Beaters:* 'An Agonizing New Life,' " an examination of the changed, highly complex Self that emerges in this volume; and R. V. Cassill's "The Most Dangerous Game of the Poet James Dickey," a personal response to the man behind the public image. The special issue also includes some poems that purportedly relate to Dickey, though the relationship is often not clear. Some of the essays in this special number of the *South Carolina Review* will be treated at greater length below.

Critical Studies: Major Articles and Book Sections

Dickey's artistic success and popularity result from his ability to stir strong emotional and intellectual responses in his audience. The critical reception of his work reflects comparable reactions: his advocates and his few but vociferous detractors are equally emphatic in their judgments on his work. The critical views range from N. Michael Niflis's proclamation, in "A Specialized Kind of Fantasy: James Dickey on the Razor's Edge," that "Dickey is our greatest poet" to Robert Bly's vitriolic 1967 attack, which labels Dickey's poetry (especially in *Buckdancer's Choice*) morally and politically "repulsive." Other voices, Laurence Lieberman's and Harold Bloom's among them, salute Dickey as a mystic celebrator of the individual's triumph over destructive forces outside and within the Self. An appreciative but darker view is held by such critics as Joyce Carol Oates. Still others, notably Richard J. Calhoun, Robert W. Hill, and Paul Carroll, regard the poet's relationship with nature as the primary thrust of his work.

Perhaps the single most important discussion of Dickey's works remains H. L. Weatherby's 1966 essay "The Way of Exchange in James Dickey's Poetry." Appearing quite early in Dickey's career, Weatherby's analysis has proven extremely influential to other studies. The critic identifies Dickey's central thematic method as the Self's exchange of identity with the Other—with inanimate objects, animals, and human beings—to achieve a renewed perspective on the world. Weatherby asserts that a writer's desire to gain the insights of someone or something other than himself is a feature at once ancient and modern: "the perfect union of man and his opposites, the *me* and the *not me*, is what poetry always tries to express. But the effort to resolve these paradoxes through the process of exchange . . . may very well be unique with Dickey. If that is true it may be safe to say that he has achieved a new way of doing what all poets do or try to do in some way or another . . . to throw light on the world which will show it as the poet knows it must be."

The process of exchange involves much more than the simple projection of a poet-speaker into another being, Weatherby shows. First of all, exchange may operate in both directions—from Self to object, and from object to Self—creating a composite, double vision in a poem. The speaker, for example, may adopt the point of view of an animal, while the animal assumes the perspective of the human. Such a double vision proceeds throughout the work until a dramatic climax occurs, and the process is reversed. Furthermore, underlying this process is a profound intellectual/emotional necessity within the poet. Such works as "Slave Quarters" and "The Firebombing," for example, have raised the ire of some critics, since Dickey's attitudes toward the controversial subjects treated are highly ambiguous. Yet, as Weatherby contends, these complex poems represent Dickey's honest attempts to probe his uncertainties about his region's legacy of slavery and his own involvement in war. Weatherby's excellent discussion of Dickey's central method should be the beginning point for students of the writer's canon, not only for what the essay offers but equally for its influence on later critical studies.

Picking up on Weatherby's views, Laurence Lieberman determines that Dickey's process of exploration eventually identifies him as a mystical visionary and, most importantly, a celebrator of life. As Lieberman states in his commentary for *The Achievement of James Dickey* (1968), "The poetic vision in James Dickey's fifth volume of poems, *Falling* [first published in book form as the final section of *Poems 1957-1967*], contains so much joy that it is incapable of self-pity or self-defeat." This emphasis on the "condition of joy" and ecstasy in the poet's works, an emphasis that permeates all of Lieberman's writings on Dickey, may elicit a degree of skepticism; but the critic also contends that Dickey's affirmation is not easily won. In "The Worldly Mystic" (1967), for example, Lieberman says that the poems of *Buckdancer's Choice* and *Falling* feature a "moral guilt" that paralyzes and frustrates the writer's Self; however, Dickey transcends this condition through a series of "life-saving" connections, a process of reconciliation between "worldliness and the inner life of the spirit," Lieberman declares. Through this process he achieves his position as a "worldly mystic," which allows him to celebrate life while remaining aware of the world's pain. Dickey's capacity to overcome agony and achieve celebration is also central to Lieberman's distinction, in his 1968 essay, between confessional and expansional poets. In "The Expansional Poet: A Return to Personality," the critic characterizes such confessional writers as Anne Sexton, W. D. Snodgrass, and Robert Lowell as "all surface" and therefore restricted to a limited exploration of the Self, usually in terms of that Self's personal agonies. The expansional poet, on the other hand—John Berryman, William Stafford, Dickey—projects the Self beyond the surface to complete an alliance with the "outer—or inner—limits of joy and terror." Lieberman's assessments of Dickey as a visionary who expresses profound but not easily won joy form a major cornerstone of criticism on the poem.

In his essay "James Dickey: From 'The Other' through *The Early Motion*" (1985), Harold Bloom agrees with Lieberman's perspective. Bloom regards Dickey as an "heroic celebrator," "a throwback to . . . the bards of divination." This critic also shares with Lieberman the conviction that guilt is central to Dickey's work, though Bloom identifies guilt's source as a feeling of betrayal in "the family romance," the poet's realization that he has been given life to replace a dead older brother. Dickey's guilt then leads him "to a mind-body schism," a thematic duality that occurs throughout Dickey's poetry and that in turn informs his mystical vision. Bloom provides an extensive array of ancient and modern literary connections in his close reading of "The Other." He points out that "Dickey's natural religion has always been Mithraism, the traditional faith of soldiers, and certainly the most masculine and fierce of all Western beliefs. Despite the Persian origins of Mithra, Rome assimilated him to Apollo, and Dickey's major alteration is to make the Incarnation of the Poetical Character into a Mithraic ritual." This essay demonstrates Bloom's extraordinary ability to connect the contemporary poet's works with ancient and modern world literature; his commentary provides readers insights into Dickey's art while it also demonstrates the workings of a first-rate critical mind.

Although Dickey is also regarded as a celebrator of experience in Richard Howard's "On James Dickey" (1966), this critic does not emphasize the affirmative voice of Dickey as fully as does Lieberman. Rather, Howard sees the poet as Orphic, the "telluric [earthly] maker Wallace Stevens had called for in prophesying that the great poems of heaven and hell have been written and the great poem of the earth remains. . . ." Howard believes that Dickey is the teller who writes "images of the earth." Focusing on obsession, madness, and excess in the writer's celebration, particularly in *Poems 1957-1967*, Howard declares that these motifs reflect Dickey's "pervasive terror of extinction." The critic notes that for Dickey "History is a nightmare from which the Self, struggling yet damned, may not escape" and that the poet dramatizes his reliance on his personal and his region's history in order to escape them and thereby to gain control over his life. In his early poetry, especially that collected in *Into the Stone* and *Drowning with Others*, Dickey seeks control through his connection with nature, but as he matures he turns increasingly toward his own Self as a subject for exploration, Howard says. Although the critic's ornate language and often labyrinthine sentences may discourage some readers, his commentaries are thoughtful considerations that provide valuable insights.

Joyce Carol Oates's "Out of Stone, Into Flesh: The Imagination of James Dickey" (1974) provides an overview of the poet's works that seems very accurately to capture Dickey's intent and tone. Oates declares that the poet's work treats "the frustration that characterizes modern man . . . the frustration and its necessary corollary, murderous rage." Perceiving the "increasing disorder" in contemporary life as various systems fail or falter, Dickey develops what Oates identifies as his aesthetic of "entropy," or systematic breakdown. Throughout his early work, she notes, the poet seeks connection and reconciliation with forces outside of himself; beginning with "The Firebombing," however, Dickey's darker themes emerge. The critic believes that "The Firebombing" establishes an aesthetic stance that does not allow reconciliation but instead leads to a perpetual state of guilt. As Oates convincingly argues, Dickey's primary defense against the powers of entropy is his art, his using "the human activity of creating and organizing language in a coherent, original structure" to ward off the helplessness that occurs when unthinking, unfeeling systems bear down on the individual. Because Oates's analysis clearly emanates from a close consideration of the poet's works, her conclusions reflect his vantage point rather than seeming an arbitrarily imposed critical view. This essay, an excellent complement to Weatherby's discussion, is an essential critical assessment of Dickey's poetry through *The Eye-Beaters*.

Demonstrating a variation on Weatherby's concept of exchange is Ralph J. Mills, Jr.'s "The Poetry of James Dickey" (1968), a treatment of the writer's use of transformation (metamorphosis and metempsychosis—the passing of a soul from the dead to the living) in his work. Mills centers his discussion on Louis Simpson's claim that many contemporary poets—Robert Bly, James Wright, W. S. Merwin, Donald Hall, and Dickey—employ a surrealism found in "images . . . connected in a dream," as Simpson states. Mills regards this emphasis on dream-like surrealism as part of the move away from the confines of rationalistic poetry. Such a tendency and "a preoccupation . . . with ritual and archetypal modes of experience confirm Dickey as a poet who possesses an imagination of a primitive, magical type. Obviously, he is at the same time a modern man of considerable sophistication; but the fact that he hunts with a bow and arrow and that he has been a decorated fighter pilot in both World War II and the Korean War indicates something of the broad spectrum of his experience." Dickey's themes, Mills notes, "have a timeless aura about them" while still employing the settings and features of recognizably contemporary existence.

Mills's laudatory discussion of Dickey's poetry takes a surprising turn when he voices agreement with Robert Bly's "just criticism" of the poet's moral stance in such poems as "The Firebombing" and "Slave Quarters." In a 1967 review-essay, *"Buckdancer's Choice"* (listed in the table of contents as "The Collapse of James Dickey"), Bly had argued that these poems demonstrate an American penchant for exerting power over and destroying racial minorities. Concurring with Bly, Mills asserts that Dickey's poetic skills are "broken in the poems which are morally insensate." Further, he finds the vast majority of poems in *Falling* to be "boring," and he sounds an early warning about the alleged fading of Dickey's powers: "I believe we must find notable instances of a diminishing of Dickey's poetic intensity, though such a comment does not everywhere apply. Nonetheless, a regrettable straining after material and effect—perhaps really after novelty— seems to me fatally injurious to most of the longer pieces. . . ." This shortsightedness aside, Mills's comments about the poet's treatment of transformation are particularly instructive.

Moreover, the following year Mills returns to the subject of Dickey's art in an excellent study entitled *Creation's Very Self: On the Personal Element in Recent American Poetry* (1969). Here the critic contends that American poets since World War II have increasingly rejected T. S. Eliot's notion of poetry as an escape from the writer's personality and from emotion; Mills says that most contemporary poets instead have placed the Self at the center of their art. He uses Dickey's "Second Birth" to illustrate how the Self becomes the "informing principle" for his experience. While acknowledging that the writer does not belong to any one poetic school, Mills identifies Dickey as one of the major voices announcing a new aesthetic in American poetry.

Dickey's rebellion against the tenets of Eliot is more specifically treated in an essay written for the 1978 special Dickey number of *South Carolina Review*. George Lensing's "The Neo-Romanticism of James Dickey" declares that whereas Eliot wished to connect to a "cumulative mythic construct" through "tradition" and the "historical sense," Dickey desires the opposite: "instead of making the personal myth universal, as Eliot does, Dickey moves conversely from the universal to the personal. . . . Instead of escaping *from* personality, there is an eager surrender to it." Citing examples from the Dickey canon through *The Zodiac,* Lensing argues that metaphor is the poet's principal means of fusing outer and inner states, the object and the poet.

Another consideration of Dickey's relationship to a general literary tradition appears in Monroe K. Spears's *Dionysus and the City: Modernism in Twentieth-Century Poetry* (1970). Spears declares that "discontinuity"—metaphysical, aesthetic, rhetorical, and temporal—separates modern poetry from that of the past. The metaphysical emphasizes the separation between the human and the natural worlds; the aesthetic asserts a schism between art and life; the rhetorical proclaims the differences in logic between poetry and prose; and the temporal involves both spatial and historical disruptions. Spears also states, "I am tempted to add another category—Psychological—to cover both awareness of discontinuity in general and specific awareness of division within the psyche." The critic then discusses modern writers' Apollonian adherence to or Dionysian rejection of "the 'classical' wisdom of moderation, self-knowledge and self-control." He suggests that Dickey both embodies and tries to bridge currents of discontinuity through Dionysian impulses that allow him "to identify with non-human creatures and with the mysterious forces that they embody," particularly in "moments of ultimate confrontation, of violence and truth."

Peter Davison's "The Difficulties of Being Major: The Poetry of Robert Lowell and James Dickey" (1967) finds in these two important poets philosophical and aesthetic differences that help define opposing tendencies in contemporary American poetry. Davison declares that Dickey does not turn toward and probe the "civilized past," as Lowell does; instead, "no less learned than Lowell, [Dickey] carries the literary past more lightly, but his poems explore our overgrown forest of archetypal scenes and situations; they deal with animals and hunting, with war and wounds, with drowning and flying; with domestic life rather than family history; with pantheism rather than Catholicism; with death and transfiguration rather than funerals; with transformations of shapes and states of being rather than with the dream wrought by time and society. . . . Lowell looks to the Atlantic Ocean and across it, Dickey to the great American wilderness and within the continent." Thus, like Mills, Lensing, and Spears, Davison attempts to locate Dickey's place within twentieth-century poetic traditions.

Many of the essays treating Dickey, especially during the 1970s and 1980s, focus upon single subjects, themes, techniques, or works. Ronald Baughman's "James Dickey's War Poetry: 'A Saved, Shaken

Life' " (1983), the thesis of which is carried over into Baughman's later book on Dickey, examines the poet's handling of the guilt resulting from his survival of combat. The critic finds in the war poetry a movement from confrontation with death, to reordering of the poet's perceptions of death and his own guilt, to his eventual renewal to life. For example, Baughman shows that in his most important war poem, "The Firebombing," Dickey records profound ambiguities about his actions during World War II bombing missions; by refusing to simplify his responses, to espouse a "correct" political or moral position, the poet honestly assesses his situation and thereby prepares for the renewal that more fully comes in the later war poetry.

If Baughman's essay implicitly counters the Bly/Mills contention that Dickey in such poems as "The Firebombing" celebrates militaristic power and racism, two articles on "May Day Sermon" defend him from the as frequently advanced charge of sexism. Thomas O. Sloan's "The Open Poem Is a Now Poem: Dickey's May Day Sermon" (1969) and Maxine S. Rose's "On Being Born Again: James Dickey's 'May Day Sermon to the Women of Gilmer County, Georgia, by a Woman Preacher Leaving the Baptist Church' " (1978) develop very similar arguments, with Rose frontally attacking those who label the poet "shamelessly chauvinistic" not only in the sermon but also in many of the other works in *Poems 1957-1967*. These critics perceive that in "May Day Sermon" both the lady preacher and the young woman at the center of her story are associated with natural processes and passions, with a drive for freedom. Males in the poem—the enraged Southern Baptist father and the God he serves, for example—are seen as unnatural, arbitrary, and repressive. The poem ultimately celebrates, in Sloan's words, the "breaking down [of] barriers, including those imposed by rigid categories of thought"; and in Rose's words, it "infuses new hope in the hearts of women everywhere who are repressed and tortured for being sexual creatures."

A pair of essays are representative of those treating Dickey's handling of important symbolic settings or devices. David C. Berry's "Harmony with the Dead: James Dickey's Descent into the Underworld" (1974) argues that the poet's recurrent interest in the dead is caught through an Orpheus motif. Descending into the underworld, the poet-speaker fails to achieve complete union with the dead; yet the knowledge gained through his descent helps him attain a midpoint between the living and the dead and therefore a degree of harmony of "celebration" in his own life, Berry states. Daniel L. Guillory, in "Water Magic in the Poetry of James Dickey" (1970), shows that the poet employs water—rivers, streams, the sea—both as a source for the renewal of life and as a conduit to the world of the dead. As the critic explains, water "represents a force at once beneficial and maleficent," and death by water gives "the dead person new life since he is absorbed by the life-giving energy of the water and thereby is immortalized." Dickey develops his own experimental symbolic system, Guillory says, that becomes "a significant frame of reference for all worthwhile events."

Almost all studies of Dickey's poetry necessarily touch on his relationship to the natural world. Most critics emphasize the sense of joy, of ecstasy, of spiritual renewal implicit in this relationship. However, in "The Smell of Blood in Paradise" (1968) Paul Carroll defines a different current. Focusing on the poem "The Heaven of Animals," Carroll examines the "unnaturalness of nature's heaven," the Platonic ideal of earthly nature. Beneath its placid surface the poem conveys a disorienting emotion, "the ecstasy of violence," Carroll declares. The perfect, eternal cycle created for "joyous violence only" between predator and prey implies much about the earthly vision of this ideal, as well as about the god that created "an eternal and ceaseless cycle of maiming, rebirth, and maiming again." Therefore, the critic suggests, Dickey's "celebration" has a more ominous quality than most commentators concede.

A substantial part of the criticism on Dickey treats his only novel to date, *Deliverance*. Several significant essays examine the nature of the suburbanites'—particularly Ed Gentry's—transformation in the wilderness. Mark Royden Winchell's "The River Within: Primitivism in James Dickey's *Deliverance*" (1977) argues that the writer has created "an authentic primitive hero whose initiation into manhood involves the shedding of human blood." Paralleling Gentry to the heroic figures described in Joseph Campbell's *The Hero with a Thousand Faces*, Winchell shows that Ed undergoes ten of the seventeen experiences that Campbell says transform the initiate into a hero. Through these experiences Gentry is changed "from a sterile and insulated suburbanite into a being who is at least in touch with animal nature," Winchell declares.

Donald J. Greiner, in "The Harmony of Bestiality in James Dickey's *Deliverance*" (1972), asserts that Ed is forced to evolve into a bestial figure to save himself and the others in the wilderness. In this regard he undercuts the primitivist conception of the benevolent noble savage. But in order to save his life upon his return to civilization, Gentry must, Greiner says, establish a "harmonious relationship between the two sides of his nature, the bestial and the human, . . . a balance between his animal nature and his human personality."

Charles E. Davis's discussion "The Wilderness Revisited: Irony in James Dickey's *Deliverance*" (1976) regards the novel as Dickey's conscious reversal of one of the most persistent themes in American literature: the Romantic belief that man can return to nature for "strength, truth, and virtue." Portraying a nature that is "mindless, flatly indifferent, and impersonal" and whose lesson for man is "amoral," Dickey gives the wilderness such traditionally masculine qualities as aggressiveness and strength; in contrast, he describes the men, with the exception of Lewis Medlock, as embodying the traditionally feminine traits of tenderness and submissiveness, Davis argues. Because these men are dependent upon the technology and morality of the city, Gentry's deliverance depends less on primitive skills of survival than on his employment of a device of civilization—"a lie, the fabrication Ed concocts concerning the death of Drew Ballinger" and others, the critic says. Davis thereby determines that Dickey's theme is that "twentieth-century man may attempt to turn and may even succeed in turning to nature for renewal. But such a renewal will not entail a moral cleansing or a spiritual rebirth." Instead, man must finally rely on the city and civilization for well-being.

Another critical question raised by studies of *Deliverance* concerns the role of various art forms in the novel. Peter G. Beidler's " 'The Pride of Thine Heart Hath Deceived Thee': Narrative Distortion in Dickey's *Deliverance*" (1972) asserts that Gentry has killed an innocent hunter rather than Bobby Trippe's sodomizer or Drew's murderer. Ed's act thus "shows what a monster man becomes when he takes upon himself the roles of prosecuting attorney, jury, judge, and executioner." To maintain his own equilibrium, Gentry purposely deceives himself about his own guilt; using imaginative devices, particularly those drawn from movies, he distorts the truth in his own mind and in narrative, thereby allowing himself to assume a heroic rather than demonic self-image, Beidler says.

In "Art and Nature in *Deliverance*" (1979), Edward Doughtie counters Beidler's charge that Gentry has killed the wrong man but agrees that Ed depends on art forms to accomplish the killing required to deliver him from danger. Doughtie convincingly discusses the ways in which "Dickey shows art to be a necessary mediator between nature—both the exterior nature of woods and rivers and the interior nature of man's drives and dreams—and modern urban 'civilized' life." Again, the critic treats the movies as Gentry's primary art form;

but in Doughtie's view Gentry's reliance on art allows him to bring "a kind of order to chaos" and therefore to insure his survival.

Linda Tarte Holley's "Design and Focus in James Dickey's *Deliverance*" (1978) demonstrates how Gentry's training as a graphic artist, which causes him to focus on design and arrangement, helps him to save himself and his companions. Ed "frames" with his eye and mind crucial events that occur—his shooting of the mountain man, for example; similarly, the novel is structured around such frames, thus creating a thematic pattern that connects voice and action in the novel, Holley says. Gentry's deliverance comes "because his creative imagination has sharply defined the relationship between form and matter and has delivered him from lassitude and death."

Treatments of sexuality have also appeared in discussions of the novel. Don Kunz, in "Learning the Hard Way in James Dickey's *Deliverance*" (1978), argues that in this work Dickey consciously works against the tradition of "the woman-despising American dream" of males. The mountain men's sexual domination of the four suburbanites forces Gentry and his friends to assume the conventional female role of submission. Consequently, Ed and other characters learn the hard way that their deliverance, especially upon their return to the city, depends upon their transcending the "prison of gender" and achieving a balance of male-female attributes in order to gain a more complete humanity, Kunz declares.

The novel's explicitly sexual motif becomes the primary concern of Paul G. Italia's "Love and Lust in James Dickey's *Deliverance*" (1975). Italia asserts that the central pattern of the work is one of "struggle, copulation, and death" and that "what results from this whirlwind weekend courtship with death is love." Much of the narrative, Italia contends, is a working out of dream-fantasy states linking the hunt with sexual pursuit. Ultimately, the critic says, Gentry's physical and sexual confrontations that lead to death also become the means by which he gains his own sense of humanity.

Finally, an extremely instructive essay concentrates on a character whom many critics have neglected or found baffling. John Jolly's "Drew Ballinger as 'Sacrificial God' in James Dickey's *Deliverance*" (1985) finds thematic connections between Ballinger and the mythic Greek figure Orpheus. Using Sir James G. Frazier's concept in *The Golden Bough* of the sacrificial god, Jolly demonstrates the similarities between Drew and Orpheus by noting their associations with music, their deaths and apparent resurrections in water, and their powers of prophesy. For example, after his death Ballinger sits among the river rocks as if resurrected and as if offering a prophetic warning to the other men, while in the Greek myth Orpheus's dismembered head is caught in rocks but continues to deliver oracles. Both figures, Jolly concludes, are sacrificed so that others may survive and prosper.

That Dickey's poetry and novel have inspired so many fine critical commentaries suggests the complex vision and artistry of his work. From whatever perspective his canon has been approached, it has yielded fruitful insights into the human condition and the function of literature in America since World War II. It is safe to predict that James Dickey's poetry and prose will continue to attract significant critical attention.

Robert Hayden
(1913-1980)

Fred M. Fetrow
United States Naval Academy

PRIMARY BIBLIOGRAPHY

Books

Heart-Shape in the Dust. Detroit: Falcon Press, 1940. Poems.
The Lion and the Archer, by Hayden and Myron O'Higgins. Nashville, Tenn.: Hemphill Press, 1948. Poems.
Figure of Time: Poems. Nashville, Tenn.: Hemphill Press, 1955. Poems.
A Ballad of Remembrance. London: Paul Breman, 1962. Poems.
Selected Poems. New York: October House, 1966. Poems.
Words in the Mourning Time. New York: October House, 1970. Poems.
The Night-Blooming Cereus. London: Paul Breman, 1972. Poems.
Angle of Ascent: New and Selected Poems. New York: Liveright, 1975. Poems.
American Journal. Taunton, Mass.: Effendi Press, 1978; enlarged edition, New York: Liveright, 1982. Poems.
The Collected Prose, ed. Frederick Glaysher. Ann Arbor: University of Michigan Press, 1984. Essays.
Robert Hayden: Collected Poems, ed. Frederick Glaysher. New York: Liveright, 1985. Poems.

Edited Books

Kaleidoscope: Poems by American Negro Poets, ed. with an introduction by Hayden. New York: Harcourt, Brace & World, 1967. Anthology.
Afro-American Literature: An Introduction, ed. Hayden and others. New York: Harcourt Brace Jovanovich, 1971. Anthology.
The United States in Literature, ed. Hayden and others. Glenview, Ill.: Scott Foresman, 1973. Anthology.

SECONDARY BIBLIOGRAPHY

Bibliographies and Checklists

Nicholas, Xavier. "Robert Hayden: A Bibliography," *Obsidian*, 7 (Winter 1980), 109-127. Primary and secondary.

_____."Robert Hayden: A Bibliography," *Obsidian*, 8 (Spring 1981), 207-210. Supplement; primary and secondary.

Biographies: Articles and Book Sections

Greenberg, Robert M. "Robert Hayden 1913-1980." In *American Writers: A Collection of Literary Biographies,* Supplement II, Part 1, ed. A. Walton Litz. New York: Scribners, 1981, 316-383.

Williams, Pontheolla T. "Robert Hayden: A Life Upon These Shores," *World Order,* 16 (Fall 1981), 11-34.

Selected Interviews

"Conversations with Americans: A Conversation During the Bicentennial," *World Order,* 10 (Winter 1975-1976), 46-53.

Layman, Richard. "Robert Hayden." In *Conversations with Writers,* vol. 1. Detroit: Gale Research, 1977, 156-179.

McCluskey, Paul. "The Poet and his Art: A Conversation." In *How I Write/*1. New York: Harcourt Brace Jovanovich, 1972, 133-213.

O'Brien, John. "A Romantic Realist." In his *Interviews with Black Writers.* New York: Liveright, 1973, 109-123.

Critical Studies: Books

Fetrow, Fred M. *Robert Hayden.* Boston: Twayne, 1984.

Hatcher, John. *From the Auroral Darkness: The Life and Poetry of Robert Hayden.* Oxford, U.K.: George Ronald, 1984.

Critical Studies: Special Issues of Journals

Obsidian, 8 (Spring 1981).

World Order, 16 (Fall 1981).

Critical Studies: Articles and Book Sections

Davis, Arthur P. "Robert Hayden." In *From the Dark Tower: Afro-American Writers 1900 to 1960,* ed. Arthur P. Davis. Washington, D.C.: Howard University Press, 1974, 174-180.

Davis, Charles T. "Robert Hayden's Use of History." In *Modern Black Poets,* ed. Donald B. Gibson. Englewood Cliffs, N.J.: Prentice-Hall, 1973, 96-111.

Faulkner, Howard. " 'Transformed by Steeps of Flight': The Poetry of Robert Hayden," *CLA Journal,* 21 (Dec. 1977), 282-291.

Fetrow, Fred M. " 'Middle Passage': Robert Hayden's Anti-Epic," *CLA Journal,* 22 (June 1979), 304-318.

_____."Robert Hayden's 'Frederick Douglass': Form and Meaning in a Modern Sonnet," *CLA Journal,* 17 (Sept. 1973), 79-84.

_____. "Robert Hayden's 'The Rag Man' and the Metaphysics of the Mundane," *Research Studies,* 47 (Sept. 1979), 188-190.

Harper, Michael S. "Remembering Robert Hayden," *Carleton Miscellany,* 18 (Winter 1980), 231-234.

_____."Remembering Robert Hayden," *Michigan Quarterly Review,* 21 (Winter 1982), 182-186.

Lester, Julius. "In Memorium: In Gratitude for Robert Hayden," *World Order,* 16 (Fall 1981), 50-55.

Lewis, Richard O. "A Literary-Psychoanalytic Interpretation of Robert Hayden's 'Market,' " *Black American Literature Forum,* 9 (Spring 1975), 21-24.

Novak, Michael P. "Meditative, Ironic, Richly Human: The Poetry of Robert Hayden," *Midwest Quarterly,* 15 (Spring 1974), 276-285.

O'Sullivan, Maurice J., Jr. "The Mask of Allusion in Robert Hayden's 'The Diver,' " *CLA Journal,* 17 (Sept. 1973), 85-92.

Parks, Gerald. "The Baha'i Muse: Religion in Robert Hayden's Poetry," *World Order,* 16 (Fall 1981), 37-48.

Pool, Rosey E. "Robert Hayden: Poet Laureate (An Assessment)," *Negro Digest,* 15 (June 1966), 39-43.

Post, Constance J. "Image and Idea in the Poetry of Robert Hayden," *CLA Journal,* 20 (Dec. 1976), 164-175.

Potter, Vilma R. "A Remembrance for Robert Hayden, 1913-1980," *MELUS,* 8 (Spring 1980), 51-55.

Stepto, Robert B. "After Modernism, After Hibernation: Michael Harper, Robert Hayden, and Jay Wright." In *Chant of Saints: A Gathering of Afro-American Literature, Art, and Scholarship,* ed. Michael S. Harper and Robert B. Stepto. Urbana: University of Illinois Press, 1979, 470-476.

Turco, Lewis. *"Angle of Ascent:* The Poetry of Robert Hayden," *Michigan Quarterly Review,* 16 (Spring 1977), 199-219.

Williams, Wilburn, Jr. "Covenant of Timelessness and Time: Symbolism and History in Robert Hayden's *Angle of Ascent."* In *Chant of Saints: A Gathering of Afro-American Literature, Art, and Scholarship,* ed. Michael S. Harper and Robert B. Stepto. Urbana: University of Illinois Press, 1979, 66-84.

Wright, John S. "Homage to a Mystery Boy," *Georgia Review,* 36 (Winter 1982), 904-911.

BIBLIOGRAPHICAL ESSAY

Bibliographies and Checklists

There exists no book-length bibliography of writings by or about Robert Hayden; indeed, the lack of such a work reflects the limited number of volumes he produced and the critical neglect he endured during his career. The few bibliographical items listed in general studies of his life and work mirror Hayden's belated recognition in that most of these items are of recent vintage.

Although brief checklists are provided in the two critical books on Hayden, the only extended primary and secondary bibliography is that by Xavier Nicholas in two successive issues of *Obsidian,* a journal devoted to black literature. Nicholas includes a full listing of Hayden's poetry volumes, his poems originally printed or since reprinted in journals, his poetry collected in anthologies, and his prose statements in print. The section on published criticism is quite extensive, and given the limited amount of Hayden scholarship to date, the Nicholas checklists are as close to definitive as possible. That a supplement was warranted is encouraging since it suggests that increasing attention is being paid to Hayden.

Biographies: Articles and Book Sections

The current biographical sources on Hayden are few in number and uneven in quality. Because no full-length biography has been published, readers must rely on introductory chapters in the two critical books presently available, upon an unusually detailed account in a reference book, and upon one purely biographical essay published in a journal.

The two critical books—discussed in detail later in this essay—contain useful summaries of the life in their introductory chapters and attempt throughout to relate Hayden's works to events in his life. A comparable source for biographical information is Robert M. Greenberg's sketch in *American Writers: A Collection of Literary Biographies* (1981). His essay begins with an account of Hayden's life, which is followed by one section on the poet's career in general and another on discussion of the major works. While the biographical segment is relatively comprehensive, including much material from interviews, it is perhaps too dependent upon the unpublished doctoral dissertation of Dennis Gendron (University of North Carolina, 1975) for its information and assumptions. The analytical commentary is adequate, but Greenberg is sometimes too diffuse in his response to the poetry, sometimes erroneous in his discussion of particular works. His thesis—that Hayden's dominant poetic theme involves an ongoing struggle between harsh reality and comforting fantasy—too often makes the writer seem a frustrated escapist, since Greenberg sees no resolution of this conflict in any of the poems. Although his discussion of "Middle Passage" seems overgeneralized, this critic does justice to several of the other important poems. His essay is strengthened by his discernment of Hayden's abiding interest in those people and places just beyond the ordinary and often out of favor with the world. And one cannot argue with Greenberg's closing remark as an epitaph for the poet: "Hayden has brought us more fully and humanly into the world. That was his purpose, his calling."

As pure biography, an essay by Pontheolla T. Williams has the strengths of comprehensive coverage and copious detail. Published in the Fall 1981 *World Order,* this article shares with other biographical sketches a tendency to tail off: the account diminishes in its amount of detail as the biography approaches the present. It is as if the early life, described by the poet himself in interviews, was more eventful and interesting than the later life, which Hayden did not so fully discuss. Yet Williams's essay is, at present, the fullest account of Hayden's early life and career (1913-1946), focusing as it does on biography rather than on analysis of the poetry. A very readable study, it is not however readily accessible, since few libraries carry *World Order.*

Selected Interviews

Of the published interviews, only four are significant enough to discuss here. Paul McCluskey's 1971 discussion with Hayden, which appeared in *How I Write / 1* (1972), is probably the fullest of the interviews in its coverage of the close correlation between the subject's personal history and his poetic canon. Using a pedagogical approach, McCluskey asks Hayden about the origin, evolution, and significant features of one poem before going on to another. Set up in five sections that distinguish among stages in the poet's development and discrete thematic concerns, the interview moves through the canon more or less chronologically.

When the interviewer begins by asking questions about the poet's early work, Hayden responds with biographical data from the 1930s, which leads to quotation and discussion of the more personal poems evoking that era ("Summertime and the living . . ." and "Those Winter Sundays"). The folkloric elements of several poems are also attributed to youthful memories of his cultural milieu. The so-called experimental phase of Hayden's career (he liked to call it the "Baroque period") is addressed through discussion of "A Ballad of Remembrance," quoted in its entirety and covered in terms of its sources, composition, revision, diction, and imagery. The interview highlights the black history poems in a section called "The Black Spear," in which are found a lengthy discussion of "Middle Passage," as well as talk about "O Daedalus Fly Away Home," "The Ballad of Nat Turner," "Runagate Runagate," and "Frederick Douglass." In the next section Hayden illuminates three of his "Mexican poems" with commentary on the experience, emotion, and conscious craft behind each work. A final segment, "The Poet's World," discusses three poems ("Full Moon," "Zeus Over Redeye," "Monet's *Waterlilies*") that are diverse in subject and technique. Throughout the discussion Hayden conveys the strong feelings informing each poem, whether about religious faith, the age of technology, or the love of art. Hayden's first published interview is and will continue to be especially enlightening for readers because McCluskey directly links the poet and his work in ways that illuminate both.

John O'Brien's 1973 interview of Hayden, which is among the briefest and least substantial of the published talks, has at least one redeeming feature. Emphasizing the "mysteries of art," O'Brien does his best to draw out his subject on this rather difficult topic. However, the interview soon gives way to a rather plodding, recurring questioning of how particular poems originated and evolved. Although Hayden seems willing to share candid assessments of his own practices and values, the interviewer's questions do not evoke such revelations. For perhaps the clearest statement of the poet's aesthetic stance and philosophy, readers should consult Hayden's own created dialogue, a mock debate between "Poet" and "Inquisitor" that he delivered as his final address as Poetry Consultant to the Library of Congress. That document, now available in the *Collected Prose* (1984), contains Hayden's most complete expression of his philosophy of art and his conception of the artist's role.

A more specialized interview—that appearing in the Winter 1975-1976 *World Order*—serves as a summary of the feelings cryptically expressed later in Hayden's *American Journal*. The focus of the interview can be indicated by its initial question: "What does America mean to you on the eve of the bicentennial?" Hayden's responses to this and other questions like it provide an understanding of the poet's views of his native land. Hayden's vision of America's past is influenced by his knowledge of the black racial experience and by his Baha'i belief in a tortuous evolution toward a better future. His commentary on the fulfillment of America's promise is fraught with the same ambivalence evident in *American Journal*. In spite of his disdain for what he terms "reactionary forces" that forestall "real social and spiritual progress," the poet's vision of America is essentially optimistic. Although grieved by racial and sectarian barriers and bothered by the American penchant to worship power and technology, he still contends that "spiritually mature" people can bring about changes in attitudes and that "redefinition will come about as the result of a renewal of transcendent belief." Thus, in contrast to his apparent pessimism elsewhere, Hayden in this instance views his country as a catalytic agent of world unification. When prompted by the interviewer, he also claims a role for art in this process, but he resists the interviewer's suggestion that he label his work quintessentially "American." Instead, he aspires to a universality of appeal that would subsume yet transcend regional or national labels. This interview may be relatively narrow in its scope and purpose, but it does provide valuable insights into its later poetic counterpart, *American Journal*.

For a biographical perspective, Richard Layman's 1977 *Conversations with Writers* interview is most detailed and informative. Beginning with questions about Hayden's early life and family background, the interview's organization remains chronological. Prompted by inquiries about those early days, Hayden elaborates his earliest memories of his elementary school fascination with words and language and describes his reading habits and experiences as a high school student. In this mode Layman and Hayden produce a delightfully anecdotal account of Hayden's early life. As the chronology progresses, more emphasis is placed on the career, with some attention to the poet's artistic and philosophic values: the years at Michigan under the tutelage of W. H. Auden, the Fisk experience, the "Baroque period," and Hayden's Baha'i conversion of the 1940s all receive their due. The wealth of detail is attributal to Hayden alone, but the interviewer skillfully draws out Hayden's responses. Perhaps after going over the same events in an interview with Dennis Gendron (which became part of Gendron's dissertation), the poet had in effect rehearsed his answers; in any event, for a reader interested in Hayden's early career, this interview is invaluable.

Critical Studies: Books

Only two book-length critical studies of Robert Hayden's poetry are currently in print. Both are comprehensive in their coverage but introductory in their premises and purposes. One circumstance of their publication characterizes the embryonic status of Hayden scholarship: Fred M. Fetrow's *Robert Hayden* and John Hatcher's *From the Auroral Darkness: The Life and Poetry of Robert Hayden* were published in rapid succession (Fetrow's in June 1984; Hatcher's in December 1984), yet neither author was aware of the other's impending publication before the two books appeared.

Fetrow's book has the advantage of availability, since most libraries subscribe to the Twayne's United States Authors Series, in which *Robert Hayden* is a number. The study itself is organized according to the standard format of that series. Beginning with a chronology, which is simply a listing of the principal events of Hayden's life and his major publications, the monograph proceeds systematically from a first chapter of biographical survey through five chapters of sustained critical discussion of the poetry. Fetrow describes his purpose and method in a brief preface:

> The analytical chapters have been ordered in the chronological sequence of Hayden's major publications and organized to treat the poems according to subject categories, thematic concerns, and poetic techniques. This progression is designed to trace and thus

clarify the poet's evolution into a major voice in modern American literature.

One of the more interesting observations that derives from this approach is Fetrow's notion that while Hayden was experimenting and evolving as an artist, he eventually came almost full circle in his treatment of his own life as poetic subject matter. Fetrow's thesis is that Hayden began his career writing personal lyrics that revealed his closest relationships and innermost feelings. He then refrained almost entirely "from purely personal utterance during midcareer, and finally returned more frequently to his own biography as the poetic subject matter that would culminate his growth as an artist." Fetrow's tracing of patterns of poetic practice and development makes his book seminal in its substance and its timing.

Hatcher's *From the Auroral Darkness* is a valuable contribution to Hayden studies primarily because of its inclusion of materials providing a complete frame of reference for understanding Hayden's life and art. Organized similarly to Fetrow's volume, Hatcher's book begins with a biographical summary that is followed by a digressive but important segment dealing with the background of "The Problem of a 'Black Aesthetic,' " "The Birth of the Hayden Stand" (against " 'the chauvinistic, the cultish . . . special pleading . . . all that seeks to limit and restrict creative expression' "), and "The Controversy" (related to Hayden's refusal to be categorized as a racial spokesman). Thereafter the book chronologically covers Hayden's life and career through examination of the published collections. Because the content is divided into brief mini-chapters, Hatcher is able to place in sharp focus significant trends or points of departure in Hayden's life or career. Moreover, the text is supplemented by seven photographs of the poet (ranging from Hayden looking somber and formal at age eight to his receiving an honorary doctorate from Brown University in 1976).

The strength of this book is its comprehensive coverage of all phases of the life and work, from Hayden's aesthetic premises to his final responses to terminal illness. If the book has a weakness, it lies in its emphasis on (and thus bias toward) the Baha'i influence on Hayden's poetry. While Hayden's faith does figure prominently in his life and work, other important artistic and critical considerations may be slighted through the heavy concentration on the Baha'i identity of the subject. The study's focus should not be unexpected, given the author's own faith and his book's having been commissioned and published by Baha'i organizations. However, the account consistently links the poet and his faith more completely than any previous work on Robert Hayden.

Critical Studies: Special Issues of Journals

Several publications contemplated special issues devoted to Hayden soon after his death in 1980; two eventually came to fruition. *World Order*, the quarterly journal of the Baha'i faith, an organ for which Hayden served as poetry editor for several years, published a memorial issue in the Fall of 1981. The most important essays therein are individually discussed in the *Major Critical Articles and Book Sections* part of this entry; also included in that special issue are a few poems in tribute to Hayden.

The Spring 1981 special issue of *Obsidian* contains a larger collection of remembrances, tributes, and brief portraits of Hayden. Most of its articles are as brief as they are poignant, but the collection is extensive (210 pages, thirty-two brief essays, six poems, and a supplementary bibliography). The essays range from reminiscences of Hayden's earliest work, to the accolades of contemporary fellow artists, to the impressions of young critics flush with relatively recent discovery and appreciation of the man and his work.

Critical Studies: Articles and Book Sections

Most of the articles published about Hayden can be conveniently classified into four major categories. In fact, the nature of these categories indirectly reflects the increasing critical attention to Hayden's work from the early 1970s to the present. Initial attention came in the form of usually brief analytical articles in explication of individual poems. Later criticism expanded coverage to treat thematic concerns represented in diverse samplings from Hayden's canon. Some essays also provided rather comprehensive overviews of Hayden's career as exemplified by major works and significant trends. Finally, in the wake of his death, eulogies and appreciations of the man, his work, and his moral vision appeared.

Two early studies treating individual poems were printed together in the September 1973 special number of the *CLA Journal* devoted to Gwendolyn Brooks, LeRoi Jones (Imamu Amiri Baraka), and Hayden. The first essay, Fred M. Fetrow's close reading of "Frederick Douglass," illustrates Hayden's innovative approach to the traditional sonnet form. The brief article was timely since there previously existed no commentary on the poem and since "Douglass" was and is still perhaps the most widely anthologized of Hayden's works. Fetrow argues that although elements of form (rhyme, meter, structure) reinforce meaning in regular sonnets, Hayden in "Frederick Douglass" eschews all the required formal properties of the sonnet, using instead alternative devices of structure, style, and language to accomplish a masterful merging of form and function. Twenty-five years after the poem first appeared in print, Fetrow demonstrates how successful Hayden was in his early experimentations with form, an interest that he shared with such other earlier innovators in sonnet form as John Keats and Gerard Manley Hopkins.

The companion essay on another individual poem is less plausible as analysis but more expansive in its implication. Maurice J. O'Sullivan, Jr., begins his interpretation of "The Diver" by decrying and rejecting what would seem to be a widespread misunderstanding of the poem resulting from overzealous application of psychoanalytic criticism. But he soon reveals that his real "target" is only a single short entry in the *Instructor's Guide* accompanying a black literature anthology containing "The Diver." O'Sullivan's alternative to psychoanalytic theorizing is an interpretation that imposes a "racial message" on the poem and denies any universal application of its other thematic implications. While acknowledging that the general outline of the poem's content ("descent, temptation, rejection, ascent") might seem to lend itself to "psychoanalyzing," O'Sullivan rejects that approach as too fraught with internal contradiction. Instead, he advocates a second kind of allusiveness, a cultural-historical analogy whereby the scuba diver's mask becomes the "tactical masquerade" necessary for racial survival. O'Sullivan thus presents the diver as a modern successor or counterpart to Paul Dunbar's speaker in "We Wear the Mask" and to Ralph Ellison's invisible man. He concludes,

> Hayden offers a modern audience the period Dunbar had implicitly promised, a time when the grinning, lying, laughing mask of anguish and forbearance has metamorphosed into the tactically expressionless mask of the emerging diver.

His conclusions are intriguing, but the poem itself will not bear them out. Only by overemphasizing some elements of "The Diver" while ignoring others can the critic sustain his thesis.

Perhaps the most substantial critical study of a single poem is

Fetrow's 1979 *CLA Journal* article on "Middle Passage." Here the author asserts that Hayden consciously designed the poem as a variation on the epic structure, what Fetrow calls an "anti-epic." By documenting the poet's interview commentary on the poem, specifically his remarks about the influence on him of Stephen Vincent Benét's *John Brown's Body* (1927) and about his ambition to sing the "black-skinned epic," Fetrow establishes an epic intent behind the work. He thereafter explicates "Middle Passage" in terms of variations on conventions of the epic mode.

Some of his critical assertions and assessments are self-evidently accurate (lists of ships' names obviously could constitute an epic catalogue); other claims seem more tenuous (Fetrow cannot seem to decide whether the pagan gods of classical myth are replaced in Hayden's poem by sharks, malevolent spirits, or simply by a lack of a benevolent Christian God. For a reader new to Hayden's "Middle Passage," the primary benefit of this essay is its glossing of the sources for most of the poem's narrative raw materials. Finally, whether or not Hayden was as methodical in his use of epic convention as this critic claims, genre study allows both critical writer and interested reader more access to a masterpiece that has an importance to American literature thus far belied by its critical neglect. If nothing else, Fetrow does justice to "Middle Passage" because he has done more with the poem than anyone else.

Another short article on a short poem is an interesting exercise in psychoanalytical criticism posing as metaphysics. In his 1979 *Research Studies* essay Fetrow approaches Hayden's "The Rag Man" as a case study in psychological projection—the phenomenon of revealing one's own emotional concerns by projecting them onto an external stimulus. The critic argues that the speaker's doubt and latent guilt about his own values are stirred alive through his response to a rag picker who seems not only indifferent but also superior to those who pity him. Such an attitude, such behavior from an impoverished beggar puzzles the speaker-narrator; this response, combined with Hayden's other references to the "Rag Man," gives the character a mysterious nature, an identity alien to the society in which he grudgingly coexists. According to Fetrow's critical conclusion, the "Rag Man" is "Hayden's version of King Lear's 'unaccommodated man,' " a symbol of modern man's subliminal guilt about his materialistic values. In view of the apparent brevity and simplicity of the poem, one may suspect that this critical response is itself a form of projection—an assumption of a moral profundity scarcely contemplated by the artist. However, the poet himself assented to the article's plausibility, either because the essay really does make sense, or because Robert Hayden was being typically kind to puzzled critics with good intentions.

While a few critics have concentrated on specific individual poems, many commentators attempt to illuminate Hayden's work by dealing with such poetic elements as characterization and style or by treating thematic concerns such as history and religion. Charles T. Davis, for example, in one of the earliest sustained critical essays on Hayden's poetry, emphasizes the poet's early and abiding interest in history in general and black history in particular. He begins "Robert Hayden's Use of History" (1973) by summarizing Hayden's purpose, "to record accurately the yearnings, frustrations, and the achievement of an enslaved but undestroyed people." Providing a historical context for Hayden's work, Davis lists several early poems about noble blacks who rise from oppression and obscurity and then documents Hayden's shift toward historical patterns that impel the reader into the present, thereby emphasizing spiritual as well as physical liberation.

Davis devotes the bulk of the essay to probing the origins and manifestations of Hayden's historical inclination. For example, his analysis of "Middle Passage" accounts for the influence of Benét and *John Brown's Body* in the 1930s and highlights Hayden's research on the slave trade era. The essay then covers other historically oriented poems such as "The Ballad of Nat Turner," "Runagate Runagate," "O Daedalus Fly Away Home," and "Frederick Douglass." Davis updates his thesis with final attention to Hayden's then recent collection, *Words in the Mourning Time* (1970). While the critic finds no sharp focus on history in this new collection, he nevertheless notes that history is an inherent concern of poems like "The Dream" and "On Lookout Mountain," both of which he explicates in those terms. The critic concludes his article by finding similarities between Hayden's poem about the life of Malcolm X and the historical account in "Middle Passage": both trace the ironies and movement of history; both trace a pattern of progression toward human understanding, reflecting the Baha'i sense of history as a painful evolution toward perfection. In sum, this essay on Hayden's use of history is an astute and sensible means for clarifying a central feature of the poet's work.

Lewis Turco in his Spring 1977 *Michigan Quarterly Review* essay examines features of Hayden's style with the intention of defending him as a black poet. Decrying the neglect experienced by Hayden and other black writers caused by the "ghettoizing" of their kind, Turco also notes the irony of Hayden's being rejected by other more militant black poets who have not understood or appreciated his determination to be judged by his art, exclusive of race. Against this backdrop, Turco sets out to prove that Hayden's work is as "black" as anyone's by applying standards of the "black aesthetic" defined by Stephen Henderson in *Understanding the New Black Poetry* (1973). Thus the entire article is devoted to a defense of Hayden as "a paradigmatic poet of the English language who has been true to his roots and history, though not circumscribed by, or limited to, what is merely racial, ethnic, or personal."

Turco systematically examines Henderson's "broad critical categories" and those specific devices of technique and content that exemplify black poetry in order to demonstrate convincingly that (1) such techniques are not uniquely black, and that (2) Robert Hayden employs virtually all of the techniques listed and illustrated by Henderson, anyway. Turco's pattern of presentation is to cite, define, and exemplify one of the devices Henderson claims is black or in the black tradition, then to show the same device or technique as used by non-black predecessors (such as the sixteenth-century English poet, John Skelton), and to cite Hayden's use or adaptation of the technique under discussion. In this convincing but repetitious fashion the critic resoundingly defends Hayden's ethnic commitment as well as his artistic expertise. He claims that the real distinction of Hayden's work is the poet's ability to go beyond the influences of form, to transform standard forms into something uniquely his own, "a masterful wedding of tradition with personal style."

Like Turco before him, Wilburn Williams, Jr., begins his "Covenant of Timelessness and Time: Symbolism and History in Robert Hayden's *Angle of Ascent*" (1979) by lamenting Hayden's neglect as an artist of demonstrated ability and importance. Williams then develops the notion that Hayden is a combination of symbolist and historian. He sees Hayden as a symbolist whose perception of a transcendent spiritual realm strives to redeem the tragedy and destruction of history, both public and private. Thus the critic views much of the poetry in terms of the conflicting claims of the ideal and the actual. Williams asserts that this preoccupation with the relationship between natural and spiritual puts Hayden in the mainstream of American literary tradition along with Ralph Waldo Emerson, Henry David Thoreau, Emily Dickinson, and Herman Melville.

In the second part of the essay Williams dwells on Hayden as a historian with a discernible and "powerful elegiac strain in his work."

Acknowledging Charles Davis's work in this regard, Williams applies the oxymoronic labels—"romantic realist," "skeptical believer"—that Hayden himself used to characterize a symbolist compelled to face the harsh realities of history. To support his thesis Williams provides close readings of several poems. He argues that Hayden's penchant for individualized portraits of racial heroes is an attempt to depict present reality through past fact. But Williams considers Hayden a traditionalist as well, a historian concerned "for the fate of myth and religion in the modern world." Here the critic perhaps overextends his premise as he tries too hard to substantiate this claim with an ingenious treatment of "Full Moon," as if one deft example could prove a case not otherwise made.

The concluding segment of the essay portrays Hayden as a historian concerned with smaller and smaller units of time, within which the poet can more fully explore the mystery of change itself. To illustrate this trend, Williams concentrates on late poems describing or contemplating metamorphoses in various forms. Finally, the critic claims a similar shift in Hayden's portraiture, a shift from past public figures to less known contemporaries. He may be overstating the case here because too many examples contradict such easy generalization. Perhaps the safest conclusion is simply to link the portraits in the poems with diminishing units of time: both are finally means to an end—to facilitate the poet's perceptive observations on life, art, and truth. In that sense these characters and those poems are indeed as timeless as Williams believes them to be, but finally not for the reasons he claims.

In another 1979 essay concerned with time and history, Robert Stepto nominates Hayden, Michael Harper, and Jay Wright as perpetuators of the legacy inherent in the view of history that informs Ralph Ellison's *Invisible Man*. Using the terms "After Modernism" and "Hibernation" in his title, Stepto defines the former as a "series of incidents in recent literary history wherein a literary exchange between modern writers and would-be post modern writers yields epilogues to the modernists' work." From there Stepto goes on to discuss several poems by Hayden, Harper, and Wright as responses to Ellison's definition of his hero's hibernation: "a covert preparation for a more overt action." Specifically, the critic treats Hayden's "Elegies for Paradise Valley" to show that such poems extend the racial legacy of Ellison's protagonist because these works extend history beyond the "modern" to the "post modern." He contends that the eight separate poems function individually and collectively to create a reality beyond the strict definitions of history. Thus Hayden's imagined and remembered worlds of Paradise Valley suggest typical thematic and spiritual links among contemporary black poets and their literary predecessors.

Gerald Parks sheds considerable light on a substantial portion of Hayden's canon by examining the poet's religious convictions generally and the doctrines of the Baha'i faith specifically. Parks's "The Baha'i Muse: Religion in Robert Hayden's Poetry" (1981) explores "the thematic development in Hayden's treatment of religion." Parks's premise is that Hayden's religious faith is an important source of tension at once sustaining and impeding the creative impulse, the artistic balance. By limiting his analysis to where and how the theme of religion occurs in Hayden's poetry, the critic establishes the presence of religious implications in the canon, but he does not get much beyond that exercise. For the reader unfamiliar with the poet's faith, Parks does provide a sound explanation of how Baha'i history and theology inform many poems; but the publication of his essay in the quarterly journal of the Baha'i faith does little to extend that knowledge to secular scholars unfamiliar with that journal. Parks does his Baha'i readership a service by quoting substantially from Hayden's diverse work, but he compromises Hayden's own determined search for truth by obstinately ignoring or minimizing some of Hayden's ambivalent views on his chosen religion.

One of the more authoritative voices providing overviews of the career and canon of Robert Hayden is that of Arthur P. Davis, who devotes to Hayden a short segment of his comprehensive study, *From the Dark Tower: Afro-American Writers 1900 to 1960* (1974). A contemporary of Hayden's concerned with an expansive view of black literature, Davis summarizes while distilling the essence of his subject. His treatment begins with a recognition of two aspects of Hayden's work and philosophy that Davis considers essential to understanding the poet: although he began writing conventionally racial poems and continues to address the black experience, Hayden also "somehow manages to lift that experience above the narrow and parochial limitations of race." After a brief synopsis of Hayden's life and career up to 1974, Davis surveys the poet's major publications and poems within those collections.

Noting the strengths and weaknesses of Hayden's early work in *Heart-Shape in the Dust* (1940), Davis chronicles the development of the "master craftsman" discernible in *A Ballad of Remembrance* (1962) and discusses in some detail the "finest poems" in that volume and in the new work in *Selected Poems* (1966). At the rate of about a paragraph per poem Davis explains the essential content and theme of such works as "Middle Passage," "A Ballad of Remembrance," "The Witch Doctor," "The Ballad of Nat Turner," and "Runagate Runagate." He also briefly catalogues poetic techniques used by Hayden in his so-called "modern phase," thereby defining differences in poetic practice between the early and later career. In addition, Davis determines that "a considerable number of poems in each of Hayden's major publications . . . have nothing to do with race," but finally contends that "though Hayden does not want to be thought of as a Negro poet, his ultimate critical assessment may be similar to that of Countee Cullen, who admitted that his strongest poems tended to deal with race."

Unlike Davis, who treats Hayden as one of many familiar twentieth-century black writers, Michael P. Novak presents his 1974 *Midwest Quarterly* overview by assuming an audience with little or no knowledge of either Hayden or black literature. Characterizing Hayden's poetry as "meditative, ironic, richly human," Novak establishes the general biographical background, the career pattern, and Hayden's basic philosophical views by devoting a single paragraph to each subtopic. Then, invoking Langston Hughes's "The Negro Artist and the Racial Mountain," he cites Hayden as the epitome of the "individualism of the black artist," as a racial spokesman whose higher calling is to his art. The essayist exemplifies this notion by notifying the reader that Hayden's poems of suffering are not limited to racial subjects; in this context he cites some of the Mexican poems and Baha'i works.

In the body of the essay Novak treats rather superficially seven or eight poems in an effort to convey the "gist" of Hayden's poetic topics, themes, and techniques. This treatment varies in its success, but many observations about specific poems and poetic devices are soundly perceptive. For example, Novak asserts that Hayden's tightly controlled narratives are also emotionally explosive and that the control derives from the same general sources as the emotion—alliteration, sound effects, extensive vocabulary. Highlighting Hayden's talent for vivid description, such as that in "Summertime and the living . . . " and "A Ballad of Remembrance," the critic notes the "racial overtones" of the latter poem and arrives at the generalization that some of Hayden's finest poems are those about Afro-American history.

With that transition, Novak continues to comment on such black poems as "Middle Passage," "Runagate Runagate," and "The Ballad of Nat Turner." He provides a brief synopsis of "Middle Passage," which he considers Hayden's best poem. The chronological account of Hayden's canon includes *Words in the Mourning Time,* although Novak finds its poems of topical subject matter inferior to Hayden's finest in *Selected Poems.* To explain Hayden's neglect (in contrast to the fame of more militant black poets), Novak discusses "Frederick Douglass," emphasizing the poem's implicit themes of pain and hope that are experienced with stoic grace. Novak's essay is primarily an introductory look, a call to pay heed to a neglected black poet whose artistry is confirmed. The adjectives of the title, while drawn from Hayden's own words in description of his friend Mark Van Doren, are not done justice by this treatment of Hayden's subjects, themes, or techniques. Nevertheless, as Novak senses, those terms are appropriate labels for both the poetry and person of Hayden.

Constance J. Post, in her "Image and Idea in the Poetry of Robert Hayden" (1976), compares Hayden with Yeats as a poet in search of a theme, but then immediately announces that she has perceived a thread of continuity through Hayden's poetry that provides him with a subject and her with a thesis. She suggests that the unifying symbol for Hayden is the star and that his dominant theme of struggle is sustained by the use of paradox and of star imagery. Thereafter the essay seems a determined effort to reduce a complex poet to a single image and theme.

Post attempts to link instances of recurring star images to the "theme of struggle," her definition of Hayden's central subject. Seeking support for her thesis by almost randomly citing examples of poems that convey notions of conflict or struggle, she then claims that paradoxes and oxymorons are the devices most frequently bearing that thematic burden. She discusses in this manner such poems as "Theme and Variation," "Richard Hunt's Arachne," and "The Night-Blooming Cereus," while citing relevant features in others—"The Ballad of Nat Turner," "El-Hajj Malik El-Shabazz," "The Diver," and "For a Young Artist." Post's method is typified in the following synopsis: Starting with the Yeatsian allusion in "Lear Is Gay," Post suggests that the resilience of old age is similarly conveyed by the figure of Bessie Smith in "Homage to the Empress of the Blues" and states that "Her song thus embodies Hayden's imagery of the stars, his theme of struggle and his use of paradox." Such linkages may indeed reside in these poems, but one suspects that they are more at home in the critic's imagination than in Hayden's thematic objectives or techniques.

Howard Faulkner's " 'Transformed by Steeps of Flight': The

Poetry of Robert Hayden" (1977) responds to *Angle of Ascent* (1975). Faulkner also alludes to Hayden's Yeatsian search for theme by quoting from "Kodachromes of the Island" as an epigraph, and he goes on to assert that the poet's dominant theme is transformation. Defining transformation as a movement upward toward or downward from beauty, the critic claims Hayden most frequently employs that process to work through a progression rather than to complete the act. He further posits that Hayden's "favorite devices" are oxymoron and paradox. Faulkner sees in this concern with transformation a poetic tension that does indeed characterize much of Hayden's mature work, but in reducing the entire canon to struggle, tension, and paradox, the critic probably makes Hayden's world view more pessimistic than it really is.

The organizing principle of the article employs major metaphoric structures as exemplified in selected poems. Faulkner identifies patterns that put Hayden in the mainstream of black literature (for example, the metaphor of flight to signify escape, freedom, imagination, as in "For a Young Artist" and "O Daedalus Fly Away Home"); but he also discerns an implicit threat in the imagery, since flight may become a falling or even a condition of stasis accompanied by a fear of falling, such as that suggested in "Crispus Attucks," "The Performers," or "The Diver." While he sometimes oversimplifies in order to make a poem fit his scheme, Faulkner also recognizes that even in the midst of several thematic instances of fearful falling or frustrated stasis, one finds ample evidence of a determined movement beyond limitation, not just the "constant constraints" this essay brings into focus. And to his credit, the critic concludes with a qualifying statement in recognition of the inadequacy of his or any similar approach: "Robert Hayden is a delicate, supple poet, and his themes and techniques are more subtle and various than a reductionist view such as this can indicate."

Rosey E. Pool calls her 1966 article on Robert Hayden "An Assessment," and there can be no doubt of her intent to single out the poet for attention and praise. Thus the essay is not analytically objective, but it is significant for being the first published response to Hayden's work beyond a brief review of a single poem or volume. Pool regrets that *The Poetry of the Negro*, edited by Langston Hughes and Arna Bontemps in 1949, has been for over a decade practically the only source to represent American black poetry (230 poems by 66 poets between 1746 and 1949). She notes, however, that eight of these poems are by Hayden and cites them by title. In her account of the appearance of *A Ballad of Remembrance* she explains that Hayden and his publisher Paul Breman included in *Ballad* five of those eight poems from fifteen years earlier because they represent Hayden's efforts at artistic experimentation, especially the title poem itself, which Pool finds typical of Hayden's work.

Having provided the background of Hayden's poetic progression, Pool fleshes out her essay with a synopsis of how Hayden's work came to be judged superior, how he came to be awarded the "prize for anglophone poetry" at the First World Festival of Negro Arts at Dakar, Senegal, in 1965. (She digresses briefly with a personal memoir of her special appreciation of Hayden's "Runagate Runagate," a poem Hayden resurrected and revised largely because of her admiration for it. The article has appended to it the two versions of that poem— the first completed in 1949, the second in 1964.) Pool concludes with excerpted quotations from the report issued by the selection jury in Dakar, a report that includes a special tribute to Hayden:

> And so, the First World Festival of Negro Arts has honored an Afro-American's artistic parity, his natural Negro-ness, which is a part of his natural human-ness, his American-ness, along with his universal-ness: the human integrity of an artist, and the artistic integrity of a fellow-man.

Another recent essay commingles the qualities of a general appreciation and a critical thesis. Vilma R. Potter's "A Remembrance for Robert Hayden" (1980), however, attempts to reduce Hayden's work (as represented by *Angle of Ascent*) to a metaphoric vision of the black American experience as a "continuing journey both communal and private." After announcing her thesis in the introductory paragraph, Potter is thereafter captive to it, so much so that she often misreads the few poems presented as evidence while she ignores the plethora of so-called "black poems" that counter her journey premise. Moreover, by wrenching Hayden's host of historic figures into the shared role of travelers, the essayist oversimplifies both the diverse character portraits and the larger implications of the poems they populate. In sum, this "remembrance" essay is almost a classic example of good intentions gone awry.

"In Memorium: In Gratitude for Robert Hayden" (1981) is a eulogy by Julius Lester, Hayden's perhaps most successful and celebrated former student. Recounting his years as Hayden's student at Fisk University, Lester illuminates the character of the man and the commitment of the artist. He emphasizes Hayden's enduring strength of spirit while, personifying the lonely vigil of a dedicated artist in an unappreciative society, he lived through personal doubts while preparing his students to cope with their own. Jumping from the 1940s to the 1960s, Lester recalls Hayden's manner of confronting the dilemma of black pride versus artistic integrity. While admiring Hayden's stand against using art as "the voice of political ideology," Lester says that he himself could not in 1966 choose between "what I had learned from Mr. Hayden and the new ethos." But he concludes his essay by honoring Hayden with an acknowledgment of the correctness of his mentor's stand: "*Words in the Mourning Time* was proof that Mr. Hayden was right: there is only good literature and bad." Lester lauds Hayden for resisting those identities others would impose upon him and attributes at least a portion of that strength of purpose to the poet's Baha'i faith. He closes his essay by quoting the ninth part of "Words in the Mourning Time" with its admonition to continue the struggle toward human brotherhood and harmony:

> We must not be frightened nor cajoled
> into accepting evil as deliverance from evil.
> We must go on struggling to be human,
> though monsters of abstraction
> police and threaten us.
>
> Reclaim now, now renew the vision of
> a human world where godliness
> is possible and man
> is neither gook, nigger, honky, wop,
>   nor kike
>
> but man
>   permitted to be man.

Without explicitly drawing out the conclusion, Lester nevertheless presents Hayden's—and his own—perception of the function of art.

Michael S. Harper's "Remembering Robert Hayden" (1980) is a brief but incisive tribute to the deceased poet from a fellow poet intimately acquainted with Hayden's life, work, and values. Harper provides a lyrical synopsis of Hayden's character and career in terms at once familiar yet respectful. He thus demystifies the poet "with a symbolist bent for mysticism and for the cryptic phrasings of the bizarre and occult" in order to emphasize his subject as a "consummate storyteller" of past suffering and future hope. Perhaps the most telling illumination in this essay is Harper's perception of Hayden's willingness to submerge himself in art. As the younger poet describes his senior, "He was a poet of the discovery of self as art, not a proponent of the confessional mode." Never overly concerned with or adept at self-promotion, Hayden received long overdue recognition in his final years at least in part because of the efforts of Harper and a few others who were similarly devoted to the man and his art. The close of Harper's brief memorial essay reminds readers of the most proper means of assessing Robert Hayden: "As a figure, who, increasingly, will earn his rightful place in our hearts, in our minds and libraries and anthologies, his epitaph ought to be the poems he gave us."

Randall Jarrell
(1914-1965)

Sister Bernetta Quinn, O.S.F.
Assisi Heights, Rochester, Minnesota

PRIMARY BIBLIOGRAPHY

Books

The Rage for the Lost Penny. In *Five Young American Poets,* ed. John
 Ciardi. New York: New Directions, 1940, 81-123. Poems.
Blood for a Stranger. New York: Harcourt, Brace, 1942. Poems.
Little Friend, Little Friend. New York: Dial, 1945. Poems.
Losses. New York: Harcourt, Brace, 1948. Poems.
The Seven-League Crutches. New York: Harcourt, Brace, 1951. Poems.
Poetry and the Age. New York: Knopf, 1953; London: Faber & Faber,
 1955. Essays.
Pictures from an Institution. New York: Knopf, 1954; London: Faber
 & Faber, 1954. Novel.
Selected Poems. New York: Knopf, 1955; London: Faber & Faber, 1956.
 Poems.
The Woman at the Washington Zoo. New York: Atheneum, 1960. Poems
 and translations.
A Sad Heart at the Supermarket. New York: Atheneum, 1962; London:
 Eyre & Spottiswoode, 1965. Essays.
The Bat-Poet. New York: Macmillan/London: Collier, 1964. Illustrated
 by Maurice Sendak. Children's poems.
Selected Poems Including the Woman at the Washington Zoo. New York:
 Atheneum, 1964.
The Gingerbread Rabbit. New York: Macmillan/London: Collier-Mac-
 millan, 1964. Illustrated by Garth Williams. Children's story.
The Animal Family. New York: Pantheon, 1965; London: Hart-Davis,
 1967. Illustrated by Maurice Sendak. Children's story.
The Lost World. New York: Macmillan/London: Collier-Macmillan,
 1965. Poems.

The Complete Poems. New York: Farrar, Straus & Giroux, 1969; London: Faber & Faber, 1971. Poems.
The Third Book of Criticism. New York: Farrar, Straus & Giroux, 1969. Essays.
Jerome: The Biography of a Poem, edited with a commentary by Mary Jarrell. New York: Grossman, 1971. Poem.
Fly by Night. New York: Farrar, Straus & Giroux, 1976. Illustrated by Maurice Sendak. Children's poems.
A Bat is Born. Garden City, N.Y.: Doubleday, 1978. Illustrated by J. Schoenherr. Children's poem.
Kipling, Auden & Company: Essays and Reviews 1935-1964. New York: Farrar, Straus & Giroux, 1980. Essays.

Letters

Randall Jarrell's Letters: An Autobiographical and Literary Selection, ed. Mary Jarrell, assisted by Stuart Wright. Boston: Houghton Mifflin, 1985.

Selected Essays

"Answers to Questions." In *Mid-Century American Poets,* ed. John Ciardi. New York: Twayne, 1950, 182-185.
"The Appalling Taste of the Age," *Saturday Evening Post,* 26 July 1958, pp. 18-19.
Six Russian Novels, introduction by Jarrell. Garden City, N.Y.: Doubleday, 1963.

Translations

Bechstein, Ludwig. *The Rabbit Catcher and Other Fairy Tales of Ludwig Bechstein,* translated by Jarrell. New York & London: Macmillan, 1962. Illustrated by Ugo Fontana.
Grimm, Jacob and Wilhelm. *The Golden Bird and Other Fairy Tales of the Brothers Grimm,* introduction and four of the tales translated by Jarrell. New York: Macmillan, 1962. Illustrated by Sandro Nardini.
Chekhov, Anton. *The Three Sisters,* translated with an afterword by Jarrell. New York: Macmillan/London: Collier-Macmillan, 1969.
Grimm, Jacob and Wilhelm. *Snow-White and the Seven Dwarfs: A Tale from the Brothers Grimm,* translated by Jarrell. New York: Farrar,

Straus & Giroux, 1972. Illustrated by Nancy Ekholm Burkert.
_____. *The Juniper Tree and Other Tales from Grimm,* translated by
    Jarrell, selected by Lore Segal and Maurice Sendak. New York:
    Farrar, Straus & Giroux, 1973; London: Bodley Head, 1974.
Goethe, Johann Wolfgang von. *Goethe's Faust, Part I,*translated by Jar-
    rell. New York: Farrar, Straus & Giroux, 1976.
The Fisherman and His Wife, translated by Jarrell. New York: Farrar,
    Straus & Giroux, 1980.

Edited Book

The Anchor Book of Short Stories, selected with an introduction by Jarrell.
    Garden City, N.Y.: Doubleday, 1958.

Recordings

Randall Jarrell, June 9, 1947. Library of Congress (6117-28).
Randall Jarrell, November 28, 1947. Library of Congress (6117-29).
The Taste of the Age. Library of Congress, 17 Dec. 1956 (2516).
Poets, Critic, and Readers. Library of Congress, 28 Oct. 1957 (2609).
Richard Wilbur Reading and Discussing His Poems, December 2, 1957, with
    Jarrell. Library of Congress (2623).
*[John Crowe] Ransom Reading and Discussing His Poems with Randall
    Jarrell, January 14, 1958.* Library of Congress (843).
Randall Jarrell Reading His Poetry, October 24, 1962. Library of Congress
    (3870, 2 & 3).
Randall Jarrell Reading. Mills Modern Poetry Readings, Wayne State
    University, 20 Nov. 1962 (MMP 661).
*Randall Jarrell Reading His Own Poems and Those of Elizabeth Bishop, with
    comment.* Library of Congress, 29 Oct. 1966 (4868).
Randall Jarrell Reads and Discusses His Poems Against War. Caedmon,
    1972 (TC 1363).
The Bat-Poet. Caedmon, 1972 (TC 1364).
Randall Jarrell Reads His Poems Against War. Caedmon, 1972 (TC 1381).

Editions and Collections

*The Achievement of Randall Jarrell: A Comprehensive Selection of His Poems
    with a Critical Introduction,* ed. Frederick J. Hoffman. Glenview,
    Ill.: Scott, Foresman, 1970.

SECONDARY BIBLIOGRAPHY

Bibliographies and Checklists

Adams, Charles M. *Randall Jarrell: A Bibliography.* Chapel Hill: University of North Carolina Press, 1958. Primary.
_____. "A Supplement to Randall Jarrell: A Bibliography," *Analects,* 1 (Spring 1961), 49-56. Primary.
Calhoun, Richard J. "Randall Jarrell (1914-1965)." In *Bibliographical Guide to the Study of Southern Literature,* ed. Louis D. Rubin, Jr. Baton Rouge: Louisiana State University Press, 1969, 226-227. Primary and secondary.
Gillikin, Dure Jo. "A Checklist of Criticism on Randall Jarrell, 1941-1970," *Bulletin of the New York Public Library,* 75 (Apr. 1971), 176-194. Secondary.
Kisslinger, Margaret. "A Bibliography of Randall Jarrell, 1958-1965," *Bulletin of Bibliography and Magazine Notes,* 24 (May-Aug. 1966), 243-247. Primary and secondary.
Meyers, Jeffrey. "Randall Jarrell: A Bibliography of Criticism, 1941-1981," *Bulletin of Bibliography,* 39 (Dec. 1982), 227-234. Secondary.

Biographies: Major Articles and Book Sections

Arendt, Hannah. "Randall Jarrell." Collected in *Randall Jarrell 1914-1965,* ed. Robert Lowell, Peter Taylor, and Robert Penn Warren, 3-9. See Collections of Essays.
Berryman, John. "Tribute at Yale," *Alumni News,* 54 (Spring 1966), 6. Collected in Lowell, Taylor, and Warren. See Collections of Essays.
Ferguson, Suzanne. "The Death of Randall Jarrell: A Problem in Legendary Biography," *Georgia Review,* 37 (Winter 1983), 866-876.
Fitzgerald, Robert. "A Place of Refreshment." Collected in Lowell, Taylor, and Warren, 70-75. See Collections of Essays.
Jarrell, Mary. "Afterword." In *The Three Sisters,* translated by Randall Jarrell, 99-101.
_____. "The Animal Family," *Alumni News,* 54 (Spring 1966), 24-25.
_____. "*Faust* and Randall Jarrell: A Reminiscence," *Columbia*

Forum, new series, 2 (Summer 1973), 24-33. Reprinted in *Goethe's Faust, Part I,* translated by Randall Jarrell.

_____. "The Group of Two," *Harper's,* 234 (Apr. 1967), 73-78. Collected in Lowell, Taylor, and Warren. See Collections of Essays.

_____. "Peter and Randall," *Shenandoah,* 28 (Winter 1977), 28-34.

Kunitz, Stanley. "Tribute at Yale," *Alumni News,* 54 (Spring 1966), 9-10. Collected in Lowell, Taylor, and Warren. See Collections of Essays.

Lowell, Robert. "Randall Jarrell: 1914-1965," *New York Review of Books,* 25 Nov. 1965, pp. 3-4. Excerpted in *Alumni News,* 54 (Spring 1966). See Special Issues of Journals. Collected in Lowell, Taylor, and Warren. See Collections of Essays. Reprinted in Jarrell, *The Lost World.*

Meyers, Jeffrey. "The Death of Randall Jarrell," *Virginia Quarterly Review,* 58 (Summer 1982), 450-467.

Moore, Marianne. "Tribute at Yale," *Alumni News,* 54 (Spring 1966), 7.

Preyer, L. Richardson. "Tribute to a Gentle Power," *Alumni News,* 54 (Spring 1966), 15.

Ransom, John Crowe. "The Rugged Way of Genius—A Tribute to Randall Jarrell," *Southern Review,* 3 (Apr. 1967), 263-281. Collected in Lowell, Taylor, and Warren. See Collections of Essays.

_____. "Tribute at Yale," *Alumni News,* 54 (Spring 1966), 8.

Rich, Adrienne. "Tribute at Yale," *Alumni News,* 54 (Spring 1966), 5.

Sharistanian, Janet. "The Poet as Humanitarian: Randall Jarrell's Literary Criticism as Self-Revelation," *South Carolina Review,* new series, 10 (Nov. 1977), 32-42. Collected in *Critical Essays on Randall Jarrell,* ed. Suzanne Ferguson. See Collections of Essays.

Tate, Allen. "Young Randall," *Alumni News,* 54 (Spring 1966), 7. Collected in Lowell, Taylor, and Warren. See Collections of Essays.

Taylor, Eleanor Ross. "A Friend Remembered," *Alumni News,* 54 (Spring 1966), 12-14. Collected in Lowell, Taylor, and Warren.

Taylor, Peter. "That Cloistered Jazz," *Michigan Quarterly Review,* 5 (Fall 1966), 237-245. Excerpted in *Alumni News,* 54 (Spring 1966). See Special Issues of Journals. Excerpt collected in Lowell, Taylor, and Warren. See Collections of Essays.

Warren, Robert Penn. "Tribute at Yale," *Alumni News,* 54 (Spring 1966), 23.

Watson, Robert. "Randall Jarrell: The Last Years." Collected in Lowell, Taylor, and Warren. See Collections of Essays.

Selected Interviews

Glick, Nathan. "About American Poetry: An Interview with Randall Jarrell," *Analects*, 1 (Spring 1961), 5-11.
Walton, Edithe. *Speak Up.* Library of Congress, WNBC (New York City) radio interview, 4 Feb. 1965.

Critical Studies: Books and Pamphlets

Beck, Charlotte. *Worlds and Lives: The Poetry of Randall Jarrell.* Port Washington, N.Y.: Associated Faculty Press, 1983.
Ferguson, Suzanne. *The Poetry of Randall Jarrell.* Baton Rouge: Louisiana State University Press, 1971.
Hagenbüchle, Helen. *The Black Goddess: A Study of the Archetypal Feminine in the Poetry of Randall Jarrell.* Bern: Francke, 1975.
Quinn, Sister Bernetta. *Randall Jarrell.* Boston: Twayne, 1981.
Rosenthal, M. L. *Randall Jarrell.* Minneapolis: University of Minnesota Press, 1972. Reprinted in *Seven American Poets from MacLeish to Nemerov: An Introduction,* ed. Denis Donoghue. Minneapolis: University of Minnesota Press, 1972.
Shapiro, Karl. *Randall Jarrell.* Washington, D.C.: Library of Congress, 1967. Collected in Lowell, Taylor, and Warren. See Collections of Essays.

Critical Studies: Collections of Essays

Ferguson, Suzanne, ed. *Critical Essays on Randall Jarrell.* Boston: G. K. Hall, 1983.
Lowell, Robert, Peter Taylor, and Robert Penn Warren, eds. *Randall Jarrell 1914-1965.* New York: Farrar, Straus & Giroux, 1967.

Critical Studies: Special Issues of Journals

Alumni News, 54 (Spring 1966).
Analects, 1 (Spring 1961).
South Carolina Review, 17 (Fall 1984), 50-96.

Critical Studies: Major Articles and Book Sections

Adams, Charles. "Collecting Randall Jarrell," *Alumni News*, 54 (Spring 1966), 29.

"After the Habit of Command," *Time*, 26 Apr. 1948, pp. 105-108. Review of *Losses*.

Angus, Sylvia. "Randall Jarrell, Novelist: A Reconsideration," *Southern Review*, new series, 2 (July 1966), 689-696. Collected in Ferguson.

Atlas, James. "Randall Jarrell," *American Poetry Review*, 4 (Jan.-Feb. 1975), 26-28.

Beck, Charlotte H. "Unicorn to Eland: The Rilkean Spirit in the Poetry of Randall Jarrell," *Southern Literary Journal*, 12 (Fall 1979), 3-17. Collected in Ferguson.

Bedient, Calvin. "Randall Jarrell and *Poetry and the Age*," *Sewanee Review*, 93 (Winter 1985), 128-135.

Bellow, Saul. "*The Bat-Poet*," *Christian Science Monitor*, 4 May 1964, p. 68. Review.

Benamou, Michel. "The Woman at the Zoo's Fearful Symmetry," *Analects*, 1 (Spring 1961), 2-4.

Bennett, Joseph. "Utterances, Entertainment and Symbols," *New York Times Book Review*, 18 Apr. 1965, p. 24. Review of *The Lost World*.

Berryman, John. "Matter and Manner," *New Republic*, 2 Nov. 1953, pp. 27-28. Review of *Poetry and the Age*. Collected in Lowell, Taylor, and Warren.

Bottoms, David. "The Messy Humanity of Randall Jarrell: His Poetry in the Eighties," *South Carolina Review*, 17 (Fall 1984), 82-95.

Broyard, Anatole. "Accursed with Infallible Taste," *New York Times Book Review*, 19 May 1985, p. 11. Review of *Randall Jarrell's Letters*.

Calhoun, Richard J. "Randall Jarrell: A Seventieth Birthday Tribute," *South Carolina Review*, 17 (Fall 1984), 50-51.

Cambon, Glauco. "Jarrell's War Poems and the Syntax of Eloquence," *Analects*, 1 (Spring 1961), 11-13.

Carruth, Hayden. "Daylight," *Poetry*, 105 (Dec. 1964), 194-195. Review of *The Bat-Poet*.

Cowley, Malcolm. "First Blood," *New Republic*, 30 Nov. 1942, pp. 718-719. Review of *Blood for a Stranger*.

_____. "Poets as Reviewers," *New Republic*, 24 Feb. 1941, pp. 281-282.

Cross, Richard K. "Jarrell's Translations: The Poet as Elective Middle European." Collected in Ferguson, 310-320.

Dickey, James. "Orientations," *American Scholar*, 34 (Autumn 1965), 646-658.

_____. "Some of All of It," *Sewanee Review*, 64 (Spring 1956), 324-348. Review of *Selected Poems*. Reprinted in his *The Suspect in Poetry*. Madison, Minn.: Sixties Press, 1964. Reprinted in his *Babel to Byzantium: Poets & Poetry Now*. New York: Farrar, Straus & Giroux, 1968.

Donoghue, Denis. "*The Lost World.*" Collected in Lowell, Taylor, and Warren, 49-62. Reprinted in Donoghue, *The Ordinary Universe.* New York: Macmillan, 1968. Reprinted in *Modern American Poetry*, ed. Guy Owen. De Land, Fla.: Everett/Edwards, 1972.

Duffey, Bernard. *Poetry in America: Expression and Its Values in the Times of Bryant, Whitman, and Pound*. Durham, N.C.: Duke University Press, 1978, 284-287.

Dunn, Douglas. "An Affable Misery," *Encounter*, 39 (Oct. 1972), 42-48.

Fein, Richard. "Randall Jarrell's World of War," *Analects*, 1 (Spring 1961), 19-23. Collected in Ferguson.

Ferguson, Frances C. "Randall Jarrell and the Flotations of Voice," *Georgia Review*, 28 (Fall 1974), 423-439. Collected in Ferguson.

Ferguson, Suzanne. "Narrative and Narrators in the Poetry of Randall Jarrell," *South Carolina Review*, 17 (Fall 1984), 72-82.

_____. "To Benton, with Love and Judgment: Jarrell's *Pictures from an Institution.*" Collected in Ferguson, 272-283.

Finney, Kathe Davis. "The Poet, Truth, and Other Fictions: Randall Jarrell as Story-Teller." Collected in Ferguson, 284-297.

Flint, R. W. "Jarrell as Critic," *Partisan Review*, 20 (Nov.-Dec. 1953), 702-708. Review of *Poetry and the Age*.

_____. "On Randall Jarrell," *Commentary*, 41 (Feb. 1966), 79-81. Collected in Lowell, Taylor, and Warren.

Foell, E. W. "*A Sad Heart at the Supermarket*," *Christian Science Monitor*, 26 Apr. 1962, p. 11. Review.

Fowler, Russell. "Randall Jarrell's 'Eland': A Key to Motive and Technique in His Poetry," *Iowa Review*, 5 (Spring 1974), 113-126. Collected in Ferguson.

Fuller, John. "Randall Jarrell," *Review*, 16 (Oct. 1966), 5-9. Reprinted in *The Modern Poet*, ed. Ian Hamilton. New York: Horizon, 1969. Review of *The Lost World*.

Graham, W. S., and Hayden Carruth. "Jarrell's *Losses*: A Controversy," *Poetry*, 72 (Sept. 1948), 302-307. Review.

Gray, Paul. "A Love Affair with Learning," *Time,* 29 Apr. 1985, p. 80. Review of *Randall Jarrell's Letters.*

Greene, George. "Four Campus Poets," *Thought,* 35 (Summer 1960), 233-236.

Hill, S. R. "Poetry and Experience," *English Journal,* 55 (Feb. 1966), 162-168.

Hirose, Michiyoshi. "Randall Jarrell and His Agony." In his *American Literature in the 1940s.* Tokyo: Tokyo Chapter of American Literature Society of Japan, 1975, 120-131.

Humphrey, Robert. "Randall Jarrell's Poetry." In *Themes and Directions in American Literature,* ed. Ray B. Browne and Donald Pizer. Lafayette, Ind.: Purdue University Press, 1969, 220-233.

Jackson, James L. "Jarrell's 'Losses,' " *Explicator,* 19 (Apr. 1961), Item 49.

Jarrell, Mary. "Ideas and Poems," *Parnassus,* 5 (Winter 1976), 213-230.

_____. "Letters to Vienna," *American Poetry Review,* 6 (July-Aug. 1977), 11-17.

_____. "Reflections on Jerome." In Randall Jarrell, *Jerome: The Biography of a Poem,* 11-18.

Jones, Peter. *A Reader's Guide to Fifty American Poets.* London: Heinemann, 1980, 275-281.

Kazin, Alfred. "Prince of Reviewers," *Reporter,* 35 (8 Sept. 1966), 45-48. Collected as "Randall: His Kingdom" in Lowell, Taylor, and Warren.

Kinzie, Mary. "The Man Who Painted Bulls," *Southern Review,* new series, 16 (Autumn 1980), 829-852. Excerpt collected in Ferguson.

Kobler, Jasper F. "Randall Jarrell Seeks Truth in Fantasy," *Forum,* 3 (Spring 1961), 17-20.

Lensing, George S. "The Modernism of Randall Jarrell," *South Carolina Review,* 17 (Fall 1984), 52-60.

Levin, Harry. "Randall Jarrell's *Faust.*" In his *Memories of the Moderns.* New York: New Directions, 1980, 166-177.

Libby, M. S. *"The Gingerbread Rabbit,"* *Book Week,* 10 May 1974, p. 25. Review.

Logan, John. "Rilkean Sense," *Saturday Review,* 28 Jan. 1961, pp. 29-30.

Lowell, Robert. "With Wild Dogmatism," *New York Times Book Review,* 7 Oct. 1951, pp. 7, 41. Review of *The Seven-League Crutches.* Collected in Lowell, Taylor, and Warren.

Maguire, C. E. "And Yet . . . *Selected Poems* by Randall Jarrell," *Renascence*, 9 (Autumn 1956), 42-43. Review.

_____. "Shape of the Lightning: Randall Jarrell," *Renascence*, 7 (Spring 1955), 115-120.

_____. "Shape of the Lightning: Randall Jarrell," part two, *Renascence*, 7 (Summer 1955), 181-186, 195.

Malkoff, Karl. *Crowell's Handbook of Contemporary American Poetry.* New York: Crowell, 1973, 146-153.

Marcus, Mordecai, and Erin Marcus. "Jarrell's 'The Emancipators,' " *Explicator*, 16 (Feb. 1968), Item 26.

Mazzaro, Jerome. "Arnoldian Echoes in the Poetry of Randall Jarrell," *Western Humanities Review*, 23 (Autumn 1969), 314-318.

_____. "Between Two Worlds: The Post-Modernism of Randall Jarrell," *Salmagundi*, no. 17 (1971), 92-113. Reprinted in *Contemporary Poetry in America*, ed. Robert Boyers. New York: Schocken, 1974. Reprinted in Mazzaro, *Postmodern American Poetry.* Urbana: University of Illinois Press, 1980.

Meredith, William. "The Adventures of a Private Eye," *New York Herald Tribune Book Week*, 14 Mar. 1965, p. 4. Review of *The Lost World.*

_____. "The Lasting Voice." Collected in Lowell, Taylor, and Warren, 118-124.

Meyers, Jeffrey. "Randall Jarrell and German Culture," *Salmagundi*, no. 61 (Fall 1983), 71-89.

_____. "Randall Jarrell: The Paintings in the Poems," *Southern Review*, new series, 20 (Spring 1984), 300-315.

Monroe, Keith. "Principle and Practice in the Criticism of Randall Jarrell." Collected in Ferguson, 256-265.

Moon, Samuel. "Finding the Lost World," *Poetry*, 106 (Sept. 1965), 425-426. Review of *The Lost World.*

Moran, Ronald. "Randall Jarrell as Critic of Criticism," *South Carolina Review*, 17 (Fall 1984), 60-65.

Morse, S. F. "Seven Poets, Present Tense," *Virginia Quarterly Review*, 37 (Spring 1961), 291-296. Review of *The Woman at the Washington Zoo.*

Nemerov, Howard. "What Will Suffice?," *Salmagundi*, no. 27 (Winter 1975), 90-103.

Nitchie, George. "Randall Jarrell: A Stand-in's View," *Southern Review*, new series, 9 (Autumn 1973), 883-894.

"A Poet Who Was There," *Time*, 15 Sept. 1967, p. 102. Review of *Randall Jarrell 1914-1965.*

Pritchard, William H. "Randall Jarrell: Poet-Critic," *American Scholar*, 52 (Winter 1982-1983), 67-77. Revised and collected in Ferguson.

Quinn, Sister Bernetta. "Jarrell's Desert of the Heart," *Analects*, 1 (Spring 1961), 24-28.

_____. "Randall Jarrell and Angels: The Search for Immortality," *South Carolina Review*, 17 (Fall 1984), 65-71.

_____. "Randall Jarrell: His Metamorphoses." In her *The Metamorphic Tradition in Modern Poetry*. New Brunswick: Rutgers University Press, 1955, 168-207. Excerpt collected in Lowell, Taylor, and Warren. Excerpt collected in Ferguson.

_____. "Randall Jarrell: Landscapes of Life and LIFE," *Shenandoah*, 20 (Winter 1969), 49-78. Collected in Ferguson.

_____. "Thematic Imagery in the Poetry of Randall Jarrell," *Southern Review*, new series, 5 (Autumn 1969), 1226-1235.

_____. "Warren and Jarrell: The Remembered Child," *Southern Literary Journal*, 8 (Spring 1976), 24-40.

Ransom, John Crowe. "The Rugged Way of Genius—A Tribute to Randall Jarrell," *Southern Review*, 3 (Apr. 1967), 263-281. Collected in Lowell, Taylor, and Warren.

Ray, David. "The Lightning of Randall Jarrell," *Prairie Schooner*, 35 (Spring 1961), 45-52.

_____. "*The Woman at the Washington Zoo*," *Epoch*, 11 (Winter 1961), 58-60. Review.

Rideout, Walter. " 'To Change, to Change!': The Poetry of Randall Jarrell." In *Poets in Progress*, ed. Edward Hungerford. Evanston, Ill.: Northwestern University Press, 1962, 156-178.

Sale, Roger. "New Poems, Ancient and Modern," *Hudson Review*, 18 (Summer 1965), 299-308. Review of *The Lost World*.

Scannell, Vernon. "American Poets of the Second World War." In his *Not Without Glory: Poets of the Second World War*. London: Woburn Press, 1976, 176-237.

Schwartz, Delmore. "The Dream from Which No One Wakes," *Nation*, 161 (1 Dec. 1945), 590-592. Review of *Little Friend, Little Friend*. Collected in Lowell, Taylor, and Warren.

Seidler, Ingo. "Jarrell and the Art of Translation," *Analects*, 1 (Spring 1961), 37-48. Excerpt collected in Ferguson.

Shapiro, Karl. "The Death of Randall Jarrell." In his *The Poetry Wreck: Selected Essays, 1950-1970*. New York: Random House, 1975, 268-299.

Smith, W. J. "The New Books," *Harper's,* 231 (Aug. 1965), 109-110. Review of *The Lost World.*

Spears, Monroe. "Randall Jarrell: An American Original," *Washington Post,* 28 Apr. 1985, pp. 1, 10-11.

Spender, Stephen. "Randall Jarrell's Complaint," *New York Review of Books,* 23 Nov. 1967, pp. 26-31. Review of *The Lost World.*

_____. "Randall Jarrell's Landscape," *Nation,* 1 May 1948, pp. 475-476. Review of *Losses.*

Staples, H. B. "Randall Jarrell," *Contemporary Literature,* 15 (Summer 1974), 423-427. Review of Ferguson, *The Poetry of Randall Jarrell.*

Stauffer, D. B. *A Short History of American Poetry.* New York: Dutton, 1974, 369-373.

Steele, P. "A Dialogue with the Father," *Meanjin,* 41 (Sept. 1982), 410-419.

Stepanchev, Stephen. "Randall Jarrell." In his *American Poetry since 1945.* New York: Harper & Row, 1965, 37-52.

Travers, P. L. "*The Animal Family* by Randall Jarrell," *New York Times Book Review,* 21 Nov. 1965, p. 56. Review. Collected in Lowell, Taylor, and Warren.

Tyler, Parker. "The Dramatic Lyricism of Randall Jarrell," *Poetry,* 79 (Mar. 1952), 335-346. Collected in Ferguson.

Vendler, Helen. "Randall Jarrell." In her *Part of Nature, Part of Us: Modern American Poets.* Cambridge, Mass.: Harvard University Press, 1980, 111-118.

Wallace-Crabbe, C. "Randall Jarrell's Plain Speaking," *New Poetry,* 29 (Dec. 1971), 3-9.

Walsh, T. J. "Second World War Poetry: The Machine and God." In his *American War Literature, 1914 to Vietnam.* New York: St. Martin's Press, 1982, 152-184.

Weisberg, Robert. "Randall Jarrell: The Integrity of His Poetry," *Centennial Review,* 17 (Summer 1973), 237-256.

Wilcott, P. "Randall Jarrell's Eschatological Vision," *Renascence,* 18 (Summer 1966), 210-215.

Winters, Yvor. "Three Poets," *Hudson Review,* 1 (Autumn 1948), 402-406. Reprinted in his *Uncollected Essays and Reviews,* ed. F. Murphy. Chicago: Swallow Press, 1973. Review of *Losses.*

Wright, Stuart. "Jarrell Reconsidered," *Sewanee Review,* 92 (Summer 1984), lxviii-lxx. Review of Ferguson, *Critical Essays on Randall Jarrell.*

BIBLIOGRAPHICAL ESSAY

Bibliographies and Checklists

The initial and most outstanding bibliography to date is *Randall Jarrell: A Bibliography*, prepared in 1958 and updated in a 1961 *Analects* supplement by Jarrell's colleague Charles M. Adams, librarian at the Women's College of the University of North Carolina, Greensboro. It is divided into "Books," arranged by date of first editions; "Collections indexed for contributions by Randall Jarrell," listed alphabetically; "Poems," alphabetized but with special attention to chronology and to the various places where each appeared; "Prose," arranged alphabetically by title with mention of chronology for the various appearances; "Book Reviews," listed by date of publication; and "Translations," arranged alphabetically by author, with cross references to the poems in the third section. A two-page list of important dates concludes Adams's work, which is introduced by Robert Humphrey, another colleague of Jarrell.

The volume is based upon a Special Collection in the Walter Clinton Jackson Library at the University of North Carolina in Greensboro: fourteen boxes contain manuscripts, correspondence, galley proofs, plate proofs, teaching materials, holograph notebooks, textbooks with marginalia, dust jackets, binding dummies, biographical material, awards and citations, periodical articles, and drawings (Jarrell frequently interspersed poems with pen-and-ink illustrations). Beginning in 1955 he donated books, and the rest of the archive came from such sources as the Friends of the Library. Copies of the Hume-Fogg High School *Echo* and the Vanderbilt *Masquerader*, photographs, tributes after the poet's death, and tapes make the collection particularly important for Jarrell scholarship.

Adams's preface to *Randall Jarrell: A Bibliography* refers to Duke University and the Library of Congress for additional resources, but since the date of his research the bulk of Jarrell papers has been bought by the Berg Collection of the New York Public Library. This Jarrell collection includes letters, drafts of stories, essays, poems, lyrics composed in memory of Jarrell, annotated books and other teaching materials, personal biographical items (such as his second-grade report card), speeches, typescripts, clippings, reviews, and any number of other aids to a study of the poet.

Richard J. Calhoun contributed "Randall Jarrell (1914-1965)," a two-page index of useful Jarrell background items, to Louis D.

Rubin, Jr.'s *Bibliographical Guide to the Study of Southern Literature* (1969). Dure Jo Gillikin published in the April 1971 *Bulletin of the New York Public Library* a checklist of criticism on Jarrell from 1941 to 1970. Margaret Kisslinger covered some of the same years in her 1966 "A Bibliography of Randall Jarrell, 1958-1965." Both Gillikin's and Kisslinger's studies have been updated by Jeffrey Meyers's 1982 "Randall Jarrell: A Bibliography of Criticism, 1941-1981," with 325 entries.

Among critical works Karl Shapiro's 1967 pamphlet *Randall Jarrell* (originally a lecture delivered when Shapiro was Poetry Consultant) ends with a good descriptive list of Jarrell material available at the Library of Congress. Helen Hagenbüchle's full-length critical study, *The Black Goddess: A Study of the Archetypal Feminine in the Poetry of Randall Jarrell* (1975), has a bibliographical appendix (eight pages of the primary works and secondary materials relating to them). Both Sister Bernetta Quinn in her Twayne *Randall Jarrell* (1981) and Suzanne Ferguson in her *Critical Essays on Randall Jarrell* (1983) provide useful short assessments of significant criticism on the poet. Stuart Wright is reportedly working on a full-scale descriptive bibliography to be published by the University Press of Virginia.

Biographies: Major Articles and Book Sections

As of 1985 no full-length biographies have appeared on Jarrell, although William Pritchard has been named authorized biographer. Commentary on Jarrell's life is available in Sister Bernetta Quinn's Twayne volume, in the memorial issue (Spring 1966) of the University of North Carolina at Greensboro *Alumni News*, in Janet Sharistanian's essay "The Poet as Humanitarian: Randall Jarrell's Literary Criticism as Self-Revelation," in the articles on Jarrell's death by Jeffrey Meyers and Suzanne Ferguson, in Mary Jarrell's accounts of her husband in several journal articles and in *Randall Jarrell's Letters,* and in *Randall Jarrell 1914-1965,* the memorial volume edited by Robert Lowell, Peter Taylor, and Robert Penn Warren.

Among the most valuable chapters in *Randall Jarrell 1914-1965* are Mary Jarrell's "The Group of Two," a reminiscence of their ten years of marriage; the article by his Greensboro colleague Robert Watson; the essay of his Vanderbilt teacher and Kenyon friend, John Crowe Ransom, who evokes the 1930s and 1940s they shared and offers an insightful reading of *The Lost World;* and the recollections of his companion at Vanderbilt, Gambier, and Greensboro, Peter Taylor. Also of special biographical interest are the reminiscences by

Hannah Arendt, dedicatée of *Pictures from an Institution;* John Berryman, a friend since their encounter at Princeton in the 1950s (details from Jarrell's life appear in "Dream Songs" 90, 121, 127, 153, 198, 250, 282, and 338); and Robert Fitzgerald, who describes their shared experiences at the Kenyon School of Letters, at Sarah Lawrence College, and in Liguria, Italy. Among the collection's best portraits of Jarrell at various stages of his life are Allen Tate's "Young Randall" and Robert Lowell's "Randall Jarrell," the first of his two essays in the volume.

Jarrell himself disliked the idea of autobiography, as he indicates in his preface to his poems in John Ciardi's *Five Young American Poets* and in Ciardi's *Mid-Century American Poetry.* His conviction that writing should stand on its own merits led to his not returning data sheets for reference works so that some do not even mention his first marriage of twelve years. The biographical material provided by book-length critical studies is therefore particularly useful. For example, Sister Bernetta Quinn, in the opening chapter of *Randall Jarrell* (1981), heads its sections "Childhood," "Jarrell the Adolescent," "The Vanderbilt Days," "At Kenyon as Instructor and Graduate Student," "From Kenyon to the Armistice," "The Man Who Gladly Taught," and "In the Glass of Memory: The Greensboro Graduates Look Back," in which memories of former students of Jarrell are featured.

Jeffrey Meyers's "The Death of Randall Jarrell" (1982) is one of several articles this critic has published on Jarrell. A controversial account of the poet and his fatal accident on 14 October 1965, it is the most biographical of Meyers's Jarrell essays and is ably refuted point-by-point by Suzanne Ferguson in "The Death of Randall Jarrell: A Problem in Legendary Biography" (1983). What evidence Meyers has for the "excessive drinking" of the 1940s, which led to alcoholism as "proved" by liver damage at the autopsy (explained by Ferguson as the result of hepatitis, for which Jarrell was hospitalized in 1962), is not specified, only one instance where speculation replaces fact. There can be no doubt of this critic's deep interest in the poet, and some of his details are welcome, even painful ones, such as the effect on Jarrell of cruel reviews after *The Lost World* came out. Yet Meyers's conclusions—particularly that the poet "willed" his own death—are highly debatable.

An excellent source of biographical information is Janet Sharistanian's "The Poet as Humanitarian: Randall Jarrell's Literary Criticism as Self-Revelation" (1977). This essay treats Jarrell's character, his attitudes toward reality, good, and evil, his poetic theory, his religion—the poet's interior landscape. A highly important study, Sharistanian's article also traces the influences of the philosopher Spinoza and Sigmund Freud on Jarrell's poetry.

The most significant source for biographical research to date is *Randall Jarrell's Letters,* edited by Mary Jarrell, about which Robert Penn Warren says on the dust jacket: "This book will be of great interest to anyone concerned with modern American poetry. Jarrell's tragic death twenty years ago cut off the work of a splendid poet, certainly one of the finest of his generation." In reviewing the collection for the 28 April 1985 *Washington Post,* Monroe Spears ranked it second only to the letters of Flannery O'Connor; Anatole Broyard in the 19 May 1985 *New York Times Book Review* was not so enthusiastic about the volume or so perceptive about its author. Broyard, for example, calls "The Death of the Ball Turret Gunner" bad and bathetic. That *Time* devoted a whole page of its 29 April issue to Paul Gray's review of the *Letters* suggests its worth. The reviewer brings out some of the ways in which the letters—beginning with one to Robert Penn Warren in 1935 and using throughout Jarrell's work as a guide to selection—capture a sense of the human being behind the artifacts.

Mary Jarrell clearly sees the letters as autobiography: "In seeking to preserve the letters as an endangered species—which letters surely have become—I felt a responsibility to use them to fill Randall's biographical space in the 'American Bloomsbury Circle' of the fifties. I also valued them to memorialize the poignant, enduring affection that existed between Jarrell and Taylor and Lowell. Finally, I saw his letters as an autobiographical source in which he tells us what it was like for him to read and teach and write for thirty years."

Since almost all of the correspondence is undated, its chronology must remain uncertain; yet Mary Jarrell provides a readable running commentary on the approximately 400 letters, which cover many facets of Jarrell's life: his affection for Amy Breyer, the Vanderbilt medical student who broke off their engagement while he was at Kenyon but with whom he continued to correspond during his Army Air Force service; his relationship with Mackie Langham; his love for Mary von Schrader Jarrell; his literary friendships with such writers as Lowell, Taylor, and Warren; his kindness to Sister Bernetta Quinn (the "nun" of "A Conversation with the Devil"), to whom he gave written replies regarding her study of his work; his responses to Edmund Wilson; and his concern for his last correspondent, Adrienne Rich (to whom he wrote shortly before his death). Jarrell inhabits these pages of fine scholarship, which results from the intelligent and painstaking devotion of its editor.

Selected Interviews

In Nathan Glick's Spring 1961 *Analects* conversation, "About American Poetry: An Interview with Randall Jarrell," the poet emphasizes the good of the work itself, rather than money or audience, as the motivation for writing: poets would write if on a desert island, he asserts. He names Robert Frost and Walt Whitman as closest to American poet laureates and calls Herman Melville a poet in *Moby-Dick*. Wallace Stevens and William Carlos Williams, he tells his questioner, are examples of self-supporting artists; Emily Dickinson goes with Silence as surely as Robinson Crusoe with Friday. Perceptively, he indicates how some poets notice the world outside, whereas others are preoccupied with that inside.

Jeffrey Meyers, in a footnote to "Randall Jarrell and German Culture" (1983), speaks of a 1981 interview he himself had with Karl Shapiro, in which such episodes as Jarrell's summer in Salzburg were discussed. The Library of Congress archives have many of Jarrell's recorded conversations with visitors: for examples, with Richard Wilbur in 1957, and with John Crowe Ransom in 1958. The archives also contain Edithe Walton's radio interview with Jarrell on 4 February 1965, in which he discussed his methods of work, his themes, the background of *The Lost World,* the children's books, the "scenes" behind *Pictures from an Institution* and *A Sad Heart at the Supermarket,* the Actor's Studio presentation of his translation of *The Three Sisters,* and his enthusiasm for Russian literature. To Walton, Jarrell also spoke of the trip he was planning to take to Russia that summer (it never materialized), of his intention to translate "The Inspector General," of his new poems since *The Lost World,* and of the English version of Goethe's *Faust,* which Jarrell had begun in 1957. Once again, he praised the profession of teaching as something he would pay to do if he had a fortune.

Critical Studies: Books and Pamphlets

The first book-length study of Jarrell was Suzanne Ferguson's *The Poetry of Randall Jarrell* (1971), an interesting and sensitive reading of the life and poems. H. B. Staples in *Contemporary Literature* called it "comprehensive and illuminating" in its concentration on change

as a theme running through the verse—"truly a pioneering achievement," though he wished that Ferguson had done more with the
worksheets available in Greensboro and elsewhere. Generously illustrated with photographs from Jarrell's early childhood on, the book
presents a just portrait of the person Ferguson finds in the lyrics that
have gradually won for their author the title of major poet. Her
reaction to his genius is characterized by astute analysis and a spirit
sympathetic to Jarrell's interior landscapes. About "The Lost Children" and "Thinking of the Lost World," Ferguson writes: "In a very
special way they bring together the 'real' world of things with the 'real'
world of the mind, no longer needing the masks provided in the early
poems by myths or märchen, since by then the individual's own world
has become mythical and magical." She is especially good at explicating
the lyrics, such as "Burning the Letters" and "The Bronze David of
Donatello," giving to the latter four pages growing out of her study
of the worksheets.

In the same year as Ferguson's volume, a year (1971) that also
saw Mary Jarrell's edition of *The Complete Poems*, Helen Hagenbüchle,
a Swiss scholar, published in Europe a thesis called in translation
"Randall Jarrell's Dark Poetry: Epiphanies of Death," a forerunner
of her full-length book, *The Black Goddess: A Study of the Archetypal
Feminine in the Poetry of Randall Jarrell* (1975). Hagenbüchle examined
the poems in relation to certain archetypes, a scrutiny implying that
Jarrell walked habitually in "the valley of the shadow of death," perhaps an overstatement of his darker themes. Chapter titles are suggestive of Hagenbüchle's thrust: for example, "Horrid Nurse," "Blind
Mother," "The Secret of the Widowed House," "The Futile Quest,"
"Birds of Death & Night." The name of the section "The Devouring
Unconscious" summarizes her psychoanalytic approach, as does her
variation on the title of Jarrell's first separate volume of verse, *Blood
for a Stranger*, the last word of which she changes to *Muse*, "Blood for
a Muse." Yet Hagenbüchle's scholarship is assiduous and her work,
on the whole, of genuine assistance.

Between Ferguson's and Hagenbüchle's studies, two briefer
books appeared: Frederick Hoffman's *The Achievement of Randall Jarrell* (1970), in the Modern Poet series edited by William J. Martz; and
M. L. Rosenthal's *Randall Jarrell* (1972), a University of Minnesota
pamphlet. Hoffman's work reprints forty-one poems from six Jarrell
books, headed by a nineteen-page critical introduction and a biographical note. Though often seminal, his comments in the essay are
sometimes too negative or capricious, an example of the latter being

his praise of the poet's childhood as ideally happy. The forty-eight-page study by Rosenthal, reprinted in Denis Donoghue's *Seven American Poets from MacLeish to Nemerov: An Introduction,* shows feeling for Jarrell, though its expression regarding individual poems ("Lady Bates," in particular) leaves something to be desired. "The Skaters" Rosenthal regards as a suicidal projection of the symbolic search for the lost mother, a theme Maurice Sendak and others were later to note; unquestionably the lyric *is* highly autobiographical. Rosenthal's exegesis on "The Death of the Ball Turrett Gunner," Jarrell's most widely anthologized poem, is unusually good, as is his commentary on "A Hunt in the Black Forest."

Charlotte Beck's *Worlds and Lives: The Poetry of Randall Jarrell* (1983), which is unfortunately marred by misprints, is a development of her Princeton University thesis. Beck expresses its purpose in the sentence "Those who have read and savored *The Complete Poems* of Randall Jarrell generally believe they have access to all the worlds and lives, but not so." Toward the end of her book she discusses uncollected lyrics now at the Berg Collection (the New York Public Library owns thirteen folders of poems, some of them new to scholarship). Beck speaks of Jarrell's "constant interest in the problem of identify [*sic*] and self-evaluation" and develops in some detail the soldier, woman, and child observers as the central figures in the dramatic monologues. As Beck shows through her examination of the unpublished manuscripts, "A Man Meets a Woman in the Street" was originally set in the aisle of a plane; other works not in *The Complete Poems* include "There Was an Old Witch Who Came Home Drunk," "The New Ghost," "A Girl Leaning Out of the Window," and "From All the Hands of the Hillbilly Ranch."

Critical Studies: Collections of Essays

Two book-length collections of critical essays have appeared thus far, though in the first, *Randall Jarrell 1914-1965* (1967), as has been shown above, the biographical emphasis dominates. Yet several fine assessments of Jarrell's work are printed in the collection. Irish critic Denis Donoghue in his original article on *The Lost World* relates its spirit to the Thomas Hardy lyric, "During Wind and Rain," that Jarrell rescued from oblivion. Proust was also one of the American poet's favorites, and Donoghue says that "Jarrell is a little Proust, to whom, as someone has said, the only real paradises are lost paradises, spectrally recovered in memory and vision." The critic sees Shakespeare's

King Lear in the structure of *The Lost World;* indeed, the poetry collection does have resemblances to the play, including the five "noth-
ings" that are condensed in the collection's enigmatic ending, of which
John Crowe Ransom makes such clear sense in his long 1967 essay,
"The Rugged Way of Genius," reprinted in the commemorative volume.

Lowell, Taylor, and Warren clearly chose as contributors people
most qualified to assess Jarrell's work. Mary Jarrell's 1967 "The Group
of Two," besides providing biographical details, casts light on "The
Old and New Masters." R. W. Flint's essay reprinted from the February 1966 *Commentary,* declares that none "came within shouting
distance of" Jarrell as war poet and reinforces this judgment with
original discussion of individual lyrics. Lowell's "With Wild Dogmatism," a reprint of a 1951 review of *The Seven-League Crutches,* praises
"A Girl in the Library" and says of "The Knight, Death, and the Devil"
that it is one of the most remarkable word pictures in English verse
or prose; he regards the rather melancholy "The Orient Express" as
a sequel to Matthew Arnold's "Dover Beach."

The other anthology is *Critical Essays on Randall Jarrell* (1983),
edited and with very useful introduction and notes by Suzanne Ferguson. Stuart Wright in his 1984 *Sewanee Review* assessment of the
collection says quite rightly that it "comes at a time marked by vigorous
renewal of interest in the man and his work." Wright praises William
H. Pritchard's "Randall Jarrell: Poet-Critic" as caring and nonaca-
demic, reflecting Jarrell's own tone in *Poetry and the Age;* on the other
hand, Wright dislikes Keith Monroe's "Principle and Practice in the
Criticism of Randall Jarrell," though the affirmations made by Monroe
are interesting. Among other essays written specifically for this book
is Kathe Davis Finney's "The Poet, Truth, and Other Fictions," which
explores Jarrell's reasons for writing prose, his fictional theory. In
discussing *Pictures from an Institution,* she makes the arresting point
that Gertrude, the sophisticated cynic, "sees through" life instead of
seeing it. Another original essay appearing in this volume is Ferguson's
own, "To Benton, with Love and Judgment: Jarrell's *Pictures from an
Institution,*" about which she says, "The greatest evil is finally unkind-
ness." The glittering *Pictures,* Ferguson says, is the surface of the
"outer reality," and its antiheroine Gertrude Johnson akin to both
Satan and the Witch of folklore. Also written for *Critical Essays on
Randall Jarrell* is Richard K. Cross's "Jarrell's Translations: The Poet
as Elective Middle European"; though he touches on Goethe, Cross

also gives unusual and worthwhile attention to Jarrell's translations of Eduard Mörike and Ferdinand Gregorovius.

One of the most illuminating essays in the Ferguson collection is Parker Tyler's "The Dramatic Lyricism of Randall Jarrell." The essay originally appeared in the March 1952 *Poetry*, only a decade after *Blood for a Stranger* and a year after *The Seven-League Crutches*, in the days when to estimate "Jarrell's poetry one of the most mature and rewarding bodies of verse produced in our time" was as radical as Sister Bernetta Quinn's devoting a long chapter to Jarrell in a 1955 book that also dealt with Wallace Stevens, William Carlos Williams, T. S. Eliot, W. B. Yeats, Hart Crane, and Ezra Pound. Tyler stresses the symbolism of the Nemian wood, which he considers an image of the world, even linking it loosely with Jarrell as "the ax-man"; he also introduces the ideas of Jean-Paul Sartre into his text, a fertile parallel when existentialism was a strong influence in university circles. Though she abridges Sister Bernetta Quinn's chapter on metamorphosis and Jarrell (see Critical Studies: Major Articles and Book Sections), Ferguson prints in its entirety Quinn's "Randall Jarrell: Landscapes of Life and LIFE," a venture into symbolic landscape. Taken from *Shenandoah*, the essay stresses the important place that French painter Edouard Vuillard had in the later technique. The word *life*, while not so prevalent as *world*, is an important term throughout *The Complete Poems*, Quinn asserts. This piece on landscapes develops the role that inner and outer "scenery" play in Jarrell, as does Quinn's "Jarrell's Desert of the Heart" in *Analects* (see below).

Special Issues of Journals

So far there has been no newsletter or journal given over exclusively to Jarrell, although three journals have had Jarrell issues. The Spring 1961 *Analects*, published by the Women's College of the University of North Carolina at Greensboro, appeared during the poet's lifetime and thus not only anticipated later enthusiasm for his work but provided him with considerable encouragement. One of its best articles is Richard Fein's "Randall Jarrell's World of War," which stresses the dreamlike nature of experience for the persons who live in Jarrell's world, a place "where they are lost like frightened children." Striking, indeed, is the way that Fein fastens on the motif of lostness, key to the last of his books published during Jarrell's lifetime: "It is this theme of entrapment, this perennial and wistful sense of unfulfillment, of being lost, which dominates" the poetry. The critic goes into the alienation-from-Mother idea that Maurice Sendak and others detect in the children's books; Fein calls it "the mother's inability to protect the child," as this failure informs the war poems—the view of children who hunch in fear, unable to control their destinies or understand the feelings of the adults who inhabit this world with them. Jarrell's world, Fein feels, is as different from Wordsworth's as "We Are Seven" is different from "The Black Swan." Glauco Cambon also discusses, in *Analects,* the war poetry from the point of view of "the syntax of eloquence."

The University of North Carolina at Greensboro *Alumni News* for Spring 1966, dedicated to Jarrell, is mostly reminiscences. It contains articles, many of them memorial tributes, by Peter Taylor, Adrienne Rich, John Berryman, Allen Tate, Marianne Moore, John Crowe Ransom, Stanley Kunitz, Robert Lowell, Eleanor Ross Taylor, L. Richardson Preyer, Robert Penn Warren, Mary Jarrell, Charles Adams, and nine students.

The only other Jarrell special issue to date is the Fall 1984 *South Carolina Review,* which published papers given during a seventieth birthday celebration at the University of North Carolina, Chapel Hill. In his introduction, editor Richard J. Calhoun writes: "We trust that in a day of critical specialists, rather than poet-critics, these essays will contribute to an understanding of Randall Jarrell's importance." Suzanne Ferguson's "Narrative and Narrators in the Poetry of Randall Jarrell" stresses the transformation of painful life into the permanence of art, as in the last, obviously autobiographical poems. In exploring narrative, Ferguson takes up setting, dialogue, characters; in narrators, she treats primarily the "focus of narration," as in "The Night before the Night before Christmas." This Christmas lyric is also one of the sixteen Jarrell poems about angels—which most prominently appear in "A Girl in a Library," "In the Ward: The Sacred Wood," "The Angels at Hamburg," "The Place of Death," and "Lady Bates"— explicated by Sister Bernetta Quinn in "Randall Jarrell and Angels: The Search for Immortality." Quinn concludes that an angel is for this poet "a link between a visible and an invisible reality, a reality brightened by the Star of Hope." George S. Lensing, in "The Modernism of Randall Jarrell," insists effectively that, however much Jarrell might protest in prefaces and elsewhere against modernism, he was deeply influenced by it, even though possessing a voice of his own. Ronald Moran on Jarrell as critic and David Bottoms, "moderating" a series of views of the poetry, complete the Jarrell section of the *South Carolina Review* special issue.

Critical Studies: Major Articles and Book Sections

At Vanderbilt and Kenyon, Jarrell's poems won magazine acceptance as fast as he could send them out, most of them going to the *Southern Review*, which Robert Penn Warren and Cleanth Brooks were then editing. Before long—and especially after *Five Young American Poets* in 1940 and *Blood for a Stranger* two years later—such anthologies as *War and the Poet*, edited by Richard Eberhart and Seldon Rodman in 1945, began including Jarrell poems. Malcolm Cowley's "First Blood" praised *Blood for a Stranger* in the 30 November 1942 *New Republic*.

Losses, which came out while its author was in the Army Air Force, was very favorably reviewed; Harcourt quickly sold out its edition but much to Jarrell's disappointment did not reprint it. *Time* covered the book in "After the Habit of Command" (26 April 1948), crediting Jarrell with using language "with the abstract compassion of a surgeon." In the September 1948 issue of *Poetry*, W. S. Graham and Hayden Carruth totally disagreed on its worth, the former saying that *Losses* is a "collection of poems which are mostly spun from what should be the involuntary incidentals of a poem, rather than the poem's being made first for the poetic action." Graham called Jarrell's prosody old-fashioned and objected to such conversational devices as dots. Carruth defended the poet, though in 1964 he was to review *The Bat-Poet* with a burst of venom. The most insightful early evaluation was Stephen Spender's May 1948 "Randall Jarrell's Landscape." Spender made the point that an American poet's landscape is necessarily different from a European artist's landscape; the former is characterized by the actuality of his or her physical surroundings, while the latter is preoccupied with disintegration. Spender finds Jarrell a first-rate intelligence and his comments on the nature of man deep. Spender declares, "What gives his poetry its extraordinary cohesion and strength is the sense of a resolute, sharp-featured landscape, with the dreadful scene [the war] taking place on the islands, beyond the hills, out at sea, in the sky." Spender aptly compares Jarrell to Alfred Lord Tennyson and Robert Browning and also to Rainer Maria Rilke and Federico Garcia Lorca. "Orestes at Tauris" seems to the poet-critic overlong, an odd failure, and indeed it has never caught on, even with Jarrell enthusiasts.

A rather amusing critical response is that of Yvor Winters to *Losses*, perhaps the result of Jarrell's review of *Maule's Curse* in a 1937

Kenyon Review and his 1947 *New York Times* evaluation of *In Defense of Reason*. After quoting fourteen lines of "Pilots, Man Your Planes," Winters calls the lyric trite and obvious, going on to say that not only he but any Stanford teacher (he is not so sure about the institutions on the east side of the Mississippi) would have marked it up in blue pencil as a hopeless mess: "The passage is dead; furthermore, one will find nothing appreciably better in Jarrell." Though Mary Jarrell in her 1977 article on Peter Taylor and Jarrell calls the former a romantic and the latter an intellectual, Jarrell was romantic enough to draw down lightning from this czar of classicism. Moreover, about "When I Was Home Last Christmas," which recounts an incident from a love affair, Winters declares that it is "the sort of thing one would expect to be published by a female genius in a country newspaper." And he goes on to say that "Randall Jarrell is wholly without the gift of language. With the best of intentions and some reasonably good topics [love, death, pain, wisdom], he displays, line by line, from beginning to end of his book, an utter incapacity to make serious topics appear anything but ludicrous." Winters ridicules those who like Jarrell and elevates J. V. Cunningham far above him and John Berryman, who shares the review.

It is hard to overestimate the effect of *Poetry and the Age* (1953) on American criticism. As an example of the pleasure it gave the literary world, R. W. Flint's 1953 *Partisan Review* critique is outstanding: "Mr. Jarrell is a provoking critic in all senses of the word, one who can be counted on to scatter the unctuous fog which usually surrounds the middle-academic study of letters. . . . Qualify and dissent as we may, the fact is plain that Mr. Jarrell is a critic who brings more loving care, more intelligent good will, to his criticism than most of us can afford." Praising the writer for the life his poems have, Flint calls him an elegist by nature and cites "Nestus Gurley," "Lady Bates," and "Say Good-bye to Big Daddy" as examples. Anticipating Sister Bernetta Quinn's 1984 essay on Jarrell and angels, he includes this quotation from *Poetry and the Age:* "Around the throne of God, where all angels read perfectly, there are no critics—there is no need for them." Just as laudatory is John Berryman, who writes in the 2 November 1953 *New Republic* that Jarrell's criticism is the best of its kind since R. P. Blackmur's and Yvor Winters's.

As Suzanne Ferguson has noted in the history of Jarrell criticism prefacing her 1983 anthology, Sister Bernetta Quinn was the first scholar to publish a long study of the poetry, "Randall Jarrell: His Metamorphoses," which constitutes chapter five in Quinn's *The Met-*

amorphic Tradition in Modern Poetry (1955). She begins by naming Jarrell as perhaps the most likely among younger writers for a permanent place in American letters (he was then forty-one). The opening part of the essay deals at length with the märchen and other fairy tales as these involve metamorphosis, the most complete poetic instance of which is "Hohensalzburg: Fantastic Variations on a Theme of Romantic Character." The second poem to be scrutinized is "The Night before the Night before Christmas," which Quinn calls "a case-history of adolescent heartbreak" and ties to the Hansel and Gretel story, casting light upon a lyric wherein fantasy and truth mingle and metamorphosis is a shining interlude of escape from unpleasantness. Next comes a lyric, "The Black Swan," about a young girl who tries to understand—by means of a hallucinatory imagination linked to the myth of the swan-maidens and to the world of Tchaikovsky's *Swan Lake* ballet—her sister's death; similarly, "The Girl Dreams that She Is Giselle" is linked to the Coralli ballet. Other lyrics are taken up from the angle of dream or half-dream, "The Venetian Blind" proving memorable in its discovery "that the true nightmare is the wide-awake one." "A Quilt-Pattern" appears as the most thorough use of the Grimm brother-sister imprisonment in the witch's house, here a way of making concrete the boy-hero's psychological state. An extensive group of war poems, including "The Dream of Waking" and "1914," highlights the split-in-the-ego dramatized by metamorphic techniques. The problem of identity and the explanation of reality itself dominate the examination here of "The Face" and "The Place of Death."

The conclusion of Quinn's essay regards metamorphosis as "an attempt to go back to that principle of change, natural to the child and common in dreams, in order to live more adequately our mortal measure of years": "one of Randall Jarrell's ways of voicing that unfathomable disillusion which informs his poetry and at the same time of reaching a wisdom beyond that proffered by science, a wisdom which may yet successfully oppose those forces seeking the blood of Man." Jarrell's own suggestions as expressed in the *Letters* and unpublished correspondence at Greensboro and the Berg Collection increase the value of Quinn's chapter to scholarship.

In the extremely enjoyable early essay "Shape of the Lightning: Randall Jarrell," C. E. Maguire, in the Spring and Summer 1955 issues of *Renascence*, gives a reading of *Pictures from an Institution* that sees Gertrude Johnson as an individual to whom "the world was one of those stupid riddles whose only point is that they have no point."

Gertrude treats other human beings as scientists do things, this article judges: about *Poetry and the Age,* the essay is particularly cogent in its account of Jarrell's reaction to his friend Robert Lowell's entrance into the Catholic Church, which he regarded as a frame of reference far more useful than science.

Walter Rideout's fine " 'To Change, To Change!': The Poetry of Randall Jarrell" appeared in Edward Hungerford's *Poets in Progress* (1962). Commenting on Jarrell's early echoes of Auden and Eliot in the 1942 *Blood for a Stranger,* Rideout emphasizes the influence of modernism, especially Ransom's during the two years that he was Jarrell's "boss" at Kenyon, citing their appreciative essays on each other's poetry. The title poem of the article is about suffering childhood, which in Rideout's view functions as a synecdoche for human suffering in general in a world subject to the authority of Necessity, as powerful as a parent's over a child. The critic's favorite among the lyrics is "90 North." Rideout's analysis of the little-explicated "A Lullaby" is also memorable. He stresses individual responsibility in regard to killing in "Second Air Force" and other war poems, and he feels that *Little Friend, Little Friend* is a distinct advance over the first collection of verse. He singles out for commendation "A Camp in the Prussian Forest," admirable from "the necessarily ugly images in the first stanza to the speaker's horrified hysteria in the last." The critic points out that in *The Seven-League Crutches* humor characterizes the poet's way of looking at life, ironically helping the reader understand its seriousness and sadness. In reference to the 1955 *Selected Poems,* Rideout calls attention to the fact that the volume contains only two new lyrics; he also notes that in the 1960 collection, the National-Book-Award-winning *The Woman at the Washington Zoo,* thirty poems had already appeared in magazines a decade or so earlier and twelve are translations.

George Greene, analyzing the one-third of *Selected Poems* dealing with war for the Summer 1960 *Thought,* defines Jarrell's response to setting. In the essay "Four Campus Poets" he writes: "A limbo, where one accepts insensitiveness in order to survive, is the central locale of Randall Jarrell's poetry." Fellow-poet John Logan contributed "Rilkean Sense" to the 28 January 1961 *Saturday Review,* its tone positive enough to have delighted any author, as in the first paragraph where Logan says that every single lyric in *The Woman at the Washington Zoo* can be returned to with pleasure and that the translations are good English poems like the rest. Logan exaggerates somewhat when he refers to Nestus Gurley as a vender perceived as a god, although

Jarrell has several poems wherein resurrection figures. And by mentioning the introduction to the *Anchor Book of Short Stories* Logan uncovers a fruitful source for understanding Jarrell's use of dream and fairy tale. The end of the article is challenging, asserting that here is a poet who, more than any other, "assumes supremely well a central responsibility of art: the conjuring of spirits."

One of the key articles to come out before Jarrell's death was that by David Ray in the Spring 1961 *Prairie Schooner*. In "The Lightning of Randall Jarrell" Ray interprets "The Death of the Ball Turret Gunner" through a startling metaphor: "The dominant image of the poem is that of an abortion, and the narrator speaks with the anger which an aborted foetus might express if he could feel, and if he could speak out against those who would deny him a chance to be born, to come to the full development of his potentialities." Ray continues: "All the anger and resentment of a man subjected to less than a child's role, to that of a mere foetus dependent on another's ambition, is expressed in the description of the fighter hunched in an obscene and humiliating position. . . . But he has also touched a deeper anger— an anger against an even crueler father and mother, a father and mother who have refused to summon him even to exist, to the minimum of life itself." To apply this interpretation to "the man who loved children" seems just and appropriate.

Regarding figures of speech used in Jarrell lyrics, Ray is also very good, defining poetry as "the transmission of coded messages," in which both sender and addressee are often unaware of what is being sent and received. The importance of such a theory is that in a horrifying few lines (for example, those treating the ball turret gunner) the poet can say by the indirection of metaphor what perhaps would never otherwise be tolerated. Such evils as the holocaust can also come through vividly in poetry, Ray contends—for example, "a child laughing unwittingly while her father is bundled off to the gas chamber." The ghastly fact of totalitarianism, says this critic, becomes, in "Variations," "a play with grisly results." The boy in that lyric, caught in a web of malice, can be thus described: "A child who perceives adult political reality as the terror of a fairy tale has the same message as that of the ball turret gunner." As a summing up, Ray asserts that "Jarrell may well prove to be the poet of our time who has best profited from Freudism."

That Stephen Stepanchev in *American Poetry since 1945* (1965) would devote fifteen pages of prose to Jarrell is significant. Speaking of the juvenilia accepted in the late 1930s by the *Southern Review*, he singles out "The Orient Express," describing its subject as "a train that suddenly assumes a metaphysical character": "The end of motion is a rest or a death as the cycle renews." The poem, he declares, gives an "essentially science-conditioned view of reality," not surprising in view of Jarrell's grounding in science at Vanderbilt. Furthermore, Stepanchev finds in "1789-1939" "the horrors and betrayals of European history." "The Winter's Tale," to him, has "the bitterness of Picasso's mural about the bombing of Guernica," that painting so important to the 1930s. "Fear" he sees as representative of the betrayal of children, a theme frequently mentioned by Jarrell critics. Stepanchev also emphasizes how Jarrell learned from Auden ways to describe the modern world and also "how to join the processes of the heart and the mind," a phrase evoking Nathaniel Hawthorne.

Some of the reviews of *The Lost World* might best be described either as examples of obtuseness or as petty attempts at vengeance for the writers or their friends whose work had come under Jarrell's critical eye. Joseph Bennett's in the 18 April 1965 *New York Times Book Review* is an outstanding specimen of the angry review. As Jeffrey Meyers shows in "The Death of Randall Jarrell," these harsh reviews disturbed Jarrell greatly. Fortunately, not all the evaluations preceding his October accident during the year of its publication were of this type.

William Meredith's "The Adventures of a Private Eye" in the 14 March 1965 *New York Herald Tribune Book Week* remarks on Jarrell's progress "toward greater awareness of what he can call his own." Sensibly rejecting "The Three Bills," Meredith warmly lauds "Field and Forest," "Hope," and especially "Well Water," wherein dailiness is seen as drama. Whatever James Dickey's reservations, he treats the new book kindly in the omnibus review "Orientations" in the Autumn 1965 *American Scholar:* the piece ranks Jarrell and his friend Berryman above the other six poets discussed. Dickey attributes to Jarrell wit, intelligence, and compassion and calls him a poet interested in the reader's having the experience that the poem itself is trying to have. Dickey likens the poem to a pane of glass, distinctly unlike the product of Berryman's lyric gift. But then he blames Jarrell for being incapable of the telling phrase, of the exact rhythm to match an emotion. Whereas many have warmly praised "Next Day," Dickey considers it an ordinary poem about an ordinary woman. "A Hunt in the Black Forest," however, he warmly commends, as he does "Woman," which he considers a perfect example of "literalizing" experience.

Alfred Kazin, represented in the Lowell, Taylor, and Warren

memorial anthology by "Randall, His Kingdom," first published in the 8 September 1966 *Reporter* as "Prince of Reviewers," describes his impression of the poet as critic: "Jarrell could be cruel as a child is cruel—but he was wittily so." His honesty was the sort, Kazin declares, that "can sometimes make man feel lonelier on a modern highway than if he were lost in the Antarctic." Another Jarrellian role, as fiction-writer, is also treated in a 1966 essay: Sylvia Angus's "Randall Jarrell, Novelist: A Reconsideration," written for a reissue of *Pictures from an Institution*. In Angus's opinion Jarrell will be remembered best for his achievement in the novel—for this "mythic vision of heaven and hell"—than for his poetry. The inhabitants of Benton are "universal as Everyman," and one of them, Gertrude, is clearly among the damned.

Jerome Mazzaro has shown decided interest in Jarrell, though his two major essays do not contain unqualified enthusiasm. The earlier work, "Arnoldian Echoes in the Poetry of Randall Jarrell" (1969), compares the writer to Matthew Arnold, just as by others he has been linked to Tennyson and Browning. The other essay, "Between Two Worlds: The Post-Modernism of Randall Jarrell" (1971), is quite querulous, as when Mazzaro states that Jarrell's poetry appears "unreal and valueless." Yet in his description of the influence of Sartre, Auden, and Freud, and in his commentaries on "The State," "A Story," and other poems, he is excellent. However, on the whole, Mazzaro's desire to push Jarrell's "post-modernism" gets in the way of the poems themselves.

Sister Bernetta Quinn's 1969 *Southern Review* response to *The Complete Poems*, "Thematic Imagery in the Poetry of Randall Jarrell," traces through the themes of star, dream, and wish. In editing *Jerome: The Biography of a Poem* two years later, Mary Jarrell adds a fascinating essay called "Reflections on Jerome," memorable because of her co-experiencing with Jarrell so many paintings and etchings of the Vulgate translator who is portrayed as a Washington, D.C., psychiatrist in this companion-poem to "The Woman at the Washington Zoo." Douglas Dunn in his 1972 *Encounter* essay echoes his countryman Stephen Spender. His affirmation in "An Affable Misery: On Randall Jarrell" is restrained and persuasive in its admiration, highlighting the master Rilke and calling Jarrell's art "almost like happiness in spite of itself," while rejecting the not-uncommon accusation of sentimentality.

Robert Weisberg's "Randall Jarrell: The Integrity of His Poetry" (1973) stresses the poet's striving for truth, but the critic is not blind to the dangers confronting his subject: "For Jarrell, and this most noticeably in his later poetry, was so in love with the world as it simply appeared to him that he always wrote on the brink of banality." Children, says Weisberg, possessed, even haunted the poet: "And what is revealed for modern man is the infantile core of his life, the child that is father to him." Quite correctly this critic defines Jarrell's aim in his searching to be religious, "since its goal is the discovery of absolute truth."

Mary Jarrell's *"Faust* and Randall Jarrell: A Reminiscence"was published in the Summer 1973 *Columbia Forum* three years before its inclusion in Randall Jarrell's English version, which she guided into print. (The translation is treated briefly in Richard Cross's contribution to Ferguson's *Critical Essays on Randall Jarrell.*) The essay is one of Mary Jarrell's best works, illuminating the difficult eight-year process of putting Goethe's masterpiece into a form that the twentieth century would find good theater. She links Jarrell in some respects with Dr. Faustus: "To open Randall's *Complete Poems* at any page is to find in some degree a Faustian world-disappointment or self-disappointment." The whole article, followed by excerpts from Scene IV, is a truly scholarly and readable contribution.

Although his title does not suggest a comprehensive treatment, Russell Fowler's "Randall Jarrell's 'Eland': A Key to Motive and Technique in His Poetry" (1974) treats the whole career from *Blood for a Stranger* on, bringing out how important emotion was to the poet and dwelling on his increased use of dramatic figures, as in the thoroughly Rilkean parable "Seele im Raum." Another 1974 essay, Frances C. Ferguson's "Randall Jarrell and the Flotations of Voice," originally published in the *Georgia Review* and reprinted in Suzanne Ferguson's collection, brilliantly interprets some of the lyrics, for instance "Eighth Air Force" and " Jerome." The first half of the essay concentrates on fictional technique, the relation of truth and art in story, and the strategy of focus of narration. A single line from the article's final section illustrates the sensitivity of Ferguson's reading of poetry: "Voice becomes a register of the loss of all consciousness, all objects of consciousness and concern."

Karl Shapiro's long essay on Jarrell in *The Poetry Wreck* (1975) warrants close attention. With a poet's gift for the vivid phrase, Shapiro says: "His [Jarrell's] bookplate might be a question mark." Some of the text is biographical, but much is critical: Shapiro declares that he himself was influenced by figures whom Jarrell assimilated (Frost, Grimm, Corbiere, Rilke, Auden, Whitman). Shapiro's comments on

Pictures from An Institution are also acute: "a horn-book of avant-gard-ism, sophisticated to the point of philistinism, . . . the kind of novel the age demanded, the exposé of sensibility. . . . He attacks dehu-manized letters in his lip-smacking crucifixion of Gertrude." As a Jew, Shapiro reacts more deeply than most to "A Game at Salzburg," in which he finds "an almost unbearable sorrow," "a German-Jewish sorrow, so to speak." This is a first-class meditation on Jarrell and his work.

Poet Howard Nemerov's 1975 *Salmagundi* article, "What Will Suffice?," is pivotal in Jarrell criticism because it advances the very important belief that Jarrell is an "organic" poet: the appearance of *The Complete Poems* shows that his work develops from one lyric to another, that all the poems fit together, that the meanings of one reinforce the meanings of another in such a way as to build a coherent, articulate world. For reasons of this excellence Nemerov tends to award Jarrell the noun *greatness*. Out of the phrase "the Great Change" the poet-critic educes Jarrell's view of children "who suddenly pen-etrate behind the storybooks, the fairy tales, and see death in all its lonesomeness, its decisive and destructive effect on all that is loved, especially the self." This, the theme of "During Wind and Rain," somehow is not bleak, Nemerov believes.

Vernon Scannell considered Jarrell at length in the chapter "American Poets of the Second World War" in his *Not Without Glory* (1976). Scannell credits Jarrell with "a technical assurance that has produced some of the most relentless indictments of the evil of war since Sassoon and Owen." He is excellent on single poems, such as "Eighth Air Force" and "Burning the Letters." Although he considers Jarrell an uneven poet ("The Dead Wingman" is weak), the intensity of pain, pity, and despair builds, and the poems defining war as totally destructive and pointless win a permanent place in American letters, Scannell believes.

The first part of another 1976 essay, Sister Bernetta Quinn's "Warren and Jarrell: The Remembered Child" in the *Southern Literary Journal,* probes the layered metaphors of "Time as Hypnosis" and other works by Robert Penn Warren, wherein the poet looks back at the boy he used to be and tries to see the meaning of innocence from the vantage point of experience. The rest of the essay treats Jarrell's recollections of the child he once was, as these memories are turned into art; "The Elementary Scene," "Thinking of the Lost World," and other autobiographical pieces come back in mid-life as if one were to revisit a familiar country, Quinn shows.

Largely about the poet's concern with the drying up of his inspiration, Mary Jarrell's "Ideas and Poems" in the Winter 1976 *Parnassus* does more than offer details of the life she, the poet, and her daughters led in Greensboro: she reveals the genesis of such poems as "The Lost Children" (a dream she had about two little girls, one living, one dead); the birth of "A Meteorite" in Colorado when the terror of inability to compose again was freezing Jarrell; analyses of feminine personae, such as that in "Seele im Raum," the voice of which she considers to be Jarrell's in disguise.

"Letters to Vienna" (1977) by Mary Jarrell centers around the correspondence Jarrell carried on with Elisabeth Eisler, a ceramist with whom he had formed a romantic friendship during his two months in Salzburg in 1948 lecturing at the Seminar in American Civilization. Important as its biographical side is, the essay's major importance lies in the illumination it—and the Jarrell/Eisler letters—bring to the poems: "Hohensalzburg," "It Is Like Any Other" (an early version of "The Orient Express"), and other works that owe their being to this Vienna summer. The poems are included here in all their variations, and Mary Jarrell's commentary into which the letters and lyrics are set are enriched by Elisabeth Eisler's reminiscences of Jarrell during 1948.

As can be seen from this overview, much has been made of the presence of Rilke in Jarrell's work, including Charlotte H. Beck's discoveries recorded in "Unicorn to Eland: The Rilkean Spirit in the Poetry of Randall Jarrell" (1979), which originally appeared in *Southern Literary Journal* and is reprinted in Ferguson's collection. Rilke becomes a symbol of The Poet, who "stands apart and looks, Januslike, at both worlds," the child's and the adult's, Beck declares. "Seele im Raum" is examined as the selection most Rilkean in spirit, related, as it is, to the German celebration of the unearthly unicorn.

Harry Levin's chapter in *Memories of the Moderns* (1980) is titled "Randall Jarrell's *Faust*." Including much more than *Faust*, such as Jarrell's rendering of Rilke's "The Olive Garden," it does speak usefully about his translation of Goethe's work, especially the Dungeon Scene, and it describes his prosodic style as moving toward blank verse. Helen Vendler's book *Part of Nature, Part of Us: Modern American Poets*, also published in 1980, shows in its Jarrell chapter how well she understands his final volume: "The child who was never mothered enough, the mother who wants to keep her children forever, these are the inhabitants of the lost world, where the perfect filial symbiosis continues forever." What some have labeled compassion she calls pity and sees it as his link to Rilke. In "Hope" his parents become his babies, he remaining theirs only in memory, she says. Yet Vendler misses the fear-of-death motif in "Deutsch Durch Freud," which she regards as "a disarming poem of pure pleasure."

Mary Kinzie's long 1980 *Southern Review* article "The Man Who Painted Bulls," which is excerpted in Ferguson's collection, argues that Jarrell alone could write of the things and persons of war in such a way as to have them appear mystical. California seems to Kinzie a mythic place, a dream-factory, even a death-factory; in her view Jarrell is a psychologist of childhood and dream. What she says about "The Orient Express" is arresting and valid; about "The Knight, Death, and the Devil" even more striking ("Because they have the world within them, these figures become it and, after a fashion, do not need it"). *The Animal Family* she regards as Jarrell's best children's book (it is the most imaginative, certainly), and she views Jerome Mazzaro's 1971 *Salmagundi* essay as a brilliant contribution to Jarrell studies.

English critic Peter Jones has substantial coverage of Jarrell in *A Reader's Guide to Fifty American Poets* (1980). However, he is not always accurate, as when he relates how the poet was killed by a truck during the composition of his best book, *The Lost World*. Yet this six-page account, on the whole, is one of the most thoughtful, defining as it does the fairy tale as metaphor for lived experience; innocence and the loss of innocence as themes; and compassion as the dominant tone of the work. Furthermore, in a few words he summarizes what the war meant to the poet: "The war was for Jarrell a powerful symbol of loss, innocence violated, and conscience implicated."

Jeffrey Meyers's "Randall Jarrell and German Culture" (1983) supplies the following reductive summation of Jarrell's fiction and poems:

> Jarrell's sympathetic identification with and nourishing absorption in German culture—which had much more positive results than the fuzzy metaphysics of Coleridge, the ponderous style of Carlyle, the beery bombast of Mencken—provided the artistic and intellectual content of his poetry and novel, and inspired his affirmation—despite the demonic element—of the essential value of western civilization.

Meyers's literary detection, on the other hand, comes in handy for scholars; he discovers, for example, that Ludwig Wittgenstein's *Tractatus* is the source for a section-heading in *Selected Poems*. Meyers is more helpful in "Randall Jarrell: The Paintings in the Poems," a 1984 *Southern Review* essay, but more annoying, too. His notes—a wealth of valuable minutiae—make as interesting reading as his text. Reproductions of the art involved in "The Old and the New Masters" and the Dürer pieces are an undeniably fine feature of the article. Yet in his last paragraph Meyers accuses Jarrell of being inexact: his description of the Dürer etching on the Knight, Death, the Devil is unaccompanied by explanation of the meaning of the allegory; his diffusion of the focus in "Jerome" weakens the analogy; he ignores the symbolism (as of the wild flowers) in van der Goes; he is mistaken about certain important details. However, Meyers correctly discerns that "These deeply moving paintings become a perfect vehicle for Jarrell's union of Auden's and Rilke's great themes about the modern world: the loss of faith, the indifference to suffering, and the transcendent power of art."

In 1985 Calvin Bedient published in the *Sewanee Review* "Randall Jarrell and *Poetry and the Age*," in which he describes the advent of the critical book in terms of "a crystal bell shaken in celebration and giving off a gleeful, high-pitched, but vigorous ring." Each essay in Jarrell's book, he says, is "like a single sticking word, an ontic naming," similar to Adam's. In this fine article Bedient shows, as does Jarrell, that criticism exists for the sake of the art it treats. Ideally, his assertion underlies all of the criticism discussed in this essay.

Robert Lowell
(1917-1977)

Steven Gould Axelrod
University of California, Riverside

PRIMARY BIBLIOGRAPHY

Books

Land of Unlikeness. Cummington, Mass.: Cummington Press, 1944. Poems.

Lord Weary's Castle. New York: Harcourt, Brace, 1946. Poems.

Poems, 1938-1949. London: Faber & Faber, 1950. Includes poems from *Lord Weary's Castle* and *The Mills of the Kavanaughs.*

The Mills of the Kavanaughs. New York: Harcourt, Brace, 1951. Poems.

Life Studies. London: Faber & Faber, 1959. New York: Farrar, Straus & Cudahy, 1959. Poems. A 1968 Faber & Faber reprint includes a prose memoir.

For the Union Dead. New York: Farrar, Straus & Giroux, 1964; London: Faber & Faber, 1965. Poems.

The Old Glory. New York: Farrar, Straus & Giroux, 1965; London: Faber & Faber, 1966; rev. ed., New York: Farrar, Straus & Giroux, 1968. Plays.

Near the Ocean. New York: Farrar, Straus & Giroux, 1967; London: Faber & Faber, 1967. Poems.

Prometheus Bound. New York: Farrar, Straus & Giroux, 1969; London: Faber & Faber, 1970. Play.

Notebook 1967-68. New York: Farrar, Straus & Giroux, 1969. Revised and republished as *Notebook.* New York: Farrar, Straus & Giroux, 1970; London: Faber & Faber, 1970. Poems.

History. New York: Farrar, Straus & Giroux, 1973; London: Faber & Faber, 1973. Poems.

For Lizzie and Harriet. New York: Farrar, Straus & Giroux, 1973; London: Faber & Faber, 1973. Poems.

The Dolphin. New York: Farrar, Straus & Giroux, 1973; London: Faber
& Faber, 1973. Poems.
Selected Poems. New York: Farrar, Straus & Giroux, 1976; rev. ed.,
New York: Noonday, 1977. Poems.
Day by Day. New York: Farrar, Straus & Giroux, 1977; London: Faber
& Faber, 1978. Poems.

Selected Essays

"Review of T. S. Eliot, *Four Quartets,*" *Sewanee Review,* 51 (1943), 432-
435.
"A Note," *Kenyon Review,* 6 (Autumn 1944), 583-586. Reprinted as
"Hopkins' Sanctity." In *Gerard Manley Hopkins by the Kenyon Crit-
ics.* Norfolk, Conn.: New Directions, 1945.
"Current Poetry," *Sewanee Review,* 54 (Winter 1946), 143-153.
"Thomas, Bishop, and Williams," *Sewanee Review,* 55 (Summer 1947),
493-503.
"On Stanley Kunitz's 'Father and Son,'" *New World Writing,* no. 20
(1962), 206-210. Reprinted in *Contemporary Poet as Artist and
Critic,* ed. Anthony Ostroff. Boston: Little, Brown, 1964.
"On 'Skunk Hour,'" *New World Writing 21* (1963), 155-159.
"After Reading Six or Seven Essays on Me," *Salmagundi,* no. 37 (Spring
1977), 112-115.

Translations

Racine, Jean Baptiste, and Pierre Beaumarchais. *Phaedra and Figaro,*
trans. Lowell and Jacques Barzun. New York: Farrar, Straus &
Cudahy, 1961; London: Faber & Faber, 1963. *Phaedra,* reprinted
separately. London: Faber & Faber, 1963; New York: Octagon,
1971. Plays.
Imitations, trans. and ed. Lowell. New York: Farrar, Straus & Cudahy,
1961; London: Faber & Faber, 1962. Poems.
The Voyage and Other Versions of Poems by Baudelaire, trans. Lowell. New
York: Farrar, Straus & Giroux, 1968; London: Faber & Faber,
1968. Poems.
The Oresteia of Aeschylus, trans. Lowell. New York: Farrar, Straus &
Giroux, 1978. Plays.

Edited Book

Randall Jarrell 1914-1965, ed. Robert Lowell, Peter Taylor, and Robert Penn Warren. New York: Farrar, Straus & Giroux, 1967. Essays.

Filmed Interview

Robert Lowell. National Educational Television, 1964.

Recordings

The Poetry of Robert Lowell. J. Norton, 1974. Recording of 1968 reading in New York City.
Robert Lowell: A Reading. Caedmon, 1978. Recording of reading on 8 Dec. 1976.
Robert Lowell Reading his Own Poems. Twentieth-Century Poetry in English series, Library of Congress, 1978.

Editions and Collections

The Achievement of Robert Lowell: A Comprehensive Selection of His Poems, ed. William J. Martz. Glenview, Ill.: Scott, Foresman, 1966.
Robert Lowell's Poems: A Selection, ed. Jonathan Raban. London: Faber & Faber, 1974.

SECONDARY BIBLIOGRAPHY

Concordance

Rehor, Rosalind. "This Round Dome: An Analysis of Theme and Style in the Poetry of Robert Lowell." Unpublished dissertation, Case Western Reserve University, 1972. Concordance to fifty-four poems.

Bibliographies and Checklists

Axelrod, Steven Gould, and Helen Deese. *Robert Lowell: A Reference Guide.* Boston: G. K. Hall, 1982. Secondary.
Mazzaro, Jerome. *The Achievement of Robert Lowell: 1939-1959.* Detroit: University of Detroit Press, 1960. Primary and secondary.
Zin, Annamaria. "Italian Bibliography on Robert Lowell." Collected in *Robert Lowell: A Tribute,* ed. Rolando Anzilotti, 172-180. See Collections of Essays. Primary and secondary listings of Italian

translations of Lowell and of Italian secondary material.

Biography: Book

Hamilton, Ian. *Robert Lowell: A Biography.* New York: Random House, 1982.

Biographies: Major Articles and Book Sections

Atlas, James. "Robert Lowell in Cambridge: Lord Weary," *Atlantic Monthly,* 250 (July 1982), 56-64.

_____. "Unsentimental Education," *Atlantic Monthly,* 251 (June 1983), 79-92.

Baumel, Judith. "Robert Lowell: The Teacher," *Harvard Advocate,* 113 (Nov. 1979), 32-33.

Bell, Vereen M. "Robert Lowell 1917-1977," *Sewanee Review,* 86 (Winter 1978), 102-105.

Betocchi, Carlo. "L'amico Lowell." Collected in *Robert Lowell: A Tribute,* ed. Anzilotti, 23-32. See Collections of Essays.

Bidart, Frank. "Robert Lowell," *Harvard Advocate,* 113 (Nov. 1979), 12.

Booth, Philip. "Summers in Castine/Contact Prints: 1955-65," *Salmagundi,* no. 37 (Spring 1977), 37-53.

Brooks, Esther. "Remembering Cal." Collected in Anzilotti, 37-44. See Collections of Essays.

Clark, Blair. "On Robert Lowell," *Harvard Advocate,* 113 (Nov. 1979), 9-11.

Elman, Richard. "A Life Study of Lowell," *American Book Review,* 1 (Dec. 1978-Jan. 1979), 7-8.

Fitzgerald, Robert. "The Things of the Eye," *Poetry,* 132 (May 1978), 107-111.

Heaney, Seamus. "On Robert Lowell," *New York Review of Books,* 25 (9 Feb. 1978), 37-38.

Heymann, C. David. *American Aristocracy: The Lives and Times of James Russell, Amy, and Robert Lowell.* New York: Dodd, Mead, 1980, 283-513.

Kazin, Alfred. *New York Jew.* New York: Knopf, 1978, 202-205.

Kunitz, Stanley. "The Sense of a Life," *New York Times Book Review,* 16 Oct. 1977, pp. 3, 34-36.

McClatchy, J. D. "Some Photographs of Robert Lowell," *American Poetry Review,* 7 (Sept.-Oct. 1978), 28-29.

Mailer, Norman. *The Armies of the Night.* New York: New American Library, 1968, 18-22, 40-46, 63-68, 73-74, 82-84, 89, 109, 124-129, 139.

O'Connor, Flannery. *The Habit of Being,* ed. Sally Fitzgerald. New York: Farrar, Straus & Giroux, 1978, throughout.

Parker, Francis S. "Brantwood Camp," *Harvard Advocate,* 113 (Nov. 1979), 8.

Ransom, John Crowe. "A Look Backward and a Note of Hope," *Harvard Advocate,* 145 (Nov. 1961), 22-24.

"The Second Chance," *Time,* 2 June 1967, pp. 67-74.

Sexton, Anne. *Anne Sexton: A Self-Portrait in Letters,* ed. Linda Gray Sexton and Lois Ames. Boston: Houghton Mifflin, 1977, throughout.

Simpson, Eileen. *Poets in their Youth: A Memoir.* New York: Random House, 1982, throughout.

Spivack, Kathleen. "Robert Lowell: A Memoir," *Antioch Review,* 43 (Spring 1985), 189-193.

Stein, Jean, and George Plimpton, eds. *American Journey: The Times of Robert Kennedy.* New York: Harcourt Brace Jovanovich, 1970, 36, 192-193, 113, 268-270, 302-304, 309-310, 321-322, 340-341.

Taylor, Peter. "Robert Trail [*sic*] Spence Lowell: 1917-1977," *Ploughshares,* 5, no. 2 (1979), 74-81.

Thompson, John. "Robert Lowell 1917-1977," *New York Review of Books,* 27 Oct. 1977, pp. 14-15.

Tillinghast, Richard. "Robert Lowell in the Sixties," *Harvard Advocate,* 113 (Nov. 1979), 14-16.

Vendler, Helen. "Lowell in the Classroom," *Harvard Advocate,* 113 (Nov. 1979), 22-26, 28-29.

Williamson, Alan. "Robert Lowell: A Reminiscence," *Harvard Advocate,* 113 (Nov. 1979), 36-39.

Lowell in Fiction, Poetry, and Drama

Berryman, John. "Dream Song 15." In his *The Dream Songs.* New York: Farrar, Straus & Giroux, 1969, 17. Poem.

Bishop, Elizabeth. "North Haven." In her *Complete Poems 1927-1979.* New York: Farrar, Straus & Giroux, 1983, 188-189. Poem.

Eberhart, Richard. "The Mad Musician." In his *Collected Verse Plays.* Chapel Hill: University of North Carolina Press, 1962, 131-160. Play.

Hardwick, Elizabeth. *Sleepless Nights: A Novel.* New York: Random House, 1979, throughout.

Heaney, Seamus. "Elegy." In his *Field Work.* Boston & London: Faber & Faber, 1979.

Richards, I. A. "For a Miniature of Robert Lowell," *Harvard Advocate,* 145 (Nov. 1961), 4. Poem.

Stafford, Jean. "A Country Love Story." In her *Collected Stories.* New York: Dutton, 1984, 133-146. Story.

Taylor, Peter. "1939." In his *Collected Stories.* New York: Farrar, Straus & Giroux, 1969, 326-359. Story.

_____. "An Influx of Poets," *New Yorker,* 54 (6 Nov. 1978), 43-58. Story.

Voznesensky, Andrei. "Family Graveyard" and "Lines to Robert Lowell." In his *Nostalgia for the Present.* Garden City: Doubleday, 1978, 7, 109-115. Poems.

Selected Interviews

Alvarez, A. "A Poet Talks About Making History into Theater," *New York Times,* 4 Apr. 1976, sec. II, pp. 1, 5.

_____. "Robert Lowell in Conversation," *London Observer,* 21 July 1963, p. 19. Revised and republished in *Review,* 8 (Aug. 1963), 36-40. Collected in *Profile of Robert Lowell,* ed. Jerome Mazzaro. See Collections of Essays.

_____. "A Talk with Robert Lowell," *Encounter,* 24 (Feb. 1965), 39-43. Republished in his *Under Pressure.* London: Penguin, 1966. Collected in Mazzaro. See Collections of Essays.

Billington, Michael. "Mr. Robert Lowell on T. S. Eliot and the Theatre," *London Times,* 8 Mar. 1967, p. 10. Collected in Mazzaro. See Collections of Essays.

Brooks, Cleanth, and Robert Penn Warren. "Robert Lowell, Cleanth Brooks, and Robert Penn Warren." In *Conversations on the Craft of Poetry,* ed. Brooks and Warren. New York: Holt, Rinehart & Winston, 1961, 33-47.

Carne-Ross, Donald S. "Conversation with Robert Lowell," *Delos,* 1 (Apr. 1968), 165-175. Collected in Mazzaro. See Collections of Essays.

Gilman, Richard. "Life Offers No Neat Conclusions," *New York Times,* 5 May 1968, sec. II, pp. 1, 5. Collected in Mazzaro. See Collections of Essays.

Hamilton, Ian. "A Conversation with Robert Lowell," *Review,* no. 26

(Summer 1971), 10-29. Reprinted in *Modern Occasions*, 2 (Winter 1972), 28-48; *American Poetry Review*, 7 (Sept.-Oct. 1978), 23-27.

"In Bounds," *Newsweek*, 12 Oct. 1964, pp. 120-122.

Kunitz, Stanley. "Talk with Robert Lowell," *New York Times Book Review*, 4 Oct. 1964, pp. 34-39. Collected in Mazzaro. See Collections of Essays.

Lieberson, Goddard. "An Interview with the Author." *Benito Cereno by Robert Lowell*, Columbia Records, 1965, liner notes.

McCormick, John. "Falling Asleep over Grillparzer: An Interview with Robert Lowell," *Poetry*, 81 (Jan. 1953), 269-279.

Naipaul, V. S. "Et in America ego," *Listener*, 4 Sept. 1969, pp. 302-304. Collected in Mazzaro. See Collections of Essays.

Seidel, Frederick. "Interview with Robert Lowell," *Paris Review*, 25 (Winter-Spring 1961), 56-95. Reprinted in *Writers at Work*, 2nd Series, ed. George Plimpton. New York: Viking Press, 1963. Collected in *Robert Lowell: A Collection of Critical Essays*, ed. Thomas Parkinson and in *Robert Lowell: A Portrait of the Artist in His Time*, ed. Michael London and Robert Boyers. See Collections of Essays.

Young, Dudley. "Talk with Robert Lowell," *New York Times Book Review*, 4 Apr. 1971, pp. 31-32.

Critical Studies: Books and Pamphlets

Axelrod, Steven Gould. *Robert Lowell: Life and Art*. Princeton: Princeton University Press, 1978.

Bell, Vereen M. *Robert Lowell: Nihilist as Hero*. Cambridge: Harvard University Press, 1983.

Cooper, Phillip. *The Autobiographical Myth of Robert Lowell*. Chapel Hill: University of North Carolina Press, 1970.

Cosgrave, Patrick. *The Public Poetry of Robert Lowell*. London: Gollancz, 1970; New York: Taplinger, 1972.

Crick, John. *Robert Lowell*. Edinburgh: Oliver & Boyd, 1974.

Fein, Richard J. *Robert Lowell*. New York: Twayne, 1970; rev. ed., Boston: Twayne, 1979.

Martin, Jay. *Robert Lowell*. Minneapolis: University of Minnesota Press, 1970.

Mazzaro, Jerome. *The Poetic Themes of Robert Lowell*. Ann Arbor: University of Michigan Press, 1965.

Meiners, R. K. *Everything to Be Endured: An Essay on Robert Lowell and Modern Poetry*. Columbia: University of Missouri Press, 1970.

Perloff, Marjorie G. *The Poetic Art of Robert Lowell.* Ithaca: Cornell
    University Press, 1973.
Procopiow, Norma. *Robert Lowell: The Poet and the Critics.* Chicago:
    American Library Association, 1984.
Raffel, Burton. *Robert Lowell.* New York: Ungar, 1981.
Rudman, Mark. *Robert Lowell: An Introduction to the Poetry.* New York:
    Columbia University Press, 1983.
Smith, Vivian. *The Poetry of Robert Lowell.* Sydney, Australia: Sydney
    University Press, 1974.
Staples, Hugh. *Robert Lowell: The First Twenty Years.* London: Faber &
    Faber, 1962; New York: Farrar, Straus & Cudahy, 1962.
Williamson, Alan. *Pity the Monsters: The Political Vision of Robert Lowell.*
    New Haven, Conn.: Yale University Press, 1974.
Yenser, Stephen. *Circle to Circle: The Poetry of Robert Lowell.* Berkeley:
    University of California Press, 1975.

Critical Studies: Collections of Essays

Anzilotti, Rolando, ed. *Robert Lowell: A Tribute.* Pisa, Italy: Nistri-Lis-
    chi, 1979.
Axelrod, Steven Gould, and Helen Deese, eds. *Robert Lowell: Essays
    on the Poetry.* New York: Cambridge University Press, forthcom-
    ing 1986.
London, Michael, and Robert Boyers, eds. *Robert Lowell: A Portrait of
    the Artist in His Time.* New York: David Lewis, 1970.
Mazzaro, Jerome, ed. *Profile of Robert Lowell.* Columbus: Merrill, 1971.
Parkinson, Thomas, ed. *Robert Lowell: A Collection of Critical Essays.*
    Englewood Cliffs, N.J.: Prentice-Hall, 1968.
Price, Jonathan, ed. *Critics on Robert Lowell.* Coral Gables, Fla.: Uni-
    versity of Miami Press, 1972; London: Allen & Unwin, 1974.

Critical Studies: Special Issues of Journals

Agenda, 18 (Autumn 1980).
Harvard Advocate, 95 (Nov. 1961).
Harvard Advocate, 113 (Nov. 1979).
Salmagundi, no. 4 (1966-67).
Salmagundi, no. 37 (Spring 1977).

Critical Studies: Major Articles and Book Sections

Allen, Carolyn. "Lowell's 'After the Surprising Conversions': Another Look at the Source," *Notes on Modern American Literature,* 3 (Summer 1979), Item 17.

Altieri, Charles. *Enlarging the Temple: New Directions in American Poetry During the 1960s.* Lewisburg, Pa.: Bucknell University Press, 1979, 60-80.

_____. "Poetry in a Prose World: Robert Lowell's 'Life Studies,' " *Modern Poetry Studies,* 1, no. 4 (1970), 182-199. Collected in Mazzaro.

Alvarez, A. *Beyond All This Fiddle.* London: Allen Lane, Penguin Press, 1968, 3-21.

_____. "Robert Lowell 1917-1977," *London Observer,* 18 Sept. 1977, p. 24.

Antin, David. "Modernism and Postmodernism: Approaching the Present in American Poetry," *Boundary 2,* 1 (Fall 1972), 98-133.

Arrowsmith, William. "Five Poets," *Hudson Review,* 4 (Winter 1952), 619-627. Collected in London and Boyers and in Parkinson.

Axelrod, Steven Gould. "Baudelaire and the Poetry of Robert Lowell," *Twentieth Century Literature,* 17 (Oct. 1971), 257-274.

_____. "Colonel Shaw in American Poetry: 'For the Union Dead' and Its Precursors," *American Quarterly,* 24 (Oct. 1972), 523-537. Revised and reprinted in his *Robert Lowell: Life and Art.*

_____. "Introduction: Lowell's Living Name." Collected in Axelrod and Deese, forthcoming.

_____. "Lowell's *The Dolphin* as a 'Book of Life,' " *Contemporary Literature,* 18 (Autumn 1977), 458-474. Reprinted in his *Robert Lowell: Life and Art.*

_____. "Robert Lowell and Hopkins," *Twentieth Century Literature,* 31 (Spring 1985), 55-72.

_____. "Robert Lowell and the New York Intellectuals," *English Language Notes,* 11 (Mar. 1974), 206-209.

Barry, Jackson G. "Robert Lowell's 'Confessional' Image of an Age: Theme and Language in Poetic Form," *Ariel,* 12 (Jan. 1981), 51-58.

Bayley, John. "If Life Could Write," *New Statesman,* 10 Mar. 1978, pp. 322-323.

_____. "Robert Lowell: The Poetry of Cancellation," *London Magazine,* new series, 6 (June 1966), 76-85. Collected in London and Boyers.

_____. *The Uses of Division-Unity and Disharmony in Literature.* London: Chatto & Windus, 1976, 157-171.

Bedient, Calvin. "Illegible Lowell (The Late Volumes)." Collected in Axelrod and Deese, forthcoming.

Belitt, Ben. *"Imitations:* Translation as Personal Mode," *Salmagundi,* no. 4 (Winter 1966-1967), 44-56. Collected in London and Boyers.

Berryman, John. "Lowell, Thomas &C," *Partisan Review,* 14 (Jan.-Feb. 1947), 73-85. Reprinted in Berryman, *The Freedom of the Poet.* New York: Farrar, Straus & Giroux, 1976.

_____. "On Robert Lowell's 'Skunk Hour': Despondency and Madness." In *The Contemporary Poet as Artist and Critic,* ed. Anthony Ostroff. Boston: Little, Brown, 1964, 99-106. Reprinted in Berryman, *The Freedom of the Poet.* Collected in Parkinson.

Bidart, Frank. "On Robert Lowell," *Salmagundi,* 37 (Spring 1977), 54-55.

Blackmur, R. P. "Notes on Eleven Poets," *Kenyon Review,* 7 (Spring 1945), 339-352. Collected in London and Boyers and in Parkinson.

Bloom, Harold. "Harold Bloom on Poetry," *New Republic,* 20 Nov. 1976, pp. 20-26.

_____. "Harold Bloom on Poetry," *New Republic,* 26 Nov. 1977, pp. 24-26.

Bly, Robert. "The Dead World and the Live World," *The Sixties,* 8 (Spring 1966), 2-7.

Bogan, Louise. "Verse," *New Yorker,* 30 Nov. 1946, pp. 137-140. Reprinted in her *A Poet's Alphabet.* New York: McGraw-Hill, 1970.

_____. "Verse," *New Yorker,* 9 June 1951, pp. 109-113.

Borroff, Marie. "Words, Language, and Form." In *Literary Theory and Structure Essays in Honor of William K. Wimsatt,* ed. Frank Brady, John Palmer, and Martin Price. New Haven: Yale University Press, 1973, 63-79.

Bowen, Roger. "Confession and Equilibrium: Robert Lowell's Poetic Development," *Criticism,* 11 (Winter 1969), 78-93.

Boyers, Robert. "On Robert Lowell," *Salmagundi,* no. 13 (Summer 1970), 36-44. Collected in Mazzaro.

Branscomb, Jack. "Robert Lowell's Painters: Two Sources," *English Language Notes,* 15 (Dec. 1977), 119-122.

Breslin, James E. B. *From Modern to Contemporary: American Poetry, 1945-1965.* Chicago: University of Chicago Press, 1984, xiv-xvi, 18-30, 110-142, 247-251.

Brustein, Robert. "Introduction." In *The Old Glory* by Robert Lowell. Collected in London and Boyers and in Price.

_____. *Seasons of Discontent-Dramatic Opinions 1959-1965.* New York: Simon & Schuster, 1965, 252-259.

Calder, Alex. "*Notebook 1967-68:* Writing the Process Poem." Collected in Axelrod and Deese, forthcoming.

Calhoun, Richard J. "The Poetic Metamorphosis of Robert Lowell," *Furman Studies,* 13 (Nov. 1965), 7-17.

Cambon, Glauco. "Robert Lowell: History as Eschatology." In his *The Inclusive Flame: Studies in American Poetry.* Bloomington: Indiana University Press, 1963, 219-228, 242-245.

Cargas, Harry J. *Daniel Berrigan and Contemporary Protest Poetry.* New Haven: College & University Press, 1972, 47-61.

Carne-Ross, Donald S. "The Two Voices of Translation." Collected in Parkinson, 152-170.

Carruth, Hayden. "An Appreciation of Robert Lowell," *Harper's,* 255 (Dec. 1977), 110-112.

Cohen, B. Bernard. "Tragic Vision in the Sixties," *Genre,* 3 (Sept. 1970), 254-271.

Cooper, Philip. "Lowell's Motion: *Notebook* and After," *South Carolina Review,* 12 (Spring 1980), 18-30.

_____. "Lowell's 'The Quaker Graveyard in Nantucket,' " *Explicator,* 38 (Summer 1980), 43.

Corcoran, Neil. "Lowell's *Retiarius:* Towards *The Dolphin,*" *Agenda,* 18 (Autumn 1980), 75-85.

Davie, Donald. "A Private Life Lived in Public," *New York Times Book Review,* 18 July 1976, pp. 23-26.

Deese, Helen. "Lowell and the Visual Arts." Collected in Axelrod and Deese, forthcoming.

"The Destructive Element," *Times Literary Supplement,* 14 Oct. 1960, p. 660.

Doherty, Paul C. "The Poet as Historian: 'For the Union Dead' by Robert Lowell," *Concerning Poetry,* 1 (Fall 1968), 37-41.

Dolan, Paul J. "Lowell's *Quaker Graveyard:* Poem and Tradition," *Renascence,* 21 (Summer 1969), 171-180, 194.

Donoghue, Denis. *Connoisseurs of Chaos—Ideas of Order in Modern American Poetry.* New York: Macmillan, 1965, 150-157.

_____. "Does America Have a Major Poet?," *New York Times Book Review,* 3 Dec. 1978, pp. 9, 88.

Dover, K. J. "Translation: The Speakable and the Unspeakable," *Essays in Criticism,* 30 (Jan. 1979), 1-7.

Dubrow, Heather. "The Marine in the Garden: Pastoral Elements in

Lowell's 'Quaker Graveyard,' " *Philological Quarterly*, 62 (Spring 1983), 127-145.

Duffey, Bernard. *Poetry in America—Expression and Its Values in the Times of Bryant, Whitman, and Pound.* Durham, N.C.: Duke University Press, 1978, 289-295.

Dyck, Reginald. "Lowell's 'The Drinker,' " *Explicator*, 40 (Winter 1982), 7-9.

"Eastern Personal Times," *Times Literary Supplement*, 1 July 1965, p. 558.

Eberhart, Richard. "Four Poets," *Sewanee Review*, 55 (Apr.-June 1947), 324-336. Collected in Parkinson.

Eddins, Dwight. "Poet and State in the Verse of Robert Lowell," *Texas Studies in Literature and Language*, 15 (Summer 1973), 371-386.

Edwards, Thomas R. *Imagination and Power—A Study of Poetry on Public Themes.* London: Chatto & Windus, 1971, 3-6, 210-225.

Ehrenpreis, Irvin. "The Age of Lowell," *American Poetry*, Stratford-upon-Avon Series, no. 7 (1965), 68-95. Collected in London and Boyers, in Parkinson, and in Price.

Estrin, Mark W. "Robert Lowell's *Benito Cereno*," *Modern Drama*, 15 (Mar. 1973), 411-426.

Eulert, Donald. "Robert Lowell and W. C. Williams: Sterility in 'Central Park,' " *English Language Notes*, 5 (Dec. 1967), 129-135.

Fein, Richard J. "*Lord Weary's Castle* Revisited," *PMLA*, 89 (Jan. 1974), 34-41. Revised and reprinted in his *Robert Lowell*, 2nd ed.

_____. "The Life of *Life Studies*," *Literary Review*, 23 (Spring 1980), 326-338.

Feldman, Burton. "Robert Lowell: Poetry and Politics," *Dissent*, 16 (Nov.-Dec. 1969), 550-555.

Fender, Stephen. "What Really Happened to Warren Winslow?," *Journal of American Studies*, 7 (Aug. 1973), 187-190.

Fitzgerald, Robert. "Aiaia and Ithaca: Notes on a New Lowell Poem," *Salmagundi*, no. 37 (Spring 1977), 25-31.

Fraser, G. S. "Amid the Horror. A Song of Praise," *New York Times Book Review*, 4 Oct. 1964, pp. 1, 38. Collected in Mazzaro.

_____. " 'Near the Ocean,' " *Salmagundi*, no. 37 (Spring 1977), 73-87.

Furia, Philip. " 'IS, the whited monster': Lowell's Quaker Graveyard Revisited," *Texas Studies in Literature and Language*, 17 (Winter 1976), 837-854.

Gelpi, Albert. "Robert Lowell: The Fall from Prophecy to Irony." Collected in Axelrod and Deese, forthcoming.

Gilbert, Sandra M. "Mephistophilis in Maine: Rereading 'Skunk Hour.' " Collected in Axelrod and Deese, forthcoming.

Gray-Lewis, Stephen W. "Too Late for Eden—An Examination of Some Dualisms in 'The Mills of the Kavanaughs,' " *Cithara*, 5 (May 1966), 41-51.

Hagopian, John V. "Robert Lowell's 'Skunk Hour.' " In *Insight III*, ed. Reinhold Schiffer and Hermann Weiland. Frankfurt: Hirschgraben-Verlag, 1968, 171-180.

Hall, Donald. "Robert Lowell and the Literature Industry," *Georgia Review*, 32 (Spring 1978), 7-12.

_____. "Two Poets Named Robert," *Ohio Review*, 18 (Fall 1977), 110-125.

Hartman, Geoffrey H. "The Eye of the Storm," *Partisan Review*, 32 (Spring 1965), 277-280. Collected in London and Boyers.

Hass, Robert. "Lowell's Graveyard," *Salmagundi*, no. 37 (Spring 1977), 56-72.

Hill, Geoffrey. "Robert Lowell: 'Contrasts and Repetitions,' " *Essays in Criticism*, 13 (Apr. 1963), 188-197. Collected in Price.

Hirsh, John C. "The Imagery of Dedication in Robert Lowell's 'For the Union Dead,' " *Journal of American Studies*, 6 (Aug. 1972), 201-205.

Hochman, Baruch. "Robert Lowell's *The Old Glory*," *Tulane Drama Review*, 11 (Summer 1967), 127-138.

Hoffman, Daniel. "The Greatness and Horror of Empire: Robert Lowell's *Near the Ocean*." In *The Sounder Few: Essays from the Hollins Critic*, ed. R. H. W. Dillard, George Garrett, and John Rees Moore. Athens: University of Georgia Press, 1971, 213-244.

Hoffman, Steven K. "Impersonal Personalism: The Making of a Confessional Poetic," *English Literary History*, 45 (Winter 1978), 687-709.

Holder, Alan. "Going Back, Going Down, Breaking: *Day by Day*." Collected in Axelrod and Deese, forthcoming.

_____. *The Imagined Past*. Lewisburg, Pa.: Bucknell University Press, 1980, 20-22, 221-222, 255-283.

Holloway, John. "Robert Lowell and the Public Dimension," *Encounter*, 30 (Apr. 1968), 73-79.

Holton, Milne. "Maule's Curse and My-Lai: Robert Lowell's *Endecott*." In *Proceedings of a Symposium on American Literature*, ed. Marta Sienicka. Poznan, Poland: Uniw. Im. Adama Mickiewicza, 1979, 175-186.

Ilson, Robert. *"Benito Cereno* from Melville to Lowell," *Salmagundi,* no. 4 (1967), 78-86. Collected in Parkinson.

Jarrell, Randall. "Fifty Years of American Poetry," *Prairie Schooner,* 37 (Spring 1963), 1-27. Reprinted in his *The Third Book of Criticism.* New York: Farrar, Straus & Giroux, 1969.

_____. "From the Kingdom of Necessity," *Nation,* 18 Jan. 1947, pp. 74-77. Reprinted in his *Poetry and the Age.* New York: Knopf, 1953. Collected in London and Boyers, in Parkinson, and in Price.

_____. "Poetry in War and Peace," *Partisan Review,* 12 (Winter 1945), 120-126. Reprinted in his *Kipling, Auden & Co.* New York: Farrar, Straus & Giroux, 1980.

_____. "A View of Three Poets," *Partisan Review,* 18 (Nov.-Dec. 1951), 691-700. Reprinted in his *Poetry and the Age.*

Kalstone, David. *Five Temperaments: Elizabeth Bishop, Robert Lowell, James Merrill, Adrienne Rich, John Ashbery.* New York: Oxford University Press, 1977, 41-76.

Kazin, Alfred. "In Praise of Robert Lowell," *Reporter,* 25 June 1959, pp. 41-42. Reprinted in his *Contemporaries.* Boston: Little, Brown, 1962.

Kinsie, Mary. "The Prophet Is a Fool: On 'Waking Early Sunday Morning,' " *Salmagundi,* no. 37 (Spring 1977), 88-101.

Kramer, Lawrence. "Freud and the Skunks: Genre and Language in *Life Studies.*" Collected in Axelrod and Deese, forthcoming.

Kroll, Jack. "New Glory," *Newsweek,* 3 May 1976, pp. 83-84.

_____. "Sense of Mortality," *Newsweek,* 26 Sept. 1977, pp. 81-82.

Lane, Lauriat, Jr. "Robert Lowell: The Problems and Power of Allusion," *Dalhousie Review,* 60 (Winter 1980-1981), 697-702.

Leibowitz, Herbert. "Robert Lowell: Ancestral Voices," *Salmagundi,* no. 4 (1967), 25-43. Collected in London and Boyers.

Lensing, George. " 'Memories of West Street and Lepke': Robert Lowell's Associative Mirror," *Concerning Poetry,* 3 (Fall 1970), 23-26.

_____. "Robert Lowell and Jonathan Edwards: Poetry in the Hands of an Angry God," *South Carolina Review,* 6 (Apr. 1974), 7-17.

Lipking, Lawrence. *The Life of the Poet: Beginning and Ending Poetic Careers.* Chicago: University of Chicago Press, 1981, 184-188, 228-232.

Lunz, Elizabeth. "Robert Lowell and Wallace Stevens on Sunday Morning," *University Review,* 37 (Summer 1971), 268-272.

McCall, Dan. "Robert Lowell's 'Hawthorne,' " *New England Quarterly,* 39 (June 1966), 237-239.

McFadden, George. " 'Life Studies'—Robert Lowell's Comic Breakthrough," *PMLA,* 90 (Jan. 1975), 96-106.

_____. " 'Prose or This'—What Lowell Made of a Diminished Thing." Collected in Axelrod and Deese, forthcoming.

McWilliams, John P., Jr. "Fictions of Merrymount," *American Quarterly,* 29 (Spring 1977), 3-30.

Mahony, Patrick J. " 'La Ballade des pendus' of Francois Villon and Robert Lowell," *Canadian Review of Comparative Literature,* 1 (Winter 1974), 22-37.

Malkoff, Karl. *Escape from the Self: A Study of Contemporary American Poetry and Poetics.* New York: Columbia University Press, 1977, 98-124, 174-175.

Manousos, A. " 'Falling Asleep over the Aeneid': Lowell, Freud, and the Classics," *Comparative Literature Studies,* 21 (Spring 1984), 16-29.

Martin, Jay. "Grief and Nothingness: Loss and Mourning in Lowell's Poetry." Collected in Axelrod and Deese, forthcoming.

Mazzaro, Jerome. "The Classicism of Robert Lowell's *Phaedra,*" *Comparative Drama,* 7 (Summer 1973), 87-106.

_____. "*Imitations,*" *American Poetry Review.* 2 (Sept.-Oct. 1973), 35-41.

_____. "*Prometheus Bound:* Robert Lowell and Aeschylus," *Comparative Drama,* 7 (Winter 1973), 278-290.

_____. "Robert Lowell and the Kavanaugh Collapse," *University of Windsor Review,* 5 (Fall 1969), 1-24.

_____. "Robert Lowell's 'Benito Cereno,' " *Modern Poetry Studies,* 4 (Autumn 1973), 129-158.

_____. "Robert Lowell's Early Politics of Apocalypse." In *Modern American Poetry,* ed. Mazzaro. New York: David McKay, 1970, 321-350.

_____. "Robert Lowell's Notebooks," *American Poetry Review,* 10 (Jan.-Feb. 1981), 39-47.

Meek, Martha George. "Lowell's 'The Mills of the Kavanaughs,' " *Explicator,* 38 (Winter 1980), 46-47.

Miles, Josephine. *The Continuity of Poetic Language; Studies in English Poetry from the 1540's to the 1940's.* Berkeley: University of California Press, 1951, 385, 436-439, 505.

Miller, James E., Jr. *The American Quest for a Supreme Fiction: Whitman's*

Legacy in the Personal Epic. Chicago: University of Chicago Press, 1979, 3-11.

Miller, Terry. "The Prosodies of Robert Lowell," *Speech Monographs,* 35 (Nov. 1968), 425-434.

Mills, Ralph J. *Cry of the Human: Essays on Contemporary American Poetry.* Urbana: University of Illinois Press, 1975, 1-47.

Molesworth, Charles. *The Fierce Embrace: A Study of Contemporary American Poetry.* Columbia: University of Missouri Press, 1979, 37-60.

Moore, Andy J. "Frost—and Lowell—at Midnight," *Southern Quarterly,* 15 (Apr. 1977), 291-295.

Moore, Stephen C. "Politics and the Poetry of Robert Lowell," *Georgia Review,* 27 (Summer 1973), 220-231.

Nelles, William. "Saving the State in Lowell's 'For the Union Dead,' " *American Literature,* 55 (Dec. 1983), 639-642.

Nelson, Rudolph L. "A Note on the Evolution of Robert Lowell's 'The Public Garden,' " *American Literature,* 41 (Mar. 1969), 106-110.

Newmyer, Stephen. "Robert Lowell and the Weeping Philosopher," *Classical and Modern Literature,* 1 (Winter 1981), 121-131.

North, Michael. "The Public Monument and Public Poetry: Stevens, Berryman, and Lowell," *Contemporary Literature,* 21 (Spring 1980), 267-285.

Oberg, Arthur. *Modern American Lyric: Lowell, Berryman, Creeley, and Plath.* New Brunswick: Rutgers University Press, 1978, 5-47, 175-178.

"Open Sores," *Times Literary Supplement,* 3 Aug. 1967, p. 705.

Parkinson, Thomas. *"For the Union Dead,"* *Salmagundi,* no. 4 (1967), 87-95. Collected in Parkinson.

Pearson, Gabriel. "Robert Lowell," *Review,* no. 20 (Mar. 1969), 3-36.

Perloff, Marjorie G. "Death by Water: The Winslow Elegies of Robert Lowell," *English Literary History,* 34 (Mar. 1967), 116-140. Revised and reprinted as "The Voice of the Poet: The Winslow Elegies" in her *The Poetic Art of Robert Lowell.*

_____. "The Dolphin; History; For Lizzie and Harriet," *New Republic,* 7-14 July 1973, pp. 24-26.

_____. " 'Fearlessly Holding Back Nothing': Robert Lowell's Last Poems," *Agenda,* 18 (Autumn 1980), 104-114.

_____. *"Poetes Maudits* of the Genteel Tradition: Lowell and Berryman." Collected in Axelrod and Deese, forthcoming.

_____. "Realism and the Confessional Mode of Robert Lowell," *Contemporary Literature,* 11 (Autumn 1970), 470-487. Revised and reprinted in her *The Poetic Art of Robert Lowell.*

Pinsky, Robert. "The Conquered Kings of Robert Lowell," *Salmagundi*, no. 37 (Spring 1977), 102-105.

_____. *The Situation of Poetry*. Princeton: Princeton University Press, 1976, 16-23.

Poirier, Richard. "Our Truest Historian," *New York Herald Tribune Book Week*, 11 Oct. 1964, pp. 1, 16. Collected in Price.

Price, Jonathan. "Fire Against Fire," *Works*, 1 (Autumn 1967), 120-126. Collected in Price.

Procopiow, Norma. " 'Day by Day': Lowell's Poetics of Imitation," *Ariel*, 14 (Jan. 1983), 4-14.

_____. "William Carlos Williams and the Origins of the Confessional Poem," *Ariel*, 7 (Apr. 1976), 63-75.

Prunty, Wyatt. "Allegory to Causality: Robert Lowell's Poetic Shift," *Agenda*, 18 (Autumn 1980), 94-103.

Raizis, M. Byron. "Robert Lowell's *Prometheus Bound*," *Papers on Language and Literature*, 5 (Supplement, Summer 1969), 154-168.

Reed, John R. "Going Back: The Ironic Progress of Lowell's Poetry," *Modern Poetry Studies*, 1, no. 4 (1970), 162-181. Collected in Mazzaro.

Remaley, Peter P. "Epic Machinery in Robert Lowell's *Lord Weary's Castle*," *Ball State University Forum*, 18 (Spring 1977), 59-64.

_____. "The Quest for Grace in Robert Lowell's *Lord Weary's Castle*," *Renascence*, 28 (Spring 1976), 115-122.

Rich, Adrienne. "Carydid: A Column," *American Poetry Review*, 2 (Sept.-Oct. 1973), 42-43.

Ricks, Christopher. "The Poet Robert Lowell," *Listener*, 21 June 1973, pp. 830-832.

_____. "The Three Lives of Robert Lowell," *New Statesman*, 26 Mar. 1965, pp. 496-497. Collected in Price.

Rollins, J. Barton. "Robert Lowell's Apprenticeship and Early Poems," *American Literature*, 52 (Mar. 1980), 67-83.

_____. "Young Robert Lowell's Poetics of Revision," *Journal of Modern Literature*, 7 (Sept. 1979), 488-504.

Rosenthal, M. L. "Our Neurotic Angel: Robert Lowell (1917-77)." Collected in Anzilotti, 143-155. Reprinted in *Agenda*, 18 (Autumn 1980), 34-45.

_____. "Poetry as Confession," *Nation*, 19 Sept. 1959, pp. 154-155. Collected in London and Boyers and in Price.

_____. "Robert Lowell and 'Confessional' Poetry." In his *The New Poets: American and British Poetry Since World War Two*. New York: Oxford University Press, 1967, 25-78.

_____. "Robert Lowell and the Poetry of Confession." In his *The Modern Poets: A Critical Introduction.* New York: Oxford University Press, 1960, 225-237. Collected in Parkinson.

Russo, J. P. " 'I Fish Until the Clouds Turn Blue': Robert Lowell's *Late Poetry,*" *Papers on Literature and Languages,* 20 (Summer 1984), 312-325.

Saffioti, Carol Lee. "Between History and Self: The Function of the Alexander Poems in Robert Lowell's *History,*" *Modern Poetry Studies,* 10 (1981), 159-172.

Shaw, Robert B. "Lowell in the Seventies," *Contemporary Literature,* 23 (Fall 1982), 515-527.

Simon, John. "Abuse of Privilege: Lowell as Translator," *Hudson Review,* 20 (Autumn 1967), 543-562. Collected in London and Boyers.

Souza, Maria Helena de. "Robert Lowell's 'Dropping South: Brazil': An Analysis," *Estudos Anglo-Americanos,* 5-6 (1981-1982), 145-151.

Spacks, Patricia Meyer. "From Satire to Description," *Yale Review,* 58 (Winter 1969), 232-248.

Spears, Monroe K. *Dionysus and the City—Modernism in Twentieth-Century Poetry.* New York: Oxford University Press, 1970, 90-93, 236-248.

Spender, Stephen. "Robert Lowell's Family Album," *New Republic,* 8 June 1959, p. 17. Collected in Parkinson.

Sterne, Richard Clark. "Puritans at Merry Mount: Variations on a Theme," *American Quarterly,* 22 (Winter 1970), 846-858.

Stone, Albert E. "A New Version of American Innocence: Robert Lowell's *Benito Cereno,*" *New England Quarterly,* 45 (Dec. 1972), 467-483.

Strand, Mark. "Landscape and the Poetry of Self," *Prose,* 6 (1973), 169-183.

Sullivan, Rosemary. *"Notebook:* Robert Lowell as a Political Poet," *Etudes Anglaises,* 27 (July-Sept. 1974), 291-301.

Tate, Allen. "Introduction" to *Land of Unlikeness* by Robert Lowell. Cummington, Mass.: Cummington Press, 1944, i-ii. Collected in London and Boyers, in Parkinson, and in Price.

Tokunaga, Shozo. "Private Voice, Public Voice: John Berryman and Robert Lowell," *John Berryman Studies,* 1 (Apr. 1975), 18-23.

Twombly, Robert G. "The Poetics of Demur: Lowell and Frost," *College English,* 38 (Dec. 1976), 373-392.

Von Hallberg, Robert. *American Poetry and Culture: 1945-1980.* Cambridge: Harvard University Press, 1985, 148-174, 243-244.

Waggoner, Hyatt H. *American Poets from the Puritans to the Present.* Boston: Houghton Mifflin, 1968, 577-585.

Weatherhead, A. Kingsley. *"Day by Day:* His Endgame." Collected in Axelrod and Deese, forthcoming.

_____. *The Edge of the Image.* Seattle: University of Washington Press, 1967, 20, 24-57, 183, 187, 227, 229.

Wiebe, Dallas E. "Mr. Lowell and Mr. Edwards," *Contemporary Literature,* 3 (Spring-Summer 1962), 21-31.

Wilbur, Richard. "On Robert Lowell's 'Skunk Hour.' " In *The Contemporary Poet as Artist and Critic,* ed. Anthony Ostroff. Boston: Little, Brown, 1964, 84-87.

Williams, William Carlos. "In a Mood of Tragedy," *New York Times Book Review,* 22 Apr. 1951, p. 6. Reprinted in his *Selected Essays.* New York: Random House, 1954. Collected in London and Boyers, in Parkinson, and in Price.

Williamson, Alan. *Introspection and Contemporary Poetry.* Cambridge: Harvard University Press, 1984, 15-25, 149-153.

_____. "The Reshaping of 'Waking Early Sunday Morning,' " *Agenda,* 18 (Autumn 1980), 47-62.

Willis, Gary. "The Masculine and the Feminine as Seen in the Poetry of Robert Lowell," *English Studies in Canada,* 6 (1980), 444-459.

Willis, G. D. "Afloat on Lowell's *Dolphin," Critical Quarterly,* 17 (Winter 1975), 363-376.

Woodson, Thomas. "Robert Lowell's 'Hawthorne,' Yvor Winters and the American Literary Tradition," *American Quarterly,* 19 (Fall 1967), 575-582.

Yankowitz, Susan. "Lowell's *Benito Cereno:* An Investigation of American Innocence," *Yale/Theatre,* 1 (Summer 1968), 81-90.

Yenser, Stephen. "Half Legible Bronze?," *Poetry,* 123 (Feb. 1974), 304-309.

Zapatka, F. E. "Moreana in the Poetry of Robert Lowell," *Moreana,* 51 (1976), 148-152.

BIBLIOGRAPHICAL ESSAY

Bibliographies and Checklists

Jerome Mazzaro's *The Achievement of Robert Lowell: 1939-1959* (1960) is a descriptive bibliography divided into four parts: books by Lowell; books containing Lowell contributions not previously published in his own volumes; uncollected poems, articles, reviews, and letters; and materials about Lowell. Although it contains 347 items in all, the volume's main drawback is that it is now decades out of date. Unfortunately, it remains the only bibliography of Lowell's individual poems yet to see print; readers interested in journal publication of Lowell's poems from 1960 onward have no single source to consult. Checklists of Lowell's volumes, articles, and reviews have appeared, but there is still a need for a comprehensive bibliography of primary materials.

Steven Gould Axelrod and Helen Deese's *Robert Lowell: A Reference Guide* (1982), which supersedes Mazzaro's book as a source for secondary material, is a fully annotated bibliography of works about Lowell from 1943 (the first year such material appeared) through 1980. In principle, it includes every book, dissertation, article, chapter, and review written in English about the poet during those years, as well as significant references to the poet in books not centrally concerned with him. Interviews with Lowell are treated, as are articles by him if they refer directly to his life or work. This *Reference Guide* contains 1,736 entries, each of which includes a description of the item's contents. In addition, the book lists significant editions of Lowell's books and features an introductory essay analyzing main currents in Lowell criticism.

In sum, Mazzaro's bibliography is an essential reference tool for primary materials through 1959, and Axelrod and Deese's bibliography is indispensable for secondary materials through 1980.

Biography: Book

Thus far, only one biography devoted solely to Lowell has appeared: Ian Hamilton's *Robert Lowell: A Biography* (1982). This work serves an important function for any reader interested in Lowell's life, but it should be used with caution. Detailing the day-to-day events in Lowell's life, it rarely examines the internal drama of his psyche and imagination. Its resultant superficiality is a major drawback, since for a poet like Lowell the true center of his life was not in outward happenings but in the movements of his mind. In addition, Hamilton occasionally uses creative works—Lowell's poems and memoirs, and short stories by his friends—as if they were trustworthy guides to what really happened. But poems, stories, and even memoirs (when they are written by someone as creative as Lowell) are essentially works of design rather than truth; they ought not to be mistaken for accurate representation. This biography is a mausoleum of facts and "factoids" (as Norman Mailer would say), but the real, living Lowell makes only occasional appearances.

The reader of Hamilton's biography should be on guard for three different but related kinds of distortion. First, the book is subtly slanted against Lowell. From its opening portrait of the little boy who alternately bullied his classmates and sulked, to the later depictions of the man who behaved "callously" to his parents, friends, wives, and lovers and who, in his last years, engaged in a series of "winter antics" and "Easter dramas," this book casts a consistently negative light on everything Lowell said, did, and felt. Yet between the lines, one glimpses a very different Lowell: the young boy who was tortured by his parents' neurotic behavior; the man who cared deeply for those who loved him and who felt ashamed of hurting them during episodes of mental illness; and the dying poet who faced his end with dignity, eloquence, generosity, and wisdom. One must read against the thrust of Hamilton's narrative to discover this more attractive and fully rounded figure.

In addition to deprecating Lowell as a person, Hamilton tends to undervalue Lowell's accomplishments as a poet. He calls *Lord Weary's Castle* a "welter of grabbed myths and pseudosymbols" and *The Mills of the Kavanaughs* a collection of "cardboard characters" and "dramatic monologues that all sound the same." He finds *Life Studies* frequently "pedestrian" though also "shrewd" and "revolutionary"; *Imitations* full of "mechanical poeticizing"; *For the Union Dead* "over-deliberate and without . . . energy and grace"; *The Old Glory* "threadbare"; *Near the Ocean* "facile" and "complacent"; *Notebook* "sprawling" and "uneven"; and *Day by Day* "almost meandering" and a sort of confession of life-long failure. Hamilton is one of the most severe critics Lowell has had. He fully approves of only a handful of poems— "Waking in the Blue," "Soft Wood," half of "Night Sweat," "perhaps thirty" lines in *Lord Weary's Castle*, possibly "Waking Early Sunday Morning"—about ten pages of Lowell's work. While reading this biography, one should keep in mind that it was written not by an advocate and supporter but by a skeptic, even perhaps an opponent.

Finally, Hamilton shows little understanding of Lowell's interior world and imagination. He labels the poet's mental disorder "almost certainly incurable" but makes no attempt to fathom its causes or content. Similarly, although Lowell obsessively claimed that writing was central to his existence—"if I stop writing, I stop breathing" (*History*, p. 169)—Hamilton pays little attention to the role poetry played in Lowell's life. Indeed, the critic seems to devalue the kind of imagination Lowell possessed. For Hamilton, poetry is allied to rhetoric; it is a matter of "wit and wordplay." For Lowell, on the other hand, poetry was a matter of self-creation, an all-consuming passion, a quest for the truth of existence. He once said that "the artist finds new life in his art and almost sheds his other life" (A. Alvarez, "A Talk with Robert Lowell, 1965").

Thus Hamilton lacks sympathy with Lowell's life, his poetry, and his conception of art. His biography is densely packed with factual details, but it is unreliable in its assumptions and its evaluations.

Biographies: Major Articles and Book Sections

The only work that presently competes with Hamilton's biography is C. David Heymann's *American Aristocracy* (1980), a composite biography of the Lowell family that devotes several hundred pages to Robert Lowell. This work shares many of the weaknesses of Hamilton's biography: it too is superficial, it too is unsympathetic to Lowell and his poetry (though less so than Hamilton's book), and it too conveys little understanding of the poet's imaginative life. Furthermore, containing much less detail than does Hamilton's book, it tells Lowell's story from a distance. Although Heymann's account does occasionally provide useful information about episodes in the poet's life—for example, his imprisonment for draft refusal during World War II and his early, disastrous marriage to Jean Stafford—the book does not substantially contribute to an understanding of Lowell's life.

The memoirs of Lowell's friends and associates provide warmly human insights into the poet, thereby helping to dispel the chill created by the major biographies. The reminiscences of James Atlas, Frank Bidart, Philip Booth, Esther Brooks, Richard Elman, Seamus Heaney, John Crowe Ransom, and John Thompson are especially thoughtful and revealing.

In addition, Lowell serves as the model for characters in a number of impressive imaginative works: "Jim Prewitt" in Peter Taylor's

"1939"; "Daniel" in Jean Stafford's "A Country Love Story" and "Theron" in her "An Influx of Poets"; "Lowell" in Norman Mailer's "nonfiction novel" *The Armies of the Night;* and the mysterious "he" in Elizabeth Hardwick's *Sleepless Nights.* Although one must remember that these are works of fiction rather than biography, they nevertheless reveal fascinating sidelights on Lowell at various stages of his life, as does Elizabeth Bishop's memorial poem, "North Haven," which concludes:

> And now—you've left
> for good. You can't derange, or re-arrange,
> your poems again. (But the Sparrows can their song.)
> The words won't change again. Sad friend, you cannot change.

Selected Interviews

Lowell's interviews often rise to the status of creative texts, on a par with his poems and plays (and his best essays, too). In addition, they function as invaluable sources of information.

Perhaps best is the 1961 interview conducted by Frederick Seidel for the *Paris Review.* Lowell speaks to Seidel about a wide range of topics: his genesis as a poet; his sense of the interrelations between art and experience; his debts to other poets; the poems of *Lord Weary's Castle, Life Studies,* and *Imitations;* and, above all, the stylistic upheaval that produced *Life Studies.* This interview is the source of Lowell's comment that poetry has "become a craft, purely a craft, and there must be some breakthrough back into life," and many other oft-quoted remarks.

A. Alvarez's 1963, 1965, and 1976 interviews are noteworthy in a slightly different way. Probably the most sympathetic of all Lowell's interviewers, Alvarez encourages his subject to speak frankly and confidently about confessional poetry and contemporary politics. In the *London Observer* interview, which was revised for the *Review,* Lowell primarily discusses *Life Studies:* "The needle that prods into what really happened may be the same needle that writes a good line." In *Encounter,* he speaks mostly of cultural and political topics: John Kennedy, Sigmund Freud, Abraham Lincoln, the American character, American obsessions, and the American style of poetry. Lowell's role as a critic of culture emerges more clearly in this interview than almost anywhere else.

As an interviewer, Ian Hamilton is far less sympathetic than Alvarez, yet his distance from Lowell's viewpoint produces lively exchanges. In this 1971 interview, Lowell covers much ground: his decision to take up residence in England; his poems in *For the Union*

Dead, Life Studies, Near the Ocean, and *Notebook;* his feelings about other poets and his own career; his politics; his audience; *Benito Cereno;* and more. Hamilton tries to lead Lowell into literary gossip, and occasionally succeeds, but he also elicits serious commentary from his subject. When Lowell describes Flaubert, for example, he implies his ego-ideal for himself: "I feel he was ferociously in it, in his misses as well as his successes . . . he believed in form, a form not like the Goncourts and Maupassant, but irregular and heart-stained—the grace of anonymity, the gross of one person."

Stanley Kunitz's 1964 *New York Times Book Review* interview is also valuable, especially for revealing the poet's thoughts at the time *For the Union Dead* was published. Lowell broaches a variety of familiar themes: his attitudes toward other poets, especially ones who influenced him; the difference between prose and poetry; the "kind of poet" he is, the kind of poetry he writes, and his purposes in writing poetry at all.

John McCormick's 1953 interview is similarly helpful, in revealing Lowell's thoughts at the time *The Mills of the Kavanaughs* was published. V. S. Naipaul's interview explores the evolution of Lowell's ideas sixteen years later when *Notebook 1967-68* (1969) appeared. (Naipaul, incidentally, is a sympathetic interviewer, and again, as in the case of Alvarez, one can sense the poet opening up in response.) The interviews by Lieberson (1965), Billington (1967), and Gilman (1968), and a final interview with Alvarez (1976) focus on Lowell's dramaturgy. Donald S. Carne-Ross's 1968 *Delos* interview is the best guide to the poet's attitudes toward translation. Lowell's 1961 "conversation" with Cleanth Brooks and Robert Penn Warren is relaxed and informal, if not particularly informative.

A 1971 *New York Times Book Review* encounter with Dudley Young perhaps caused Lowell to resist granting other interviews. For much of its length, it resembles a dialogue of the deaf:

> Q: If someone found important public meanings in ["For the Union Dead"] and said "This poem strikes deeply in the body politic," wouldn't you be pleased?
>
> A: But I don't know what "strikes deeply" means.

Still, Lowell does make some telling remarks about *Notebook* and about being in England. Although only the 1976 conversation with Alvarez followed the Young interview, Lowell allowed Christopher Ricks to quote from a conversation about *The Dolphin* in his 1973 critical essay. The poet himself summed up his life in art in the last essay he published in his lifetime, "After Reading Six or Seven Essays About Me" (1977).

Critical Studies: Books and Pamphlets

There are six introductory books on Lowell, all of them reliable and helpful. Jay Martin's Minnesota Pamphlet, *Robert Lowell* (1970), is the briefest and most elegant of these. This extended essay views Lowell's work as a poetry of contraries, in which the experience of an apocalyptic present interacts with a powerful sense of the past. Perceptively discussing Lowell's poetry both in its own terms and as a reflection of larger cultural issues, the essay's major drawback is that it covers Lowell's work only through *Notebook 1967-68*.

Richard J. Fein's Twayne book, *Robert Lowell* (1970; revised edition, 1979), contains full and intelligent readings of Lowell's poetry and plays. Like Martin's essay, Fein's volume focuses on "both a private and a common world": the poems as elaborate and conscious verbal constructions that express the poet's unique viewpoint, and as reflections of our time and place. Fein provides an almost ideal guide for the first-time reader of Lowell. Although the first edition of this book discusses Lowell's work only through *Near the Ocean*, the revised edition has been expanded to encompass Lowell's whole career and has been strengthened in other ways; yet it unfortunately omits any extended discussion of *Near the Ocean* and somewhat slights Lowell's final volumes as well.

John Crick's *Robert Lowell* (1974) provides well-balanced and insightful commentary on Lowell's poetic works. In general terms, it identifies in the poetry a movement from religious dramas to a more colloquial treatment of a wide variety of psychological, political, and universal themes. This book covers Lowell's work through *Notebook* (1970). Vivian Smith's *The Poetry of Robert Lowell*, published the same year as Crick's book, is a workmanlike compendium of interpretation and explication similarly designed for new readers of Lowell. It too covers Lowell's work through *Notebook*.

Two introductory books of the 1980s are Burton Raffel's entry in the Ungar Modern Literature series, *Robert Lowell* (1981), and Mark Rudman's contribution to the Columbia Introductions to Twentieth-century American Poetry series, *Robert Lowell: An Introduction to the Poetry* (1983). Both can be recommended, though neither offers any spectacular insights beyond those contained in the books by Martin, Fein, and Crick. Raffel's study is valuable for its discussion of Lowell's theory and practice of imitation. Rudman's is written with eloquence and imagination, and is often highly sensitive to linguistic and thematic nuance. Both treat Lowell's whole career, including the last volumes.

Eleven specialized studies of Lowell have thus far been published, ranging from excellent to misguided. The first of these works to appear was Hugh Staples's *Robert Lowell: The First Twenty Years* (1962), a preliminary but enduringly valuable assessment. This study, written in the style of the New Criticism, emphasizes verbal exegesis and source identification. It also pays some attention to Lowell's thematic movement from "dissatisfaction," to "rebellion," and finally to a "partial acceptance of the order of things." Although Staples's comments on such matters are relatively brief, they are intelligent and serious.

Staples's book has two limitations. The first is that it emphasizes technical questions at the expense of ideas and theories; the second is that, because of its publication date, it treats only three of Lowell's major texts—*Lord Weary's Castle, The Mills of the Kavanaughs,* and *Life Studies.* Nevertheless, Staples's book is frequently distinguished on the subject of *Lord Weary's Castle* and remains an essential commentary on that volume. Especially noteworthy is its reading of "The Quaker Graveyard in Nantucket" as a late addition to "the great tradition of the English elegy." Staples's major insights have been repeated—and inevitably diluted—in the work of most subsequent critics of Lowell's early work.

The second specialized study to appear was Jerome Mazzaro's *The Poetic Themes of Robert Lowell* (1965). This valuable book is in some ways the perfect complement to Staples's. It alludes to a wide variety of contexts that illuminate the works: Roman Catholic belief, ritual, and tradition; classical myth; twentieth-century theories of art; comparative literature; the history of ideas. Mazzaro's thesis is that in Lowell's first major texts (*Lord Weary's Castle* and *The Mills of the Kavanaughs*), he sought to "merge" techniques from the Catholic meditative-contemplative tradition with those from literary tradition, whereas in his subsequent volumes (*Life Studies* and *For the Union Dead*), he dealt with disordered, secular experience without these supporting schema. In the latter volumes, Mazzaro declares, Lowell eliminated "the archetypal framework of meditation" and broke with "Joycean ideas" as well.

One problem for readers of this book is that Mazzaro occasionally loses control of his argument or extends it too far, lapsing into self-contradiction on the one hand or dubious assertion on the other. Another problem is that the book, like Staples's, is best on Lowell's early volumes. Nevertheless, it remains highly important for students of the early works; its discussions help form the basis for all informed study of the first phase in Lowell's career.

Phillip Cooper's *The Autobiographical Myth of Robert Lowell* (1970) finds formal and thematic "ambivalence" to be the principle that governs Lowell's poetry and unifies the canon in spite of its apparent diverseness. Unfortunately, Cooper discovers ambivalence and ironies proliferating everywhere. His thesis, though essentially sound, leads to some poems being misread. Despite this defect, Cooper's modest book is often rewarding. Lowell himself liked it: in a letter to Steven Axelrod he called it "sensitive" though not authoritative. It covers Lowell's work through *Notebook 1967-68* and is perhaps most interesting (though often furthest out on a limb) when discussing *For the Union Dead.*

Patrick Cosgrave's *The Public Poetry of Robert Lowell* (1970) seems misguided. The opposite of Cooper's study, this one is self-intoxicated and grandiose. Working through the canon from *Lord Weary's Castle* to *Near the Ocean,* Cosgrave insistently measures Lowell's poems against his own preference for clear, public, traditional meaning and judgment, and finds the works generally wanting. This kind of procedure seems a no-win strategy for analyzing poetry—not just Lowell's but anyone's. Either the poem measures up to the critic's ideas or it does not; either readers agree with the critic's viewpoint, in which case they find themselves affirmed, or they disagree, in which case they find themselves unenlightened. In either case, readers learn little about the poetry.

Nor do they even learn about the critic's viewpoint, since it is largely a matter of assumption and assertion rather than argument. Cosgrave mimics the attitudes of F. R. Leavis and, especially, Yvor Winters, but does not share their learning or wisdom. The moments of openness and discovery that occur in Winters's best criticism do not occur in Cosgrave's work; instead, it projects a self-congratulatory, self-preserving voice intent on hectoring its subject.

R. K. Meiners's brief *Everything to Be Endured: An Essay on Robert Lowell and Modern Poetry* (1970) sees Lowell's poetry as a struggle between estrangement and transcendence. Comparing Lowell to the nineteenth-century English poet and critic Matthew Arnold (who refused to write a poetry reflecting a condition in which there was "everything to be endured and nothing to be done") and to the American fugitive poet Allen Tate (who did write such a poetry), Meiners traces Lowell's desperate but frustrated poetic efforts to move beyond solipsistic despair. This critic asserts that although Lowell's poetry characteristically exposes "the personality pushed to its last limits," his best work (in *Lord Weary's Castle* and *Life Studies*) nonetheless contains moments of affirmation that point toward Christian transcendence. Readers interested in religious studies or the history of ideas should find this essay thought provoking. They may, however, be disappointed by its "cryptic" conclusion expressing, but not elaborating, a wish for "a vision which, if not of something so large as the whole, is yet more than a point edging into Nothing."

Marjorie G. Perloff's *The Poetic Art of Robert Lowell* (1973) is a book that every student of Lowell will want to read. At its best, it contains some of the most illuminating and innovative analyses of Lowell's artistry ever committed to print. It is at its worst in its attack on *Imitations*, momentarily sacrificing light for heat. Its best is contained in its chapter analyzing the metonymic mode of *Life Studies*— the volume's method of exposing character and meaning through "selected, patterned detail." This chapter is the essential starting point for all sophisticated thinking about Lowell's stylistic breakthrough in *Life Studies*. Nearly as important are the chapters on imagery, on syntax, and on the "Winslow elegies." The methodology of these chapters varies, but the perceptiveness is constant.

Perloff's study generally avoids a volume-by-volume approach, instead moving back and forth among Lowell's texts in order to investigate the "purely literary aspects" of his work. It finds *Life Studies* and *For the Union Dead* to be his greatest achievements. By its interpretive subtlety and theoretical sophistication, this book pushed Lowell criticism well beyond previously established frontiers. It remains a central study.

Despite its title, Alan Williamson's *Pity the Monsters: The Political Vision of Robert Lowell* (1974) is less interested in narrowly political issues than in the psychoanalysis of culture. The influential texts behind this work are Freud's *Civilization and its Discontents*, Herbert Marcuse's *Eros and Civilization*, and Norman O. Brown's *Life Against Death*. Williamson portrays Lowell's poetry as a deeply pessimistic questioning of civilization. He acknowledges the visionary power of *Lord Weary's Castle* and the emotional profundity of *Life Studies*, but for him Lowell's most important achievements are in his subsequent volumes. Williamson contends that *For the Union Dead* begins to forge a public conscience compounded of pacifism, skepticism, primordial energy, and moral righteousness; *Near the Ocean* constitutes an achieved prophetic text; while *Notebook* approximates an "absolute language" that can make use of every moment of private and public experience.

All three volumes, the critic believes, are based on a psychoanalytical conception of self and history, and they express an authentic desire for political change.

Although the theoretical framework of *Pity the Monsters* may no longer be current, it is not by any means irrelevant to contemporary concerns. In a sense, this book forges a valuable link between the intellectual life of the late 1960s and that of the present day. What Williamson sees and likes in Lowell's poetry are "its uncertainty and openness, its skepticism about ideas of order that amount to national or class self-ratification, its hesitation to exclude anyone from the bounds of empathy." In addition, Williamson's readings of individual poems are always thoughtful and often provocative. The limitations of *Pity the Monsters* are that it does not interest itself in specific political events and that (since it was published in 1974) it does not take Lowell's final volumes into account. The book's strengths are its serious intellectual ambitions and its illuminating commentary on texts—especially "The Quaker Graveyard in Nantucket," "Memories of West Street and Lepke," and the whole of *Near the Ocean* and *Notebook*.

Stephen Yenser's *Circle to Circle: The Poetry of Robert Lowell* (1975), which confines itself to matters of form, style, and theme, gives Lowell's poems probably the most intensive and sustained aesthetic scrutiny that they have ever received. Since Yenser is a resourceful, subtle, and adventurous critic, *Circle to Circle* serves as an excellent guidebook to the verbal features of Lowell's poetry. Yenser sees the poems of *Lord Weary's Castle* and *The Mills of the Kavanaughs* as characterized by dialectical symbolism and the use of contradiction. In later volumes, Yenser argues, Lowell extends his structural principles beyond the boundaries of individual poems: *Life Studies* is a sustained sequence, while *For the Union Dead, Imitations,* and *Notebook 1967-68* are shaped as circles or inverted cones. Throughout Yenser's book, the reader witnesses the drama of Lowell's effort "to fulfill an epic ambition with essentially lyric means."

Circle to Circle contains a series of close readings of poems and whole volumes, and this narrow focus is the book's strength, since it allows the critic to investigate linguistic and structural matters in great depth. This constructed focus also produces some inevitable limitations, which are the price of its strength: the book does not emphasize ideas or contexts, and, because it is tied so closely to Lowell's works, it cannot easily be read straight through as a narrative. Yet its individual passages and chapters do effectively stimulate readers' own thinking about particular Lowell works. For that purpose, there may be no better book.

Steven Gould Axelrod's *Robert Lowell: Life and Art* (1978) provides a well-rounded portrait of Lowell as a working artist, from the beginning of his career to the end. It is, in a sense, a biography of his imagination, of his creative life. As a work of criticism, this volume may suffer from excessive caution: it is intended to get things right, not to make a splash. Such a strategy exacts a toll, for if the book contains no bizarre misreadings, neither does it offer many critical milestones. Still, it does provide unusually sustained readings of Lowell's major poems, and in its analysis of *The Dolphin*—that Axelrod, unlike most other critics, regards as a masterwork—it proves quite innovative as well.

As a work of scholarship, *Robert Lowell: Life and Art* merits attention in several respects. It carefully analyzes Lowell's discipleship first to Allen Tate and then to William Carlos Williams; it uncovers the complex genealogy of the poem "For the Union Dead"; and it attempts to place Lowell, despite appearances to the contrary, in the American tradition of Ralph Waldo Emerson. Readers should find this book valuable for its information, its interpretations, its conceptual framework, and its evocation of the Lowell spirit.

Vereen M. Bell is a man with a thesis, and he rides it hard; he speaks at one point of being "obedient" to it. The thesis of *Robert Lowell: Nihilist as Hero* (1983) is that "Lowell's poetry is identifiable by nothing so much as its chronic and eventually systematic pessimism. One is hard pressed to come forward with even remotely sanguine or assuaging poems from Lowell's canon." There is some truth in this assertion, and readers must be grateful to Bell for elaborating on it. Nevertheless, when he converts pessimism (which Lowell had in abundance) into an absolute nihilism, he carries his argument too far.

Most readers sense that one of Lowell's aims in writing poetry was to "support"—and a nihilist does not normally wish to support. Lowell's "Epilogue" contains a prayer for "grace" of accuracy, and the poem's conclusion beautifully mixes pessimism with affirmation. Readers similarly recall poems like "For the Union Dead," which balances its images of "savage servility" with portraits of human exemplars (Colonel Shaw and his black troops, William James, and the brave Negro schoolchildren), and "Skunk Hour," which ends with the celebrated image of a mother skunk that "will not scare"—an implication that the speaker will not either. (Bell, incidentally, skews his otherwise fine interpretation of "Skunk Hour" by refusing to acknowledge the element of freedom that makes the speaker's ultimate choice meaningful.) These poems that assert or imply centers of redemptive value are not unusual, as Bell suggests, but are characteristic of Lowell.

For its insight Bell's book is well worth reading. He has unique eloquence and something serious to say. Still, readers must be careful not to suspend their disbelief. Bell himself seems aware of his propensity to go to extremes and frequently undermines his own argument. For example, he speaks in one sentence of Lowell's willingness "to yield to the implications of a nihilism of such an absolutized form," only to speak in the very next of Lowell's "wholly understandable reluctance to accept the consequences of his own vision." It is that second, qualifying Bell who is the more convincing critic.

Norma Procopiow's *Robert Lowell: The Poet and the Critics* (1984) provides a useful summary of forty years of criticism, yet Procopiow mixes penetrating comments on the criticism with more introductory comments on the poetry itself, as if she were not wholly sure of the needs of her audience. In its introductory mode, the book at times reads like a study aid; in its more sophisticated mode, however, it should appeal to, and be genuinely illuminating for, scholars who are interested in the poet and his critics. It probes a larger number of issues concerning Lowell than does any other book in existence.

Procopiow has organized her book around themes in Lowell's canon rather than around trends and motifs in the critical discourse. Chapters focus on Lowell's imitations and re-creations; his religious positions; his Matthew Arnold-like critiques of public mores; his stylistic development from "modern" to "postmodern"; and his prose essays. As a result, critics are trotted in to ornament the discussion of whatever Lowell text happens to be center stage at that particular moment—they are props rather than leading characters in the book. Nevertheless, despite what seems a structural limitation, Procopiow's study is rich in ideas and throws much new light on the intellectual context that has grown up around Lowell's work. Just as the book valuably recapitulates forty years of words about words, so will it inevitably initiate many more years of debate.

Critical Studies: Collections of Essays

Of the six collections of essays that have appeared to date, the first four are comprised largely or entirely of reprinted material and are very worth consulting. The earliest, Thomas Parkinson's *Robert*

Lowell: A Collection of Critical Essays (1968), is probably the most significant, since most of the reviews and essays in it have become standard. The collection gathers articles by Randall Jarrell on *Lord Weary's Castle*, Irvin Ehrenpreis on "the Age of Lowell," M. L. Rosenthal on Lowell's "poetry of confession," John Berryman on "Skunk Hour," Thomas Parkinson on *For the Union Dead,* and Donald S. Carne-Ross on Lowell's translations (see Critical Studies: Major Articles and Book Sections). In addition, Parkinson's volume contains Seidel's interview with Lowell, and Lowell's own analysis of "Skunk Hour."

Michael London and Robert Boyers's *Robert Lowell: A Portrait of the Artist in His Time* (1970) also provides a generous selection of valuable material. It too reprints material that has become standard, including the Jarrell and Ehrenpreis discussions, the Seidel interview, and a revised version of Rosenthal's essay, all of which had earlier appeared in the Parkinson collection. London and Boyers also include, among other notable articles, Herbert Leibowitz's study of Lowell's sense of history, discussed below.

Jerome Mazzaro's *Profile of Robert Lowell* (1971) collects most of the major interviews of Lowell, omitting only those by Seidel and Hamilton. It contains the interviews conducted by Alvarez, Kunitz, Billington, Gilman, Carne-Ross, and Naipaul. Among its noninterview contents, it reprints Charles Altieri's excellent analysis of the style of *Life Studies.*

Jonathan Price's *Critics on Robert Lowell* (1972) rounds up many of the usual suspects, including, again, Jarrell, Ehrenpreis, and Rosenthal. In addition, this volume reprints Christopher Ricks's illuminating study of *For the Union Dead.*

The first collection of new material, Rolando Anzilotti's *Robert Lowell: A Tribute* (1979), is aptly subtitled. The product of a reunion held a year after the poet's death by people who "wanted to do homage to his memory," the book contains anecdotal memoirs and informal appreciations. It is valuable primarily for readers interested in Lowell as a man or in the Italian reception of his work.

Steven Gould Axelrod and Helen Deese's forthcoming *Robert Lowell: Essays on the Poetry* (1986) features new articles that seek to expand critical horizons. After an introduction by Axelrod and a psychoanalytical study by Jay Martin, essays by Albert Gelpi, Sandra M. Gilbert, Lawrence Kramer, Marjorie Perloff, Alex Calder, Calvin Bedient, Alan Holder, Helen Deese, A. Kingsley Weatherhead, and George McFadden proceed through Lowell's poetic canon in roughly chronological order. All of these articles are discussed below.

Critical Studies: Special Issues of Journals

There are no journals or newsletters wholly devoted to the study of Lowell. Three journals, however, have devoted one or two individual issues to the poet. The two special issues of the *Harvard Advocate* are largely personal, anecdotal, and informal; the 1979 number is intended as a memorial tribute. The two issues of *Salmagundi* and the single issue of *Agenda* are critically more substantial. Articles by Herbert Leibowitz and Thomas Parkinson in the first *Salmagundi*, Robert Hass in the second *Salmagundi*, and Wyatt Prunty, Alan Williamson, and Neil Corcoran in *Agenda* are mentioned in the discussion below.

Critical Studies: Major Articles and Book Sections

Virtually all the articles and book sections listed in the accompanying checklist offer valuable insights and information, but for readers just beginning study of Lowell, three articles, taken together, provide an excellent introduction to the arc of the poet's career. These essays are Jay Martin's "Grief and Nothingness," Randall Jarrell's "From the Kingdom of Necessity," and Lawrence Kramer's "Freud and the Skunks."

Martin's "Grief and Nothingness," a psychoanalytical study, sympathetically traces the process by which Lowell attempted to redeem his debilitating sense of abandonment, loss, and mourning through his poetry. In addition to identifying a motive and theme revealed to be dominant in Lowell's major texts, this essay tells us more in twenty-five pages about Lowell the man than Hamilton's biography is able to do in 500. It thus proves the superiority of insight over the mere amassing of biographical detail. This new essay, which appears in the Axelrod and Deese collection, is the first to see Lowell's life and art as intimately related parts of a whole. It is sure to become a standard critical interpretation.

Jarrell's "From the Kingdom of Necessity" is already standard; indeed, it is generally recognized as the instigation of the Lowell critical industry. Despite its classic status, it is as fresh as the day it first appeared in 1947. Brilliantly written and wonderfully perceptive, it reads the poems of *Lord Weary's Castle* as developing the conflict between a "kingdom of necessity," where all is closed and turned inward, and a "realm of freedom," where everything is open to change and possibility. This essay has powerfully conditioned thirty years of critical reading of Lowell's first major volume. Furthermore, it seems to have conditioned or prophesied Lowell's ensuing career, which exposes a recurrent struggle to move from necessity to freedom.

Kramer's "Freud and the Skunks" is an important reading of *Life Studies*, the volume in which Lowell most dramatically broke away from his "kingdom of necessity" and moved toward liberation. Kramer argues that Lowell's ironic poetic rhetoric does not contrast with his painful and passionate content, as most earlier critics have implied, but rather is allied with it in an evasion of psychoanalytical cure. In some respects a challenge to Martin's thesis and in other respects a confirmation of it, this essay is studded with insights into individual poems and is unified by a provocative and sophisticated argument. Making its first appearance in the Axelrod and Deese collection, Kramer's article too is sure to become a standard reading.

Among general studies are those provided by five excellent book-length studies of post-World War II American poetry: Charles Altieri's *Enlarging the Temple: New Directions in American Poetry During the 1960s* (1979), James E. B. Breslin's *From Modern to Contemporary: American Poetry, 1945-1965* (1984), Karl Malkoff's *Escape from the Self: A Study of Contemporary American Poetry and Poetics* (1977), Alan Williamson's *Introspection and Contemporary Poetry* (1984), and Robert von Hallberg's *American Poetry and Culture: 1945-1980* (1985). All five devote substantial sections to Lowell. Williamson's and von Hallberg's books, which focus on *The Dolphin* and *History* respectively, will be discussed below. Altieri's, Breslin's, and Malkoff's volumes include more general treatments of Lowell's poetry. The three are related to each other, since they compose a sort of dialogue, an absorbing one, about the character of contemporary poetry and about Lowell in particular.

Altieri, in his study of the "aesthetic of presence" in the poetry of the 1960s, examines Lowell's canon from *Lord Weary's Castle* through *Notebook*, noting the ways Lowell's break from Modernism and humanism seems to him powerful but also "solipsistic and extreme." Malkoff, adopting a critical perspective derived from Norman O. Brown, Stanley Burnshaw, and Marshall McLuhan, argues that Lowell's poetry is not self-involved but the opposite, an "abandonment of the . . . traditional ego." Focusing on *Life Studies* and the sonnet sequences, Malkoff suggests that Lowell's merging of the boundaries of the self and the other eliminates solipsism as even a theoretical possibility. Breslin argues that Lowell sought to "renovate" his art by "going outside literature to a referential language and an open poetics." Like his predecessors, this critic emphasizes *Life Studies* as the apex of Lowell's career, and like Malkoff, he denies that Lowell's confessional poetry is solipsistic. For Breslin, *Life Studies* is an "effort to find a way of writing that would preserve, rather than annihilate, his life." All three of these studies focus on the poet's creation in language of a "self," though the conclusions Malkoff and Breslin draw about that self oppose those of Altieri.

Among the other general essays, three—all excellent—concentrate on Lowell as a public poet. Alan Holder's chapter on Lowell in *The Imagined Past* (1980), which studies the poet's ongoing concern with the American and New England past, finds a fruitful ambivalence in Lowell's best historical works—"In Memory of Arthur Winslow," "The Quaker Graveyard in Nantucket," and "For the Union Dead." Herbert Leibowitz's "Robert Lowell: Ancestral Voices" (1967) also examines the poet's sense of history—which, the critic suggests, takes the form of a "talking contest" with voices from the past. Dwight Eddins's "Poet and State in the Verse of Robert Lowell" (1973) explores Lowell's changing attitudes toward the state, attitudes that range from a Christian sense of justice in *Lord Weary's Castle* to a moral, stoical refusal of engagement in *Notebook*.

In 1965 Irvin Ehrenpreis provided an influential overview of Lowell's career to that date in his essay "The Age of Lowell." More recently, Monroe K. Spears has reviewed Lowell's development from *Life Studies* through *Near the Ocean* in *Dionysus and the City* (1970); Robert Pinsky has discussed Lowell's use of voices in "For the Union Dead" and *History* in *The Situation of Poetry* (1976); Robert G. Twombly, in "The Poetics of Demur: Lowell and Frost" (1976), has analyzed Lowell's rhetorical relationship to his reader in "Terminal Days at Beverly Farms" and "Dolphin"; and Steven Gould Axelrod has analyzed the fate of the poet's reputation in an "era of biography" in the introduction to *Robert Lowell: Essays on the Poetry.* Two other essays by Axelrod, "Baudelaire and the Poetry of Robert Lowell" (1971) and "Robert Lowell and Hopkins" (1985), chart Lowell's shifting relations to those two precursors, whom the American poet himself linked together in one of his earliest prose essays, "Hopkins and Baudelaire." Finally, Marjorie G. Perloff, in the Axelrod and Deese collection, has traced the personal affiliations between Lowell and John Berryman in "*Poetes Maudits* of the Genteel Tradition," and Shozo Tokunaga has compared the two poets' early poetry in "Private Voice, Public Voice" (1975).

Among more specialized studies of Lowell's separate phases, Jarrell's "From the Kingdom of Necessity" (1947) is, of course, the inevitable starting point for anyone concerned with Lowell's early volumes. His evaluation of *The Mills of the Kavanaughs* in "A View of Three Poets" (1951) is important too. Appearing in the Axelrod and Deese collection, Albert Gelpi's thoughtful "Robert Lowell: The Fall from Prophecy to Irony" seeks to revise upward the position of *Lord Weary's Castle* in Lowell's canon. Carefully and sympathetically explicating many of the volume's poems, Gelpi finds a committed witness to the world and a spiritual resonance that is absent from the poet's later work.

A more personal reconsideration is Richard J. Fein's eloquent *"Lord Weary's Castle* Revisited" (1974), a revised version of which has been incorporated into the second edition of his *Robert Lowell.* The most thorough analysis of the political background of the early volumes is Jerome Mazzaro's "Robert Lowell's Early Politics of Apocalypse" (1970). This fascinating article sheds considerable light on the rightist milieu of the poet's young manhood.

Other valuable essays include A. Kingsley Weatherhead's study of Lowell's Coleridgean imagination in *The Edge of the Image* (1967) and J. Barton Rollins's analysis of "Young Robert Lowell's Poetics of Revision" (1979). Two especially noteworthy readings of "The Quaker Graveyard in Nantucket" are Heather Dubrow's "The Marine in the Garden" (1983) and Robert Hass's "Lowell's Graveyard" (1977). George Lensing's "Robert Lowell and Jonathan Edwards" (1974) examines the two poems about Edwards in *Lord Weary's Castle.* Finally, Jerome Mazzaro's "Robert Lowell and the Kavanaugh Collapse" (1969) explicates the title poem of *The Mills of the Kavanaughs* in terms of its Ovidian motifs, and Wyatt Prunty's "Allegory to Causality" (1980) discovers in the poem evidences of Lowell's shift from a Christian to an empiricist concept of the world.

Life Studies has generally been judged a milestone in Lowell's career, and it has inspired some superb critical writing—for example, Kramer's, Malkoff's, and Breslin's discussions, previously treated in this essay. Two pioneering studies are M. L. Rosenthal's examination of Lowell's "Confessional" art, the perfected version of which appears in *The New Poets* (1967), and Marjorie Perloff's "Realism and the Confessional Mode of Robert Lowell" (1970), which was later revised and reprinted in her *Poetic Art of Robert Lowell.* Rosenthal was the first to insist that the seemingly personal poetry of *Life Studies* has a crucial public dimension as well—that the poet makes his psychological anguish embody the predicament of his civilization. Perloff focuses on Lowell's formal innovations in *Life Studies.* She argues that Lowell begins with the lyrical "I" of Romantic convention and fuses it with the "metonymic" descriptive mode of prose realism. One or both of these essays can be detected in the substratum of virtually every subsequent treatment of *Life Studies*.

Charles Altieri's "Poetry in a Prose World" (1970) has been another important and influential essay on *Life Studies*. Writing from an implicitly phenomenological perspective, Altieri arrives at conclusions congruent with those of both Rosenthal and Perloff. He finds that in *Life Studies* Lowell exchanged his earlier symbolic mode supporting "vertical" levels of meaning for an experience-centered mode projecting only "horizontal," secularized meanings.

Other major interpretations include George McFadden's " 'Life Studies'—Robert Lowell's Comic Breakthrough" (1975), which emphasizes Lowell's use of the "Freudian myths" of maturation and the family romance, as well as his comic strategy; and Steven K. Hoffman's genre study, "Impersonal Personalism" (1978). Finally, there are some important individual readings: John Berryman's imaginative and highly influential study, "On Robert Lowell's 'Skunk Hour' " (1964); Sandra M. Gilbert's recent discussion in the Axelrod and Deese collection, "Mephistophilis in Maine," which stresses Lowell's anxieties about himself; and George Lensing's brief but resonant essay, " 'Memories of West Street and Lepke': Robert Lowell's Associative Mirror" (1970).

Lowell's next volume, *Imitations,* has been the subject of relatively few critical essays, and most of those that have appeared have focused on the quality and theory of Lowell's art of translation. Perhaps the definitive defense of the volume is Donald S. Carne-Ross's "The Two Voices of Translation" (1968), which treats Lowell's translations as "the probing encounter between two linguistic and cultural mediums" rather than as transcriptions that strive merely for accuracy. Ben Belitt has written another significant defense in "*Imitations:* Translation as Personal Mode" (1966-1967), while John Simon has articulated the prosecution's case in "Abuse of Privilege: Lowell as Translator" (1967).

Perhaps the best introduction to Lowell's *For the Union Dead* remains Gabriel Pearson's "Robert Lowell" (1969). This essay argues that "many of Lowell's later poems are, as it were, frayed, have holes or chunks eaten out," but that they remain "upright, columnar assertions of the human will to survive its own madness and self-destruction." The title poem itself is "militantly braced against the dissolution it utters." Eloquently pointing up the stylistic and thematic play of order and chaos, Pearson's essay illuminates not merely *For the Union Dead* but Lowell's poetic practice in general.

Other useful essays are Christopher Ricks's admiring and sensitive "The Three Lives of Robert Lowell" (1965) and Thomas Parkinson's thought provoking attack on Lowell's language, *"For the Union Dead"* (1967). Many studies of the volume's title poem have appeared, most of which trace its allusions and ancestry. The most thorough of these is Steven Gould Axelrod's "Colonel Shaw in American Poetry" (1972), parts of which are reprinted in his *Robert Lowell: Life and Art.* Michael North's "The Public Monument and Public Poetry" (1980) finds that Lowell's poem elevates the St. Gaudens bas-relief of Colonel Shaw and his men to the level of moral lesson.

Daniel Hoffman's "The Greatness and Horror of Empire" (1971) provides a sound overview of Lowell's next book of poetry, *Near the Ocean.* It focuses on Lowell's parallel between the Roman and American Empires, and it branches out to discuss *Imitations* and *The Old Glory* as well. Three essays that provide helpful interpretations of *Near the Ocean*'s first poem, "Waking Early Sunday Morning," are Elizabeth Lunz's "Robert Lowell and Wallace Stevens on Sunday Morning" (1971), Mary Kinsie's "The Prophet Is a Fool" (1977), and Alan Williamson's "The Reshaping of 'Waking Early Sunday Morning'" (1980). In "From Satire to Description" (1969) Patricia Meyer Spacks compares Lowell's version of Juvenal's "The Vanity of Human Wishes" to Samuel Johnson's.

Of Lowell's four dramatic texts, the first and the last—*Phaedra* and *The Oresteia*—have received very little critical attention. Only Jerome Mazzaro's "The Classicism of Robert Lowell's *Phaedra*" (1973) stands out as a sustained analysis, and it is vitiated by an overemphasis on Lowell's "Ovidian views." A number of essays have valuably analyzed the plays of *The Old Glory* trilogy in terms of their political perspectives and their literary and historical sources. These include Albert E. Stone's "A New Version of American Innocence: Robert Lowell's *Benito Cereno*" (1972), which compares Lowell's drama to Captain Delano's narrative and Melville's novella; Baruch Hochman's "Robert Lowell's *The Old Glory*" (1967), which focuses on the trilogy's presentation of "antithetical impulses"; Mark W. Estrin's "Robert Lowell's *Benito Cereno*" (1973); Robert Ilson's *"Benito Cereno* from Melville to Lowell" (1967); and John P. McWilliams, Jr.'s "Fictions of Merrymount" (1977). Helpful readings of Lowell's penultimate play are Jerome Mazzaro's *"Prometheus Bound:* Robert Lowell and Aeschylus" (1973); M. Byron Raizis's "Robert Lowell's *Prometheus Bound*" (1969); and Jonathan Price's "Fire Against Fire" (1967).

Lowell's sonnet sequences of 1969-1973 received mixed to hostile notices when they appeared, but their critical reputations have subsequently risen. Two essays in the forthcoming Axelrod and Deese collection testify to renewed interest in these works. By closely examining Lowell's revisions, Alex Calder in *"Notebook 1967-68:* Writing the Process Poem" arrives at a number of fresh observations about the structure and significance of that volume and of its successors, *Notebook* and *History.* Calder finds Lowell closer to Derridean and Foucaultian notions of textuality than other poets with whom he might be compared—for example, Charles Olson or John Berryman. Calvin Bedient in "Illegible Lowell" provides the most thorough and perceptive analysis available of Lowell's style in his sonnet sequences. He focuses on the poet's use of metonymy, metaphor, heteroglossia, and his multiple linguistic nuances.

Robert von Hallberg's chapter on *History* in his 1985 *American Poetry and Culture, 1945-1980* provides a superb reading of that volume. Equally sensitive to style and to culture (though less so to overall form), von Hallberg examines *History*'s verbal and tonal characteristics as well as its ideological allegiances. He portrays Lowell as a consensus liberal—both optimistic about man's ability to change his world for the better and cosmopolitan in his vision—who maintained a powerful integrity by defending such values at a time when liberalism was under attack from every direction. Von Hallberg concludes that "postwar liberalism had sufficient range of vision and intelligence, and commanded enough emotional power, to enable a poet of unusual ability to write the sort of book that guarantees him the status of major poet." Although considerably more modest in scope, Carol Lee Saffioti's "Between History and Self " (1981) supplies a useful sidelight on *History* by examining the function of its Alexander poems.

The Dolphin has also received a number of sophisticated commentaries. Alan Williamson's 1984 *Introspection and Contemporary Poetry* examines how Lowell, in turning on himself, "casts himself into the round" and defines his whole consciousness in a humbling yet ultimately liberating fashion. Steven Gould Axelrod's "Lowell's *The Dolphin* as a 'Book of Life' " (1977), reprinted in his *Robert Lowell: Life and Art,* treats the volume not only as the telling of a story but as a self-reflexive story of telling. A third valuable essay is Neil Corcoran's "Lowell's *Retiarius:* Towards *The Dolphin*" (1980).

Lowell's last book of poetry, *Day by Day,* is the subject of a number of significant essays appearing in the Axelrod and Deese collection. George McFadden's " 'Prose or This'—What Lowell Made of a Diminished Thing" provides probably the best overview of the volume. Placing it in the context of Lowell's completed canon, McFadden examines its use of prose resources and its development of strategies to compensate for creative loss. Alan Holder's somewhat more stringent "Going Back, Going Down, Breaking" arrives at conclusions that are in the main congruent with McFadden's. Like McFadden, Holder compares this volume to Lowell's earlier work and discovers in the book recurring patterns that manifest a sense of diminishment. A. Kingsley Weatherhead, taking the most stringent view of all in *"Day by Day:* His Endgame," laments the loss of imaginative power that he detects in the volume.

Finally, there are three more specialized studies of *Day by Day* worth noting. Robert Fitzgerald provides an early but illuminating close reading of "Ulysses and Circe" in "Aiaia and Ithaca" (1977). In their collection of critical essays, Steven Gould Axelrod concludes his "Introduction: Lowell's Living Name" with an interpretation of "George III," and Helen Deese, in "Lowell and the Visual Arts," underscores the findings of both McFadden and Holder by pointing out pastoral elegy motifs throughout *Day by Day.* Deese also studies Lowell's relationship to the artists Vermeer, Van Eyck, and Rembrandt and to photography, principally in *Day by Day* but also in *History.* This essay is essential reading for anyone interested in the significance of Lowell's allusions to painting and photography in his poetry.

Howard Nemerov

(1920-)

Deborah S. Murphy and Gloria Young
Kent State University

PRIMARY BIBLIOGRAPHY

Books

The Image and the Law. New York: Holt, 1947. Poems.

The Melodramatists. New York: Random House, 1949. Novel.

Guide to the Ruins. New York: Random House, 1950. Poems.

Federigo, or, the Power of Love. Boston: Little, Brown, 1954; London: Gollancz, 1955. Novel.

The Salt Garden. Boston & Toronto: Little, Brown, 1955. Poems.

The Homecoming Game. New York: Simon & Schuster, 1957; London: Gollancz, 1957. Novel.

Mirrors & Windows. Chicago: University of Chicago Press, 1958. Poems.

A Commodity of Dreams & Other Stories. New York: Simon & Schuster, 1959; London: Secker & Warburg, 1960. Stories.

New & Selected Poems. Chicago: University of Chicago Press, 1960. Poems.

Endor: Drama in One Act. New York & Nashville: Abingdon Press, 1961. Play.

The Next Room of the Dream: Poems and Two Plays. Chicago: University of Chicago Press, 1962. Poems, plays.

Poetry and Fiction: Essays. New Brunswick, N.J.: Rutgers University Press, 1963. Essays.

The Blue Swallows. Chicago & London: University of Chicago Press, 1967. Poems.

The Winter Lightning: Selected Poetry. London: Rapp & Whiting, 1968. Poems.

Stories Fables & Other Diversions. Boston: Godine, 1971. Stories.

Reflexions on Poetry & Poetics. New Brunswick, N.J.: Rutgers University Press, 1972. Essays.
Gnomes & Occasions. Chicago: University of Chicago Press, 1973. Poems.
The Western Approaches: Poems. Chicago & London: University of Chicago Press, 1975. Poems.
The Collected Poems of Howard Nemerov. Chicago: University of Chicago Press, 1977. Poems.
Figures of Thought: Speculations on the Meaning of Poetry and Other Essays. Boston: Godine, 1978. Essays.
Sentences. Chicago: University of Chicago Press, 1980. Poems.
Inside the Onion. Chicago: University of Chicago Press, 1984. Poems.
New and Selected Essays. Carbondale: Southern Illinois University Press, 1985. Essays.

Journal

Journal of the Fictive Life. New Brunswick, N.J.: Rutgers University Press, 1965.

Selected Essays

Barfield, Owen. *Poetic Diction: A Study in Meaning,* introduction by Nemerov. New York: McGraw-Hill, 1964, 1-9.
Williams, Miller. *A Circle of Stones,* foreword by Nemerov. Baton Rouge: Louisiana State University, 1964, vii-x.
"The First Count[r]y of Places." In *Images and Ideas in American Culture: The Functions of Criticism, Essays in Memory of Philip Rahv,* ed. Arthur Edelstein. Hanover, N.H.: Brandeis University Press, 1979, 158-168.

Translations

Dante. *Convito,* Dissertation 2, Canzone 1, translated by Nemerov as "The Banquet," *Wake,* 10 (1951), 98-100. Reprinted in *Lyric Poetry of the Italian Renaissance,* ed. L. R. Ling. New Haven: Yale University Press, 1954. Reprinted in *Lyrics of the Middle Ages,* ed. Hubert Creekmore. New York: Grove, 1959. Reprinted in *The Western Approaches: Poems.*
Rilke, Rainer Maria. *Kindheit,* translated by Nemerov as "Childhood,"

Silo, 13 (Spring 1968), 71-72. Reprinted in *The Western Approaches: Poems.*

Edited Books

Longfellow, Henry Wadsworth. *Longfellow, Selected Poems*, edited with an introduction by Nemerov. New York: Dell, 1959.
Moore, Marianne. *Poetry & Criticism*, ed. Nemerov. Cambridge, Mass.: Adams House & Lowell House Printers, 1965.
Poets on Poetry, ed. with a preface and essay by Nemerov. New York: Basic Books, 1966.

Filmed Interview

One on One. Kent, Ohio: Kent State University Television Center, 5 Oct. 1979.

Recordings

The Poetry of Howard Nemerov, 2 audiocassettes. Jeffrey Norton, 1962.
The Spoken Arts Treasury of 100 Modern Poets, Volume 14. Spoken Arts, 1978. Nemerov, William Meredith, May Swenson, Richard Wilbur, Lawrence Ferlinghetti, and Howard Moss read from their own poetry.
Howard Nemerov. Tapes for Readers, 1978.
Howard Nemerov. Tapes for Readers, 1979.

SECONDARY BIBLIOGRAPHY

Bibliographies

Duncan, Bowie. *The Critical Reception of Howard Nemerov: A Selection of Essays and a Bibliography.* Metuchen, N.J.: Scarecrow Press, 1971, 145-211. Primary and secondary. See also Collection of Essays.
Wyllie, Diana E. *Elizabeth Bishop and Howard Nemerov: A Reference Guide.* Boston: G. K. Hall, 1983. Primary and secondary.

Selected Interviews

Bowers, Neal, and Charles L. P. Silet. "An Interview with Howard Nemerov," *Massachusetts Review,* 22 (Spring 1981), 43-57.

Bowers and Silet. "An Interview with Howard Nemerov," *Poet and Critic,* 11 (1979), 35-38.

Boyers, Robert. "An Interview with Howard Nemerov," *Salmagundi,* nos. 31, 32 (Fall/Winter 1975), 109-119.

Cargas, Harry James. "An Interview with Howard Nemerov," *Webster Review,* 1 (Spring 1974), 34-39.

Castro, Jan. "Interview with Howard Nemerov," *Webster Review,* 5 (Fall 1980), 5-15.

Crinklaw, Donald. "Vibrations of a Literary Misanthrope: An Interview with Howard Nemerov," *St. Louisan,* 7 (Sept. 1975), 52-55, 66-69. Reprinted in *Biography News,* 2 (Nov./Dec. 1975), 1294-1297.

Gerstenberger, Donna. "An Interview with Howard Nemerov," *Trace,* no. 35 (Jan./Feb. 1960), 22-25. Collected in *The Critical Reception of Howard Nemerov,* ed. Bowie Duncan. See Collection of Essays.

"An Interview of Howard Nemerov," *Island,* 4 (Fall 1966), 2-8.

Labrie, Ross. "Howard Nemerov in St. Louis: An Interview," *Southern Review,* new series, 15 (Summer 1979), 605-616.

Critical Studies: Books

Bartholomay, Julia A. *The Shield of Perseus: The Vision and Imagination of Howard Nemerov.* Gainesville: University of Florida Press, 1972.

Labrie, Ross. *Howard Nemerov.* Boston: Twayne, 1980.

Meinke, Peter. *Howard Nemerov.* Minneapolis: University of Minnesota Press, 1968. Reprinted in *Seven American Poets from MacLeish to Nemerov,* ed. Denis Donoghue. Minneapolis: University of Minnesota Press, 1975.

Mills, William. *The Stillness in Moving Things: The World of Howard Nemerov.* Memphis, Tenn.: Memphis State University Press, 1975.

Critical Studies: Collection of Essays

Duncan, Bowie, ed. *The Critical Reception of Howard Nemerov: A Selection of Essays and a Bibliography.* Metuchen, N.J.: Scarecrow Press, 1971.

Critical Studies: Major Articles and Book Sections

Adams, Robert M. "Everyone's Miscellany," *Hudson Review,* 17 (Spring 1964), 146-148.
Benoit, Raymond. "The New American Poetry," *Thought,* 44 (Summer 1969), 201-218.
Bewley, Marius. "Books," *Partisan Review,* 28 (Winter 1961), 141-142.
Boyers, Robert. "Howard Nemerov's True Voice of Feeling," *American Poetry Review,* 4 (May/June 1975), 4-9. Reprinted in *Excursions: Selected Literary Essays,* ed. Boyers. Port Washington, N.Y.: Kennikat Press, 1975.
Burke, Kenneth. "Comments on Eighteen Poems by Howard Nemerov," *Sewanee Review,* 60 (Winter 1952), 117-131.
_____. "Introduction." In Nemerov. *New and Selected Essays.* Carbondale: Southern Illinois University Press, 1985, vii-xxx.
_____. "Recommended Summer Reading," *American Scholar,* 37 (Summer 1968), 518.
Ciardi, John. "Dry and Bitter Dust," *Saturday Review,* 44 (Fall 1961), 66.
Conarroe, Joel. "Visions and Revisions," *Shenandoah,* 19 (Summer 1968), 78-81. Collected in Duncan.
Davidson, Peter. "New Poetry: The Generation of the Twenties," *Atlantic,* 221 (Feb. 1968), 142.
DeMott, Benjamin. "Assertions, Appreciations," *New York Times Book Review,* 16 Apr. 1978, p. 11.
Deutsch, Babette. "Chiefly Ironists," *New Republic,* 28 Apr. 1973, pp. 25-26.
Dickey, James. "The Death and Keys of the Censor," *Sewanee Review,* 69 (Spring 1961), 331-332.
_____. "Some of All of It," *Sewanee Review,* 64 (Spring 1956), 333-336. Reprinted in his *The Suspect in Poetry.* Madison, Minn.: Sixties Press, 1964. Reprinted in his *Babel to Byzantium: Poets & Poetry Now.* New York: Farrar, Straus & Giroux, 1968.
Dickey, William. "Hopes for Explosions," *Hudson Review,* 16 (Summer 1963), 307-310.

Dobie, Ann B. *"The Poet as Critic,* The Stillness in Moving Things: The World of Howard Nemerov," *Southern Review,* new series, 12 (Fall 1976), 891-894.

Eagleton, Terry. "New Poetry," *Stand,* 17 (Fall 1975), 69-70.

Eberhart, Richard. "Five Poets," *Kenyon Review,* 14 (Winter 1952), 174-175.

Flint, R. W. "Holding Patterns," *Parnassus,* 3 (Spring/Summer 1975), 27-34.

Gage, John T. Review of *Figures of Thought, Journal of Aesthetics and Art Criticism,* 37 (Spring 1979), 373-376.

Galassi, Jonathan. "Determined Forms," *Poetry,* 129 (Dec. 1976), 164-166.

Gilman, Harvey. "Unassuming Virtuoso," *Chicago Review,* 25 (1973), 193-195.

Goldberg, Maxwell H. "The Reticulum as Characteristic Metaphor." In *Images and Innovations: Update 1970's,* ed. Malinda R. Maxfield. Spartanburg, S.C.: Center for the Humanities, Converse College, 1979, 68-84.

Golffing, F. C. "Question of Strategy," *Poetry,* 71 (Nov. 1947), 94-97. Collected in Duncan.

Gordon, Ambrose, Jr. Review of *New and Selected Poems, Carleton Miscellany,* 2 (Winter 1961), 116-120. Collected in Duncan.

Gunn, Thom. "Outside Faction," *Yale Review,* 50 (Summer 1961), 586-588.

_____."Seeing and Thinking," *American Scholar,* 28 (Summer 1959), 394-396.

Hartman, Geoffrey H. "Words and Things," *Partisan Review,* 32 (Winter 1965), 137-139.

Harvey, Robert D. "A Prophet Armed: An Introduction to the Poetry of Howard Nemerov." In *Poets in Progress: Critical Prefaces to Ten Contemporary Americans,* ed. Edward B. Hungerford. Evanston, Ill.: Northwestern University Press, 1962, 116-133. Collected in Duncan.

Hecht, Anthony. "Writers' Rights and Readers' Rights," *Hudson Review,* 21 (Spring 1968), 213-315.

Hillyer, Robert. "A Dark, Bleak Spaciousness," *New York Times Book Review,* 17 July 1955, p. 4. Collected in Duncan.

Howard, Richard. "Comment." In *Preferences,* ed. Howard. New York: Viking, 1974, 205-207.

_____. "Some Poets in Their Prose," *Poetry,* 105 (Mar. 1965), 400-403.

Jacobsen, Josephine. Review of *Figures of Thought, Modern Language Notes,* 93 (Dec. 1978), 1089-1091.

Jarrell, Randall. "Recent Poetry," *Yale Review,* 45 (Autumn 1955), 126-128. Collected in Duncan.

Jerome, Judson. "A Poetry Chronicle—Part 1," *Antioch Review,* 23 (Spring 1963), 113-115.

Johnson, Tom. "Ideas and Order," *Sewanee Review,* 86 (Summer 1978), 445-453.

Johnson, W. R. Review of *The Next Room of the Dream, Carleton Miscellany,* 4 (Spring 1963), 120-124. Collected in Duncan.

Kiehl, James M. "The Poems of Howard Nemerov: Where Loveliness Adorns Intelligible Things," *Salmagundi,* nos. 22/23 (Spring/Summer 1973), 234-257. Reprinted in *Contemporary Poetry in America: Essays and Interviews,* ed. Robert Boyers. New York: Schocken Books, 1974.

Kinzie, Mary. "The Judge is Rue," *Poetry,* 138 (Sept. 1981), 344-350.

_____. "The Signature of Things: On Howard Nemerov," *Parnassus,* 6 (Fall/Winter 1977), 1-57.

Kizer, Carolyn. "Nemerov: The Middle of the Journey," *Poetry,* 93 (Dec. 1958), 178-181. Collected in Duncan.

Koch, Vivienne. "The Necessary Angels of Earth," *Sewanee Review,* 59 (Autumn 1959), 674-675. Collected in Duncan.

Kumin, Maxine. "On Howard Nemerov's *Journal of the Fictive Life.*" In her *To Make a Prairie: Essays on Poets, Poetry, and Country Living.* Ann Arbor: University of Michigan Press, 1979, 69-71.

Kunitz, Stanley. "Many Exertions, Some Excellences," *New York Times Book Review,* 21 July 1963, pp. 4-5.

Lieberman, Laurence. "New Poetry in Review," *Yale Review,* 58 (Autumn 1968), 140-141. Reprinted in *Unassigned Frequencies: American Poetry in Review, 1964-77,* ed. Lieberman. Urbana: University of Illinois Press, 1977.

Malkoff, Karl. "Howard Nemerov." In *Crowell's Handbook of Contemporary American Poetry,* ed. Malkoff. New York: Crowell, 1973, 220-222.

Meinke, Peter. "Howard Nemerov." In *Seven American Poets from MacLeish to Nemerov: An Introduction,* ed. Denis Donoghue. Minneapolis: University of Minnesota Press, 1975, 250-286.

_____. "Twenty Years of Accomplishment," *Florida Quarterly,* 1 (Oct. 1968), 81-90. Collected in Duncan.

Oates, Joyce Carol. "Finding Again the World," *University of Windsor Review,* 4 (Spring 1969), 70-76.

_____. Review of *Figures of Thought, New Republic,* 8 Apr. 1978, pp. 29-31.

Olsen, Douglas H. "Such Stuff as Dreams: The Poetry of Howard Nemerov." In *Imagination and the Spirit: Essays in Literature and the Christian Faith Presented to Clyde S. Kilby,* ed. Charles Huttar. Grand Rapids, Mich.: Eerdmans, 1971, 365-385.

Perkins, David. "The Collected Nemerov," *Poetry,* 132 (Sept. 1978), 351-355.

Pettingell, Phoebe. "Frozen and Fluid Images," *New Leader,* 67 (30 Apr. 1984), 16-17.

_____. "Irony, Tragedy, and Violence," *New Leader,* 5 Dec. 1977, pp. 14-15.

Price, Martin. "Open and Shut: New Critical Essays," *Yale Review,* 53 (Summer 1964), 598-599.

Prunty, Wyatt. "Permanence in Process: Poetic Limits that Delimit," *Southern Review,* new series, 15 (Winter 1979), 265-271.

Ramsey, Paul. "To Speak, or Else to Sing," *Parnassus,* 4 (Spring/Summer 1976), 130-138.

Randall, Julia. "Genius of the Shore: The Poetry of Howard Nemerov," *Hollins Critic,* 6 (June 1969), 1-12. Reprinted in *The Sounder Few: Essays from the Hollins Critic,* ed. R. H. W. Dillard, George Garrett, and John R. Moore. Athens: University of Georgia Press, 1971. Collected in Duncan.

_____. "Howard Nemerov." In *Contemporary Poets,* ed. James Vinson. New York: St. Martin's Press, 1980, 1094-1097.

_____. "Saying the Life of Things," *American Poetry Review,* 5 (Jan.-Feb. 1976), 46-47.

Robinson, James K. "Sailing Close-hauled and Diving into the Wreck: From Nemerov to Rich," *Southern Review,* new series, 11 (Summer 1975), 669-671.

Rosenthal, M. L. *The Modern Poets: A Critical Introduction.* New York: Oxford University Press, 1961, 255-261.

_____. *The New Poets: American and British Poetry Since World War II.* New York: Oxford University Press, 1967, 310-312, 319.

_____. " 'Something that Might Simply Be,' " *Reporter,* 12 Sept. 1963, pp. 54-56.

Rosten, Norman. Review of *Mirrors & Windows, Venture,* 3 (Spring 1959), 75-77. Collected in Duncan.

Rubin, Louis D., Jr. "Revelation of What is Present," *Nation,* 13 July 1963, pp. 38-39.

_____. "Well Worth the Saying," *Kenyon Review,* 26 (Spring 1964), 411-414. Collected in Duncan.

Schaefer, Anita. "Nemerov's *Mot juste* and the Fashionable Poetic," *Publications of the Arkansas Philological Association,* 8 (Fall 1982), 68-76.

Shaw, Robert B. "Making Some Mind Out of What Was Only Sense," *Nation,* 25 Feb. 1978, pp. 213-215.

Smith, Raymond. "Nemerov and Nature: 'The Stillness in Moving Things,'" *Southern Review,* new series, 10 (Winter 1974), 153-169.

Spiegelman, Willard. "Alphabeting the Void: Poetic Diction and Poetic Classicism," *Salmagundi,* no. 42 (Summer/Fall 1978), 132-145.

Stock, Robert. "The Epistemological Vision of Howard Nemerov," *Parnassus,* 2 (Fall/Winter 1973), 156-163.

Van Duyn, Mona. "The Poet as Novelist," *Poetry,* 109 (Feb. 1967), 332-339.

Vendler, Helen. "Wisdom Poetry," *New York Times Book Review,* 18 Dec. 1977, pp. 14, 29. Reprinted in her *Part of Nature, Part of Us: Modern American Poets.* Cambridge: Harvard University Press, 1980.

Waggoner, Hyatt. *American Poets from the Puritans to the Present.* Boston: Houghton Mifflin, 1968, 610-614.

Whitehill, Karen. "A Virtuoso Versifier," *Virginia Quarterly Review,* 54 (Spring 1978), 368-372.

Whittemore, Reed. "Introduction." Collected in Duncan, xi-xii.

_____. "Observations of an Alien," *New Republic,* 23 May 1958, pp. 27-28. Collected in Duncan.

Williams, Miller. "Transactions with the Muse," *Saturday Review,* 9 Mar. 1968, p. 32. Collected in Duncan.

Wright, James. "Some Recent Poetry," *Sewanee Review,* 66 (Fall 1968), 666-668.

Young, Gloria L. " 'The Fountainhead of All Forms': Poetry and the Unconscious in Emerson and Howard Nemerov." In *Artful Thunder: Versions of the Romantic Tradition in American Literature in Honor of Howard P. Vincent,* ed. Robert J. DeMott and Sanford E. Marovitz. Kent, Ohio: Kent State University Press, 1975, 241-267.

BIBLIOGRAPHICAL ESSAY

Kenneth Burke's introduction to Howard Nemerov's *New and Selected Essays* (1985), which also may serve as an introduction to this essay, provides an overview of Nemerov's "tripartite psychic economy." Burke defines the "harmonious relationship" of Nemerov's roles as poet, critic, and teacher. Discussing the "Poeticizer" in terms of "what it is like to be a poet," particularly a Nemerovian poet, Burke uses Nemerov's essay "Thirteen Ways of Looking at a Skylark" (*Figures of Thought*, 1978) to equate his poetic practice with "power." Asking "what it is to be poetry," the critic discusses the essay "Poetry and Meaning" (*New and Selected Essays*) to show that Nemerov's prose theorizing is "wisdom." Addressing "what it is to be a really great poem," Burke treats Nemerov's "The Dream of Dante" (*New and Selected Essays*) to show how the teacher—the connoisseur of poetry—is the one who communicates through "classroom homiletics" the greatness of the poem. The teacher ties together the poet and the critic and thus complements power and wisdom with "spirit," the "communicative bond between them," Burke declares. Through these and his other essays, the critic discusses what he considers to be the main characteristics of Nemerov's poetry—"Complexity, Complicity, Duplicity, Perplexity"—subjects that constantly reappear in the criticism of Nemerov's work.

Bibliographies

There are two bibliographies of Nemerov's work, both of which are valuable. Bowie Duncan's *The Critical Reception of Howard Nemerov: A Selection of Essays and a Bibliography* (1971) consists of three parts, with an introduction by Reed Whittemore. Part I, "Overviews," reprints four excellent assessments of Nemerov's work: Julia Randall's "Genius of the Shore" (1969); Peter Meinke's "Twenty Years of Accomplishment" (1968); Donna Gerstenberger's "An Interview with Howard Nemerov" (1960); and Robert Harvey's "A Prophet Armed" (1962). Part II collects two or three reviews on every book published by Nemerov from his first, *The Image and the Law,* through his twelfth, *The Blue Swallows.* These reviews provide excellent discussions of Nemerov's poetry as well as illuminate the evolving critical opinion on his work. Part III, the bibliography, extending to 1970, is quite useful. For each collection of Nemerov's poems or essays, Duncan identifies material printed for the first time; works that were published earlier in periodicals are listed chronologically in the section recording periodical appearances. Yet another part of the bibliography shows Nemerov's poems reprinted in anthologies. Duncan's book contains thirty-one pages of primary items and thirty-two pages of secondary, carefully annotated items.

Diana E. Wyllie's *Elizabeth Bishop and Howard Nemerov: A Reference Guide* (1983) devotes 116 pages to a primary and secondary bibliography of Nemerov. Commenting in her introduction that both Nemerov and Bishop work "outside the various 'schools' of contemporary poetry," Wyllie finds Nemerov's "enormous variety" his most characteristic element: "He writes funny, meditative, bitter, thoughtful, cynical, amusing, light-hearted, deeply moving, and, at times, pontifical works." She labels each new book surprising in its juxtaposition of lyric poems with ironic aphorisms, and she is fascinated by the range of his subject matter. The reference guide itself is well organized, carefully annotated, and easy to use. The items in the secondary bibliography are listed alphabetically for each year, beginning with 1947 and going through 1981, although Wyllie warns the reader that the 1981 entries are not complete. This guide both updates and, in some instances, corrects the Duncan bibliography.

Selected Interviews

Of the many interviews with Nemerov, those of Robert Boyers, Ross Labrie, and Neal Bowers/Charles L. P. Silet reveal the most about his life, personality, thought, and poetry. Filled with quotations from and discussions of literature, philosophy, science, and linguistics, these interviews demonstrate Nemerov's erudition, humility, humor, and sensitivity.

In his 1975 *Salmagundi* interview, Boyers asks Nemerov about his process of composition. The poet replies that he usually thinks in blank verse, that he had written all of his free verse when he was young and thus did not have to do any later, and that a new poem starts with a "line not an idea: if I get an idea I'm pretty sure I can't write it . . . whereas a poem just speaks itself in me when I'm composing. It's really kind of uncanny, though mind you I'm not claiming heaven-sent inspiration . . . but it feels like some kind of privileged condition." Nemerov goes on to say that he does not deny the need for "a little skill at carpentering the stuff together, so you find the rhyme at the right time, the rhyme that maybe gives you an idea you wouldn't have had if you didn't have to find a rhyme."

What the poem says, according to Nemerov, should be "as clear as you can make it" in its literal meanings, but what it means may be mysterious "because the universe is mysterious and vast, and doesn't need to mean one thing." The great writers must be committed to both clarity and mysteriousness, and the really great ones, Nemerov declares, are Dante, Socrates, Shakespeare, sixteenth-century French essayist Michel Eyquem de Montaigne, and Sigmund Freud—Freud because "he tells you always the process of his thought," and Montaigne because of his lack of arrogance in saying, "I have no subject but ignorance and profess nothing but myself."

In this interview Nemerov also discusses the origins of such poems as "Bee-Keeper," "The Mud Turtle," and "Celestial Globe." He expresses his opinion of Auden (a decent middle-range voice) and of "naked" poetry (it had better be a warm climate and beautiful), defines his method of writing (fast), lays down a law for poets and politics (say what the world is, not what it ought to be), and comments on his influences ("I was influenced by everybody. . . . What is marvelous is . . . how the poem can sound like all the others and still be itself "). He says he became a poet instead of a novelist when Bennington College hired Malamud as its "novelist" and kept him as its "poet."

Covered in Labrie's "Howard Nemerov in St. Louis" (1979) are many subjects, ranging from Nemerov's war experience ("boredom and terror") to his use of imagery from both Judaism and Christianity. Nemerov declares that he believes poetry relates to religion but that he is suspicious of moral systems. He says that he grew up with the New Criticism, which he regards as good and sensible but perhaps worn out; on such "new new criticism" as structuralism, he comments, "it's remarkable how little of it seems new when you cut through the enormous vocabulary and apparatus for milling around confusedly." Nemerov discusses his rule for reading a poem—"Read what's in the poem; don't read what's not in the poem"—but he also says that he modifies this approach in his teaching because "once you understand what the poem says, you can have fun ranging as widely as possible." The interview rapidly addresses additional subjects such as art as obsession, Nemerov's preoccupation (according to Labrie) with perception, and Nemerov's patterning of the "prosaic with violence" and of the serious with the comic. Other subjects touched upon are nominalism and realism, Thomas Mann, science, mathematical language, Wallace Stevens, riddles, physics and biology, and imagism. All in all, this twelve-page conversation provides insights into Nemerov's thought but Labrie tries to make one interview do too much.

The questions asked by Bowers and Silet in their 1981 *Massachusetts Review* interview clearly stimulate Nemerov to lengthy reminiscences and ruminations, and when the poet is allowed to ramble, the trip with him is worth the taking. On his writing he declares: "When it's there it's wonderful and it's easy, and when it's not there it's impossible. . . . It's always remarkable to me that one thing should follow another. . . . Those little epigrams, gnomes, they tell you I'm not going to be the *Iliad.*" On rhyme Nemerov says that because of laziness he tends to write longer poems in blank verse but shorter ones in rhyme. On the development of his poetry he declares that there's no point in being embarrassed about the "silly" things he did when he was young: "Of course you live life forward and think about it backwards." Bowers and Silet ask Nemerov to respond to a list of adjectives describing qualities of his poetry: to "reflective," he says, "Yes, meditative"; to "emotional," he declares, "sometimes dramatic, but not very"; to "pessimistic," he answers, "pessimism has gone out of fashion"; and to "the serious and the funny," he replies, "must be both or else we'd fly apart."

When asked if he is "mellower," Nemerov says, "Well, you're looking at the complacent, smug old slob instead of the nasty, mean young slob." Questioned about how he reacts to criticism of his poetry, he responds that one gets "inured to that" but admits being annoyed by "public contumely followed by private apologies . . . guys writing sneaky little letters saying, 'I didn't really mean to destroy your book.' Well, they didn't destroy my book." One of the most enjoyable features of this conversation is the sense conveyed of Nemerov's simply enjoying himself and chatting with friends. When one of the interviewers asks him if he thinks his poetry is getting simpler—and adds, "I don't mean to say simpleminded"—Nemerov answers, "I would accept simpleminded." This is a charming, useful discussion.

Critical Studies: Books

Peter Meinke in his University of Minnesota Pamphlet *Howard Nemerov* (1968), provides an excellent forty-five page discussion. One of the earliest critics to discuss at length Nemerov's work, Meinke also includes useful biographical information. He details Nemerov's early life as a privileged young man who attended the Fieldston School and then Harvard University, who joined the Royal Canadian Air Force as a fighter pilot and later the Eighth U.S. Army Air Forces. Meinke notes that Nemerov married Margaret Russell, an Englishwoman, and that they have three sons. He outlines the poet's teaching career at Hamilton College in New York, at Bennington College in Vermont, at the University of Minnesota, at Hollins College in Virginia, at Brandeis University in Massachusetts, and at Washington University in St. Louis, where he has remained since 1969.

Meinke believes Nemerov's background in both the city and the country has set up the "deeply divided personality," the "opposed elements" in his character, the tensions in his "romantic and realistic visions" that affect his work. According to Meinke, Nemerov, "more than any other contemporary poet," is the spokesman for the "existential, science-oriented (or science-displaced), liberal mind of the twentieth century." The critic asserts that the poetry reflects Nemerov's Jewishness, his Puritanism, his wit, and his intelligence. Of the World War II poets, Meinke believes Nemerov and Lowell have held up the best.

In discussing many of the poems in Nemerov's first seven books of poetry, concluding with *The Blue Swallows*, Meinke defines polarities of Nemerov's thought: physics/theology; reality/imagination; pain/ significance; terror/beauty; hopelessness/indomitability. In addition, the critic reveals the progression of Nemerov's major themes: in *The Image and the Law* (1947) the poet develops the structure of the eye as "image" and the mind as "law"; in *Guide to the Ruins* (1950) he writes the war out of his system along with the influence of Eliot, Yeats, and Stevens; in *The Salt Garden* (1955) he reaches his poetic maturity, finds his voice—a brooding, lyrically beautiful, tragically lonely voice. In all of these first three books, Meinke views Nemerov as a "nonpracticing Jew engaged in a continual dialogue with Christianity . . . testing its relevance in the modern world," yet always affirming his essential Jewishness. *The Salt Garden* also deepens Nemerov's sense of the primitive, "brute" world, the unknown Other of the phenomenal world as well as of the unconscious. The idea of death has moved from the death of war to death as a part of nature, "time's ruining stream," the critic asserts.

In the following four books Meinke shows a poet becoming a "master of his craft" in which rhythm, image, and sound fuse. *Mirrors & Windows* (1958) reveals that Nemerov can control "internal despair with external craftsmanship," the critic says. Many of his best poems— "To Lu Chi," "Painting a Mountain Stream," "Writing," for example— are about the craft of writing poetry; the major images of the book are "life-reflecting mirrors, and windows through which we see with the poet's 'infinitely penetrant' eye." In *New & Selected Poems* (1960) the central work is "Runes," a dream fantasy whose theme is mutability. *The Next Room of the Dream* (1962), according to Meinke, is directed toward philosophy and includes the two plays *Cain* and *Endor*, which are more successful as verse than as drama; the poem that summarizes the philosophy of the book, in Meinke's opinion, is "Nothing Will Yield," in which art smashes on the rocks of reality, and interpretation itself is only "the next room of the dream." *The Blue Swallows* (1967) shows progression both in art and in theme, Meinke contends. Nemerov has become less "bitter and more sad" and employs specifically contemporary imagery: Auschwitz, burning monks, cybernetics, "light years and nebulae, the speed of light, electrodes, a heterodyne hum, physicists and particles." Meinke's book is an excellent study of the first seven collections of poetry.

The second full-length work is Julia A. Bartholomay's *The Shield of Perseus: The Vision and Imagination of Howard Nemerov* (1972). The title implies that one must "mirror" the world, not confront it nakedeyed. Art is a mirroring, and truth is "reflected and limited by imagination which is not only a mirror but also a shield to protect us from the blinding light of reality," says Bartholomay. Speaking as "A Predecessor of Perseus" Nemerov describes the "amateur" who thinks he can approach the Gorgon without the shield, "All guts no glass," but who will be "stricken." Throughout the book Bartholomay relies heavily—and usefully—on Nemerov's *Journal of the Fictive Life* as well as on his essays. Her interpretations of the poems are occasionally Freudian, but she relies even more on Swiss psychologist Carl Jung's concepts of the unconscious and its archetypes.

The first chapter, "A Doctrine of Signatures," treats Nemerov's ideas of the creative process, imagination as the agent of reality, and the "reflexive image." The universe for Nemerov is a "doctrine of signatures" that the poet tries to translate, Bartholomay asserts. She begins with the essay "The Swaying Form," in which Nemerov quotes the French painter Eugène Delacroix as saying: "Nature is a dictionary. Everything is there but not in the order one needs." The imagination of the poet/painter is to listen/look and then say/paint; nature is transformed by the imagination, resulting in the work of art. Yet the voice of the imagination (the truly creative) cannot always be clearly distinguished from echo (the merely imitative). Bartholomay quotes the *Journal* passage in which Nemerov uses the analogy of the pond as the source of the creative imagination from which come the "artefacts and representations," with "*seeing*" as the mediator between the source and the work of art. In another analogy, art is the "creative aspect of vision; photography the imitative aspect."

Bartholomay explains her use of the word *reflexive,* as distinguished from *reflective,* to describe Nemerov's imagery. Both terms suggest mirroring, but *reflexive* imagery not only mirrors an object but also acts upon itself, "thereby emitting a response which generates a still different third response but one that retains continuity with all previous responses." To illustrate her claim, the critic uses stanza XIV from "Runes," in which the first six lines of the poem present two different images of a threshold: one where "the strider walks on drowning waters," and the second, "That tensed, curved membrane of the camera's lens/Which darkness holds against the battering light." The last nine lines present a third image of a threshold, "The water of the eye where the world walks," an image of the mind imagining the world, which unites the first two, extends them, and makes them richer.

Chapter two, "The Running Water and the Standing Stone," presents an excellent discussion of major dichotomies in Nemerov's poetic vocabulary. The contrast of running water/standing stone imagery extends to water/cloud/fire versus earth/stone/statue, with each set of images defining the other. These images pose the flowing, liquid, creative process against the rigidity of tradition, myth, legends, law. Bartholomay uses such poems as "Deep Woods," "Shells," "Salt Garden," "The Pond," and "Painting a Mountain Stream" to illustrate her thesis. The third chapter, "Fire in the Diamond, Diamond in the Dark," sets the images of fire/sun/light/reason/Apollo/eye/mind—all images of energy—against images of space/air/breath/spirit. Bartholomay points out that *extremes* of mind or imagination result in solipsism (a belief that only the self exists) or phenomenalism (a theory that knowledge results only from observed facts or events); however, the mind of the scientist and the imagination of the poet reveal "two different ways of the mind to draw nearer to the shadow of an external world." For Nemerov, the critic declares, light often represents that moment when "form and substance become one" in the moment of revelation. Chapter four, "The Third Voice," consists of an excellent explication of "Runes," which Bartholomay considers to be "the greatest poem by an American poet in the 20th century—epic, timeless, and universal." The balance of *The Shield of Perseus* is conclusion and summary.

The third book-length study of Nemerov's poetry is William Mills's *The Stillness in Moving Things: The World of Howard Nemerov*

(1975), an excellent study of Nemerov's craft, sources, relation to his audience, and relation to the world of objects. Dealing with more than one hundred of Nemerov's poems by focusing on their philosophical implications, Mills contends that Nemerov's response to the "challenges of scientism and some forms of positivism" places him in the school of the phenomenologists, specifically the German philosophers Edmund Husserl and Martin Heidegger.

Chapters one and two are highly philosophical. Chapter one, "Because the mind's eye lit the sun," deals with phenomenology, the going back in the poetry "to the things," to the concretely experienced phenomena, free of conceptual presuppositions. However, for Nemerov, as for other phenomenologists, the "essence" of the thing is not restricted to sense experience but includes relations, values, and intuitions, and does not reject even universals, Mills suggests. Whereas rationalism deals with the conceptual reasoning *over* experience, phenomenology is concerned with the intuitive foundation and verification of concepts. Chapter one deals with the poetry making the point that "the mind's eye" does, in fact, "light the sun"; it names, says, makes the world—or, at least, the poet likes to think it does. Chapter two, "Running and standing still at once is the whole truth," is an explication of the title of the book—the stillness in moving things. This chapter explores the influence on Nemerov of English philosopher Alfred North Whitehead. Nemerov's "study this rhythm, not this thing," declares Mills, indicates that truth is neither in mind nor in object but in the flowing, the rhythm in which "running and standing still at once/is the whole truth." The critic also deals with the poem sequence "Runes" in its extended metaphorical sense of an outward journey (opposite to the inward journey of the earlier poem sequence "Scales of the Eyes," so admirably dealt with by Kenneth Burke in his 1952 essay "Comments on Eighteen Poems by Howard Nemerov").

The third chapter, "Language, Mirrors, and the Art," focuses on the concepts of perception, things, and words—how language unites thing and thought. Mills, relying on the poetry and Nemerov's own discussions of critical theory, stays close to the poet's ideas of an independent world that may be chaos but that is yet responsive to the word. In the authentic "saying" of the poem, Mills believes, the real world may be evoked so that the "thing" is on one side of the word and the "thought" on the other, and one's "being is both thought/and thing." Mirrors reflect, but water reflects even more accurately since, like the world itself, it is always moving and changing, the critic contends. And, finally, there are those shapes that "cannot be seen in a glass," that cannot be brought into the garden of civilization "where relations grow" but, as Nemerov says, remain "outside the garden" in the "wild abyss." The book's last two chapters deal with Nemerov as a poet of nature (chapter four) and as a poet of the urban landscape (chapter five). The discussion of the writer's best nature poems and urban poems is worthwhile, though it seems these poems would fit as well into the scheme of thought dominating the earlier sections of the book.

Ross Labrie's *Howard Nemerov* (1980) is the most comprehensive of the full-length studies of the writer. It includes biographical information, critical interpretation, an excellent chronology, a bibliography, and a very useful index. Labrie covers hundreds of Nemerov's poems, discussing them in terms of his range as a poet; his philosophies of art, science, perception, and language; his artistic form, especially his use of metaphor; and his belief in the prophetic role of the artist in society. In the process, Labrie conveys Nemerov's understanding of "contemporary epistemology," or theories of knowledge, his "skepticism and metaphysical loneliness," and his eclectic, solitary personality.

Chapter one, "Nemerov's Approach to Art," defines the writer's theories in preparation for relating them to specific poetry. Labrie explains the philosophical, metaphysical, and epistemological backgrounds of Nemerov's work, and then discusses the major influences on that work: Kenneth Burke, Freud, Shakespeare, Dante, and a host of others. The author also discusses Nemerov's definition of myth and history—myth being patterns of human experience, history being the continuum of experience. (Chapter two, "The Fiction," relates some of the fiction to the poetry.) In chapter three, "Poems of the 1940s and 1950s," Labrie discusses the first four collections (*The Image and the Law, Guide to the Ruins, The Salt Garden,* and *Mirrors & Windows*), pointing out progressive changes in thought and style as Nemerov continues to find his own voice. Images of gulls, gardens, oceans, mirrors, thresholds, borders, perimeters suggest a philosophical dualist—a thin line or space between two worlds, the Self and the Other or the Mind and the World, Labrie says. Sometimes, he continues, these two worlds seem irreconcilable while at other times they appear reciprocally responsive: they seem gradually to merge into a point where "world and spirit wed," where the "autonomy of art as a third force between mind and world" can unify the dualism.

Chapter four, "The Later Poems" (*New & Selected Poems, The Next Room of the Dream, The Blue Swallows, Gnomes & Occasions, The*

Western Approaches, and *The Collected Poems*), indicates a growing and continuous change in Nemerov's way of thinking. Labrie notes the salutary effect on Nemerov of the dream's registering the "mind's total response to its surroundings without the need for rational interpretation." Through this means, the critic contends, Nemerov avoids epistemological discussions about the validity of his perceptions but instead records "impressionistically the look of things"; he skirts the problem of dualism "by focusing holistically on the experience of the present moment." His hunger for meaning, for validity, persists, Labrie believes, but the poetry records "the moment's inviolable presence." In fact, many of the poems show a growing belief that consciousness itself is the primary source of pain in contrast to the "toy kingdom" of the insects where "nobody thinks" ("These Words Also"). In this chapter, Labrie's interpretation of "Runes" adds to the growing body of interpretative work on these fine poems.

In the poem "The Blue Swallows" Labrie shows Nemerov moving further into "reflexiveness," as the poetic process becomes a way of exploring imagination itself. In addition, the critic explains how Nemerov—sometimes meditatively, sometimes wittily—uses science as a metaphor to play off scientific truths against imaginative ones. Labrie helps the reader understand the poet's allusions to or metaphorical use of such subjects as mathematics, physics, astronomy, the entropic theme of the running down of the world, the second law of thermodynamics, Darwin's spiraling evolution of being, gyroscopes, the laws of relativity, and the logarithmic spiral. Finally, however, the critic declares that science is seen by Nemerov as "just another mask," as "beginning and ending in myth," as simply another "pathway for the mind." Labrie sums up this chapter by suggesting that "the phenomenal world has become as much a part of an enveloping cosmic dream as the laws drawn from it. While taking care to preserve the concreteness and individuality of phenomena, Nemerov is no longer haunted by the question of epistemological validity."

The last chapter, "A Final Approach," reveals that Nemerov is more and more becoming recognized as a major poet. Although the critic admits that Nemerov's resistance to sentimentality, his complexity, and his erudition have contributed to his belated recognition, Labrie points out that the poet's work is not that of a cloistered academic but instead records an "intellectual and moral break with the past." Modern man has undergone an intellectual crisis, and Nemerov's way of confronting this crisis has been his introspective, unflinching way of looking at the world, the culture, the philosophical problems; what he has seen and shown has been the isolated self trying to piece together the world, Labrie declares. In Nemerov's earlier work, the mood is futile, unsubstantial, even bitter; in his later work, the poems become more relaxed, with an acceptance that the "world seen by the eye and the mind is the only world worth knowing." Labrie sees Nemerov as a "religious poet with no religion, a philosophical poet with no philosophy, and a satirist filled with compassion." For this critic, "Nemerov has . . . trenchantly captured the spirit of his time."

Critical Studies: Major Articles and Book Sections

Kenneth Burke's "Comments on Eighteen Poems by Howard Nemerov" (1952), designed to be published with the poems, is an early critical essay on Nemerov's work and still one of the best. It is also the fullest explication of the poem sequence "The Scales of the Eyes: a poem in the form of a text and variations." The work itself and "Runes," Nemerov's other major poetic sequence, are among his best creations and are often listed among the best poems since World War II. Together, "The Scales of the Eyes" and "Runes" chronicle Nemerov's inward and outward journeys. Burke finds in "The Scales of the Eyes" variations on a theme or themes—a journey to the center of the self, or to the "furthest circumference"; or "typical moments of the poeticizing self as motive"; or "radiations from a single center"; or "moments of a single motive (properties of a single essence)."

Burke summarizes the moments of the self developed in each of the poems in the sequence: the reflexive, the continuum, the abyss, the appetition, the dream, the blindness as vision, the underground, the guilt and cleansing, the cultivating within, the exaltation, the encountering of monsters, the self-sickness, the inexorable joining of first and last things, the translations of the within into terms of the without, the self split from the self, and the self in its "final finale-like freshness, its sprout nature." The poem and its variations, says Burke, are all told with "a considerable ranging and modifying of the theme, without loss of consistency." According to the critic, these works bring together "eloquently, many motivational strands basic to a poetic eschatology."

Burke also discusses the structure of the poem sequence, the purpose behind the imagery ("psychologistic and intellectualistic"), and Nemerov's style (the "Biblical resonance," the "musicality," the "narrative epigram"). The commentator points out that the "greatest defect of the verse is in the excess of its virtue": the profusion of imagery and of overtones, and the clustering of the images from poem to poem. An example of the kind of close reading Burke offers is revealed in his discussion of the title, "The Scales of the Eyes." He gets the reader to see/hear the "I-eye," the "scale"-"caul" links, cognate with the "gull-girl-gall" images in the poem. He notes how the word "shale" flutters around "scale," and how "scale" bridges "shale" on one side and "caul" on the other. He reminds the reader that scales serve as a device to weigh objects as well as an emblem of justice and that the eye connects to Emerson's and to the neo-Platonists' concept of God's omnipotence. Burke then moves, by inversion, to "The Eyes of the Skull" ("scales"-"Skull"). He duplicates exactly the kind of thinking/hearing Nemerov himself offers through language as he tries to construct and/or discover the world through the word.

M. L. Rosenthal in *The Modern Poets* (1961) discusses many of Nemerov's best poems ("The Lives of Gulls and Children," "The Scales of the Eyes," "The Goose Fish," "The Murder of William Remington," "Storm Windows," "Lore," "A Day on the Big Branch," "The Town Dump," "Orphic Scenario") to show that Nemerov, like Thomas Hardy, desires to believe and searches for a return to religion, myth, primitive rituals, yet finds belief impossible. Nemerov, sometimes humorously, sometimes sadly, says much about what has happened to the Romantic view of a perfectible world; he wishes to report the horror of the world frankly but also "to put the case for melioristic faith," Rosenthal declares. Thus the poet's desire for meaning "compels a return to sources of myth and ritual" from which "the liberal mind derives comfort." In its own way, says Rosenthal, Nemerov's poetry is "a memorandum on the subject of despair."

Six years later Rosenthal in *The New Poets* (1967) announces: "Many figures, including the American poet Howard Nemerov, . . . are independent of movements yet embody important tendencies at the same time." By "independent," he means "in the sense that they have worked on their own, in the manner of many artists, without being closely involved with the momentary 'centers' of most intense poetic influence and perhaps without attracting much critical attention." Rosenthal considers Nemerov "versatile," with "an extraordinarily varied body of excellent work." Ranging from the satirical to the serious, this work is handled with "sheer humane intelligence" and irony revealing "a sensibility such as marks the best of the confessional poets." The critic believes that since World War II, poetry has taken on a "new coloration," a new sense of "unease and disorder,"

perhaps because the "humanistic way" may have been already de-
feated and because "remorseless brutality is a condition not only of
the physical universe but also of man himself." Rosenthal discusses
"The Scales of the Eyes" as a poem of terror, like the "first awareness
of horror of death felt by children." He considers the "ominousness
of all things" a condition of Nemerov's poetry.

Robert D. Harvey in "A Prophet Armed: An Introduction to
the Poetry of Howard Nemerov" (1962) writes a fine summary of
Nemerov's work through the first five volumes of poetry, culminating
in *New & Selected Poems.* Harvey deals with three major poetic themes
reflecting Nemerov's life up to age forty: city childhood, wartime
violence, and the natural world of the sea and the Vermont hills.
Discussing the early war poems ("Redeployment," "The Soldier Who
Lived Through the War," and "Life Cycle of Common Man"), Harvey
notes a movement from almost hysterical paralysis, with Nemerov's
using nightmarish, surrealist technique, to a kind of stoical courage,
with greater control of irony, rhythms, compression.

The critic asserts that, beginning with *The Salt Garden,* Nemerov's
concept of war shifts from the battlegrounds of World War II to the
conflicts between city and nature, between mind and chaos, between
human consciousness and brute forces. Through this movement the
poet attains a degree of order, an awareness of a larger reality containing both mind and matter. Harvey uses "The Town Dump" to
illustrate this progression and cites also Nemerov's Emersonian statement calling "poetry a doctrine of signatures." The critic comments
that in Nemerov's best work he "presents adumbrations, not a 'ratio,'
'signatures rather than the Name Itself.' " Harvey uses "Boom" and
"Suburban Prophecy" to exemplify the early and striking use of verbal
play, the tonal qualities of "the serious and funny" being one; he
discusses "Trees," "Writing," "Painting a Mountain Stream," and
"Brainstorm" to show Nemerov's increasing "mastery of his rhythms."
Harvey accurately describes Nemerov as both a sardonic and an inspired prophet armed with "patience, good humor and a mature
awareness of his powers."

Hyatt Waggoner in *American Poets from the Puritans to the Present*
(1968) considers Ralph Waldo Emerson as central to American poetry,
particularly in his essays "The Poet" and "Representative Men," and
Nemerov as "unabashed" in his romanticism and his philosophical
kinship to Emerson. Waggoner believes Kenneth Burke's discovery
of Emerson's method of "transcendence—'I-Eye-Aye' " directly influenced Nemerov. In a letter to Waggoner, Nemerov says that he had

a "sort of illusion of having come at" his Emersonian ideas by himself but that since he was a student of Burke—"and through him of both Coleridge and Emerson"—he could not, of course, quite claim this lack of influence. Waggoner sees Nemerov as turning to the natural world, to landscape which is "comtemplative" rather than practical, and he quotes Nemerov's description in his essay "Attentiveness and Obedience": "consciousness of nature as responsive to language or, to put it the other way, of imagination as the agent of reality." The critic also includes Nemerov's definitions of poetry from "Thirteen Ways of Looking at a Skylark": "Everything we think we know was once a figure of speech. Poetry perceives the world as a miracle transcending its doctrine. . . . Poetry speaks of the spirit's being compelled to renew itself. . . . Every word in the dictionary was beautiful once. . . . What you look hard at, looks hard at you. . . . In the highest range the theory of poetry would be the theory of the Incarnation, which seeks to explain how the Word became Flesh."

Julia Randall's "Genius of the Shore" (1969) is a fine essay for those readers who know Nemerov's work sufficiently to make the leaps Randall makes. She shows Nemerov trying to find the relationship between two worlds: between the sea and the city with the poet on the shore, or between the sea and the land with the poet in between. She notes the problem of the "thing in itself," when thought—whether resulting from theology or physics—erects a rigid world that may have little relationship to the fluid thing-in-itself. The poet, according to Randall, must "unwrite," go back to the things as they are and name them again freshly. She points out that Nemerov "does not seek to impose a vision upon the world so much as to listen to what it says." She classes him as a romantic, religious, prophetic poet who writes of history from the point of view of the "losers" in a world without heroes or in which heroism is simply to stick it out. Randall cites Nemerov's hesitancy to claim moral values for poetry, except occasionally as in "To Lu Chi," but she supports his claim that "poetry's power" can bear new parts of a world up to consciousness out of "an unmindful sleep of causes." The critic turns frequently to her subject's obsession with the inside and outside of things—"the eyes turned into the skull are blind until thought illuminates the objects inside as the sun illuminates those outside." She points out that psychic or subject form can be recognized only through its likeness to natural or objective form, which can be conveyed only through the "medium of the living art-form." Nemerov's lines, "The way a word does when/It senses on one side/A thing and on the other/A thought," mean to Randall—as to Nemerov—that this is "one way of doing/One's being in a world/ Whose being is both thought/And thing, where neither thing/Nor thought will do alone/Till either answers other." In the process of "doing one's being," language is a partner, not merely a stenographer.

Raymond Benoit in "The New American Poetry" (1969) deems Nemerov a Romantic in his reconciliation of idea and image. The critic acknowledges how Nemerov's "casual-serious meditation from nature" takes him from his schooled intelligence into the "brute Fact." In this essay Benoit shows that such poems as "Writing," "Carol," and "To Lu Chi" exemplify the theme that to know is to polarize while to imagine may be to reconcile. He concludes that if contemporary American poetry owes a "series of footnotes" to anyone, it is to Samuel Taylor Coleridge.

In a lengthy essay, "Such Stuff as Dreams: The Poetry of Howard Nemerov" (1971), Douglas H. Olsen argues that Nemerov is a religious poet, not because his work forms a theology or systematic philosophy, but because it is "a re-creation of a situation" in which the poet perceives chaos as "the ongoing process of life." This act, for Olsen, is the "working of God himself." The loneliness, alienation, and meaninglessness of the world that Nemerov perceives and describes are transcended, according to Olsen, and this transcendence is in itself a kind of religious experience. Among the poems the critic explicates to develop his thesis are "Storm Windows," "Moment," parts of "Runes," "Death and the Maiden," and "The View from an Attic Window."

Karl Malkoff in his *Crowell's Handbook of Contemporary American Poetry* article (1973) views Nemerov as a poet of assertion, if not of transcendence. To illustrate Nemerov's sense of the relationship between the subjective self and the objective world, Malkoff discusses "The Goose Fish," which shows the lovers' movement from Eden to their fall from grace into the world of "time and decay" whose patriarch is the dead goose fish. Initially in harmony with nature, they ultimately confront an unsympathetic natural world. Another poem, "The Pond," illustrates not only the dichotomy between man and nature but also nature's own history of catastrophe and renewal. The cycle of birth, death, and rebirth provides no affirmation, but perhaps an "uneasy truce": "not consolation, but our acquiescence." Similarly, Malkoff states that in "The Blue Swallows" Nemerov comes to terms with the "painful limitations of the human intellect" and reacts with the "anticipation of a new awakening," which suggests a kind of affirmation.

In his essay "Nemerov and Nature: 'The Stillness in Moving Things' " (1974) Raymond Smith maintains that the poet is essentially pessimistic, resigned, and passive and that he believes nature is running down. Smith treats many poems in terms of the poetic process itself, or the theme "of how to hold the axe/to make its handle." Many of his poems reveal Nemerov's ordering the flux of reality to reveal "the wedding of world and spirit in the act of the imagination," the critic declares. Smith specifically focuses on "To Lu Chi," "Writing," "Lion & Honeycomb," "The Winter Lightning," "Painting a Mountain Stream," "Elegy for a Nature Poet," "A Spell Before Winter," "Between the Window and the Screen," "The Sanctuary," "Zalmoxis," "The View from the Attic Window," "Death and the Maiden," "Brainstorm," "The Human Condition," "The View," "The Blue Swallows," and "Runes." He perceives the fifteen stanzas of "Runes" as carrying out the theme of perception and process. Smith notes that the poem's structure consists of paired stanzas—1-15, 2-14, 3-13, for example—as reflections of each other, with stanza eight as the poem's center. He declares that the poem sequence moves from late summer to spring and from an inward to an outward thrust. The "runic message," the "stillness in moving things," is death, according to Smith. In summary, he says that "Nemerov's world is a world of process, though the inevitability of completion in the sense of death is always present." The theme of mortality is pervasive, and man's distance from the world of nature—the isolation of his individual consciousness—brings a sense of "sterility, and impotence," and limitation to the poetic narrators, Smith suggests.

In "Howard Nemerov's True Voice of Feeling" (1975) Robert Boyers points out that the writer's best work occurs in two kinds of poems: those of the mind pondering itself and those of lyric evocations of beekeepers or street-cleaners. Both types—"sustained reflection" and "celebratory invocation"—are highly developed. Boyers considers Nemerov's "The Beekeeper Speaks . . . And Is Silent" his best poem because it presents "a tropism toward meaning, order and form," as Nemerov says, rather than a "definitive elucidation." Meaning emerges "beyond, beyond"; rather than transcending the limitations of the human condition, the poem embraces those limitations creatively. Boyers treats "The Beekeeper" in terms of Nemerov's essay "The Protean Encounter" (*Reflexions on Poetry & Poetics*), in which Menelaus, consulting Proteus, hangs on "to the powerful and refractory spirit in its slippery transformations of a single force." Boyers follows the transformations of the beekeeper as he is "lifted out of " his limited identity and "confronted with the enigmatic at the heart of all experience." Imagination helps to heal the gap between mind and world by "dreaming in harmony with the archetypes rooted in the human unconscious," Boyers declares; thus the poet does not have to "revise" his visions "conformable with fact." The poet cannot suppress the intellect, but he can operate on many levels at once, "inviting reverie and the critical faculty to work freely in the smithy of his imagination."

Boyers believes that Nemerov's best poems are not the "trained and polished ambiguities of metaphysical wit so much as simple and profound uncertainty" expressed in a context of "lucid meditation and frequently ecstatic illumination." Elaborating this thesis, the critic discusses "The Mud Turtle" and "The Blue Swallows." In these and such other fine poems as "Writing," "The Breaking of Rainbows," and "Beginner's Guide," Boyers finds that Nemerov's "voice is so immaculately singular that it constitutes a true signature. Only a handful of poets ever come to such a signature," and Nemerov's involves a "curious mixture of intellectual candor, a really impressive probity of mind, and a species of tenderness touched by sorrow."

Complementing Nemerov's immaculate voice, Boyers says, is the poet's "tutelary impulse," his desire to tell readers of something he knows or suspects. Boyers declares that what Nemerov wishes to teach his audience is "how to be sincere, to be what we are, and to express what we feel in a way that will make those feelings available to others like us," or—as Coleridge said—"to cultivate and predispose the heart of the reader." When, for example, Nemerov takes readers into the "Deep Woods," he gives them an apprehending truth—not the truth of the deep woods but the way that "intelligence and wit are liberated in the encounter" with its "awesome self-possession and impenetrability," Boyers believes; the poet must be "possessed by subjects," or, as Nemerov's mentor Owen Barfield says, "man becomes only a "collector, a . . . connoisseur" of limited truths and glib sensations. Boyers suggests that the poem "Beginner's Guide" instructs readers in how to approach volumes yet to come. The poem asserts that neither collecting nor learning names, nor pressing samples is enough: "the world was always being wider/And deeper and wiser than his little wit," while the collector remained "Still to this world its wondering beginner." Such a perspective is Nemerov's true signature, his "true voice of feeling," Boyers shows.

In " 'The Fountainhead of All Forms': Poetry and the Unconscious in Emerson and Howard Nemerov" (1975), Gloria L. Young traces sources for Nemerov's conception of the importance of the unconscious in providing archetypes for poetry. Her thesis is that Emerson's "ideas of the unconscious anticipate certain psychological, linguistic, and aesthetic theories of Carl Jung . . . and Howard Nemerov." Part one of the essay discusses Emerson's, Jung's, and Nemerov's descriptions of the unconscious; part two explains how the three quite different thinkers gained access to the unconscious; and part three explains the confrontation and interaction with the unconscious of all three writers. In addition, Young offers statements from other contemporary poets to indicate their views of the role of the unconscious in recent American poetry.

Paralleling Emerson's and Jung's descriptions of the unconscious, Nemerov uses images of water to symbolize the ground of being, the unconscious, the alien, the Other, Young declares. Discussing his poem "Painting a Mountain Stream," Nemerov describes the Other "whose independent existence might be likened to that of the human unconscious, a sleep of causes. . . . The image most appropriate for this notion . . . is the image of a stream, a river, a waterfall, a fountain, or else of a still and deep reflecting pool" ("Attentiveness and Obedience"). Young shows that "In 'The Sanctuary,' Nemerov envisions a trout sanctuary as the 'pool of the skull' where images swim." For Emerson and Jung, such a source is tapped through a variety of devices, including dream, hallucination, or the occult, while for Nemerov access is gained through "attentiveness and obedience," through something like Keats's "negative capability, when a man is capable of being in . . . mysteries. . . . One looks, listens, and transforms." In "The Scales of the Eyes" Nemerov describes the world of "mind" as being "mined" with archetypes of the unconscious which must themselves be "mined." Emerson called the unconscious the "fountainhead of all forms" from which comes poetry—the magic of Merlin's "artful thunder." Jung says the creative process consists "in the unconscious activation of an archetypal image" that is then consciously shaped and transformed. For Nemerov, the archetypes of the unconscious may be "dammed in artifice," but what one can capture is only the flowing, not the essence, Young contends. However, nature is, as Nemerov puts it, "responsive to language," and imagination can be seen as the "agent of reality." Emerson's metaphor of inspiration as a quick "flash of light" followed by darkness is echoed in Nemerov's "Winter Lightning" in which language may reveal the world. The poet "in the lightning second's sight" reveals three aspects of the creative process: instantaneousness, illumination, and magic.

Like both Emerson and Jung, Nemerov acknowledges that this process is magical, but, he says, "Our proper magic is the magic of language."

Mary Kinzie's "The Signature of Things: On Howard Nemerov" (1977) is an excellent study of *The Collected Poems*, the *Journal of the Fictive Life*, and the critical essays. Exploring Nemerov's poetry through theories expressed in his essays, Kinzie offers a particularly valuable discussion of Nemerov's techniques. She treats such pervasive symbols as statues, water, eye, threshold, tapestry, snow, mirror, diamond, veins, arteries, and salt in terms of the "special cadence" in Nemerov's poetry between the image and the interpretation that lends subtlety to his "doctrine of the forms swaying through the changing materials." She also discusses his division of *mind* into two different methods of dealing with the phenomena of the world, which she calls the "This" and the "That." The "This" is innocent, lyrical, fertile, romantic—a believer and an experiencer. The "That" is intellectual, satirical, realistic, sterile, and skeptical. The "This" represents *mind* a bit "muddled and unhouseled," trying to scrape together a meaning, while the "That" wants to solve the problem at once. In the best of the poems, the temptations to a partial vision are resolved into a third, unified way of glimpsing reality, or at least an intuition of vision's limits, Kinzie says. In her discussion of Nemerov's "small felicities of observation," she culls from his poetry examples of his lyrical descriptions of the natural world.

Kinzie defines four different ways that Nemerov makes the reader "see," processes which he calls "getting something right in language." First is his use of metaphor, of contiguity, and of the objective correlative. Second is his knowledge of language through which he makes the "commonplace word refer back to its livelier origins," his knowledge of the Elizabethan turn on words, and of the puns inherent within words. A third of his strategies is his "positing the metaphoric theme in a capsule or miniature form, and then moving out and away to the particular textures of the contributing parts." Last is his use of "similitudes" through which he lets his "ideas unfold, piece by piece" and thereby achieves "the sublime by way of the minute." Kinzie specifically illustrates all of these techniques through Nemerov's poems. Although some of his descriptive-meditative lyrics may meander, she comments, the real subject emerges, like a "deep syntax," clearly, concretely, and effectively.

Kinzie also relates Nemerov's work to his Jewish, Old Testament heritage, to emblems of the apocalypse, to Saint Augustine's *City of God*, to Joseph Conrad's "Heart of Darkness," to mythology, and to other important literary influences. She says that literary critics Owen Barfield and Kenneth Burke have most significantly shaped his poetic theory and practice; that Dante, Shakespeare, William Blake, and William Butler Yeats are his crucial poetic inspirations; and that Wallace Stevens, Robert Frost, Ezra Pound, Theodore Roethke, and Allen Tate are his poetic brothers. She concludes, however, that Nemerov sounds only like himself, having long ago found his own voice. Kinzie finally asserts that this poet "has been able to bring forth out of death and irony a species of bravery, illumination, and delight."

In "Ideas and Order" (1978), Tom Johnson discusses and then dismisses two stereotypes often used for Nemerov's work: that he is a "good academic poet," by which is meant difficult and dull; and that he is a "competent suburban poet," by which is meant middle-class and dull. Nemerov, says Johnson, is an excellent teacher who writes some of the best criticism appearing today. He is, moreover, "a master of the craft of poetry." Using "Equations of a Villanelle" and "Sarajevo" to exhibit the subtlety and breadth of Nemerov's craft, Johnson then discusses the sound values and rhythms in Nemerov's work, concluding that he is a "master of the American colloquial" voice. That Nemerov is intellectual simply means there are "ideas in his poems"; that he is "difficult" suggests that there are too many ideas, a view which Johnson calls "ridiculous." Just as the word *imagination* is commonly connected with Wallace Stevens, the word *thought* is often associated with Nemerov; and the density of his thought and of its symbolic expression is Nemerov's strength, Johnson believes. He points out that when poetry is about "aesthetics, writing itself, and painting," it necessarily contains a certain difficulty, and that if critics object to intelligence and its intelligent expression, they may find themselves objecting to Nemerov. For Johnson, however, Nemerov has "written more incisively of science and its place in our imaginations than anyone else has yet managed to do in good (or even readable) poems." He adds that Nemerov also has succeeded in writing poems about nature, "at once sharply seen and felt, as both Emerson and Frost tried to do and failed."

"The Reticulum as Characteristic Metaphor" (1979) by Maxwell H. Goldberg defines the "epistemic primacy" of Nemerov's metaphoric images of reticulation—of networks, patterns, weaving. Goldberg begins by discussing Nemerov's *Figures of Thought,* which, he says, consists of essays that are both an inquiry into metaphor and a collection of metaphorical figures. Then he defines reticulum-related metaphors in Nemerov's work that may be "explicit, full-fledged imagings—synecdochic, metonyomic, derivation, associative." Among many such images, Goldberg mentions "webs and webbing, fabrics and weaving; nets, netting, and mesh; seines and cages; threads and threading; reeling and raveling; tackle; brain and other neural systems; latticing and lacing; veils; ropes, fibers, hair; circulatory systems . . . ; branches and vines."

Goldberg treats two poems at length as exhibiting reticular patterning: "Angel and Stone" and "Deep Woods." In "Angel and Stone" the poet has the reader imagine dropping a stone into a pool and observing the ripples, thus initiating the reticulating process. Then, two stones are dropped, forming "a more complicated/Pattern, a kind of reticulation regular and of/simple origins." When, however, a handful of sand is thrown into the pond, the antithesis of reticulum imagery occurs—confusion rather than patterning. Such confusion is the result of the limits of perception—not of the phenomenon itself, which does have pattern. Thus, Nemerov has moved from thesis to antithesis to synthesis, the critic says. Similarly, Goldberg compares Nemerov's imagery of the reticulum in "Deep Woods" to Melville's use of it in *Moby-Dick*—particularly Melville's imagery of "looms and flying shuttles, of spindles, and weavings, of fabrics and tapestries"; the critic concludes that "both of them draw on organismic, biological metaphor. Both of them utilize reticulum-related imagings." Melville and Nemerov use this metaphor for "epistemic instrumentality" rather than embellishment, and in both the imagery transforms "traditional, conventional imagery into fresh creations" to enhance knowing and to expand the range of experience, Goldberg says.

The 1980s have, to date, produced the very fine Labrie book, the Wyllie bibliography, good interviews of Nemerov by Jan Castro and Bowers and Silet, and a number of reviews of Nemerov's recent books, but few noteworthy critical articles. Much work remains to be done with Nemerov's poetry, especially with the three books published in the early 1980s, *Sentences, Inside the Onion,* and *New and Selected Essays.* Nemerov is a poet who is continually changing and growing, becoming more complex in subject matter and apparently simpler in style. His work deserves further critical attention.

Charles Olson

(1910-1970)

Alan Golding
University of Mississippi

PRIMARY BIBLIOGRAPHY

Books

Call Me Ishmael. New York: Reynal & Hitchcock, 1947; London: Cape, 1967. Criticism.

Y & X. Washington, D.C.: Black Sun Press, 1948. Poems.

In Cold Hell, In Thicket. Dorchester, Mass.: Origin, 1953; San Francisco: Four Seasons Foundation, 1967. Poems.

The Maximus Poems 1-10. Stuttgart: Jonathan Williams, 1953. Poems.

The Maximus Poems 11-22. Stuttgart: Jonathan Williams, 1956. Poems.

O'Ryan 2 4 6 8 10. San Francisco: White Rabbit Press, 1958. Poems.

Projective Verse. New York: Totem Press, 1959. Essay.

The Maximus Poems. New York: Jargon/Corinth, 1960; London: Centaur Press, 1960. Poems.

The Distances. New York: Grove, 1960; London: Evergreen, 1960. Poems.

Maximus, From Dogtown-I. San Francisco: Auerhahn, 1961. Poem.

A Bibliography on America for Ed Dorn. San Francisco: Four Seasons Foundation, 1964. Essay.

Human Universe and Other Essays, ed. Donald Allen. San Francisco: Auerhahn Society, 1965. Essays.

Proprioception. San Francisco: Four Seasons Foundation, 1965. Essay.

O'Ryan 1 2 3 4 5 6 7 8 9 10. San Francisco: White Rabbit Press, 1965. Poems.

Reading at Berkeley, transcribed by Zoe Brown. Bolinas, Cal.: Coyote, 1966. Lecture/reading.

Selected Writings of Charles Olson, ed. Robert Creeley. New York: New

Directions, 1966. Essays, letters, play, poems.

West. London: Goliard, 1966. Poems.

The Maximus Poems IV, V, VI. London: Cape Goliard, 1968; New York: Grossman, 1968. Poems.

Causal Mythology. San Francisco: Four Seasons Foundation, 1969. Lecture.

Archaeologist of Morning. London: Cape Goliard, 1970; New York: Grossman, 1973. Poems.

The Special View of History, ed. Ann Charters. Berkeley: Oyez, 1970. Lectures.

Poetry and Truth: The Beloit Lectures and Poems, trans. and ed. George F. Butterick. San Francisco: Four Seasons Foundation, 1971. Lectures/readings.

Additional Prose: A Bibliography on American, Proprioception & Other Notes & Essays, ed. George F. Butterick. Bolinas, Cal.: Four Seasons Foundation, 1974. Essays.

Charles Olson in Connecticut: Last Lectures As Heard by John Cech, Oliver Ford, [and] Peter Rittner. Iowa City: Windhover Press, 1974. Lectures.

In Adullam's Lair. Provincetown, Mass.: To the Lighthouse Press, 1975. Essay.

The Maximus Poems, Volume Three, ed. Charles Boer and George F. Butterick. New York: Grossman, 1975. Poems.

The Post Office: A Memoir of His Father. Bolinas, Cal.: Grey Fox Press, 1975. Memoir.

Spearmint and Rosemary. Berkeley: Turtle Island, 1975. Poems.

The Horses of the Sea. Santa Barbara: Black Sparrow, 1976 [*Sparrow* 43]. Poem.

The Fiery Hunt and Other Plays. Bolinas, Cal.: Four Seasons Foundation, 1977. Plays.

Some Early Poems. Iowa City: Windhover Press, 1978. Poems.

Muthologos: The Collected Lectures and Interviews, ed. George F. Butterick. 2 vols. Bolinas, Cal.: Four Seasons Foundation, vol. 1, 1978; vol. 2, 1979. Lectures/interviews.

The Maximus Poems, ed. George F. Butterick. Berkeley: University of California Press, 1983. Poems.

Letters

Mayan Letters, ed. Robert Creeley. Palma de Mallorca: Divers Press, 1954; London: Cape, 1968.

Pleistocene Man: Letters from Charles Olson to John Clarke During October 1965. Buffalo, N.Y.: Institute of Further Studies, 1968.

Letters for Origin: 1950-1956, ed. Albert Glover. London: Cape Goliard, 1969; New York: Grossman, 1970.

"Charles Olson/Joyce Benson: First Round of Letters," *Boundary 2,* 2 (Fall 1973/Winter 1974), 358-367.

Charles Olson and Robert Creeley: The Complete Correspondence, ed. George F. Butterick. vols. 1- . Santa Barbara, Cal.: Black Sparrow, 1980- .

"The Letters of Edward Dahlberg and Charles Olson. Part I: The Early Years (1936-1948)," ed. Paul Christensen. *Sulfur,* no. 1 (1981), 104-168.

"The Letters of Edward Dahlberg and Charles Olson. Part II: An Unraveling Friendship (1949-1950)," ed. Paul Christensen. *Sulfur,* no. 2 (1981), 65-166.

"The Letters of Edward Dahlberg and Charles Olson. Part III: The Final Feud (1950-1955)," ed. Paul Christensen. *Sulfur,* no. 3 (1982), 122-223.

Notebook

"Notes for *Maximus Poems IV, V, VI,*" ed. Roy Skodnick. *All Area,* no. 2 (1983), 46-63.

Journal

Charles Olson and Ezra Pound: An Encounter at St. Elizabeths, ed. Catherine Seelye. New York: Grossman, 1975.

Selected Poems

"Charles Olson: Eight Poems," *American Poetry Review,* 11 (May/June 1982), 3-5.

"From *The Collected Poems of Charles Olson:* 1940-1949," ed. George F. Butterick. *Sulfur,* no. 11 (1984), 141-157.

"From *The Collected Poems of Charles Olson:* 1950-1957," ed. George F. Butterick. *Sulfur,* no. 12 (1985), 75-95.

"From *The Collected Poems of Charles Olson:* 1958-1964," ed. George F. Butterick. *Sulfur,* no. 13 (1985), 4-20.

Selected Essays

"Lear and Moby-Dick," *Twice A Year,* 1 (Fall/Winter 1938), 165-189.

"Dostoevsky and the Possessed," *Twice A Year,* 5-6 (Fall/Winter 1940-Spring/Summer 1941), 230-237.

"People v. The Fascist, U.S. (1944)," *Survey Graphic,* 33 (Aug. 1944), 356-357, 368.

"This is Yeats Speaking," *Partisan Review,* 13 (Winter 1946), 139-142. Reprinted in *Charles Olson and Ezra Pound: An Encounter at St. Elizabeths,* ed. Seelye. See Journal.

"A Syllabary for a Dancer," *Maps,* no. 4 (1971), 9-15.

"Notes for the Proposition: Man is Prospective," *Boundary 2,* 2 (Fall 1973/Winter 1974), 1-6.

"Definitions by Undoings," *Boundary 2,* 2 (Fall 1973/Winter 1974), 7-12.

"D. H. Lawrence, & the High Temptation of the Mind," *Chicago Review,* 30 (Winter 1979), 27-29.

Recording

Charles Olson Reads from Maximus Poems IV, V, VI. New York: Folkways Records, 1975.

SECONDARY BIBLIOGRAPHY

Bibliographies and Checklists

Butterick, George F. "An Annotated Guide to *The Maximus Poems.*" Dissertation, State University of New York at Buffalo, 1970. Primary and secondary.

_____. "A Bibliography of Writings by Charles Olson: Posthumous Publications," *OLSON,* 7 (Spring 1977), 43-60. Primary.

Butterick, and Albert Glover. *A Bibliography of Works by Charles Olson.* New York: Phoenix Book Shop, 1967. Primary.

Maud, Ralph. "Charles Olson: Posthumous Editions and Studies," *West Coast Review,* 14 (Jan. 1980), 27-33. Primary.

_____. "Charles Olson: Posthumous Editions and Studies (Part 2)," *West Coast Review,* 15 (Winter 1981), 37-42. Secondary.

Biographies: Books

Boer, Charles. *Charles Olson in Connecticut.* Chicago: Swallow Press, 1975.

Cech, John. *Charles Olson and Edward Dahlberg: A Portrait of a Friendship.* ELS Monograph Series, no. 27. Victoria, B.C.: English Literary Studies, University of Victoria, 1982.

Biographies: Articles and Book Sections

Dawson, Fielding. *The Black Mountain Book.* New York: Croton, 1970.

_____. "On Olson, with References to Guy Davenport," *Sagetrieb,* 1 (Spring 1982), 125-132.

_____. "The Pork Chop Incident," *Chicago Review,* 30 (Winter 1979), 100-109.

Duberman, Martin. *Black Mountain: An Exploration of Community.* New York: Dutton, 1972, 385-407.

Finch, John. "Dancer and Clerk," *Massachusetts Review,* 12 (Winter 1971), 34-40.

Metcalf, Paul. "Big Charles: A Gesture Towards Reconstitution," *Prose,* 8 (Spring 1974), 163-177.

Snow, Wilbert. "A Teacher's View," *Massachusetts Review,* 12 (Winter 1971), 40-44.

Selected Interviews

Clayre, Alasdair. "BBC Interview." In *Muthologos: The Collected Lectures and Interviews,* ed. Butterick, vol. 2.

"Interview in Gloucester, August 1968." In *Muthologos: The Collected Lectures and Interviews,* ed. Butterick, vol. 2.

Kenny, Herbert A. " 'I know men for whom everything matters': Charles Olson in conversation with Herbert A. Kenny," *OLSON,* 1 (Spring 1974), 7-44. Reprinted in *Muthologos: The Collected Lectures and Interviews,* ed. Butterick, vol. 2.

Leinoff, Andrew S. "Black Mountain (II)," *OLSON,* 8 (Fall 1977), 66-107.

Malanga, Gerard. "The Art of Poetry XII: Charles Olson," *Paris Review,* 13, no. 49 (1970-1971), 177-204. Reprinted as *"Paris Review* Interview" in *Muthologos: The Collected Lectures and Interviews,* ed. Butterick, vol. 1.

Critical Studies: Books

Butterick, George F. *A Guide to the Maximus Poems of Charles Olson.* Berkeley: University of California Press, 1978.

_____. *Editing the Maximus Poems: Supplementary Notes.* Storrs: University of Connecticut Library, 1983.

Byrd, Don. *Charles Olson's Maximus.* Urbana: University of Illinois Press, 1980.

Charters, Ann. *Olson/Melville: A Study in Affinity.* Berkeley: Oyez, 1968.

Christensen, Paul. *Charles Olson: Call Him Ishmael.* Austin: University of Texas Press, 1978.

Meachen, Clive. *Charles Olson, His Only Weather.* London: Spanner, 1979.

Merrill, Thomas F. *The Poetry of Charles Olson: A Primer.* Newark: University of Delaware Press, 1982.

Paul, Sherman. *olson's push: origin, black mountain, and recent american poetry.* Baton Rouge: Louisiana State University Press, 1978.

Selerie, Gavin. *To Let Words Swim Into the Soul: An Anniversary Tribute to the Art of Charles Olson.* London: Binnacle Press, 1980.

Von Hallberg, Robert. *Charles Olson: The Scholar's Art.* Cambridge, Mass.: Harvard University Press, 1978.

Critical Studies: Special Journal

OLSON: The Journal of the Charles Olson Archives. Storrs: University of Connecticut Library, 1974-1978.

Critical Studies: Special Issues of Journals

Boundary 2, 2 (Fall 1973/Winter 1974).

Io, nos. 22-23 (1976).

The Iowa Review, 11 (Fall 1980).

Maps, no. 4 (1971).

Massachusetts Review, 12 (Winter 1971).

Critical Studies: Articles and Book Sections

Aiken, William. "Charles Olson and the Vatic," *Boundary 2*, 2 (Fall 1973/Winter 1974), 27-38.

_____. "Charles Olson: A Preface," *Massachusetts Review*, 12 (Winter 1971), 57-68.

_____. "The Olson Poetics: Some Effects," *Contemporary Poetry*, 3 (1978), 62-80.

Altieri, Charles. "Olson's Poetics and the Tradition," *Boundary 2*, 2 (Fall 1973/Winter 1974), 173-188.

Apsel, Maxine. " 'The Praises,' " *Boundary 2*, 2 (Fall 1973/Winter 1974), 263-268.

Ballew, Steve. "History as Animated Metaphor in the *Maximus Poems*," *New England Quarterly*, 47 (Mar. 1974), 51-64.

Barua, Dibakar. "One and Many: The Paradox of 'Methodology' in Charles Olson's *Maximus*," *Massachusetts Studies in English*, 9 (Spring 1983), 1-21.

Bedient, Calvin. "Pushing Olson," *Parnassus*, 7 (Spring/Summer 1979), 187-202.

Bernstein, Michael André. *The Tale of the Tribe: Ezra Pound and the Modern Verse Epic*. Princeton: Princeton University Press, 1980, 227-270.

Bertholf, Robert. "On Olson, His Melville," *Io*, no. 22 (1976), 5-36.

_____. "Righting the Balance: Olson's *The Distances*," *Boundary 2*, 2 (Fall 1973/Winter 1974), 229-249.

Blackwell, Henry. "Amiri Baraka's Letters to Charles Olson," *Resources for American Literary Study*, 10 (Spring 1980), 56-70.

Bové, Paul A. *Destructive Poetics: Heidegger and Modern American Poetry*. New York: Columbia University Press, 1980, 217-281.

Bowering, George. "The New American Prosody," *Kulchur*, 4 (Autumn 1964), 3-15.

Breslin, James E. B. *From Modern to Contemporary: American Poetry, 1945-1965*. Chicago: University of Chicago Press, 1984, 66-76.

Burns, Gerald. "How Olson Does Impress," *Boxcar*, no. 2 (1983), 69-71.

_____. "In Medias [Olson's] K," *Sagetrieb*, 4 (Spring 1985), 109-113.

Butterick, George F. "Charles Olson and the Postmodern Advance," *Iowa Review*, 11 (Fall 1980), 4-28.

_____. "Editing Postmodern Texts," *Sulfur*, no. 11 (1984), 113-140.

_____. "Modern Literary Manuscripts and Archives: A Field Report," *Credences*, 1, no. 1 (1981), 81-104.

_____. "Olson's Reading: A Preliminary Report (A-Z)," *OLSON*, 1-6 (Spring 1974-Fall 1976).

_____. "Olson's Reading: A Preliminary Report (Addenda)," *OLSON*, 7 (Spring 1977), 61-69.

Byrd, Don. "The Open Form of Charles Olson's *Maximus*," *Athanor*, no. 6 (Spring 1975), 1-19.

_____. "The Possibility of Measure in Olson's *Maximus*," *Boundary 2*, 2 (Fall 1973/Winter 1974), 39-54.

Cech, John. "Olson Teaching," *Maps*, no. 4 (1971), 72-78.

Charters, Ann. "I, Maximus: Charles Olson as Mythologist," *Modern Poetry Studies*, 2, no. 2 (1971), 49-60.

Charters, Samuel. *Some Poems/Poets: Studies in American Underground Poetry Since 1945*. Berkeley: Oyez, 1971, 21-35.

Christensen, Paul. *"In Cold Hell, In Thicket."* In *A Book of Rereadings in Recent American Poetry—30 Essays*, ed. Greg Kuzma. Lincoln, Neb.: Best Cellar Press, 1979, 54-78.

_____. "The New American Romances," *Twentieth-Century Literature*, 26 (1979), 269-277.

Churchill, Tom. "From Melville to Olson to Metcalf: The Double Play," *Review of Contemporary Fiction*, 1 (Summer 1981), 273-285.

Clarke, Graham. "The Poet as Archaeologist: Charles Olson's Letters of Origin." In *Modern American Poetry*, ed. R. W. (Herbie) Butterfield. Totowa, N.J.: Barnes & Noble, 1984, 158-172.

Combs, Maxine. "Charles Olson's 'The Kingfishers': A Consideration of Meaning and Method," *Far Point*, 4 (Spring/Summer 1970), 66-76.

Corman, Cid. "On Poetry as Action," *Maps*, no. 4 (1971), 66-71.

Corrigan, Matthew. "Materials for a Nexus," *Boundary 2*, 2 (Fall 1973/Winter 1974), 201-228.

_____. "The Poet as Archaeologist," *Boundary 2*, 2 (Fall 1973/Winter 1974), 273-278.

Creeley, Robert. " 'An Image of Man . . . ': Working Notes on Charles Olson's Concept of Person," *Iowa Review*, 11 (Fall 1980), 29-43.

_____. *A Quick Graph: Collected Notes and Essays*, ed. Donald Allen. San Francisco: Four Seasons Foundation, 1970, 151-194.

Davenport, Guy. "Scholia and Conjectures for Olson's 'The Kingfishers,' " *Boundary 2*, 2 (Fall 1973/Winter 1974), 250-262.

Davey, Frank. "Six Readings of Olson's *Maximus*," *Boundary 2*, 2 (Fall 1973/Winter 1974), 291-321.

Davidson, Michael. "Archeologist of Morning: Charles Olson, Edward Dorn and Historical Method," *English Literary History*, 47 (Spring 1980), 158-179.

Dembo, L. S. "Charles Olson and the Moral History of Cape Ann," *Criticism*, 14 (Spring 1972), 165-174.

_____. *Conceptions of Reality in Modern American Poetry*. Berkeley: University of California Press, 1966, 208-214.

_____. "Olson's *Maximus* and the Way to Knowledge," *Boundary 2*, 2 (Fall 1973/Winter 1974), 279-289.

Doria, Charles. "Pound, Olson, and the Classical Tradition," *Boundary 2*, 2 (Fall 1973/Winter 1974), 127-143.

Dorn, Edward. *What I See in* The Maximus Poems. Ventura, Cal. & Worcester, Eng.: Migrant Press, 1960. Reprinted in *Kulchur*, no. 4 (1961), 31-44. Reprinted in *The Poetics of the New American Poetry*, ed. Donald Allen and Warren Tallman. New York: Grove, 1973.

Duncan, Robert. "Notes on Poetics Regarding Olson's 'Maximus,' " *Black Mountain Review*, 6 (Spring 1956), 201-211. Reprinted in *The Poetics of the New American Poetry*, ed. Donald Allen and Warren Tallman. New York: Grove, 1973.

Eggers, Philip. "Old Mother Smith: The Offshore Hero of Charles Olson's Counter-Epic," *Contemporary Poetry*, 5 (1982), 30-44.

Faas, Egbert [*sic*]. "Olson and D. H. Lawrence: The Aesthetics of the 'Primitive Abstract,' " *Boundary 2*, 2 (Fall 1973/Winter 1974), 113-126. Rev. as "Charles Olson" in his *Towards a New American Poetics: Essays and Interviews*. Santa Barbara: Black Sparrow, 1978.

Ferrini, Vincent. "A Frame," *Maps*, no. 4 (1971), 47-60.

Ford, O. J. "Charles Olson and Carl Sauer: Towards a Methodology of Knowing," *Boundary 2*, 2 (Fall 1973/Winter 1974), 145-150.

_____. "Repairing the Primordial (Charles Olson as Teacher)," *Athanor*, no. 1 (Winter/Spring 1971), 5-52.

Géfin, Laszlo K. *Ideogram: History of a Poetic Method*. Austin: University of Texas Press, 1982, 85-98.

Golding, Alan. "Charles Olson's Metrical Thicket: Toward a Theory of Free-Verse Prosody," *Language and Style*, 14 (Winter 1981), 64-78.

Greenspan, Cory. "Charles Olson: Language, Time and Person," *Boundary 2*, 2 (Fall 1973/Winter 1974), 340-357.

Grossinger, Richard. "Origin of the Human World (A Chronicle)," *Io*, no. 23 (1976), 5-91.

Groves, Percilla. "Archival Sources for Olson Studies," *Line*, 1 (Spring 1983), 94-102.

Gunderson, Keith. "What Is Projective Verse?," *Burning Water*, 2 (Fall 1964), 21-26.

Hise, Daniel G. "Noticing 'Juan de la Cosa,' " *Boundary 2*, 2 (Fall 1973/ Winter 1974), 323-332.

Hogg, Robert. "Okeanos Rages," *Sagetrieb*, 3 (Spring 1984), 89-104.

Hutchinson, George. "The Pleistocene in the Projective: Some of Olson's Origins," *American Literature*, 54 (Mar. 1982), 81-96.

Ingber, Richard. "Number, Image, Sortilege: A Short Analysis of 'The Moon is the Number 18,' " *Boundary 2*, 2 (Fall 1973/Winter 1974), 269-272.

James, David. "The Film-Maker as Romantic Poet: Brakhage and Olson," *Film Quarterly*, 35 (Spring 1982), 35-42.

Karlins, Mark. "The Primary of Source: The Derivative Poetics of Charles Olson's *The Maximus Poems* (vol. 1)," *Sagetrieb*, 4 (Spring 1985), 33-60.

Kavka, Jerome. " 'Olson Saved My Life': Ezra Pound," *Paideuma*, 14 (Spring 1985), 7-30.

Kiernan, Robert F. *American Writing Since 1945: A Critical Survey*. New York: Frederick Ungar, 1983, 125-126.

Knapp, James F. "The Undivided World of Pleistocene Eden: Charles Olson's *Maximus*," *Cithara*, 19 (May 1980), 55-65.

Kyle, Carol. "The Mesoamerican Cultural Past and Charles Olson's 'The Kingfishers,' " *Alcheringa*, nos. 1, 2 (1975), 68-77.

Lieberman, Marcia R., and Philip Lieberman. "Olson's Projective Verse and the Use of Breath Control as a Structural Principle," *Language and Style*, 5 (Fall 1972), 287-298.

McPheron, William. "Charles Olson: Mythologist of History," *Boundary 2*, 2 (Fall 1973/Winter 1974), 189-199.

Maier, John R. "Charles Olson and the Poetic Uses of Mesopotamian Scholarship," *Journal of the American Oriental Society*, 103 (Jan.-Mar. 1983), 227-233.

Malkoff, Karl. *Escape from the Self: A Study in Contemporary American Poetry and Poetics*. New York: Columbia University Press, 1977, 79-91.

Melnick, David. "On 'Quantity in Verse, and Shakespeare's Late Plays,' " *Maps*, no. 4 (1971), 79-82.

Metcalf, Paul. "A Seismic Rift," *Parnassus*, 4 (Spring/Summer 1976), 260-274.

Miller, James E., Jr. *The American Quest for a Supreme Fiction: Whitman's*

Legacy in the Personal Epic. Chicago: University of Chicago Press, 1979, 202-233.

Paul, Sherman. "Birds, Landscape, Place, Cosmicity," *Iowa Review*, 11 (Fall 1980), 45-61.

_____. "Clinging to the Advance: Some Remarks on 'Projective Verse,' " *North Dakota Quarterly*, 47 (Spring 1979), 7-14.

_____. "In and About the Maximus Poems," *Iowa Review*, 6, no. 1 (Winter 1975), 118-130; 6, no. 3 (Summer/Fall 1975), 74-96.

_____. "A Letter on Olson and Burke," *All Area*, no. 2 (Spring 1983), 64-65.

_____. *"Maximus:* Volume III or Books VII and After," *Boundary 2*, 5 (Winter 1977), 557-572.

Perloff, Marjorie. "Charles Olson and the 'Inferior Predecessors': 'Projective Verse' Revisited," *English Literary History*, 40 (Summer 1973), 285-306.

_____. "The Greening of Charles Olson," *Criticism*, 21 (Summer 1979), 251-260.

Philip, J. B. "Charles Olson Reconsidered," *Journal of American Studies*, 5 (Dec. 1971), 293-306.

Pops, Martin L. "Melville: To Him, Olson," *Boundary 2*, 2 (Fall 1973/Winter 1974), 55-84. Reprinted in *Contemporary Poetry in America: Essays and Interviews*, ed. Robert Boyers. New York: Schocken, 1974. Rev. as "Charles Olson: Obeying the Figures of the Present Dance" in his *Home Remedies*. Amherst: University of Massachusetts Press, 1984.

Riddel, Joseph N. "De-Centering the Image: The 'Project' of American 'Poetics'?," *Boundary 2*, 8 (Fall 1979), 159-188. Reprinted in *Textual Strategies: Perspectives in Post-Structuralist Criticism*, ed. Josué V. Harari. Ithaca, N.Y.: Cornell University Press, 1978.

Rosenthal, M. L. *The New Poets: American and British Poetry Since World War II*. New York: Oxford University Press, 1967, 160-173.

_____. "Olson/His Poetry," *Massachusetts Review*, 12 (Winter 1971), 45-57.

Rosenthal, and Sally M. Gall. *The Modern Poetic Sequence: The Genius of Modern Poetry*. New York: Oxford University Press, 1983, 331-349.

Scoggan, John. " 'Gravel Hill,' " *Boundary 2*, 2 (Fall 1973/Winter 1974), 333-339.

_____. "The Larger Setting," *Maps*, no. 4 (1971), 83-96.

Sealts, Merton M., Jr. *Pursuing Melville: 1940-1980*. Madison: University of Wisconsin Press, 1982, 91-151.

Smith, Philip E., II. "Descent into Polis: Charles Olson's Search for Community," *Modern Poetry Studies,* 8 (Spring 1977), 13-21.

Sossaman, Stephen. "Olson's Sequence: The 1960 *Maximus Poems,*" *John Berryman Studies,* 3 (Fall 1977), 70-77.

Spanos, William. "Charles Olson and Negative Capability: A Phenomenological Interpretation," *Contemporary Literature,* 21 (Winter 1980), 38-80.

Stein, Charles. "Olson and Jung: The Projection of Archetypal Force Onto Language," *New Wilderness Letter,* 2 (Spring 1980), 47-55.

_____. "Projection." In *Code of Signals: Recent Writing in Poetics,* ed. Michael Palmer. Berkeley: North Atlantic Press, 1983, 67-78.

Stepanchev, Stephen. *American Poetry Since 1945.* New York: Harper & Row, 1965, 124-145.

Stimpson, Catharine R. "Charles Olson: Preliminary Images," *Boundary 2,* 2 (Fall 1973/Winter 1974), 151-172.

Tuttle, Siri. "The Stopping of the Battle: Syntactic Deviation in 3 Poems by Charles Olson," *Io,* no. 22 (1976), 37-47.

Wagner, Linda W. "Call Me Maximus." In her *American Modern: Essays in Fiction and Poetry.* Port Washington, N.Y.: National University Publications/Kennikat Press, 1980, 152-157.

Waldrop, Rosemarie. "Charles Olson: Process and Relationship," *Twentieth-Century Literature,* 23 (Dec. 1977), 467-486.

Watten, Barrett. "Olson in Language." In his *Total Syntax.* Carbondale: Southern Illinois University Press, 1985, 115-139.

_____. "Olson in Language: Part II." In *Writing/Talks,* ed. Bob Perelman. Carbondale: Southern Illinois University Press, 1985, 157-165.

Williams, Jonathan. "AM-O," *Parnassus,* 4 (Spring/Summer 1976), 243-250. Reprinted in *The Magpie's Bagpipe: Selected Essays,* ed. Thomas Meyer. San Francisco: North Point Press, 1982.

Williams, William Carlos. "Review of *The Maximus Poems 11-22.*" *Maps,* no. 4 (1971), 61-65.

Wong, Shelley. "Unfinished Business: The Work of 'Tyrian Businesses,'" *Sagetrieb,* 3 (Winter 1984), 91-106.

BIBLIOGRAPHICAL ESSAY

Bibliographies and Checklists

Although no complete primary or secondary bibliography on Olson exists, a full primary bibliography can be compiled by combining two sources: George F. Butterick and Albert Glover's *A Bibliography of Works by Charles Olson* (1967) and Butterick's "A Bibliography of Writings by Charles Olson: Posthumous Publications" (1977). Both of these checklists provide succinct but thorough annotations, and "Posthumous Publications" gives composition dates for poems and lists reviews of Olson's books. Scholars interested in the poet's publishing history will find Butterick and Glover's text especially useful because of the information it provides on the frequently obscure magazines and presses with which the poet first published. "Posthumous Publications," meanwhile, provides striking evidence of Olson's immense productivity, of how much writing he left at his death, and of the limited acknowledgment, in the form of publication, that he received during his lifetime. Some telling statistics: while Olson contributed 186 poems or essays to periodicals in the twenty-eight years from 1938 to 1966, another 134 items appeared in the seven years following his death. Fourteen books and pamphlets also were published during those same seven years, of which at least nine are major works.

Even the combination of works described above, however, leaves no complete, readily available primary bibliography for 1967-1970, the years between the publication of the Butterick-Glover book and Olson's death, or for posthumous publications after 1977. Butterick's unpublished and hence not easily obtainable 1970 dissertation, "An Annotated Guide to *The Maximus Poems,* does include a primary bibliography through 1968, thus adding one year of citations to *A Bibliography of Works by Charles Olson.* In "Charles Olson: Posthumous Editions and Studies" (1980), Ralph Maud limits himself to discussion of book-length primary texts edited by other hands and published between 1966 *(Selected Writings)* and 1978 *(Muthologos).* He concerns himself mainly with textual matters, often suggesting detailed emendations of texts. Thus Maud emphasizes the uncertain status of some oft-quoted Olson texts, particularly *The Special View of History* and the original *Paris Review* interview (revised considerably for reprinting in *Muthologos).* Since Maud's bibliography includes only books and substantial pamphlets, however, it does not compensate for the absence of a complete primary bibliography.

Perhaps the biggest gap in Olson studies is the lack of a substantial secondary bibliography. Butterick's dissertation contains a complete but unannotated secondary bibliography through 1968; Maud's "Charles Olson: Posthumous Editions and Studies (Part 2)," which appeared in 1981, is the only annotated secondary bibliography available. Maud corrects factual errors in the handful of books on Olson and questions what he sees as doubtful interpretations, but because he mentions very few of the many articles on Olson and covers biographical and critical books only briefly, his essay is of limited use.

Biographies: Books

While many short biographical essays or memoirs are available and both Thomas Merrill's 1982 and Paul Christensen's 1978 critical studies include brief accounts of the life, as of 1985 no definitive biography of Olson exists. Closest to a book-length biographical treatment is Charles Boer's memoir *Charles Olson in Connecticut* (1975). A former graduate student of Olson's and later a colleague at the University of Connecticut, Boer recounts the last few months of Olson's life, during which the poet taught at Connecticut and shared Boer's house for some time before succumbing to liver cancer in January 1970. Boer intends the book as his collection of " 'Olson stories' " and states that he decided soon after the poet's death "to write down all the conversations with Olson that I could remember." He structures his memories as a conversation, speaking as "I" and addressing Olson as "you." This device recreates Olson's living presence as more conventional biographies rarely do. The passages that Boer devotes to providing hard data on Olson's life are few and brief, but he captures fully, sympathetically, and movingly the spirit of that life in its final months.

A partial biography also emerges from John Cech's *Charles Olson and Edward Dahlberg: A Portrait of a Friendship* (1982), which covers the relationship of Olson and novelist-literary critic Dahlberg from 1936 to their final quarrel in 1955. Cech's picture of the men's clashing personalities and tempestuous friendship, their periods of silence, their sometimes overlapping and sometimes divergent interests, reveals Dahlberg's influence on Olson (especially on his prose style), their consistent mutual respect, and Olson's push for intellectual independence from a constantly demanding literary father figure. Cech quotes extensively from both men's letters to provide a carefully balanced discussion of nineteen crucial years in Olson's intellectual life.

Biographies: Articles and Book Sections

Most of the essay-memoirs written on Olson are brief and anecdotal, with the usual strengths and weaknesses of their genre. They are affectionate in tone and often make lively reading, but provide little solid information on or thoughtful insight into Olson's life and work. The best of these essays is Paul Metcalf's "Big Charles: A Gesture Towards Reconstitution" (1974), a superbly written, touching account of Metcalf's long friendship with Olson. Metcalf says little about Olson's work but much about his compelling, contradictory personality. The essay is a rich source of sometimes amusing, sometimes painful, but always revealing stories covering the period from the late 1940s until Olson's death.

In his chapter on Olson in *Black Mountain: An Exploration of Community* (1972), Martin Duberman complements extended quotations from Olson's former students at Black Mountain College with his own personal impressions to illustrate Olson's qualities as a teacher. Those qualities also powerfully affected Fielding Dawson, as he makes clear in *The Black Mountain Book* (1970), and his observation that "the story of Black Mountain from 1949 until 1956 is Charley's story" is close to Duberman's thesis. Important though Olson was to its author, however, *The Black Mountain Book* is finally more about Dawson than about Olson, again more a source of anecdotes about the poet than of solid information on him.

Selected Interviews

Most interviews with Olson are more useful to those seeking a sense of his personal presence than to those interested in his comments on his life and work. While Olson says little about his writing in any of his conversations, he addresses that topic most consistently in the "Interview in Gloucester, August 1968." This piece seems closer to monologue than interview, with Olson claiming that "the only way I can deal with these kinds of questions [about his work] is to talk like this." He speaks at some length about his reading in the late 1960s and his interest in Norse history, literature, and mythology. He also comments briefly on oral poetry, on his "Letter to Elaine Feinstein" (the 1959 postscript to "Projective Verse"), and on the historic "Reading at Berkeley."

Olson is less forthcoming in the only other interview devoted mainly to his writing, Gerard Malanga's April 1969 interview for the *Paris Review* (1970-1971). Many critics cite Olson's comments about the influences on his work of Ezra Pound and William Carlos Williams, but generally Malanga's questions seem ill-conceived or complex to the point of being unanswerable, while Olson is both uncooperative and incoherent.

The poet appears to greater advantage in Andrew S. Leinoff's April 1969 interview published in 1977 as "Black Mountain (II)." This interview shows Olson's prodigious memory for both the practical details and the intellectual atmosphere of life at Black Mountain College. The early pages of the interview reveal much about Olson's goals as a teacher, and the rest concentrates heavily on the closing of Black Mountain. Much of the account makes dull reading, as Leinoff compiles a mass of details to no clear overall purpose. Except for its beginning, the interview holds little interest for readers other than historians of Black Mountain.

Olson's memory and grasp of historical detail also shine through his August 1969 interview with Herbert A. Kenny, published in the spring of 1974. While not directly literary in its concerns, this interview is the most useful one available for readers of *The Maximus Poems*. Kenny and Olson discuss the site of *The Maximus Poems*, Gloucester, Massachusetts—its current state, its history, and Olson's reading in that history. Although Olson says little about *The Maximus Poems* themselves, he demonstrates vividly the spirit of sympathy with Gloucester and the breadth and depth of information out of which the poems grew.

Critical Studies: Books

Despite its brevity (ninety pages) and its informality of approach and style, Ann Charters's *Olson/Melville: A Study in Affinity* (1968) qualifies as the first critical book on Olson. Charters's title defines her topic: she discusses Olson's writings on Melville, in particular his first published book, *Call Me Ishmael*. After a short introduction on early drafts of Olson's critical study and on the research that lay behind it, Charters spends two chapters on a close reading of the book. Treating Olson as "a blend of philosopher and poet," she considers *Call Me Ishmael* an ideal introduction to Olson's ideas and style. The connections she makes between *Call Me Ishmael* and Olson's later poetic and critical works are sketchy, but her discussion of *Call Me Ishmael* itself is insightful. Charters comments briefly on Olson's later review-essays on Melville scholarship, which she ranks below *Call Me Ishmael* in quality and importance, and on his broadside "Letter for Melville 1951," a poem that she rates more highly than most critics. She concludes with selections from two lectures on Melville that Olson gave at Black Mountain College in the 1950s. This material, as well as Charters's use of personal correspondence and conversation with the poet, has made her book a valuable resource for later Olson scholars.

A ten-year lull followed Charters's book, but then book-length criticism on Olson began again with a rush in 1978. In that year three studies appeared: Paul Christensen's *Charles Olson: Call Him Ishmael,* Sherman Paul's *olson's push: origin, black mountain, and recent american poetry,* and Robert von Hallberg's *Charles Olson: The Scholar's Art.*

Christensen, in the best scholarly introduction to Olson's canon, analyzes carefully all the major prose and poetry and extends his discussion into some final comments on the Black Mountain "school." This final chapter is Christensen's weakest in that he tries to say too much about too many poets in too little space and thus often fails to connect the other poets adequately with Olson. Readers may also question the category "Black Mountain poets" on which Christensen's discussion depends, since many of the writers themselves have denied its validity.

The rest of Christensen's book, however, is extremely useful. His first two chapters give a biographical and intellectual introduction that helps orient new readers of Olson. Christensen sensibly acknowledges the charges of obscurity and imitativeness often made against the poet but defends him by stressing Olson's rebellion against traditional (including modernist) philosophical and poetic discourse. While the connections that Christensen draws between Olson's thinking during the late 1940s and that of contemporary philosophers and psychologists seem speculative, this intellectual context enables him to offer insightful readings of Olson's difficult essays on poetics. Christensen explains especially well Olson's philosophy of "objectism," the means by which he hoped to take poetry beyond what he saw as the limitations of ego-bound lyricism.

Christensen moves from Olson's prose to his poetry by means of the best overview available of the influential manifesto "Projective Verse." He then traces Olson's enactment of an open-form poetics through a chronological reading of the short works, arguing that by

the time of *The Distances* (1960) "Olson has come to the boundary of
the short poem" and thereafter devotes himself more and more to
the *Maximus* sequence. As he does with Olson's other work, Christensen clarifies *The Maximus Poems* without oversimplifying them; he
treats the sequence as "a drama of human consciousness seeking to
know the world around it." He contends that the increasingly ambitious acts in that drama are Olson's "interpretation of the moral history
of Gloucester," his attempt to break down barriers between subject
and object (self and city, self and world), and his use of Alfred North
Whitehead's cosmology, human migratory history, and "the history
of awareness" as manifested in myth. Christensen summarizes the
central theme of *The Maximus Poems* as "the redemption of life"—life
in all its related forms, physical and spiritual, personal and universal,
conscious and unconscious.

In *olson's push*, another introductory volume, Sherman Paul covers ground similar to that in Christensen's book. There are significant
differences between the books, however, one being stylistic: Paul often
obscures his discussion by adopting Olson's own difficult language.
The critic shows an appealing imaginative sympathy with the poet,
but within some chapters readers may find his prose impressionistic
and his focus or thesis hard to locate. Sometimes, too, Paul pushes
his sympathy to the point of adulation, not allowing himself to offer
negative criticism of Olson when it is due.

Like Christensen, Paul organizes his discussion chronologically
and begins by arguing that "Olson's essential stance is resistant." Using
this premise, he explicates much of the writer's early work as position
poems in which Olson stakes out his poetic territory. Paul pursues
this view especially through a lengthy reading of Olson's single most
important poem, "The Kingfishers," of which he offers two widely
accepted views: (1) that the work seeks cultural renewal by going
outside the European tradition, and (2) that it is an argument with
Pound, Williams, and T. S. Eliot. Here and elsewhere Paul provides
the necessary service of placing Olson's work in relation to his modernist forebears, but he sometimes overdoes this argument. The
reader grows both weary and skeptical of the thesis that virtually all
of Olson's work is preoccupied with rejecting his poetic predecessors.

Paul also speculates on the importance for Olson's emerging
poetics of the writer's 1951 trip to Yucatan, of Black Mountain College, and of *Origin* magazine, where he published much of his early
work. In this examination of Olson's early creative years, Paul offers
useful readings of "Projective Verse" and "The Praises," an important

companion poem to "The Kingfishers." He then analyzes Olson's thinking on "cosmos and history," paying particular attention to the essay "Human Universe," the rarely discussed dance-play "Apollonius of Tyana," and the important but difficult prose work *The Special View of History*.

Paul's discussion of history in Olson undergirds his analysis of *The Maximus Poems*, which—with the exception of Don Byrd's later book-length study—is the most thorough reading available of that sequence. In the first volume of *Maximus* Paul finds the poet a historian, who tests his relationship to Gloucester and engages in the recreation, redemption, or restoration of the city and the self. In the second volume, Paul contends, Olson moves from history to geology and myth, looking for a way both to include and to transcend his town's history. In the final volume, the most biographical one, Paul asserts that Olson's formal and mythic concerns stay close to those of the second volume while he also picks up again the political concerns of the first. More ordered than Christensen's, Paul's view of *The Maximus Poems* produces a suspiciously neat synthesis of themes; but in their different ways both critics describe accurately the reintegration of private, public, and mythic concerns that Olson himself pursued.

Robert von Hallberg's *Charles Olson: The Scholar's Art* is more partial than Paul's and Christensen's books in every sense of the word: it covers a smaller ground, largely ignoring the second and third volumes of *The Maximus Poems,* and it focuses on one specific feature of Olson's work—its didactic, political element. While von Hallberg's emphasis on the expository, pedagogical side of Olson leaves him no terms for appreciating the increasingly private and fragmented later *Maximus* poems (he argues that Olson simply went downhill after about 1957), it allows for a penetrating analysis of the more public, political first volume of *Maximus.* Furthermore, his interest in general problems of modern American poetics results in the most sophisticated and thought-provoking discussion available of the literary and social context of Olson's work.

Von Hallberg is concerned with Olson's poetic theory rather than with individual poems. He thinks Olson important because he redefined what is meant by poetry and raised interesting questions about the attractions and ends of an expository poetics. These questions lead von Hallberg to discuss Olson's move from a political career to an engagement, through poetry, in what the critic labels "cultural politics." In later chapters von Hallberg brings this political focus to bear on topics familiar in Olson criticism: Olson's relation to Pound,

Williams, and the American long-poem tradition (analyzed more substantially by von Hallberg than by anyone except Michael André Bernstein in *The Tale of the Tribe: Ezra Pound and the Modern Verse Epic,*
1980), the importance to Olson of the philosopher Alfred North
Whitehead, the theme of space, and the development of Olson's style,
especially his prosody. In discussing the changes in the poet's style,
von Hallberg comes up against the limits of his otherwise provocative
approach. He fails to resolve the contradiction that he finds in the
later *Maximus Poems:* what seems to him an egocentric or individualistic
stance rendered in a flat, prosaic, unindividualized voice. Critics like
Christensen and Paul, more sympathetic to Olson's mythologizing and
less convinced that the poetry becomes egocentric, are more able to
account for that later work.

For von Hallberg, then, Olson's work breaks down when "the
abstract, generalized level of understanding and statement drops out."
While some readers may feel it is von Hallberg's critical method, not
Olson's poetry, that breaks down, that method yields priceless insights.
Like Christensen, von Hallberg concludes by reviewing Olson's influence on others, and his interest in a pedagogical poetics makes possible
some valuable points about the didactic sides of poets like Edward
Dorn or the early Amiri Baraka. While von Hallberg slights everything
in Olson that deviates from what he considers the responsibilities of
a pedagogical poetics, his insights into the political side of Olson's
work and, more generally, into the problems involved in writing a
political American poetry are consistently brilliant.

Don Byrd, in *Charles Olson's Maximus* (1980), provides the only
book-length study of the complete *Maximus Poems.* He overlaps somewhat with von Hallberg in arguing that "the *Maximus* proposes a kind
of action which again allows the possibility of meaningful political
life"; yet he concurs more fully with Christensen and Paul in arguing
that to adopt this interpretation of Olson, readers must redefine their
usual ideas of political theory and political action. Like many of Olson's
critics, Byrd reads Olson as a willfully unsystematic poet, whose "politics" involve not rational argument but the development of an "idiosyncratic and personal image of man," with "the grounds for a possible
City" based on a revised human awareness of the roots of creation
and creativity.

Byrd sets up his argument by relating Olson briefly to Pound
and Williams and then lays out his three key terms: *space, fact,* and
stance. All three terms, however, remain ill-defined until the book is
well under way. (Von Hallberg's discussion of *space* is clearer and

more useful.) Byrd goes on to organize the body of his argument around these terms and other triads such as *topos* (the human and natural landscape), *typos* (the image of the hero and the ideal citizen), and *tropos* (myth, or "the deep, inhering forms"). Where such structures can be found in the poetry without distorting it, Byrd describes them usefully. Where they are less apparent, however, he can seem the most rigidly systematic of Olson's interpreters. Like Paul, he pays lip service to respecting Olson's open form but is finally seduced by the temptations of his thesis. In discussing the third volume of *Maximus,* for example, he imposes his own three-part structure on the book and seems less intent on respecting the poem's shape than on preserving his own critical paradigm. This discussion makes up Byrd's last and shortest chapter; by this point his work has lost its energy, and he sounds baffled by the poetry.

What precedes this weak last chapter, however, is very instructive. Byrd adopts the common view of *The Maximus Poems* as an unfolding drama of the self that includes but is not limited to politics. He explains especially well Olson's concept that poetic form and self are constantly open and in the process of revision. In his view Olson seeks to heal the separation that "the intrusion of man as rational, aesthetic, or moral principle" has created among "the immediate landscape, history, and the contents of the unconscious." In pursuing this thesis, Byrd captures thoroughly and sensitively the movements in the *Maximus* sequence between local and cosmic, literal and mythic, political and personal, actual city and possible City. Thus Byrd pursues themes similar to Christensen's and Paul's but treats them in greater depth. His analysis, combined with von Hallberg's skepticism, provides readers with a rich perspective on *The Maximus Poems.*

To be fair to Thomas F. Merrill, one should admit that because of his complexity Olson is a difficult poet on whom to write a primer. Nevertheless, Merrill's *The Poetry of Charles Olson: A Primer* (1982) is the weakest introduction to Olson's work. Although his own prose moves crisply, Merrill overquotes, consistently trying to explain one difficult passage in Olson with an equally difficult one. He rushes through too many reductive readings; he often limits himself to isolating one theme per poem; and, especially in discussing the shorter poetry, he says too little about Olson's style. This scattershot approach hurts the book's continuity and obscures the governing idea in each chapter.

Writing a primer also commits Merrill to considerable repetition of earlier criticism. While he says little that's original, however, he

summarizes effectively. He gives a refreshingly balanced overview of
Olson early in the book, making good use of others' mixed impressions
of the poet and combining skepticism and appreciation himself. His
subsequent discussion moves over familiar terrain: Olson's resistance
to inherited forms of discourse; his programmatic looseness in
thought, speech, and poetry; the epistemology of "objectism"; his
vision of cultural renewal in "The Kingfishers"; his view of the individual's estrangement from the self. Merrill finds this last theme in
most of Olson's shorter poetry, which he sees as trying to counter that
estrangement. Overemphasizing this theme at the expense of others,
however, Merrill makes Olson seem a far more single-minded poet
than he was.

Similarly, Merrill's discussion of *The Maximus Poems* adds little
new to readers' understanding but usefully summarizes existing interpretations. Like many commentators, he finds the ideals of personal
and civic honor and of the model city, the "polis," to be Olson's main
concerns in the first volume of *Maximus*. Although he pays less attention than others to Olson's use of history in that volume, he does note
the movement from history to myth as the main shift between volumes
one and two. In discussing the last two *Maximus* volumes, he rightly
focuses on Carl Jung's importance to Olson—an importance generally
acknowledged but not dealt with at length by previous critics. But
despite this virtue, Merrill's reading of *The Maximus Poems* has the
least depth of any available. Readers seeking a more substantial introduction to Olson should turn to Christensen or Paul; those desiring
specialized interpretations should turn to von Hallberg or Byrd.

A sensitive, accurate introduction to Olson in a format shorter
than a full-length book is Gavin Selerie's *To Let Words Swim Into the
Soul* (1980)—if the text can be obtained. Published by a small press
in London, this work is more accessible to English than to American
readers. Because it is brief (a long pamphlet rather than a book) and
because it offers the kind of introduction that Christensen and Paul
have done in more depth, scholars will find its value limited. However,
for its intended audience, the poetry reader new to Olson, the pamphlet is excellent. It covers important topics—Pound and Williams,
history and myth throughout the *Maximus* sequence, "Projective
Verse"—in a graceful style, and while Selerie lacks the space for detailed close readings, he shows broad acquaintance with Olson's canon
and comments perceptively on it.

Two books very different from those discussed so far are George
F. Butterick's *A Guide to the Maximus Poems of Charles Olson* (1978) and

Editing the Maximus Poems: Supplementary Notes (1983). The first is an essential handbook for any reader of the *Maximus* sequence, providing nearly 4,000 annotations that identify, line by line, page by page, sources and allusions in the poetry. The composition of each poem is dated as precisely as possible, and the annotations make extensive use of unpublished poems, essays, and letters as well as of published material; Butterick deliberately avoids interpretation, however, so that his own words or view will not be confused with Olson's. Butterick keys his annotations to pages in three early collections—to the 1960 Jargon/Corinth edition, to *The Maximus Poems IV, V, VI,* and to *The Maximus Poems, Volume Three*—and he reprints, in parentheses, the pagination of these collections in his own later one-volume edition so that it also can be used easily with the *Guide.*

Beyond admirably fulfilling its main goal, that of providing "the scholarship useful for reading these poems," Butterick's *Guide* contains valuable additional features. The most noteworthy is a lengthy introduction, the single most detailed account in print of the roots of *The Maximus Poems.* Butterick traces these roots through reference to letters, notebooks, unpublished poems, and Olson's reading, and then describes the poems' publishing history volume by volume. Other features of the *Guide* include a detailed chronology of Olson's life, which provides as much information in seven pages as any other biographical resource available, and a checklist of works cited in the annotations, including those texts that Olson is known to have used in writing the poems.

One area of information that Butterick covers only partly in his *Guide* is the status of Olson's texts. He provides more of that information, however, in *Editing the Maximus Poems.* In the body of the book Butterick annotates textual variants for the complete *Maximus Poems,* explaining all cases where his final edition differs from other published or unpublished versions. He devotes most of his introduction to explaining the re-editing of *The Maximus Poems, Volume Three,* which he and Charles Boer compiled following Olson's death; Butterick discusses changes from the earlier edition and justifies the addition of twenty-nine new poems. Readers who wish to assess his editorial procedures for themselves will find one appendix containing photocopies of difficult manuscripts and another containing a number of rejected poems discussed in the introduction. Butterick repeats some material from his *Guide*—the background to the poems, the listing of textual resources—but most of *Editing the Maximus Poems* is new scholarship. The book makes a valuable supplement both to the

poems and to the *Guide*—especially where the notes add dates that
were omitted from the *Guide* or emend those that later evidence has
proven incorrect. This work will mainly interest Olson specialists, but
any reader can learn much from it about the difficulties involved in
producing a definitive text of Olson's masterpiece. Readers interested
further in these textual matters should consult Butterick's articles
"Editing Postmodern Texts" (1984), a general piece on working with
Olson's texts, and "Modern Literary Manuscripts and Archives: A
Field Report" (1981), an account of the establishment, organization,
and content of the Olson Archives at the University of Connecticut.

Critical Studies: Special Journal

OLSON: The Journal of the Charles Olson Archives appeared for ten
issues from spring 1974 to fall 1978. Specializing in printing unpublished work by Olson housed in the Olson archives, it also featured
occasional notes, letters, and reminiscences by students and friends
of Olson.

The single most useful item in the journal's history is "Olson's
Reading: A Preliminary Report" (see below) which ran in the first
seven issues. The journal contained especially helpful material on *The
Maximus Poems* and on Olson's years at Black Mountain College: three
individual issues were devoted to each topic. Particularly worth noting
are reading lists, course plans, and other documents relevant to the
Black Mountain curriculum (no. 2); unpublished Olson poems from
1962-1963 (no. 4); "Background to *The Maximus Poems:* Notes and
Essays, 1945-1957" (no. 5); unpublished *Maximus* poems from 1953-
1957 (no. 6) and 1959-1963 (no. 9); Olson poems, notes, and letters
from Black Mountain, 1951-1954 (no. 8); and a series of "Lectures
in the New Sciences of Man" that Olson gave at Black Mountain in
1953 (no. 10).

Critical Studies: Special Issues of Journals

Although such journals as *Io, The Iowa Review, Maps,* and *Massachusetts Review* have produced Olson numbers, the only such essay
collection devoted exclusively to Olson is the Fall 1973/Winter 1974
double issue of *Boundary 2*. It is divided into seven sections of varying
usefulness. The first section consists of two short, previously unpublished Olson essays, "Notes for the Proposition: Man Is Prospective"
and "Definitions by Undoings"; the second section contains memoirs

and reminiscences by former colleagues or students of Olson. Beginning with an overview of Olson's style by Don Byrd, "The Possibility of Measure in Olson's *Maximus*," the third section contains some helpful essays on Olson and his predecessors. Byrd lays out general features of Olson's poetry: his use of quantitative measure (analyzed with reference to the essay "Quantity in Verse, and Shakespeare's Late Plays" collected in *Human Universe*), his breaking open of conventional syntax, and his heavy use of " 'a syntax of apposition,' which can be opposed to a syntax of subordination." Byrd also discusses Olson's ideas on oral poetry and on what the poet called "composition by field": "Olson sees the poem as a field and composition as an activity which takes place in it."

After Byrd's overview, other articles in the third section trace influences on Olson's work. In "Melville: To Him, Olson," Martin L. Pops touches on the important influence of Melville but then focuses on how *Call Me Ishmael* anticipates Olson's later work. Pops rather speculatively reads *Call Me Ishmael* "as a species of Projective Verse." Stressing the book's oral qualities, he argues that Olson sought the effect of having the print rise off the page to affect the reader as a three-dimensional object might. Pops quite validly compares the method of *Call Me Ishmael* to that of Abstract Expressionist painting and shows how *Call Me Ishmael* invites reader participation—a central principle of Olson's poetry, too. All these points are sound, but Pops belabors them until the article seems repetitive.

In "Olson and D. H. Lawrence: The Aesthetics of the 'Primitive Abstract,' " Ekbert Faas discusses the importance for Olson of Lawrence, who "anticipated the general drift of [Olson's] theorizing" and whom Olson thought a major modern artist. Arguing that Lawrence's critique of Western culture influenced Olson, Faas shows how both writers "upheld pre-Socratic and non-Western cultures as models for . . . new concepts of man." He contends that Lawrence anticipated the "primitive abstract" (Olson's term for an animistic, preclassical view of art and metaphysics), which embodied concreteness, enactments of natural energies, and a sense of "the mutual interrelatedness of all being."

Olson's view of Western culture is also central to Charles Doria's "Pound, Olson, and the Classical Tradition." Doria contrasts Olson and Pound on the basis of how they view antiquity and the classical tradition. He claims that in many respects Pound is a traditional classicist, extolling in the *Cantos* the best features of cultural conservatism and using "two rather ordinary classical forms: the encyclopedia and the lyric." Doria contends that Olson challenges the tradition's value, its discourse, and its content, from antiquity through the present. His alternative is the study of the Pleistocene era, a study designed "to attack, modify, and retrain the poetic sensibility" and to achieve "a new state of mind," as against Pound's attempted reconstitution of the old state.

In the fourth section of the collection, which consists of more general pieces on Olson, the best essay is Charles Altieri's "Olson's Poetics and the Tradition." Altieri, who stresses Olson's antitraditional bias less than other critics, sees Olson's work as an attempt to recast "Romantic organicist models of poetic experience . . . in contemporary terms." This recasting involves his separating creativity from the ego and from imagination, and his delving deeply into the "cultural and metaphysical implications" of Romantic assumptions about the uniqueness of poetic logic. Altieri also discusses Olson's attack on conventional discourse as well as the primacy that his poetry accords content and the physical elements of breath and rhythm over tightly shaped form. Although he finds Olson's prose theorizing more provocative than his poetic practice, Altieri illustrates his points with a sympathetic close reading of "Variations Done For Gerald Van De Wiele." He considers this poem a Romantic pastoral meditation that goes beyond the Romantics because Olson unites the soul with itself and with nature yet does not become trapped in either simple imagistic celebration or an internal "symbolic psychic landscape."

Close reading forms the basis of the collection's fifth section, which contains commentary both on whole books and on individual poems outside *The Maximus Poems*. The section includes Guy Davenport's "Scholia and Conjectures for Olson's 'The Kingfishers,' " the most important article yet written on Olson's most significant poem. Davenport offers a reader's guide to "The Kingfishers," alternating identification of Olson's sources ("scholia") with interpretation ("conjecture"). The essay is essential to a full understanding of the poem, and subsequent scholarship has done little to refute the accuracy of Davenport's exhaustive identifications.

Another valuable article in this section is Robert Bertholf's "Righting the Balance: Olson's *The Distances*." Moving through *The Distances* poem by poem, Bertholf argues that Olson's theme involves healing the "breakage . . . in our culture," the "fracture between thought and action." This critic thus takes what is generally recognized as a central theme in Olson's poetry and shows both how it recurs in numerous poems and how it shapes a whole volume. Bertholf's poem-

by-poem approach leaves little room for in-depth analysis, and surprisingly he neglects "The Praises," a central poem for the theme
under discussion. But since other critics have discussed this poem
adequately (including Maxine Apsel, in the same essay collection), this
weakness is not serious. Overall Bertholf's reading is clear, suggestive,
and helpful in relating *The Distances* to Olson's other work.

The central "other work" is the subject of the sixth section, which
consists of five essays on *The Maximus Poems*. This section is disappointing because its focus is limited mainly to the first volume of
Maximus and because the essays, however competent, have been
largely superseded by later scholarship. Frank Davey, for example,
devotes only a few pages of his long "Six Readings of Olson's *Maximus*"
to *The Maximus Poems IV, V, VI*, and John Scoggan's short essay on
"Gravel Hill" consists of quotations punctuated by a few impressionistic asides. Only one essay, Cory Greenspan's "Charles Olson: Language, Time and Person," says much about *Maximus IV, V, VI*, even
though that volume appeared six years before the *Boundary 2* collection. In the first volume of *Maximus*, Greenspan argues, Olson seeks
"to locate the historical in the present" by the use of historical documents, while in *Maximus IV, V, VI* he moves from historical fact to
myth and "the process of individuation," a growing self-knowledge
that takes place in a cosmic as well as a historically specific context.
Here Greenspan offers an early version of what later would become
a widely accepted interpretation of the *Maximus* sequence. Indeed,
the *Boundary 2* collection as a whole anticipates many later patterns
in Olson scholarship. Although its contents vary in quality, the collection recommends itself to all readers seeking to immerse themselves
in a wide range of approaches to Olson and in a wide range of his
work.

Critical Studies: Articles and Book Sections

One of the most useful single resources available for Olson scholars is Butterick's "Olson's Reading: A Preliminary Report," which
appeared in the first seven numbers of *OLSON*, 1974-1977. It provides
more information about the sources for Olson's work than anything
else outside of Butterick's immense critical study, *A Guide to the Maximus Poems of Charles Olson* (see above). The list consists mainly of
books and articles from Olson's personal library. It also includes items
that Olson owned but had stored and items that, from other evidence,
he is known to have read or consulted. Annotations show when Olson

acquired and/or read each text, how thoroughly he marked it, and where, if at all, he used it in his own work.

Some of the earliest important critical commentary on Olson was written by the three poets closest to and most influenced by him: Robert Creeley, Robert Duncan, and Edward Dorn. Of the three, Creeley began writing on Olson first. The sequence of Creeley's notes and reviews gathered in *A Quick Graph* (1970) and covering the period 1951-1966 still forms an excellent brief introduction to Olson's themes, goals, and style. Creeley has the knack of summarizing central principles in Olson's work accurately and concisely. Especially perceptive are his essays—"Y & X," "In Cold Hell, In Thicket," and "Some Notes on Olson's *Maximus*"—and his introduction to Olson's *Selected Writings*.

Robert Duncan was the second of this group to write formally on Olson, most notably in his "Notes on Poetics Regarding Olson's 'Maximus' " (1956). In this essay Duncan defines his own poetics as much as he comments on Olson's. But at the same time he relates his own practice to a central feature of Olson's: the stress on poetry as energy, as a form of physical activity, manifested especially in the poet's use of breath and sound.

Like Duncan, Edward Dorn reads Olson through his own preoccupations. Much of *What I See in* The Maximus Poems (1960) consists of a meditation on what it means to possess a place and to give the concept of "place" substance through art—one of Dorn's concerns in his own early poetry. He finds Olson's imaginative possession of Gloucester and his ability to bring it alive one striking feature of *The Maximus Poems;* a second is Olson's redefinition of individuality as involving something beyond personal ego. Focusing his interest on Olson's stance and content, Dorn comments only briefly on the style of *Maximus*. This chosen limitation does not weaken the essay, however, which has proven seminal for later discussions of place and self in *The Maximus Poems*.

Creeley has also written more recently on Olson in " 'An Image of Man . . .': Working Notes on Charles Olson's Concept of Person" (1980). As his title suggests, he examines what Olson meant in his constant use of the term "person." For Olson, Creeley contends, the exercise of one's "person" involved writing as an extension of the poet's physiology; using one's own experience as the authority and ground for one's poetry; bringing history into the present, as part of oneself; mending "the dislocation of mind and body"; and developing a broader sense of the human than is implied either in individualism or in classical humanism. Creeley draws these notions of "person" out of selected poems and rarely discusses prose pieces. As in his early short essays, his comments are deceptively simple on the surface, incisive and far-reaching on a second look.

As criticism on Olson has proliferated, certain themes have re-curred, both in the *Boundary 2* collection and in other work: his use of history, his interest in preclassical culture, and the major influences on his work. In "Archeologist of Morning: Charles Olson, Edward Dorn and Historical Method" (1980), Michael Davidson has written one of the most important articles available on Olson's historical con-cerns. Davidson relates those concerns to a broad literary context and shows their effect on Dorn, one of Olson's main literary descendants. Contrasting Olson's work with much recent American poetry char-acterized by an "explorative, self-conscious voice" and a strong sense of personal presence, Davidson shows how Olson's interest in history takes his poetry beyond the merely personal. He finds Olson's poetic and historical methods closely related and summarized in the term "methodology"—a problematic term in Olson's canon that Davidson defines as "the synthesis . . . of history and artistic practice." This synthesis occurs in various ways, Davidson contends: Olson acknowl-edges art itself to be a historical act; he corrects his own historical observations within the poems, showing history, like poetry, to be an ongoing process of interpreting the world; he shows historical events affecting the present, like Pound, and thus alters the linear model of history; and he conceives of his poetry as historical exploration.

Worth reading alongside Davidson's essay is Steve Ballew's "His-tory as Animated Metaphor in the *Maximus Poems*" (1974). Although *The Maximus Poems, Volume III* (published after his article) somewhat qualifies his argument, Ballew's thesis that "historical material . . . is the chief figurative language of *Maximus*" helps clarify the first volume of the poems. Focusing briefly on historical place and event and pri-marily on the poems' historical characters, Ballew asserts that char-acters who share certain traits maintain their individual identities while also forming "a larger composite figure" that represents a par-ticular life-style or moral stance. The characters fall into two such composite figures, the critic argues, becoming "animated metaphors" for two opposing sets of values. While one can imagine Olson re-sponding skeptically to this view of his historical characters as meta-phorical, Ballew has provided a useful technique for reading *The Maximus Poems*. And in conjunction with Ballew's essay, readers should also consult L. S. Dembo's "Charles Olson and the Moral History of

Cape Ann" (1972). Like Ballew, Dembo declares that Olson uses historical characters to offer social criticism and "a moral vision of history." According to Dembo, Olson's use of these figures takes his record of Gloucester's history beyond "disclosure of what happened" to "the revelation of moral truth."

Olson's interest in history takes him back to the Pleistocene era, an early geological period, and George Hutchinson discusses that topic in "The Pleistocene in the Projective: Some of Olson's Origins" (1982). Tracing "the influence on Olson's thought of his reading about the Pleistocene and the rise of the first 'city' in Sumeria," Hutchinson concentrates on Olson's study of the anthropologists Leo Frobenius and Douglas Fox, the historian Christopher Hawkes, the geographer Carl Sauer, and the art historian Max Raphael, showing how Olson used parts of that reading to formulate his theory of projective verse. Moving beyond the essay "Projective Verse" itself, however, Hutchinson argues that Olson valued the Pleistocene as a source of cultural energy throughout his career and used its study to address basic issues in his poetry: "the relation of the body to speech, of speech to education, and of education to culture."

Focusing less on Olson's reading in the Pleistocene and more on what the period meant to him, James F. Knapp, in "The Undivided World of Pleistocene Eden: Charles Olson's *Maximus*" (1980), reviews a central Olson theme: the "fragmentation of an earth that once was one" and Olson's resulting "search for wholeness." He discusses Olson's attempt to unite traditionally separate disciplines and his attraction to the Pleistocene as a world that predates the divisive categories of logical discourse. Like Hutchinson, Knapp stresses Olson's debt to Carl Sauer while drawing most of his examples from the geography and myth-based second volume of *Maximus*. Although some of what he says is covered more thoroughly by Hutchinson, his different focus makes for a helpful summary of Olson's thinking on the "irrelationship between self and world" and of what Olson meant by "self."

Other origins—not human and cultural ones but those of Olson's own poetry—have also occupied his critics, as shown by the *Boundary 2* essays and book-length studies that discuss his influences. While Paul Christensen acknowledges Olson's clear connections with Pound and Williams in his book, he also makes a sound case for Olson's originality in his essay "*In Cold Hell, In Thicket*" (1979). In this, the only essay devoted solely to the volume *In Cold Hell, In Thicket*, Christensen argues for that book as "an unheralded classic of American poetry." He reads it as documenting "Olson's emergence as a poet," its three sections reflecting "the opposition [Olson] must struggle against to find his own voice; a subject worthy of poetry; and finally, the methods and stances he must perfect to be original." Christensen concludes with comments on the book's importance for American poetry, noting Olson's experimentation with syntax, breath, sound, and typography. Since Christensen implies that *In Cold Hell, In Thicket* embodies Olson's projective principles, the essay might usefully be read alongside his discussion of "Projective Verse" in *Charles Olson: Call Him Ishmael* (see above).

Taking the opposite position, Marjorie Perloff's "Charles Olson and the 'Inferior Predecessors': 'Projective Verse' Revisited" (1973) is a seminal article on the issue of Olson's originality, if only for the debate it has sparked. For years following the article's appearance, most readers of Olson felt compelled either to refute or draw on Perloff's thesis that "Projective Verse" is a muddled rehash of the Pound-Williams aesthetic. Her close reading of "from The Song of Ullikummi" cogently isolates certain flaws in Olson's later poetry. Her argument against "Projective Verse," however, is weakened by her assertion that the essay derives partly from statements made by Pound and Williams in letters that Olson actually could not have seen, and by her failure to recognize the essay's historical context or its place in Olson's poetic development.

In "The Greening of Charles Olson," a 1979 essay-review of Christensen, Paul, and von Hallberg's books, Perloff maintains much of her skepticism about the quality, originality, and consistency of Olson's thought and poetry. The essay is most important, however, for the degree to which Perloff recants her earlier damning of her subject. While stressing that Olson's stature as a poet is by no means assured, she still considers him worthy of the attention he has received, reviews the books favorably, and admits the possibility of finding enduring value in his work.

American critics have not cornered the market on objections to Olson, as J. B. Philip shows in "Charles Olson Reconsidered" (1971). Philip writes to improve the poet's reputation in England by addressing common English misconceptions about Olson that result from a "a misreading of the 'Projective Verse' manifesto in relation to the rest of his work." He deals with these specific objections: that Olson evades "the real issues of American history" through "his concern with the processes and details of the natural world"; that he evades not only America's past but also its present; and that his tone is naively optimistic. Countering these objections, Philip argues that Olson offers "an interesting and vivid analysis of the American condition." Overall he provides both a concise review of typical objections to Olson and a convincing refutation of them.

Many commentators, of course, have discussed Olson's literary origins sympathetically. Next to his relationship to Pound and Williams, his connection with Melville has received most attention. In "On Olson, His Melville" (1976), Robert Bertholf asserts that at each stage of his poetic development Olson "returned to Melville . . . to test and rediscover the validity of [his own] new position in terms of the novels, mainly *Moby-Dick.*" The critic divides Olson's engagement with Melville into two periods: 1927-1941, when Olson wrote his M.A. thesis and some early essays on Melville, and 1941-1970, the period first of *Call Me Ishmael* and then of Olson's further short essays and poetry on Melville. Bertholf examines Olson's early published and unpublished Melville essays to show the genesis of *Call Me Ishmael* and then shows how Olson's immersion in Melville confirmed for him poetic principles that first became manifest in *Call Me Ishmael* and then later underlay "Projective Verse" and *The Maximus Poems.* Readers will still need to turn to Ann Charters's *Olson/Melville* for a close reading and structural description of *Call Me Ishmael.* But Bertholf's extensive use of unpublished materials and the connections that he draws, more tightly than Charters, between Olson's Melville work and his poetry make this the most substantial essay available on the topic.

Merton M. Sealts, Jr., gives a different slant on Olson and Melville in his *Pursuing Melville: 1940-1980* (1982), which treats Olson as Melville scholar. Olson and Sealts exchanged over eighty letters and postcards on Melville between 1940 and 1964, "with special emphasis on Melville's reading and on locating books that were once part of his library." While the bulk of the correspondence took place before 1953, extensive quotations from Olson's letters during the whole period covered show the sustained seriousness of his interest in Melville. Occasionally they cast light on his own thinking about poetry and contain ideas that appeared later in his essays on Melville.

While much Olson criticism can be categorized by its focus—on his themes, style, and influences—some can be categorized by its method. A number of commentators have drawn on linguistics and metrics to test Olson's claims about projective verse. In "Olson's Projective Verse and the Use of Breath Control as a Structural Principle" (1972), Marcia and Philip Lieberman conclude that the poetry does show him using breath to control his line, as he advocates in "Projective

Verse." Comparing a reading of Keats's "To Autumn" with readings (some by Olson himself) of Olson's poetry under careful experimental conditions, the critics suggest that whereas breathing usually reinforces syntax in the reading of traditional verse, Olson uses breath "to delimit and emphasize lines in violation of grammatical constraints." Although the Liebermans' experimental design has some minor flaws and their evidence does not always clearly support their conclusions, they do effectively refute notions that Olson was proposing "one breath per line" in "Projective Verse" or that his discussion of breath was conditioned by a "pathologic shortness of breath."

Another linguistic/metrical reading of Olson can be found in Alan Golding's "Charles Olson's Metrical Thicket: Toward a Theory of Free-Verse Prosody" (1981). In the general context of comparing traditional prosody with free verse and of suggesting a method for analyzing the latter, Golding provides the most detailed description in print of how Olson's prosody works. Through an exhaustive prosodic analysis of the early poem "In Cold Hell, In Thicket," the critic categorizes Olson's typical syntactic and rhythmic patterns. A related article using a similar approach, but doing so more briefly and focusing more specifically on Olson's syntax, is Siri Tuttle's "The Stopping of the Battle: Syntactic Deviation in 3 Poems by Charles Olson" (1976).

Recent critics have also applied the methods of contemporary critical theory, particularly deconstruction, to Olson. The results have been mixed, with dense critical language too often obscuring the power and value of Olson's work. The persistent scholarly reader can learn something from William Spanos's "Charles Olson and Negative Capability: A Phenomenological Interpretation" (1980). Spanos addresses how Olson used Keats's notion of negative capability, which Olson understood to involve a submission or commitment to life and poetry as being constantly in process. The critic notes, rightly, that the John Keats-Olson connection has never been discussed in depth and that it affects Olson's thinking both on content and on poetic form. Pursuing this connection by applying Heidegger's philosophy to Olson, Spanos summarizes the common goal: "the destruction of the Western tradition [in philosophy and literature] in order to retrieve by way of discovering that which the *hardened* tradition has covered over and forgotten." The value of Spanos's article is limited by his difficult, digressive prose style; few readers without a thorough grounding in contemporary theory will be able to understand the piece. This is unfortunate, because buried in it are some useful perceptions, and Spanos demonstrates thoroughly what it means to call Olson a "postmodern" poet.

Paul A. Bové uses an approach similar to Spanos's, and does so more readably, in *Destructive Poetics: Heidegger and Modern American Poetry* (1980). Bové sees *The Maximus Poems* as the most radical example in modern American poetry of a Heideggerian—or phenomenological—attack on the idea of "tradition." He uses selected poems from the first volume of *Maximus* to suggest that Olson sees the literary tradition as a fiction that violates "the unity of man and nature" by imposing "layers of verbal interference" on the world. Regarding the poet as a nominalist who values discrete facts over universals, Bové declares that Olson uses attention to historical and geographical detail to strip away these layers and undermine "traditional, habitual forms of language." For Olson, Bové concludes, the only authentic "tradition" is individual, "the personal record of a poet's life and discoveries." A reader should begin with some of this critic's earlier chapters to understand the philosophical basis of his case for Olson; but even with this understanding, his argument against customary notions of "tradition" sometimes seems reductive, and his redefinition of the term fanciful. The discussion, however, remains provocative, and Bové provides the most substantial philosophical reading to date of Olson.

Applying a more traditional approach to Spanos's and Bové's topic, George Butterick, in "Charles Olson and the Postmodern Advance" (1980), examines the nature of Olson's postmodernism. First he traces the term "postmodern," which the poet was the first writer to use repeatedly, through numerous Olson texts. Then, discussing how Olson uses myth to move beyond modernism, Butterick asserts that "the deeper man returns to his archaic, primordial, pre-rationalist condition, the further beyond modernism he advances." Other characteristics of Olson's work that Butterick uses to define postmodernism are a "high tolerance for disorder," often violent twistings of syntax, digressive structures, and extreme ranges and levels of diction and allusion. The essay describes effectively the "postmodern" characteristics of the poet who is often called the father of postmodern poetry.

Though Bové's is an exception, many books on recent poetry contain sections on Olson that give only a brief, superficial summary of his work. An early example of this tendency, worth noting because it demonstrates also some typical misreadings of Olson, is Stephen Stepanchev's *American Poetry Since 1945* (1965). Stepanchev distinguishes Olson from traditional poets on the basis of Olson's favoring open form and a breath-based line. The critic speaks of the "mystique of physiological process" and trust in spontaneous, organic form that he believes "Projective Verse" inspired in Olson's followers. His discussion of the essay is superficial and of little use, however, and when he confronts Olson's poetry he makes factual errors and interprets poems in ways contrary to Olson's stated intentions and poetic thinking. Like many early academic critics, he regards Olson's works as finally too fragmentary to qualify as genuine poetry (it is "pre-poetry"), but, also like these critics, he analyzes the work too briefly to support this thesis convincingly.

Historically valuable as the first sustained treatment of Olson by an influential academic critic, M. L. Rosenthal's chapter in *The New Poets* (1967) reveals his biases by valuing the "pure lyric poet" hidden in what he considers Olson's "tendentiousness." Rosenthal finds Olson at his best when a private or personal tone comes in to redeem the "expansive expositions." Hence he selects for special attention the most obviously lyrical passages of *Maximus*. His otherwise creditable reading of "The Kingfishers" is limited by his adherence to New Critical standards of excellence that many later critics—Bové, most explicitly—have shown to be inapplicable to Olson.

More recent critics who offer summaries of Olson's poetics in their books include James E. B. Breslin, in *From Modern to Contemporary: American Poetry, 1945-1965* (1984); Ekbert Faas, in *Towards a New American Poetics: Essays and Interviews* (1978); and Laszlo K. Géfin, in *Ideogram: History of a Poetic Method* (1982). All provide adequate brief introductions to Olson but nothing more substantial. Other commentators have devoted book sections to placing Olson in the American long-poem tradition. In *The American Quest for a Supreme Fiction: Whitman's Legacy in the Personal Epic* (1979), James E. Miller, Jr., traces Olson's relation to Whitman. He first compares "Projective Verse" and Whitman's 1855 Preface to *Leaves of Grass* as manifestos. Through most of his Olson chapter, however, in which he surveys *The Maximus Poems*, he barely mentions Whitman. Admitting that Whitman, although important to Olson, was far less powerful an influence than Pound and Williams, Miller does not convincingly draw any more than the most general comparisons between *Leaves of Grass* and *The Maximus Poems*.

Michael André Bernstein's *The Tale of the Tribe: Ezra Pound and the Modern Verse Epic* (1980) traces Olson's lineage much more successfully in one of the two best discussions available, along with Robert von Hallberg's, of Olson's relation to Pound and Williams. Bernstein, concentrating on the first volume of *The Maximus Poems*, proposes that the book's importance lies in its attack on the problems involved in writing a modern verse epic. He argues that in *Maximus* Olson advances on his predecessors' work by combining, as indeed he sought to do, Pound's use of historical *exempla* with Williams's adherence to a specific place—by writing, in other words, with equal emphasis on history and geography, time and space. Like von Hallberg, he values Olson as a pedagogical, argumentative poet willing to tackle complex historical and political problems in poetry. His account is "primarily descriptive rather than critical." Finally, however, Bernstein evaluates *The Maximus Poems* as a significant success as methodology or theory, a partial success "at fashioning a public rhetoric," but a stylistic failure "in the line-by-line technical execution of the verse itself." Sympathetic Olson readers will disagree with this last conclusion, especially since Bernstein applies to Olson criteria of lyric grace that cannot account for his work. Also Bernstein has disappointingly little to say about how and why Olson's poetic goals shifted in the later *Maximus* volumes. Nevertheless his account of the first volume is essential reading for anyone interested in the political dimensions of Olson's work and his unique extension of Pound's and Williams's poetics.

Theodore Roethke

(1908-1963)

James R. McLeod and Judith A. Sylte

North Idaho College

PRIMARY BIBLIOGRAPHY

Books

Open House. New York: Knopf, 1941. Poems.

The Lost Son, and Other Poems. Garden City, N.Y.: Doubleday, 1948; London: Lehmann, 1949. Poems.

Praise to the End! Garden City, N.Y.: Doubleday, 1951. Poems.

The Waking; Poems, 1933-1953. Garden City, N.Y.: Doubleday, 1953. Poems.

Words for the Wind. London: Secker & Warburg, 1957. Republished as *Words for the Wind: The Collected Verse of Theodore Roethke.* Garden City, N.Y.: Doubleday, 1958. Poems.

The Exorcism. San Francisco: Poems in Folio, 1957.

I Am! Says the Lamb, illustrated by Robert Leydenfrost. Garden City, N.Y.: Doubleday, 1961. Poems.

Party at the Zoo, illustrated by Al Swiller. New York: Crowell-Collier, 1963; London: Collier-Macmillan, 1963. Poems.

Sequence, Sometimes Metaphysical, illustrated by John Roy. Iowa City: Stonewall Press, 1963. Poems.

The Far Field. Garden City, N.Y.: Doubleday, 1964; London: Faber & Faber, 1965. Poems.

On the Poet and His Craft: Selected Prose of Theodore Roethke, ed. Ralph J. Mills, Jr. Seattle & London: University of Washington Press, 1965. Essays.

The Collected Poems of Theodore Roethke. Garden City, N.Y.: Doubleday, 1966; London: Faber & Faber, 1968. Poems.

Letters

Selected Letters of Theodore Roethke, ed. Ralph J. Mills, Jr. Seattle & London: University of Washington Press, 1968; London: Faber & Faber, 1970.

Notebooks

Straw for the Fire. From the Notebooks of Theodore Roethke: 1943-63, ed. David Wagoner. Garden City, N.Y.: Doubleday, 1972.

Essay

"Theodore Roethke—Comment." In "The Poet and His Critics: A Symposium," *New World Writing, Number 19,* ed. Anthony Ostroff. Philadelphia: Lippincott, 1961, 214-219. Republished as "On 'In a· Dark Time.' " In *The Contemporary Poet as Artist and Critic,* ed. Ostroff. Boston: Little, Brown, 1964.

Documentary Film

In a Dark Time, directed by David Meyer. New York & San Francisco: Contemporary Films, 1963.

Editions and Collections

The Achievement of Theodore Roethke: A Comprehensive Selection of His Poems with a Critical Introduction, ed. William J. Martz. Glenview, Ill.: Scott, Foresman, 1966.
Theodore Roethke: Selected Poems, ed. Beatrice Roethke. London: Faber & Faber, 1969.
Dirty Dinky and Other Creatures: Poems for Children, ed. Beatrice Roethke and Stephen Lushington. Garden City, N.Y.: Doubleday, 1973.

SECONDARY BIBLIOGRAPHY

Concordance

Lane, Gary, ed. *A Concordance to the Poems of Theodore Roethke.* Metuchen, N.J.: Scarecrow Press, 1972.

Bibliographies and Checklists

Hollenberg, Susan W. "Theodore Roethke: Bibliography," *Twentieth Century Literature*, 12 (Jan. 1967), 216-221. Primary and secondary.

McLeod, James R. "Bibliographic Notes on the Creative Process and Sources of Roethke's 'The Lost Son' Sequence," *Northwest Review*, 11 (Summer 1971), 97-111. Secondary.

_____. *Theodore Roethke: A Bibliography*. Kent, Ohio: Kent State University Press, 1973. Primary and secondary.

_____. *Theodore Roethke: A Manuscript Checklist*. Kent, Ohio: Kent State University Press, 1971. Primary.

Matheson, John William. "Theodore Roethke: A Bibliography," M.A. thesis, University of Washington, 1958. Primary and secondary.

Moul, Keith R. *Theodore Roethke's Career: An Annotated Bibliography*. Boston: G. K. Hall, 1977. Primary and secondary.

Walker, Ursula Genung. *Notes on Theodore Roethke*. Charlottesville: Bibliographic Society of the University of Virginia, 1968. Primary and secondary.

Biography: Book

Seager, Allan. *The Glass House: The Life of Theodore Roethke*. New York: McGraw-Hill, 1968.

Biographies: Major Articles and Book Sections

"Allan Seager Papers," *Bancroftiana*, no. 47 (Oct. 1970), 5.

Bogan, Louise. "Letters," *Antaeus*, no. 11 (Autumn 1973), 138-144.

Campbell, Gloria. "Roethke Remembrance," *Mill Mountain Review*, 2 (1975), 76-79.

Ciardi, John. "John Ciardi Comments on Theodore Roethke," *Cimarron Review*, no. 7 (Mar. 1969), 6-8.

Ciardi, Stanley Kunitz, and Allan Seager. "An Evening with Ted Roethke," *Michigan Quarterly Review*, 6 (Oct. 1967), 227-245. Collected in *Profile of Theodore Roethke*, ed. William Heyen. See Collections of Essays.

Everette, Oliver. "Theodore Roethke: The Poet as Teacher," *West Coast Review*, 3 (Spring 1968), 5-11.

Frank, Elizabeth. *Louise Bogan*. New York: Knopf, 1985, 225-236.

Heilman, Robert B. "Theodore Roethke: Personal Notes," *Shenan-*

doah, 16 (Autumn 1964), 55-64. Republished in *Mill Mountain Review*, 2, no. 2 (1975), 18-25.

Hellman, Lillian. *Pentimento*. Boston: Little, Brown, 1973, 213-218.

Hugo, Richard. "Stray Thoughts on Roethke and Teaching," *American Poetry Review*, 3 (Jan-Feb. 1974), 50-51.

Kunitz, Stanley. "Six Letters to Theodore Roethke," *Antaeus*, no. 23 (Autumn 1976), 165-172.

_____. "Theodore Roethke," *New York Review of Books*, 17 Oct. 1963, pp. 21-22. Republished in his *A Kind of Order, A Kind of Folly*. Boston: Little, Brown, 1975.

Stafford, William. "The Mail," *Atlantic Monthly*, 22 (Dec. 1968), 36.

Stein, Arnold. "Roethke: Man and Poet," *Virginia Quarterly Review*, 45 (Spring 1969), 361-365.

Roethke in Fiction

Wagoner, David. *Baby, Come on Inside*. New York: Farrar, Straus & Giroux, 1968. Novel loosely based on Roethke's life.

Critical Studies: Books

Blessing, Richard A. *Theodore Roethke's Dynamic Vision*. Bloomington & London: Indiana University Press, 1974.

Bowers, Neal. *Theodore Roethke: The Journey from I to Otherwise*. Columbia & London: University of Missouri Press, 1982.

Chaney, Norman. *Theodore Roethke: The Poetics of Wonder*. Washington, D.C.: University Press of America, 1981.

La Belle, Jenijoy. *The Echoing Wood of Theodore Roethke*. Princeton: Princeton University Press, 1976.

Malkoff, Karl. *Theodore Roethke: An Introduction to the Poetry*. New York & London: Columbia University Press, 1966.

Mills, Ralph J., Jr. *Theodore Roethke*. Minneapolis: University of Minnesota Press, 1963.

Parini, Jay. *Theodore Roethke: An American Romantic*. Amherst: University of Massachusetts Press, 1979.

Ross-Bryant, Lynn. *Theodore Roethke: Poetry of the Earth, Poet of the Spirit*. Port Washington, N.Y.: Kennikat Press, 1981.

Sullivan, Rosemary. *Theodore Roethke: The Garden Master*. Seattle: University of Washington Press, 1975.

Williams, Harry. *"The Edge Is What I Have": Theodore Roethke and After*. Lewisburg, Pa.: Bucknell University Press, 1977.

Wolff, George. *Theodore Roethke*. Boston: Twayne, 1981.

Critical Studies: Collections of Essays

Heyen, William, ed. *Profile of Theodore Roethke*. Columbus, Ohio: Merrill, 1971.
Stein, Arnold, ed. *Theodore Roethke: Essays on the Poetry*. Seattle: University of Washington Press, 1965.

Critical Studies: Special Issue of Journal

Northwest Review, 11 (Summer 1971).

Critical Studies: Major Articles and Book Sections

Alkalay-Gut, Karen. "The Birth of the Poet's Mind: A Study of Theodore Roethke's 'Where Knock Is Open Wide,' " *Contemporary Poetry*, 5, no. 2 (1983), 17-40.
Arnett, Carroll. "Minimal to Maximal: Theodore Roethke's Dialectic," *College English*, 18 (May 1957), 414-416.
Atlas, James. "Roethke's Boswell," *Poetry*, 114 (Aug. 1969), 327-330. Review of *The Glass House: The Life of Theodore Roethke*.
Auden, W. H. "Verse and the Times," *Saturday Review*, 23 (Apr. 1941), 30-31. Review of *Open House*.
Ayo, Nicholas. "Roethke's 'Poem': The Eternal Feminine," *University of Portland Review*, 27 (Fall 1975), 27-33.
Benedikt, Michael. "The Completed Pattern," *Poetry*, 109 (Jan. 1967), 262-266. Review of *Collected Poems*.
Bennett, Joseph. "Recent Verse," *Hudson Review*, 7 (Summer 1954), 304-305. Review of *The Waking*.
Berryman, John. "From the Middle and Senior Generations," *American Scholar*, 28 (Summer 1959), 384-390.
Blessing, Richard A. "The Shaking That Steadies: Theodore Roethke's 'The Waking,' " *Ball State University Forum*, 12 (Autumn 1971), 17-19.
_____. "Theodore Roethke: A Celebration," *Tulane Studies in English*, 20 (1972), 169-180.
_____. "Theodore Roethke's Sometimes Metaphysical Motion," *Texas Studies in Literature and Language*, 14 (Winter 1973), 731-749.

Bogan, Louise. "Stitched on Bone." In *Trial Balances,* ed. Ann Winslow. New York: Macmillan, 1935, 138-139.

_____. "Verse," *New Yorker,* 15 May 1948, pp. 118-119. Review of *The Lost Son.*

_____. "Verse," *New Yorker,* 16 Feb. 1952, pp. 107-108. Review of *Praise to the End!*

_____. "Verse," *New Yorker,* 7 Nov. 1964, p. 243. Review of *The Far Field.*

Bogen, Don. "From *Open House* to the Greenhouse: Theodore Roethke's Breakthrough," *ELH,* 47 (Summer 1980), 399-418.

_____. " 'Intuition' and 'Craftsmanship': Theodore Roethke at Work," *Papers on Language and Literature,* 18 (Winter 1982), 58-76.

Bowers, Neal. "Theodore Roethke: The Manic Vision," *Modern Poetry Studies,* 11 (Spring/Autumn 1982), 152-164. Republished in his *Theodore Roethke: The Journey from I to Otherwise.*

Bowers, Susan R. "The Explorer's Rose: Theodore Roethke's Mystical Symbol," *Concerning Poetry,* 13 (Fall 1980), 41-49.

Boyd, John D. "Texture and Form in Theodore Roethke's Greenhouse Poems," *Modern Language Quarterly,* 32 (Dec. 1971), 409-424.

Boyers, Robert. "A Very Separate Peace," *Kenyon Review,* 28 (Nov. 1966), 683-691. Review of *The Collected Poems.* Republished in *The Young American Writers,* ed. Richard Kostelanetz. New York: Funk & Wagnalls, 1967, 27-34.

Broughton, I. "A Symposium on Northwest Poetry," *Mill Mountain Review,* 2 (1975), 6-17.

Brown, Dennis E. "Theodore Roethke's 'Self-World' and the Modernist Position," *Journal of Modern Literature,* 3 (July 1974), 1239-1254.

Bullis, Jerald. "Theodore Roethke," *Massachusetts Review,* 11 (Winter 1970), 209-212. Review of *Selected Letters* and *The Glass House.*

Burke, Kenneth. "Cult of the Breakthrough," *New Republic,* 21 Sept. 1968, pp. 25-26. Review of *Selected Letters.*

_____. "The Vegetal Radicalism of Theodore Roethke," *Sewanee Review,* 58 (Jan.-Mar. 1950), 68-108. Republished in his *Language as Symbolic Action.* Berkeley & Los Angeles: University of California Press, 1966. Collected in Heyen.

Carruth, Hayden. "Requiem for God's Gardener," *Nation,* 28 Sept. 1964, pp. 168-169. Review of *The Far Field.*

Ciardi, John. "Poets of the Inner Landscape," *Nation*, 14 Nov. 1953, p. 410. Review of *The Waking*.

_____. "Theodore Roethke: A Passion and a Maker," *Saturday Review*, 31 Aug. 1963, p. 13.

Davie, Donald. "Two Ways Out of Whitman," *Review*, no. 14 (Dec. 1964), 14-19. Review of *The Far Field*.

Davis, William. "Fishing an Old Wound: Theodore Roethke's Search for Sonship," *Antigonish Review*, no. 20 (Winter 1975), 29-41.

Deutsch, Babette. "Fusing Word with Image," *Herald Tribune Book Review*, 25 July 1948, p. 4. Review of *The Lost Son*.

_____. "On Theodore Roethke's 'In a Dark Time.' " In *New World Writing, Number 19*, ed. Anthony Ostroff. Philadelphia: Lippincott, 1961, 201-206. Republished in *The Contemporary Poet as Artist and Critic*, ed. Ostroff. Boston: Little, Brown, 1964.

_____. *Poetry in Our Time*. Garden City, N.Y.: Doubleday, 1963, 197-200.

_____. "Three Generations in Poetry," *Decision*, 2 (Aug. 1941), 59-61. Review of *Open House*.

Dickey, James. "Correspondences and Essences," *Virginia Quarterly Review*, 37 (Autumn 1961), 640.

_____. "The Greatest American Poet," *Atlantic Monthly*, 222 (Nov. 1968), 53-62. Republished in his *Sorties: Journals and New Essays*. Garden City, N.Y.: Doubleday, 1971.

_____. "Theodore Roethke," *Poetry*, 105 (Nov. 1964), 119-122. Review of *Sequence, Sometimes Metaphysical*. Republished in his *Babel to Byzantium: Poets and Poetry Now*. New York: Farrar, Straus & Giroux, 1968.

Diggory, Terrence. "A Father's Authority: Theodore Roethke." In his *Yeats and American Poetry*. Princeton: Princeton University Press, 1983, 182-197.

Donoghue, Denis. "Aboriginal Poet," *New York Review of Books*, 22 Sept. 1966, pp. 14-16. Review of *Collected Poems*.

_____. "Theodore Roethke." In his *Connoisseurs of Chaos: Ideas of Order in Modern American Poetry*. New York: Macmillan, 1965, 216-245. Collected as "Roethke's Broken Music" in Stein.

Eberhart, Richard. "Deep, Lyrical Feelings," *New York Times Book Review*, 16 Dec. 1951, p. 4. Review of *Praise to the End!*

_____. "On Theodore Roethke's Poetry," *Southern Review*, new series, 1 (July 1965), 612-620. Republished in his *Of Poetry and Poets*. Urbana: University of Illinois Press, 1979.

Ferry, David. "Roethke's Poetry," *Virginia Quarterly Review*, 43 (Winter

1967), 169-173. Review of *Collected Poems*. Collected in Heyen.

Fiedler, Leslie. "A Kind of Solution: The Situation of Poetry Now," *Kenyon Review*, 26 (Winter 1964), 61-64.

Fitzgerald, Robert. "Patter, Distraction, and Poetry," *New Republic*, 8 Aug. 1949, p. 17. Review of *The Lost Son*.

Flint, F. Cudworth. "Seeing, Thinking, Saying, Singing," *Virginia Quarterly Review*, 35 (Spring 1959), 312-313. Review of *Words for the Wind*.

Forster, Louis. "A Lyric Realist," *Poetry*, 58 (July 1941), 222-225. Review of *Open House*.

Frankenberg, Lloyd. "The Year in Poetry," *Harper's Magazine*, 205 (Oct. 1952), 106. Review of *Praise to the End!*

Freer, Coburn. "Theodore Roethke's Love Poetry," *Northwest Review*, 11 (Summer 1971), 42-66.

Galvin, Brendan. "Kenneth Burke and Theodore Roethke's 'Lost Son' Poems," *Northwest Review*, 11 (Summer 1971), 67-96.

_____. "Theodore Roethke's Proverbs," *Concerning Poetry*, 5 (Spring 1972), 35-47.

Gangewere, R. J. "Theodore Roethke: The Future of a Reputation," *Carnegie Series in English*, XI. Pittsburgh: Carnegie-Mellon University, 1970, 65-73.

Goodheart, Eugene. "The Frailty of the *I*," *Sewanee Review*, 76 (Summer 1968), 516-519.

Gross, Harvey. *Sound and Form in Modern Poetry*. Ann Arbor: University of Michigan Press, 1964, 282-290.

Gunn, Thom. "Poets English and American," *Yale Review*, new series, 48 (June 1959), 623-626. Review of *Words for the Wind*.

Gustafson, Richard. "In Roethkeland," *Midwest Quarterly*, 7 (Jan. 1966), 167-174.

Hamilton, Ian. "Theodore Roethke," *Agenda*, 3 (Apr. 1964), 5-10.

Harrington, Michael. "No 'Half-baked Bacchus' from Saginaw," *Commonweal*, 21 Feb. 1969, pp. 656-657. Review of *The Glass House*.

Hayden, Mary H. "Open House: Poetry of the Constricted Self," *Northwest Review*, 11 (Summer 1971), 116-138.

Heaney, Seamus. "Canticles to the Earth," *Listener*, 22 Aug. 1968, pp. 245-246. Review of *Collected Poems*.

Heringman, Bernard. "How to Write Like Somebody Else," *Modern Poetry Studies*, 3, no. 1 (1972), 31-39.

_____. "Images of Meaning in the Poetry of Theodore Roethke," *Aegis*, no. 2 (Fall 1973), 45-57.

_____. "Roethke's Poetry: The Forms of Meaning," *Texas Studies in Literature and Language,* 16 (Fall 1974), 567-583.

_____. "Theodore Roethke," *Earlham Review,* 3 (Spring 1970), 20-30.

Heyen, William. "The Divine Abyss: Theodore Roethke's Mysticism," *Texas Studies in Literature and Language,* 11 (Summer 1969), 1051-1068. Collected in Heyen.

_____. "Theodore Roethke's Minimals," *Minnesota Review,* 8, no. 4 (1968), 359-375.

_____. "The Yeats Influence: Roethke's Formal Lyrics of the Fifties," *John Berryman Studies,* 3, no. 4 (1978), 17-63.

Hobbs, John. "The Poet as His Own Interpreter: Roethke on 'In a Dark Time,' " *College English,* 33 (Oct. 1971), 55-66.

_____. "Theodore Roethke: The Poet as Mystic," *Studies in Mystical Literature,* 3 (Jan. 1983), 18-42.

Hoey, Allen. "Some Metrical and Rhythmical Strategies in the Early Poems of Roethke," *Concerning Poetry,* 15 (Spring 1982), 49-58.

Hoffman, Frederick J. "Theodore Roethke: The Poetic Shape of Death." Collected in Stein, 94-114. Republished in *Modern American Poetry: Essays in Criticism,* ed. Jerome Mazzaro. New York: McKay, 1970.

Hoffman, Steven K. "Lowell, Berryman, Roethke, and Ginsberg: The Communal Function of Confessional Poetry," *Literary Review,* 22 (Spring 1979), 329-341.

Holmes, John. "Poems and Things," *Boston Evening Transcript,* 24 Mar. 1941, p. 9. Review of *Open House.*

_____. "Theodore Roethke," *American Poetry Journal,* 17 (Nov. 1934), 2.

Hughes, Ted. "Wind and Weather," *Listening and Writing* (Autumn 1965), 30-38.

Hummer, T. R. "Roethke and Merwin: Two Voices and the Technique of Nonsense," *Western Humanities Review,* 33 (Summer 1979), 273-280.

Humphries, Rolphe. "Inside Story," *New Republic,* 14 July 1941, p. 62. Review of *Open House.*

_____. "Verse Chronicle," *Nation,* 22 Mar. 1952, pp. 283-284. Review of *Praise to the End!*

Husband, John Dillon. "Some Readings in Recent Poetry," *New Mexico Quarterly,* 24 (Winter 1954-1955), 446-447.

Jaffe, Dan. "Theodore Roethke: 'In a Slow Up-Sway.' " In *The Fifties: Fiction, Poetry, Drama,* ed. Warren French. De Land, Fla.: Everett/Edwards, 1970, 199-207.

Kennedy, X. J. "Joys, Griefs and 'All Things Innocent, Hapless, For-saken,' " *New York Times Book Review,* 23 Aug. 1964, p. 5. Review of *The Far Field.*

Kinnell, Galway. "To the Roots: An Interview with Galway Kinnell," *Salmagundi,* no. 22-23 (Spring/Summer 1973), 206-221.

Kizer, Carolyn. "Poetry: Poetry of the Pacific Northwest," *New Republic,* 16 July 1956, pp. 18-19.

Kramer, Hilton. "The Poetry of Theodore Roethke," *Western Review,* 18 (Winter 1954), 131-146.

Kunitz, Stanley. "Four for Roethke." In his *A Kind of Order, A Kind of Folly.* Boston: Little, Brown, 1975, 77-109.

_____. " 'Imagine Wrestling with an Angel': An Interview with Stanley Kunitz," *Salmagundi,* no. 22-23 (Spring/Summer 1973), 71-83.

_____. "News of the Root," *Poetry,* 73 (Jan. 1949), 222-225. Review of *The Lost Son and Other Poems.* Republished in his *A Kind of Order, A Kind of Folly.*

_____. "Roethke: Poet of Transformations," *New Republic,* 23 Jan. 1965, pp. 23-29. Collected in Heyen. Republished in Kunitz, *A Kind of Order, A Kind of Folly.*

_____. "The Taste of Self." In *New World Writing, Number 19,* (1961), ed. Ostroff, 206-214. Republished in *The Contemporary Poet as Artist and Critic: Eight Symposia,* ed. Ostroff. Republished in Kunitz, *A Kind of Order, A Kind of Folly.*

Kusch, Robert. "The Sense of Place in Theodore Roethke's 'The Rose,' " *Contemporary Poetry,* 4, no. 4 (1982), 73-88.

La Belle, Jenijoy. "Martyr to a Motion Not His Own: Theodore Roethke's *Love Poems,*" *Ball State University Forum,* 16 (Spring 1975), 71-75.

_____. "Out of the Cradle Endlessly Robbing: Whitman, Eliot and Theodore Roethke," *Walt Whitman Review,* 22 (June 1976), 75-84. Republished in her *The Echoing Wood of Theodore Roethke.*

_____. "Theodore Roethke and Tradition: 'The Pure Serene of Memory in One Man,' " *Northwest Review,* 11 (Summer 1971), 1-18.

_____. "Theodore Roethke's Dancing Masters in 'Four for Sir John Davies,' " *Concerning Poetry,* 8, no. 2 (1975), 29-35.

_____. "Theodore Roethke's 'The Lost Son': From Archetypes to Literary History," *Modern Language Quarterly,* 37 (June 1976), 179-195. Republished in her *The Echoing Wood of Theodore Roethke.*

Lee, Charlotte I. "The Line as a Rhythmic Unit in the Poetry of Theodore Roethke," *Speech Monographs*, 30 (Mar. 1963), 15-22.

_____. "Roethke Writes About Women," *Literature in Performance: A Journal of Literary and Performing Art*, 1, no. 1 (1980), 23-32.

Levi, Peter. "Theodore Roethke," *Agenda*, 3 (Apr. 1964), 11-14.

Lewandowska, M. L. "The Words of their Roaring: Roethke's Use of the Psalms of David." In *The David Myth in Western Literature*, ed. Raymond-Jean Frontain and Jan Wojcik. West Lafayette, Ind.: Purdue University Press, 1980, 156-167.

Libby, Anthony. "Roethke, Water Father," *American Literature*, 46 (Nov. 1974), 267-288. Republished in his *Mythologies of Nothing: Mystical Death in American Poetry 1940-1970*. Urbana & London: University of Illinois Press, 1984.

Liberthson, Daniel. *The Quest for Being: Theodore Roethke, W. S. Merwin and Ted Hughes*. New York: Gordon, 1978.

Lucas, John. "The Poetry of Theodore Roethke," *Oxford Review* (University College), no. 8 (1968), 39-64.

Lupher, David A. "Lost Son: Theodore Roethke," *Yale Literary Magazine*, 135 (Mar. 1967), 9-12.

McClatchy, J. D. "Sweating Light from a Stone: Identifying Theodore Roethke," *Modern Poetry Studies*, 3, no. 1 (1972), 1-24.

McFarland, Ronald E. "Roethke's 'Epidermal Macabre,' " *Contemporary Poetry*, 4, no. 2 (1981), 16-22.

McMichael, James. "The Poetry of Theodore Roethke," *Southern Review*, new series, 5 (Winter 1969), 4-25. Collected in Heyen.

_____. "Roethke's North America," *Northwest Review*, 11 (Summer 1971), 149-159.

Maki, Jacqueline R. "The Dance: Roethke's Legacy from Yeats," *Kentucky Philological Association Bulletin* (1981), 1-23.

Malkoff, Karl. "Exploring the Boundaries of the Self," *Sewanee Review*, 75 (July-Sept. 1967), 540-542. Review of *Collected Poems*.

_____. "Roethke: The Poet as Albatross," *Southwest Review*, 54 (Summer 1969), 329-332. Review of *The Glass House* and *Selected Letters*.

Martz, Louis. "A Greenhouse Eden." Collected in Stein, 14-35. Republished in Martz, *The Poem in the Mind: Essays on Poetry English and American*. New York: Oxford University Press, 1966.

_____. "Recent Poetry: The Elegiac Mode," *Yale Review*, new series, 54 (Dec. 1964), 294-297. Review of *The Far Field*.

_____. "Recent Poetry: Roethke, Warren, and Others," *Yale Review*, 56 (Dec. 1966), 275-277. Review of *Collected Poems*.

Maxwell, J. C. "Notes on Theodore Roethke," *Notes & Queries,* new series, 16 (July 1969), 265-266.

Mazzaro, Jerome. "Theodore Roethke and the Failures of Language," *Modern Poetry Studies,* 1, no. 2 (1970), 73-96. Collected in Heyen. Republished in Mazzaro, *Postmodern American Poetry.* Urbana & London: University of Illinois Press, 1980.

Meredith, William. "A Steady Storm of Correspondences: Theodore Roethke's Long Journey Out of the Self," *Shenandoah,* 16 (Autumn 1964), 41-54. Collected in Stein.

Mills, Ralph J., Jr. "In the Way of Becoming: Roethke's Last Poems." Collected in Stein, 115-135. Republished in Mills, *Contemporary American Poetry.* New York: Random House, 1965.

_____. "Keeping the Spirit Spare," *Chicago Review,* 13 (Winter 1959), 114-122. Review of *Words for the Wind.*

_____. "Roethke's Garden," *Poetry,* 100 (Apr. 1962), 54-59. Review of *I Am! Says the Lamb.*

_____. "Towards a Condition of Joy: Patterns in the Poetry of Theodore Roethke," *Northwestern University Tri-Quarterly,* 1 (Fall 1958), 25-29. Republished in *Poets in Progress,* ed. Edward Hungerford. Evanston, Ill.: Northwestern University Press, 1962.

Molesworth, Charles. "Songs of the Happy Man: Theodore Roethke and Contemporary Poetry," *John Berryman Studies,* 2 (Summer 1976), 32-51. Republished in his *The Fierce Embrace.* Columbia & London: University of Missouri Press, 1979.

Muir, Edwin. "New Verse," *New Statesman,* 55 (18 Jan. 1958), 76-77. Review of *Words for the Wind.*

Nadel, Alan. "Roethke, Wilbur, and the Vision of the Child: Romantic and Augustan in Modern Verse," *The Lion & Unicorn: Critical Journal of Children's Literature,* 2, no. 1 (1978), 94-113.

Nelson, Cary. "The Field Where Water Flowers: Theodore Roethke's 'North American Sequence.' " In his *Our Last First Poets: Vision and History in Contemporary American Poetry.* Urbana: University of Illinois Press, 1981, 31-61.

Nemerov, Howard. "Three in One," *Kenyon Review,* 16 (Winter 1954), 148-154. Review of *The Waking.* Republished as "On Shapiro, Roethke, Winters." In his *Poetry and Fiction: Essays.* New Brunswick, N.J.: Rutgers University Press, 1963.

Ostroff, Anthony, "The Poet and His Critics: A Symposium." In *New World Writing, Number 19,* ed. Ostroff. Philadelphia: Lippincott, 1961, 189-219. Republished as "On 'In a Dark Time.' " In *The*

Contemporary Poet as Artist and Critic, ed. Ostroff. Boston: Little, Brown, 1964.

Parini, Jay. "Blake and Roethke: When Everything Comes to One." In *William Blake and the Moderns,* ed. Robert J. Bertholf and Annette S. Levitt. Albany, N.Y.: State University of New York Press, 1982, 73-91. Republished in Parini, *Theodore Roethke: An American Romantic.*

_____. "Theodore Roethke: An American Romantic," *Texas Quarterly,* 21 (Winter 1978), 99-114. Republished in her *Theodore Roethke: An American Romantic.*

_____. "Theodore Roethke: The Poetics of Expression," *Ball State University Forum,* 21 (Winter 1980), 5-11. Republished in her *Theodore Roethke: An American Romantic.*

Parker, Donald G. "The Eye of the Storm: Roethke's 'The Lost Son,' " *Contemporary Poetry,* 2, no. 1 (1975), 13-16.

Paschall, Douglas. "Roethke Remains," *Sewanee Review,* 81 (Autumn 1973), 859-864.

Pearce, Roy Harvey. "Theodore Roethke: The Power of Sympathy." Collected in Stein, 167-199.

Phillips, Robert. "The Inward Journeys of Theodore Roethke." In his *The Confessional Poets.* Carbondale & Edwardsville: Southern Illinois University Press, 1973, 107-127.

Pinsker, Sanford. "An Urge to Wrestle/A Need to Dance: The Poetry of Theodore Roethke," *CEA Critic: Official Journal of the College English Association,* 41 (May 1979), 12-17.

Pinsky, Robert. "Wonder and Derangement: 'Orchids,' 'Badger' and 'Poppies in July.' " In his *The Situation of Poetry.* Princeton: Princeton University Press, 1976, 118-133.

Porter, Kenneth. "Roethke at Harvard, 1930-1931 and the Decade After," *Northwest Review,* 11 (Summer 1971), 139-148.

Powell, Grosvenor E. "Robert Lowell and Theodore Roethke: Two Kinds of Knowing," *Southern Review,* new series, 3 (Jan. 1967), 180-185. Review of *Theodore Roethke: Essays on the Poetry.*

Pritchard, William H. "Wildness of Logic in Modern Lyric." In *Forms of Lyric,* ed. Reuben A. Brower. New York: Columbia University Press, 1970, 127-150.

Ramsey, Jarold. "Roethke in the Greenhouse," *Western Humanities Review,* 26 (Winter 1972), 35-47.

Ransom, John Crowe. "On Theodore Roethke's 'In a Dark Time.' " In *New World Writing, Number 19* (1961), ed. Ostroff, 191-201.

Republished in *The Contemporary Poet as Artist and Critic,* ed. Ostroff, 26-35.

Rodgers, Audrey T. "Dancing-Mad: Theodore Roethke." In his *The Universal Drum: Dance Imagery in the Poetry of Eliot, Crane, Roethke and Williams.* University Park: Pennsylvania State University Press, 1979, 93-137.

Rodman, Seldon. "Intuitive Poet," *New York Herald Tribune Book Review,* 2 Dec. 1951, p. 32. Review of *Praise to the End!*

Romig, Evelyn M. "An Achievement of H.D. and Theodore Roethke: Psychoanalysis and the Poetics of Teaching," *Literature and Psychology,* 28, no. 3-4 (1978), 105-111.

Rosenthal, M. L. "Closing in on the Self," *Nation,* 21 Mar. 1959, pp. 258-260. Review of *Words for the Wind.*

_____. "The Couch and Poetic Insight," *Reporter,* 25 Mar. 1965, pp. 52-53. Review of *The Far Field.*

_____. *The New Poets: American and British Poetry Since World War II.* New York: Oxford University Press, 1967, 112-118.

Schap, Keith. "A Synthetic Figure in Two Poems by Theodore Roethke," *Language and Sciences,* 11 (1978), 238-246.

Schumacher, Paul J. "The Unity of Being: A Study of Theodore Roethke's Poetry," *Ohio University Review,* 12, no. 1 (1970), 20-40.

Schwartz, Delmore. "The Cunning and the Craft of the Unconscious and the Preconscious," *Poetry,* 94 (June 1959), 203-205. Review of *Words for the Wind.* Republished in *Selected Essays of Delmore Schwartz,* ed. D. A. Dike and D. H. Zucker. Chicago: University of Chicago Press, 1971. Collected in Heyen.

Scott, Nathan A. "The Example of Roethke." In his *The Wild Prayer of Longing—Poetry and the Sacred.* New Haven: Yale University Press, 1971, 76-118.

Seymour-Smith, Martin. "Where Is Mr. Roethke?," *Black Mountain Review,* 1 (Spring 1954), 40-47. Review of *The Waking.*

Shapiro, Harvey. Review of *Praise to the End!, Furioso,* 7 (Fall 1952), 56-58.

Shapiro, Karl. "Scraping the Bottom of the Roethke Barrel," *New Republic,* 166 (4 Mar. 1972), 24. Review of *Straw for the Fire.*

Skelton, Robin. "The Poetry of Theodore Roethke," *Malahat Review,* 1 (Jan. 1967), 141-144.

Slaughter, William R. "Roethke's 'Song,' " *Minnesota Review,* 8, no. 4 (1968), 342-344.

Snodgrass, W. D. "The Last Poems of Theodore Roethke," *New York*

Review of Books, 8 Oct. 1964, pp. 5-6. Review of *The Far Field.*

_____. "Spring Verse Chronicle," *Hudson Review,* 12 (Spring 1959), 114-117. Review of *Words for the Wind.*

_____. " 'That Anguish of Concreteness'—Theodore Roethke's Career." Collected in Stein, 78-93. Republished in Snodgrass, *Radical Pursuit.* New York: Harper & Row, 1975.

_____. "W D Snodgrass: An Interview," *Salmagundi,* no. 22-23 (Spring/Summer 1973), 149-163.

Southworth, James G. "The Poetry of Theodore Roethke," *College English,* 21 (Mar. 1960), 326-330, 335-338.

_____. "Theodore Roethke: *The Far Field,*" *College English,* 27 (Feb. 1966), 413-418.

Spanier, Sandra Whipple. "The Unity of the Greenhouse Sequence: Roethke's Portrait of the Artist," *Concerning Poetry,* 12 (Spring 1979), 53-60.

Spender, Stephen. "The Objective Ego." Collected in Stein, 3-13.

_____. "Roethke: The Lost Son," *New Republic,* 27 Aug. 1966, pp. 23-25. Review of *Collected Poems.*

_____. "*Words for the Wind,*" *New Republic,* 10 Aug. 1959, pp. 21-22.

Staples, Hugh B. "The Rose in the Sea-Wind: A Reading of Theodore Roethke's 'North American Sequence,' " *American Literature,* 36 (May 1964), 189-203.

Stein, Arnold. "Introduction." In his *Theodore Roethke: Essays on the Poetry,* ix-xx.

_____. "Roethke's Memory: Actions, Visions, and Revisions," *Northwest Review,* 11 (Summer 1971), 19-31.

Sullivan, Rosemary. "A Still Center: A Reading of Theodore Roethke's 'North American Sequence,' " *Texas Studies in Literature and Language,* 16 (Winter 1975), 765-783.

Swann, Brian. "Theodore Roethke and 'The Shift of Things,' " *Literary Review,* 17 (Winter 1973-1974), 269-286.

Tate, Allen. "In Memoriam—Theodore Roethke, 1908-1963," *Encounter,* 21 (Oct. 1963), 68.

Thurley, Geoffrey. "Theodore Roethke: Lost Son." In his *The American Moment: American Poetry in the Mid-Century.* New York: St. Martin's, 1978, 91-105.

Thwaite, Anthony. "Guts, Brains, Nerves," *New Statesman,* 17 May 1968, p. 659. Review of *Collected Poems.*

Tillinghast, Richard. "Worlds of Their Own," *Southern Review,* new series, 5 (Spring 1969), 582-596. Review of *Collected Poems.*

Trudayaraj, A. Noel Joseph. "Theodore Roethke's 'Elegy for Jane': An Analysis," *CIEFL Bulletin*, 17, no. 1 (1982), 25-33.

Truesdale, C. W. "Theodore Roethke and the Landscape of American Poetry," *Minnesota Review*, 8, no. 4 (1968), 345-358.

Vanderbilt, Kermit. "Theodore Roethke as a Northwest Poet." In *Northwest Perspectives—Essays on the Culture of the Pacific Northwest*, ed. E. R. Bingham and G. A. Love. Eugene: University of Oregon Press/Seattle: University of Washington Press, 1979, 186-216.

Vanderwerken, David L. "Roethke's 'Four for Sir John Davies' and 'The Dying Man,'" *Research Studies*, 41(June 1973), 125-135.

Van Dyne, Susan R. "Self-Poesis in Roethke's 'The Shape of the Fire,'" *Modern Poetry Studies*, 10, no. 2-3 (1981), 121-136.

Vernon, John. "Theodore Roethke's *Praise to the End!* Poems," *Iowa Review*, 2 (Fall 1971), 60-79. Republished in his *The Garden and the Map: Schizophrenia in Twentieth Century Literature and Culture*. Urbana & London: University of Illinois Press, 1973.

Waggoner, Hyatt. "Centering In." In his *American Poets: From the Puritans to the Present*. Boston: Houghton Mifflin, 1968, 563-577.

Wain, John. "Half-way to Greatness," *Encounter*, 10 (Apr. 1958), 82-84. Review of *Words for the Wind*.

_____. "Theodore Roethke," *Critical Quarterly*, 6 (Winter 1964), 322-338. Collected as "The Monocle of My Sea-Faced Uncle" in Stein.

Warfel, Harry R. "Language Patterns and Literature: A Note on Roethke's Poetry," *Topic*, 6 (Fall 1966), 21-29.

Wesling, Donald. "The Inevitable Ear: Freedom and Necessity in Lyric Form, Wordsworth and After," *English Literary History*, 36 (Sept. 1969), 544-561. Republished in *Forms of Lyric: Selected Papers from the English Institute*, ed. Reuben A. Brower. New York: Columbia University Press, 1970.

Wilbur, Richard. "Poetry's Debt to Poetry," *Hudson Review*, 26 (Summer 1973), 278-280.

Winters, Yvor. "The Poems of Theodore Roethke," *Kenyon Review*, 3 (Autumn 1941), 514-516. Review of *Open House*.

Wolff, George. "Syntactical and Imagistic Distortion in Roethke's Greenhouse Poems," *Language and Style*, 6 (Fall 1973), 281-288.

BIBLIOGRAPHICAL ESSAY

Bibliographies and Checklists

A valuable forerunner of the full-scale bibliographies was John W. Matheson's 1958 University of Washington master's thesis, which listed primary and secondary material and included an index to first lines of Roethke's poems. Later works have since incorporated his bibliography: Susan W. Hollenberg's 1967 article in *Twentieth Century Literature* updates Matheson's primary and secondary list through 1965, adding the 1966 Doubleday publication of the *Collected Poems*, and Ursula Genung Walker's *Notes on Theodore Roethke* (1968) extends the list through 1967.

Preliminary to James R. McLeod's book-length works was his 1971 article on the bibliographic sources for "The Lost Son" sequence, a study which contains a 102-item catalogue of biographical and critical comments as well as manuscript locations. McLeod's *Theodore Roethke: A Manuscript Checklist*, a survey of twenty repositories in the United States and Canada holding Roethke manuscripts, notebooks, and letters, was also published in 1971. This very useful volume includes publication information on the manuscripts, lists of published and unpublished letters to and from Roethke, cross-references to significant commentary, and indexes of titles and first lines and their variations; it also assigns an approximate date of composition to each of Roethke's works.

A further joist in the emerging framework of Roethke scholarship was McLeod's 1973 *Theodore Roethke: A Bibliography*, a companion to the earlier checklist and a highly inclusive list of works by and about Roethke. In addition to the customary citation of poems, collections, and major studies, the bibliography incorporates articles and biographical notes; films, recordings, and musical settings relating to Roethke's works; and his foreign appearances in print, both in English and in translation, through April 1972. Some of these cited references will undoubtedly appear incidental to the average student of Roethke. However, they afford the biographer or historical critic a comprehensive overview of the poet's development and of the response evoked by his work from the general public as well as from the critics. The book is indexed by names and poem titles and contains significant cross references, including those to Roethke's commentaries on specific poems or sequences. A useful chronology of Roethke's life and work is also included, as well as an introductory essay sketching the growth of Roethke's reputation as a poet, teacher, and reader.

Although McLeod's bibliography contains some annotations, it was not until the 1977 publication of Keith R. Moul's *Theodore Roethke's Career: An Annotated Bibliography* that a comprehensive annotative effort appeared. While Moul does take note in his introduction of two important critical works, those by Blessing in 1974 and by Sullivan (1975, but mistakenly assigned to 1976), the absence of other significant criticism between December 1973 and Moul's work in 1977 means that Moul's bibliography covers scarcely more ground than McLeod's. However, the annotations are helpful, as is the chronological presentation of the primary and secondary material in illuminating the development of Roethke's work in relation to the criticism. Moul includes useful cross-references to reprints, but the name-only index does not include titles. Unless the reader is quite familiar with the publication history of the various works, he will not find easy access to Roethke's work through Moul's book.

Thus the relative critical silence between the publication of Malkoff's study in 1966 and Blessing's in 1974 was offset by considerable research activity. This period saw the publication of most of the scholarly tools that still provide a firm foundation for the important critical studies appearing throughout the later 1970s and the 1980s.

Biographies

Although some incidental biographical commentary was published prior to Roethke's death in 1963, the truly significant work came later. Many reminiscences in the form of dedications and poems appeared immediately after his death. Among the most notable were those done by close friends, such as Stanley Kunitz in the 17 October 1963 *New York Review of Books*. Here Kunitz affectionately traces the high marks of Roethke's life and career. Later, in the October 1967 *Michigan Quarterly Review*, he expresses many of these same sentiments as a contributor (with John Ciardi and Allan Seager) to "An Evening with Ted Roethke." Ciardi also mixes critical commentary with anecdotes illustrating Roethke's complexity as man and poet, while Seager's comments are a condensed version of his Roethke biography, which was to appear the following year, after Seager's death.

This study, *The Glass House: The Life of Theodore Roethke*, is a detailed, almost Boswellian account of the poet's life with emphasis on the Michigan years. The only book-length biography to date of Roethke, it has elicited much controversy. Seager's work presents a

wealth of information about Roethke's personal relationships, his ambitions, his career, and his bouts with mental illness. Although James
Dickey, in his 1968 essay "The Greatest American Poet," calls it "the
best biography of an American poet I have read since Phillip Horton's
Hart Crane," many of Roethke's friends, especially in the Northwest,
have dissented. Criticism of Seager's work suggests that it falls short
in its focus on Roethke's early years, in its thoroughness in delineating
Roethke's character, and in its clarification of the origins of Roethke's
art.

William Stafford, in a December 1968 *Atlantic Monthly* letter re-
sponding to Dickey's article, raised the question of Seager's relative
neglect of the Seattle years, 1947-1963. The significance of the Northwest in the development of Roethke's art has been more fully explored
by Kermit Vanderbilt in his 1979 essay "Theodore Roethke as a Northwest Poet." Articles treating the poet's years at the University of Washington—"Theodore Roethke: Personal Notes" by Robert B. Heilman
(1964), who was Roethke's department chairman, and "Roethke: Man
and Poet" (1969), by Arnold Stein, a colleague and friend at Washington—reveal that Seager failed to mine sources of information
about Roethke's later career. Moreover, Oliver Everette's sensitive
1968 *West Coast Review* portrayal of Roethke as teacher (and mental
patient) in 1949 also suggests the kind of focus that would have rendered a fuller and more satisfying biography. "Stray Thoughts on
Roethke and Teaching" (1974) by Richard Hugo, a former student
and a fellow poet and creative writing professor, is a particularly good
example of the numerous reminiscences of Roethke's unusual gifts
as a teacher, an aspect of his achievement also conveyed in the fine
documentary film "In a Dark Time" (1963). As a fictional portrait of
the poet's later years, David Wagoner's *Baby, Come on Inside* (1968),
may be of interest. Clearly, however, the influence of the Seattle experience on Roethke as poet, teacher, and man awaits more satisfying
biographical treatment.

Another weakness in the Seager biography, which Dickey and
others have pointed out, again relates to the question of thoroughness.
Dickey, who places the blame squarely at the feet of Roethke's widow
and literary executrix, Beatrice, comments on her "efforts to mitigate
certain traits of Roethke's, particularly in regard to his relations with
women." Other colleagues and friends have noted this discrepancy
between the Seager portrait and the real-life Roethke. In this connection it is interesting to note the posthumous "Letters from Louise
Bogan to Theodore Roethke" published in the Autumn 1973 *Antaeus*,

as well as the candid description of their relationship in Elizabeth Frank's excellent 1985 biography, *Louise Bogan*. Bogan's impact on Roethke's poetic development and on his personal life makes this heretofore largely unnoted relationship particularly significant; yet one examines the nineteen references to Bogan in the Seager work without finding even a hint at their romantic involvement. Comparable accounts—such as Lillian Hellman's in *Pentimento* (1973) depicting Roethke's playful and sometimes annoying attention to women—are largely missing from Seager's book. A biography dealing satisfactorily with this aspect of Roethke's life and career remains to be written.

A further concern raised by Seager's critics is that his use of psychoanalytic theory does little to clarify the origins of Roethke's art, but instead contributes to an exaggerated emphasis on the role of his mental illness in the creative process. This criticism has persisted despite Seager's declaration, in an appendix, that he is "not trying to offer here a general theory that artistic creativity depends in some measure on mental illness, nor . . . specifically that Ted was always stimulated by it." Stein's review, "Roethke: Man and Poet," objects to the biographer's psychoanalytic approach: "When Seager . . . tries to explain how the poetry came to be what it is, he falls back on conventional formulas of psychological wisdom that fuse together stubbornly individual small questions, that seem content only when they have overclarified the human problems involved." A convincing application of psychoanalytical theory to Roethke and his poetry is still to be realized.

Although critical consensus suggests that Seager's work is far from satisfactory, it remains an important point of reference in the developing critical understanding of Roethke's art. However, the University of California at Berkeley holds the Seager papers, and an anonymous commentator concludes in the October 1970 *Bancroftiana* that future biographical work might be fruitful:

> Along with drafts and galleys for the Roethke book are numerous interviews which Seager conducted with persons who had known the poet at various times in his life; as much of this latter material was not included in [*The Glass House*], and as the printed version differs in many ways from the projected biography, the files are indeed invaluable to all future Roethke studies.

Thus the possibility of a new biography—or, at the least, of a biographical study of the Seattle years—is widely and hopefully suggested. Stein in his 1969 essay has deftly expressed the shortcomings of the existing biographical work and the challenge to Roethke's future biographers:

> In short, though we end the book [*The Glass House*] knowing a great deal more about Roethke the ordinary man, the effect of our knowledge is to make it clear that Roethke the extraordinary man slips through the laborious network of external evidence, a "shape changer" from way back.

Critical Studies: Books

In his 1970 article "Roethke: The Future of a Reputation," R. J. Gangewere foresaw an explosion in Roethkeana: "With the biography and selected letters now available to the general reader, there is some reason to speculate upon a potential boom in Roethkean studies. In areas of criticism I have roughly described as biographical, psychological, philosophical, and technical, Roethke is still a poet with a future." Similarly, in "Scraping the Bottom of the Roethke Barrel," a 1972 review of David Wagoner's edition of the poet's notebook entries, Karl Shapiro reluctantly concurs: "One can discern a certain trajectory in the poetic career. Following Recognition by the poet's peers, which is really all that matters, there is (1) Cult, (2)Boom and (3) Racket. . . . Roethke is being shunted from 2 to 3." Eventually, Shapiro contends, all poets return to "mere Recognition"; however, his prophetic assessment of Roethke's declining stock has yet to be realized, as the poet's reputation continues strong into the 1980s.

Gangewere's classification of productive areas for future scholarship is useful for evaluating the course of Roethke criticism. Such early volumes as Karl Malkoff's *Theodore Roethke: An Introduction to the Poetry* (1966), Ralph J. Mills, Jr.'s 1963 Minnesota Pamphlet, and the collections of essays edited by Arnold Stein (1965) and William Heyen (1971) provide overviews of Roethke's poetic dimensions. Nine subsequent book-length studies during the 1970s and early 1980s have focused for the most part on the technical, psychological, and philosophical areas suggested by Gangewere.

Since Roethke characterized himself as "slug-nutty in the technique mines," it seems fitting that several of the major full-length studies have examined Roethke's poetics. Both Mills and Malkoff in their early works generally treat formal aspects of the poems. However, it was not until 1974 that a critical book gave full attention to what Roethke called the "minimals." Richard A. Blessing's *Theodore Roethke's Dynamic Vision* analyzes the ways in which Roethke energetically manipulated the language of his poems while writing in both free and traditional metric forms. Blessing characterizes his analysis as "a study of style: of rhythm, rhyme, diction, imagery, verb forms, the use of pun, paradox, compression, repetition, and yes, even alliteration of initial sounds and manipulation and variation of interior sounds. . . . In short, . . . Roethke's bag of tricks for getting energy into a poem." Basing his work on much unpublished material from the University of Washington collection, Blessing provides significant insight into Roethke's creative process, and the critic's emphasis on energy has been frequently reiterated by others.

Blessing has stated that "one may get hold of poetic techniques with one's critical tools, while the process by which the artist's spirit evolves remains his secret to the end"; yet, given Roethke's bouts with manic depression, which began in 1935 and continued throughout his life, many critics have been unable to resist the promise of psychoanalytic theory to offer insight into his poetic development not provided by more traditional formal criticism. However, there has been substantial disagreement not only about the validity of applying psychocriticism to Roethke's life and work, but also about which psychological theory yields the greatest understanding. This debate entails, among other issues, the fundamental question of pathology versus genius: were the demons that drove Roethke a product of illness or of a creativity of a high order?

In a 1965 article, "Roethke: Poet of Transformations," Kunitz suggested the value of a Jungian approach to understanding the poetry, an approach delineated further the following year in Malkoff's book-length survey of Roethke's work. Here Malkoff offers not so much a critical as a descriptive application of the Swiss psychologist's theories, noting—as Kunitz had earlier—the remarkable parallels. Yet Malkoff clearly is aware of the limits of this kind of approach:

> However, we must guard against taking a too exclusively psychoanalytical view of these poems. The obvious application of Jung's theories should be used as a tool to further understanding, not to limit it. And Roethke in fact places at least as much emphasis on the spiritual as on the psychological aspects of his quest (which is perhaps why Jung was more congenial to Roethke than the Freudians).

Seager's 1968 biography has further encouraged the tendency to view the poems in psychoanalytical terms because of his clear linking of Roethke's 1945 breakdown with the creation of "The Lost Son" sequence. As already noted, Seager attempts in an appendix to clarify and to some degree limit the application of this approach, but evidently his disclaimer has not been strong enough to assuage the alarm of other critics at a possibly simplistic and patronizing explanation of Roethke's creativity.

Rosemary Sullivan, in *Theodore Roethke: The Garden Master* (1975), has done much to clarify the uses and limits of the psychoanalytical approach through her intelligent discussion of Kenneth Burke's essay "Freud and the Analysis of Poetry":

> Burke's "proportional strategy" helps the critic resist the Freudian tendency to overplay the psychological factor and concentrate instead on the work of art as an act of communication with moral, intellectual, and aesthetic motives that must be given equal credence.

This more balanced view has been the standard since Sullivan, a view which tempers the use of Jung in Lynn Ross-Bryant's *Theodore Roethke: Poetry of the Earth, Poet of the Spirit* (1981), which offers a good overview of Roethke's work as well.

To date, no critic has responded to Seager's suggestion that Polish psychiatrist Kazimierz Dabrowski's theory of "positive disintegration," if intelligently applied, may well be useful for understanding Roethke and his poetry. As Seager has noted, Dabrowski believed that states of great genius and creativity could be associated with the kind of disintegration Roethke suffered, and Dabrowski, like Roethke, thought that there was some gain, some spiritual progress in such episodes. Nor did Dabrowski associate these cycles with clinically abnormal states of mind but with normal behavior consistent with great genius. The systematic application of this theory to Roethke's work would be an interesting and perhaps even highly significant endeavor.

Beyond the purely psychological concerns lie the critical issues which Gangewere might classify as philosophical: Who were Roethke's formative influences and did he transform or merely echo them? Is his a public or a private poetry? Can he be fairly labeled a romantic poet, or a mystic? What are the theological dimensions of his vision? Although Roethke himself might be inclined to dismiss such dealings in intellectual history as mere "thinky-think," these questions have occupied much of the critical dialogue.

With respect to the question of Roethke's sources, Ralph J. Mills, Jr., in a 1959 article, "Keeping the Spirit Spare," begins to refute earlier critical charges that Roethke's work was too derivative by arguing that he had gone beyond simple imitation of William Butler Yeats and T. S. Eliot. Mills continues this line of inquiry in his 1963 study, *Theodore Roethke,* by contrasting "The Lost Son" with Eliot's *Four Quartets* and declaring that "Roethke's is the more protestant approach, one that bases itself firmly on personal knowledge and evidence, on the lone individual's apprehension of the transcendant." Furthermore, Jenijoy La Belle, in *The Echoing Wood of Theodore Roethke* (1976), goes well beyond Mills in decisively countering these same charges. Utilizing the Roethke manuscripts at Washington as well as other sources, she demonstrates that his "conscious imitation of such poets as Eliot, Yeats, Whitman, Wordsworth, Smart, Donne, Sir John Davies, and Dante became components of his own distinctive voice."

Concerns with aspects of Roethke's thought beyond the matter of influences have entered increasingly into the critical discourse with the appearance of book-length studies beginning in the mid-1970s. These works include Sullivan's *Theodore Roethke: The Garden Master* (1975), Harry Williams's *"The Edge Is What I Have": Theodore Roethke and After* (1977), Jay Parini's *Theodore Roethke: An American Romantic* (1979), Norman Chaney's *Theodore Roethke: The Poetics of Wonder* (1981), Ross-Bryant's *Theodore Roethke: Poetry of the Earth, Poet of the Spirit* (1981), George Wolff's *Theodore Roethke* (1981), and Neal Bowers's *Theodore Roethke: The Journey from I to Otherwise* (1982). Among the critical issues addressed in these books have been Roethke's social relevance and breadth, his classification as a romantic and/or mystic poet, and his theological inclinations.

In her 1975 study Sullivan addresses the issue of social relevance in her chapter on "Commitment to the Self." Agreeing with M. L. Rosenthal, Stephen Spender, John Wain, and others that "Roethke is not one of the poets in whose work we encounter the whole range of the living," she refutes two conclusions that she argues do not necessarily follow from that premise: first, that Roethke "is an egocentric poet, his theme remaining entirely and only himself"; and second, that "his poetry is unable to enter into the world of public relationships." Sullivan declares that "through a process of profound subjectivity the poet arrives at what is actually objective experience." Other than George Wolff's apparent disagreement in his 1981 book,

Sullivan's arguments have gone essentially unanswered.

Despite Mills's early caution, in his 1963 Minnesota Pamphlet, about simplistic classification, the efforts to categorize Roethke as an essentially romantic, mystic, or theological poet have persisted. As Mills observes: "No doubt every one of these attempts at classification would tell us a partial truth about Roethke, but none would give us the whole of it." Yet such misgivings have not prevented other critics from placing Roethke primarily in one or another of these traditions.

The most comprehensive recent work on this question of connectedness to tradition has been Parini's fine 1979 study, which draws on a wealth of unpublished as well as published material in establishing Roethke's major standing as a poet whose ancestors were William Blake, William Wordsworth, and Yeats. Like Hyatt Waggoner in *American Poets: From the Puritans to the Present,* Parini has singled out Ralph Waldo Emerson as a particular influence, concluding that Roethke "has earned a permanent place in the literature of American Romanticism."

Some critics have gone beyond seeing Roethke as a romantic to perceiving him as an outright mystic. Although treating this issue of mysticism as only one of several concerns, Sullivan's *Theodore Roethke: The Garden Master* concurs with Malkoff's observation in his 1966 introductory study:

> [Roethke] turned to [Evelyn] Underhill's *Mysticism,* a book which, as his notebooks indicate, he considered seminal to his work. . . . [Here] Roethke found both a descriptive order and imagery which made sense out of what were obviously personal experiences of inward transmutation.

Sullivan's position has challenged some earlier critical suggestions that Roethke artificially sought the mystical experience rather than first experiencing personal revelation and then coming to understand the experience through Underhill.

Neal Bowers's study, *Theodore Roethke: The Journey from I to Otherwise* (1982), drawing to some degree on the previous work of Malkoff, Blessing, Sullivan, and Parini, has provided the most systematic study of "the relatively uncharted territory of Roethke's mysticism." Beginning with a careful consideration of the meaning of the term "mysticism," Bowers moves to an examination of the mystical tradition embodied in Henry Vaughan, Thomas Traherne, Blake, and Yeats, all of whom have been seen as influences on Roethke. The critic then traces mystical elements throughout the whole of his subject's poetry. His significant attempt to reconcile Roethke's mysticism with his manic-depression is quite illuminating. Bowers acknowledges Wagoner's observation in his introduction to *Straw for the Fire* that "Roethke was not much of a mystic if, indeed, he was one at all" but that nevertheless "the strongest impression that one brings away from the notebooks is that of how desperately Roethke sought to find God."

The first significant attention to the specifically theological dimension of the work came in Malkoff's 1966 introductory survey, in which he observes that "Roethke follows [theologian Paul] Tillich rather than the mystic tradition." The influence of Tillich and the sense of awe and wonder receive a fuller treatment in Norman Chaney's 1981 *Theodore Roethke: The Poetics of Wonder*. Arguing that the "religious character of [Roethke's] vision . . . requires more definition than it has thus far received," Chaney at the same time notes the limits of such an approach: "I am not seeking to inflate theology at the expense of poetry, nor am I offering a promiscuous intermingling of both." Although Chaney's speculations concerning religious influences are less firmly grounded in primary source research than they should be, his study wrestles with a significant issue. Thus his work belongs with the other important book-length studies of Roethke, which have tended to focus on his prosody or on the psychological and philosophical aspects of his poetry.

Critical Studies: Collections of Essays

The 1965 *Theodore Roethke: Essays on the Poetry*, edited by Arnold Stein, and the 1971 *Profile of Theodore Roethke*, compiled by William Heyen, represent two attempts to provide ready access to some of the important critical judgments of major commentators, particularly in the period immediately following Roethke's death. In his introduction Stein indicates the common thrust of the material included in his collection: "All the poets and critics who have contributed to this volume share a general conviction that Roethke was a distinctive voice in modern letters." Although Stein's collection acknowledges disagreements among contributors, such as that between Stephen Spender and W. D. Snodgrass about Roethke's originality as a poet, the genuineness of Roethke's achievement is for the most part upheld.

Likewise Heyen, in his preface, begins with the assessment that Roethke "is increasingly recognized as the first American poet of his generation." He adds, nevertheless, that "the criticism collected here is not unanimous in its praise." Both Stein's and Heyen's volumes thus seem conscious of the need to present divergence as well as convergence of views. However, with the inclusion of such detracting essays as Jerome Mazzaro's "The Failure of Language" and David Ferry's "Roethke's Poetry," the latter of which sees the art as often forced and dishonest, Heyen highlights the divergence more than Stein does while raising sharper questions—for example, "Where was Roethke at his best?" and "Where did he fail?" These questions have continued to be the focus of critical debate well into the early eighties.

The two collections focus primarily on the issues of Roethke's achievement, his originality, his absorption of influences—all matters raised by such contributors as Stephen Spender, Louis Martz, William Meredith, W. D. Snodgrass, Jerome Mazzaro, Denis Donoghue, Stanley Kunitz, John Ciardi, Kenneth Burke, Delmore Schwartz, and James McMichael. However, both collections raise, if only in passing, three other critical issues which are given considerable attention elsewhere. Kunitz, McMichael, Burke, and Meredith, in particular, note the role of Roethke's poetics, which was to become the basis for Blessing's 1974 book. On the other hand, only a little attention is given in either collection to the psychoanalytical debate raised by the Mills pamphlet (1963) and the Seager biography (1968). Except for occasional allusions, such as Roy Harvey Pearce's noting of Roethke's bouts with psychotherapy and Kunitz's reference to Roethke's familiarity with Jung, there are few references to the significance of his illness and its tie, if any, to his art. It is only fair to observe that neither Malkoff's nor Seager's works appeared until after the Stein collection, although Stein does seem well aware of the issue by the time of his 1969 review of *The Glass House.* Finally, Heyen's essay on Roethke's mysticism lays the groundwork for Bowers's later excellent study on the subject. Taken together, these two collections serve well as an introduction to many of the critical issues and provide easy access to some of the most perceptive assessments of Roethke's achievement prior to the major studies of the 1970s and 1980s.

Critical Studies: Special Issue of Journal

The Summer 1971 *Northwest Review* special issue, although not distinguished, offers a number of interesting original essays and includes some illuminating selections from the Roethke notebooks edited by David Wagoner (1972). Jenijoy La Belle's "Theodore Roethke and Tradition," which anticipates her solid 1976 study, examines

Roethke's place in the tradition of Yeats and Eliot. Stein's "Roethke's Memory," an essay on the relationship of Roethke's vision to his revision, anticipates Blessing's excellent study of 1974 and is also based on a close reading of the notebooks. Roethke's love poetry is the focus of Coburn Freer's article, which notes rightly that the thematic sources of these works have not been examined as they might be.

Both Mary H. Hayden's attention to the often neglected early volume, *Open House*, and Kenneth Porter's look at the even earlier formative years at Harvard that preceded those poems add to the growing interest in Roethke's early development. Furthermore, Brendan Galvin's analysis of the significance of Roethke's relationship to Kenneth Burke and its influence on "The Lost Son" sequences is revealing in light of Burke's later pivotal essay "The Vegetal Radicalism of Theodore Roethke." These articles frequently offer more in the way of reminiscence than of new critical insights, yet they are not without usefulness.

Critical Studies: Major Articles and Book Sections

Blessing's 1974 study of Roethke's techniques was, of course, the outgrowth of other critical discussions reaching as far back as John Holmes's brief 1934 commentary in *American Poetry Journal*. Holmes recognized, as others have, Roethke's technical craftsmanship with rhythm and diction. In his 1941 *Poetry* essay Louis Forster commented on Roethke's "exactness of epithet" but urged him to stretch his metrical muscles, as had Louise Bogan in an earlier letter. Later, with the publication of *The Lost Son, and Other Poems* in 1948, Roethke appears to have responded to such criticism. Stanley Kunitz in "News of the Root" (1949) observes of Roethke's language that "his metaphors whirl alive, sucking epithets into their centers of disturbance from the periphery of the phrase; his rhythms wrench themselves out of the fixed patterns of his earlier style." This excellent short review, along with Kenneth Burke's "The Vegetal Radicalism of Theodore Roethke," published in 1950, has become the foundation for most later studies of Roethke's poetic technique. Burke points to the dynamic nature of Roethke's imagery and the language of "sheer intuition."

Hilton Kramer's important 1954 study in the *Western Review* of "The Lost Son" narratives also underscores the vitality of the language, "the first-person protagonist frequently speaking out in anguished exclamations, nonsense songs, frenzied invocations." Howard Nemerov's *Kenyon Review* commentary on *The Waking* remarks on

Roethke's verbal sophistication and impulsive energy in "The Lost Son" poems. However, in the Spring 1954 issue of the *Black Mountain Review*, Martin Seymour-Smith finds Roethke merely an unoriginal metrical apologist for traditional verse.

William Meredith in his 1964 essay "A Steady Storm of Correspondences" continues to underscore Roethke's use of artifice to convey a kind of primal vitality and growth:

> The greenhouse poems . . . are themselves examples of vegetable
> energy. . . . Roethke is one of the few poets whose internal rhyme
> and assonance is worth thinking about.

Similarly, William J. Martz's commentary in the collection *The Achievement of Theodore Roethke* (1966) points in passing to Roethke's skillful use of metaphor and symbol and to the fact that "his rhythms are crucial to the final effect he seeks."

In contrast to Martz's brief references, John D. Boyd offers a detailed analysis of the technical aspects of the greenhouse poems. His 1971 *Modern Language Quarterly* essay emphasizes that Roethke's contribution can best be understood "through [the poems'] formal and structural properties." Like most critics, Boyd finds the dynamism and energy of Roethke's diction and rhythms remarkable, perhaps even unique. Other significant commentators on Roethke's stylistic contributions have included Brendan Galvin, who in a 1972 *Concerning Poetry* essay notes his use of proverbs, and Bernard Heringman, who in "Roethke's Poetry: The Forms of Meaning" (1974) analyzes his metrical techniques.

Perhaps the most notable post-Blessing technical comment has come in Geoffrey Thurley's chapter on "The Lost Son" sequence in *The American Moment: American Poetry in the Mid-Century* (1978). Here Thurley has diverged appreciably from the majority of critics in accusing Roethke of "rhythmic academicism" and in characterizing his poetry as "studied, academic, pre-ordained." He further asserts that "Roethke never perhaps—or only rarely—eluded the confines of a Yeatsian conception of the poet as maker: and to strive to be a maker, in poetry, is almost certain to make the striver a faker." Although Thurley's analysis is unconvincing, it is of interest in that it wittily articulates a minority position. But the critical consensus at present supports Blessing's appreciative point of view.

Perhaps the earliest encouragement of the psychological approach to Roethke criticism was offered by Kunitz's "News of the

Root" (1949), in which he describes the long poems in *The Lost Son, and Other Poems* as "the record of a psychic adventure, the poet's quest for self." Roethke's 1950 essay "Open Letter" (reprinted in *The Poet and His Craft*) refers to this psychic adventure as "a kind of struggle out of the slime; part of a slow spiritual progress; an effort to be born, and later, to become something more." Burke, a close friend of Roethke's, hints in his important "Vegetal Radicalism" article (1950) at a connection between Roethke's creative process and some kind of psychic turbulence:

> The dangers inherent in the [poetry's] regressive imagery seem to have received an impetus from without, that drove the poet still more forcefully in the same direction, dipping him in the river who loved water. His own love thus threatened to turn against him. The enduring of such discomforts is a "birth" in the sense that, if the poet survives the ordeal, he is essentially stronger, and has to this extent *forged himself* an identity.

The dangers implied by the imagery were, of course, to haunt Roethke throughout his career.

Ciardi's 1953 *Nation* review of *The Waking* more explicitly suggests the connection between the poetry and Roethke's madness. Here Ciardi considers Roethke's poetry a form of therapy (though certainly not merely that) and terms him the "medicine man" of the "inner landscape," a position also taken by Babette Deutsch in her close reading of "In a Dark Time" (1961). These critics set forth no specific theoretical foundation for a psychological approach to the work; but in "Closing in on the Self," a 1959 review of *Words for the Wind*, M. L. Rosenthal specifically applies clinical psychoanalytical references to Roethke's work. Rosenthal calls "The Lost Son" "a Freudian romance with a happy ending." Later, in his 1967 book *The New Poets*, he continues to emphasize that Roethke's long poems are "based on a program of psychological states more or less Freudian in their conception."

Kunitz, on the other hand, in his 1965 essay "Roethke: Poet of Transformations," applies not Freud's but Carl Jung's theories to the long poems in particular. Citing Roethke's statement regarding his "cyclic" method of growth—"to go forward as a spiritual man it is necessary first to go back," Kunitz observes that:

> ... these passages point straight to the door of Dr. Jung or the

door of Jung's disciple Maud Bodkin, whose *Archetypal Patterns in Poetry* was familiar to Roethke. In Jung's discussion of Progression and Regression as fundamental concepts of the Libbo-Theory in his *Contributions to Analytical Psychology,* he describes progression as the "daily advance of the process of psychological adaptation," which at certain times fails.

Early reviews by Kunitz, Deutsch, Burke, Kramer, and Carolyn Kizer of *The Lost Son* and *Praise to the End!* hail Roethke's originality. In contrast, Seymour-Smith in "Where Is Mr. Roethke?" (1954) finds little originality and certainly no breakthrough in these volumes. With the publication of *The Waking* and Roethke's apparent turn from the influence of Eliot to the cadences of Yeats, critical concern with the issue of imitation becomes even more pronounced.

W. D. Snodgrass and M. L. Rosenthal consistently label Roethke derivative, but John Berryman in his 1959 *American Scholar* essay takes a middle position. While echoing others' assessments of Roethke as a "most powerful and original" talent, Berryman expresses concern about the influences of both Eliot and Yeats. Furthermore, Delmore Schwartz argues forcefully in the June 1959 *Poetry* that Roethke was not *"merely* imitating" Yeats but transmuting his influence in a distinctively concrete way that Schwartz terms a "feat of the imagination"; he observes, "it is paradoxical and true that the most natural and frequent path to true originality, for most good poets, is through imitating the style of a very great poet."

The year after Roethke's death, with the publication of *The Far Field,* many critics were tempted to make a final assessment not only of the matter of originality, but also of the poet's place in the canon. Consensus continues to be elusive. Hayden Carruth comments in his 1964 *Nation* essay that Roethke "was too unsure of himself, technically and emotionally, to write the handful of absolute poems that one needs to enter the first rank," and Ian Hamilton in the April 1964 *Agenda* declares Roethke's later work, with its Yeatsian influence, to be self-evasive. Yet both X. J. Kennedy in a 1964 *New York Times Book Review* article and John Wain in his *Critical Quarterly* essay appearing in the Winter 1964 issue argue that Roethke had succeeded in absorbing and transcending Yeats. Similarly, William Meredith in the Autumn 1964 *Shenandoah* acknowledges that the influence of Yeats might be too strong in some poems, but that "it was perhaps because Roethke felt he had won through to a sure identity that in his later poems he made free to borrow meters, cadences, tones from other poets, but chiefly from Yeats." Denis Donoghue also maintains, in "Roethke's Broken Music" (1965), that the poet's work evolved through many voices, the last poems being "rich and humane." And whereas Snodgrass, in his October 1964 *New York Review of Books* essay, describes Roethke's career as a "remarkable achievement," he expresses disappointment in the later poems. Frederick J. Hoffman, however, traces the development of Roethke's poetic voice through four stages and declares, in "Theodore Roethke: The Poetic Shape of Death" (1965), that "from the second volume on . . . , [he] made his verse his own."

The argument continues. Although Rosenthal charges, in *The New Poets: American and British Poetry Since World War II* (1967), that the effects in the later poems "are finally unearned," Burke, in "Cult of the Breakthrough" (1968), maintains that "what he took, he would assimilate, in terms of his poetic integrity." John Lucas in his 1968 *Oxford Review* essay tosses another literary ancestor into the ring, assessing Roethke's problems with authentic voice and his echoing of Wallace Stevens and Eliot in *The Far Field*. Even more recently it has appeared that a critical consensus on the issue might be emerging: Jerome Mazzaro's 1970 "Theodore Roethke and the Failures of Language" concludes acerbically that "Roethke could do no better than to become a ventriloquist of those voices approved by his contemporaries," and J. D. McClatchy's "Sweating Light from a Stone: Identifying Theodore Roethke" (1972) argues that *The Lost Son, and Other Poems* show Roethke's "inability to construct an identity" while *The Far Field* demonstrates further that "the self [was never] authenticated." However, La Belle's 1976 book presents a formidable refutation of these charges. There has been no significant critical rejoinder to her argument other than Geoffrey Thurley's unconvincing and shrill characterization of Roethke's work in "Theodore Roethke: Lost Son" (1978) as "a confusion of self-flogging sincerity and quite blatant and factitious artistic fakery. The higher he strove, the worse he wrote. The bigger the scale attempted, the more resounding the tinkle of his bathos. . . ."

Criticism of Roethke's self-absorption and lack of social concern has come relatively late, perhaps because of the earlier hope on the part of some critics, such as Roy Harvey Pearce in his essay "The Power of Sympathy" (1965), that Roethke would "evolve." However, following the poet's death many critics have commented more freely on his characteristic inwardness of focus. Thus in his 1964 essay John Wain underscores what he regards as one of Roethke's major limitations: "[The last poetry] is too narrow in scope, too repetitious. It seeks wisdom from one source and one source only. Of the various kinds of illumination a human life needs, this poetry pursues only one kind." Moreover, Robert Phillips observes even more categorically in *The Confessional Poets* (1973):

> Theodore Roethke flourished during the years of the Great Depression, World War II, the atom bomb, the Korean War, and more—and yet made no mention of them. Of all poets discussed in this book, Roethke is the least "public," his poems almost entirely untouched by history or current events. . . . Roethke's work seems to be produced in a vacuum.

Although for some critics such an observation seems a simple statement of fact with no call to topicality or "relevance" intended, for others it is an indictment.

In *"The Edge Is What I Have": Theodore Roethke and After* (1977), Harry Williams begins from a similar premise regarding Roethke's apparent lack of social consciousness, but he reaches a different conclusion—one more in keeping with Sullivan's, which has been noted earlier in this essay. Williams cites Yeats via Robert Bly in noting that "a true political poem is a quarrel with ourselves, and . . . rhetoric is as harmful in that sort of poem as in the personal poem. . . ; like the personal poem, it moves to deepened awareness." And although Anthony Libby repeats the charge of narrowness in his 1984 *Mythologies of Nothing,* he and George Wolff, whose comments on the matter have already been noted, have been the only critics to take issue with Sullivan's and Williams's arguments.

Another concern which has received critical attention is Roethke's place in the poetic tradition. In *The New Poets* (1967) Rosenthal allocates Roethke a spot in the "confessional movement," but Malkoff qualifies this assessment in "Roethke: The Poet as Albatross" (1969), when he contends that Roethke was not just a confessional poet but created a "private world specifically calculated to bear the weight of his public vision." And while Gangewere in his important 1970 essay regards Roethke as part of the confessional tradition, Robert Phillips in his chapter on Roethke in *The Confessional Poets* (1973) concurs but adds:

> For the better part of his writing career Roethke was not content merely to swim on the surface of the unconscious. His was a

compulsion to dive down deeper and stay down longer than any other of the confessional poets. And he alone of the group attempts a poetry of mysticism.

Other critics have labeled Roethke a romantic. In his insightful 1954 essay, Hilton Kramer becomes perhaps the first to place Roethke within this movement, but he notes that Roethke carries the "Wordsworthian subject to a new extremity" and that he departs from the American tradition with his concentration on prehistory and the pre-rational. Edwin Muir in his 1958 *New Statesman* review of *Words for the Wind* places more emphasis on Roethke's distinctively American intellectual roots: he finds that Roethke's romanticism is unlike anything in traditional English poetry but belongs instead to a native American tradition that includes Emily Dickinson, Robert Frost, and others. Martz's 1966 critical introduction makes Roethke's romantic antecedents explicit without limiting them as to nationality:

> A striking characteristic of the poetry of Theodore Roethke is its relationship to the romantic tradition.... Comparisons of Roethke with other romantic poets could be multiplied indefinitely—in the twentieth century with, for example, e. e. cummings.... But finally it is toward the later Yeats, as toward Whitman, that Roethke turns.

C. W. Truesdale in "Theodore Roethke and the Landscape of American Poetry" (1968), who concurs as to the romanticism but is more specific as to its particular branch, argues that Roethke "is a distinctly 'American poet' . . . very firmly within the continuing tradition of American Romanticism" and lists Thoreau, Melville, Twain, and Whitman as ancestors. Hyatt Waggoner in his 1968 survey, *American Poets: From the Puritans to the Present,* largely agrees, citing Emerson, Whitman, and Dickinson as particular forebears. Waggoner specifically emphasizes the connection with Emerson and the American Transcendental tradition, though he also notes points of divergence. Furthermore, although seeing Roethke's romanticism as recognizably American, Waggoner does note its ties to the larger tradition embracing Rainer Maria Rilke, Blake, Yeats, and Eliot.

Oliver Everette in his 1968 memoir records a remark Roethke made after a bout with mental illness: "Do you know what I'm studying now? Christian mysticism." Such a significant biographical comment coupled with early suggestions by John Holmes in 1934 have led to considerable discussion of Roethke as a mystic. In particular, attention has focused on the influence of Evelyn Underhill's *Mysticism: A Study in the Nature and Development of Man's Spiritual Consciousness* (1955), with which Roethke was thoroughly familiar. Although critics have commented on the presence of Underhill's patterns of mystical experience in "The Lost Son" sequence and "Meditations of an Old Woman," the subject has drawn particular attention in relation to the last poems in *Sequence, Sometimes Metaphysical* and *The Far Field*, published posthumously. Much of the discussion by Kunitz, John Crowe Ransom, and Deutsch in Ostroff's symposium on "In a Dark Time" in 1961 illuminates the nature of Roethke's mysticism, as does Hugh B. Staples's "The Rose in the Sea-Wind" (1964), a sensitive reading of the "North American Sequence" that calls Roethke's mystic secrets reminiscent of Eliot's in *The Four Quartets*.

Mills in his essay "In the Way of Becoming: Roethke's Last Poems" (1965) also offers an important treatment of the same concept: "I want to call attention here to the different phases of the self's evolution as we find them treated in . . . 'North American Sequence' and 'Sequence, Sometimes Metaphysical,' in which the poet exceeds the limits of previous development and sets forth on an arduous but successful quest for mystical illumination. . . . [These poems] leave us not only some of his finest work, but a number of the most astonishing mystical poems in the language." Snodgrass in his 1964 *New York Review of Books* assessment refers to Underhill in noting Roethke's mysticism, but like several other critics he finds these last poems less successful than the earlier ones. On the other hand, James G. Southworth's 1966 essay on *The Far Field* characterizes the mystical dimension of the last poems as "the final stages in the fight between the angels and the devils for the poet's soul with temporary victories on both sides until the angels are triumphant in the end."

Although many critics have disagreed about the success of these last poems and seen the early sequences as Roethke's greatest triumph, the attention to the poet's mysticism, not only in the last works but the earlier as well, has gained momentum. William Heyen's systematic discussion, in "The Divine Abyss: Theodore Roethke's Mysticism" (1969), of Underhill's five stages of mysticism points to how closely Roethke's comments—such as those directed at "In a Dark Time" as part of the Ostroff symposium—echo Underhill. Using Roethke's poem "The Abyss" from *The Far Field* as a basis, Heyen comments briefly on its mystical connections to earlier poems as well. However, Nathan A. Scott in his long chapter in *The Wild Prayer of Longing*

(1971) argues that although mysticism is strongly present throughout Roethke's work, it is not traditional mysticism but one purified from the self-indulgent and free of easy moralizing. On the other hand, Robert Phillips in "The Inward Journeys of Theodore Roethke" (1973), which also focuses on "The Lost Son" sequence, speaks of a failed mysticism in asking: "Does Theodore Roethke finally achieve something resembling peace of mind from these traumatic confessions? Sadly not, as a reading of those poems which fill subsequent books reveals." Phillips argues that Roethke never completes the final stage of mysticism, and thus his final vision is neither earned nor attained.

Everette's interesting 1968 biographical essay, "Theodore Roethke: The Poet as Teacher," sheds further light on Wagoner's earlier suggestion that Roethke was engaged in a search for God. In a 1949 interchange between Roethke and Everette, a clergyman, regarding the need to find one's own rhythm, Roethke observed of Gerard Manley Hopkins that "no matter how he starts, he ends with God. This is true religious sense." Later at the height of a manic episode he told Everette, "This [book of poems] is my religion. But I believe in God as much as you do." Everette's suggestion of a further religious bent in Roethke's work, one which might be specifically labeled theological, also has been discussed in passing by other critics. Burke in his 1950 essay suggests that Roethke in "The Lost Son" is on the verge of some revelation, and Carroll Arnet in a 1957 *College English* article testifies to Roethke's belief in a higher realm. Later, John Crowe Ransom in his essay on "In a Dark Time" (1961) terms Roethke's vision theological, and John Wain, in his 1964 *Critical Quarterly* article, goes so far as to call him an "evangelical writer."

Although M. L. Lewandowska's 1980 study of Roethke's use of the Psalms of David is of interest, Scott's chapter in *The Wild Prayer of Longing—Poetry and the Sacred* (1971) offers the fullest account of Roethke's theological concerns. He offers a well researched reading of Roethke's "truly sacramental vision of our human inheritance" and points to Roethke's "sense of awe or wonder," which is the basis for Chaney's later full-length study.

Although much significant work has been done, Gangewere's 1970 observation that Roethke is a poet with a critical future still holds true today. Among the possibilities for further exploration is a fuller treatment of the love poetry than that afforded by Coburn Freer's good 1971 article. A study of Roethke's nonsense and children's verse, as suggested by Alan Nadel in 1978, would also be in order. As previously mentioned, a new biography, especially one concerned with the later years, would be welcomed, as would a further examination of the poet in light of Dabrowski's theory of "positive disintegration." Furthermore, although Williams's 1977 book-length study of Roethke's influence on such later poets as James Wright, Robert Bly, James Dickey, Sylvia Plath, and Ted Hughes goes far to affirm his continuing influence, and although Anthony Libby has addressed the subject in *Mythologies of Nothing* (1984), an analysis of Roethke's poetics in relation to the work of other younger writers would be fruitful. Moreover, Chaney's concentration on Roethke's theological sources could be extended to substantial treatments of the influences of Paul Tillich and Martin Buber, which have received only random notice by such critics as Malkoff, McMichael, McClatchy, and Sullivan. Yet for those readers wishing a general introduction to Roethke's work, Mills's early pamphlet (1963), Malkoff's introduction (1966), and George Wolff's 1981 Twayne volume prove both useful and enduring.

Anne Sexton

(1928-1974)

Diana Hume George
Pennsylvania State University

PRIMARY BIBLIOGRAPHY

Books

To Bedlam and Part Way Back. Boston: Houghton Mifflin, 1960. Poems.
All My Pretty Ones. Boston: Houghton Mifflin, 1962. Poems.
Eggs of Things, by Sexton and Maxine Kumin. New York: Putnam's, 1963. Children's stories.
More Eggs of Things, by Sexton and Kumin. New York: Putnam's, 1964. Children's stories.
Selected Poems. London: Oxford University Press, 1964. Poems.
Live or Die. Boston: Houghton Mifflin, 1966; London: Oxford University Press, 1967. Poems.
Poems, by Sexton, Thomas Kinsella, and Douglas Livingstone. London: Oxford University Press, 1968. Poems.
Love Poems. Boston: Houghton Mifflin, 1969; London: Oxford University Press, 1969. Poems.
Joey and the Birthday Present, by Sexton and Kumin. New York: McGraw-Hill, 1971. Children's story.
Transformations. Boston: Houghton Mifflin, 1971; London: Oxford University Press, 1972. Poems.
The Book of Folly. Boston: Houghton Mifflin, 1972; London: Chatto & Windus, 1974. Poems, stories.
The Death Notebooks. Boston: Houghton Mifflin, 1974; London: Chatto & Windus, 1975. Poems.
The Awful Rowing Toward God. Boston: Houghton Mifflin, 1975; London: Chatto & Windus, 1977. Poems.
The Wizard's Tears, by Sexton and Kumin. New York: McGraw-Hill, 1975. Children's story.
45 Mercy Street, ed. Linda Gray Sexton. Boston: Houghton Mifflin,

1976; London: Secker & Warburg, 1977. Poems.
Words for Dr. Y: Uncollected Poems with Three Stories, ed. Linda Gray
Sexton. Boston: Houghton Mifflin, 1978. Poems, stories.
The Complete Poems, ed. Linda G. Sexton. Boston: Houghton Mifflin,
1982. Poems.
No Evil Star: Selected Essays, Interviews, and Prose, edited by Steven E.
Colburn. Ann Arbor: University of Michigan Press, 1985.

Letters

Anne Sexton: A Self-Portrait in Letters, ed. Linda Gray Sexton and Lois
Ames. Boston: Houghton Mifflin, 1977.

Worksheets

" 'Suicide Note' Worksheets," *New York Quarterly,* 4 (Fall 1970), 81-94.
"Worksheets for 'Elizabeth Gone.' " Collected in *Anne Sexton: The Artist
and Her Critics,* ed. J. D. McClatchy, 51-68. See Collection of
Essays.

SECONDARY BIBLIOGRAPHY

Bibliography

Northouse, Cameron, and Thomas P. Walsh. *Sylvia Plath and Anne
Sexton: A Reference Guide.* Boston: G. K. Hall, 1974. Primary and
secondary.

Selected Interviews

Ames, Lois. "Anne Sexton: From 'Bedlam' to Broadway," *Boston Sunday Herald Traveler Book Guide,* 12 Oct. 1969, pp. 1-2, 16.
"Anne Sexton." In *Talks With Authors,* ed. Charles F. Madden. Carbondale: Southern Illinois University Press, 1968, 151-179.
Balliro, Charles. "Interview with Anne Sexton," *Fiction,* 1, no. 6 (1974),
12-13, 5.
Berg, Beatrice. " 'Oh, I Was Very Sick,' " *New York Times,* 9 Nov.1969,
pp. D1, D7.
Fitz Gerald, Gregory. "The Choir From the Soul: A Conversation
with Anne Sexton," *Massachusetts Review,* 19 (Spring 1978), 69-
88.

Green, Carol. "A Writer Is Essentially a Spy," *Boston Review of the Arts,* 2 (Aug. 1972), 30-37.
Heyen, William. "From 1928 to Whenever: A Conversation with Anne Sexton." In *American Poets in 1976,* ed. Heyen. Indianapolis: Bobbs-Merrill, 1976, 304-328.
Kevles, Barbara. "The Art of Poetry XV: Anne Sexton," *Paris Review,* 13 (Summer 1971), 159-191. Collected in McClatchy. See Collection of Essays.
Marx, Patricia. "Interview with Anne Sexton," *Hudson Review,* 18 (Winter 1965-1966), 560-570. Collected in McClatchy. See Collection of Essays.
Packard, William. "Craft Interview with Anne Sexton." In *The Craft of Poetry,* ed. Packard. New York: Doubleday, 1974, 19-23. Collected in McClatchy. See Collection of Essays.
Showalter, Elaine, and Carol Smith. "A Nurturing Relationship: A Conversation with Anne Sexton and Maxine Kumin, April 15, 1974," *Women's Studies,* 4, no. 1 (1976), 115-136.
Weeks, Brigitte. "The Excitable Gift: The Art of Anne Sexton," *Boston* (Aug. 1968), 30-32.

Critical Studies: Book

George, Diana Hume. *Oedipus Anne: The Poetry of Anne Sexton.* Champaign: University of Illinois Press, 1986.

Critical Studies: Collection of Essays

McClatchy, J. D., ed. *Anne Sexton: The Artist and Her Critics.* Bloomington & London: Indiana University Press, 1978.

Critical Studies: Special Issue of Journal

Notes on Modern American Literature, 3 (Summer 1979). Sexton and Robert Lowell number.

Critical Studies: Major Articles and Book Sections

Ames, Lois. "Remembering Anne." Collected in McClatchy, 111-114.
Axelrod, Rise B. "The Transforming Art of Anne Sexton," *Concerning Poetry,* 7 (Spring 1974), 6-13.

Bagg, Robert. "A Regime of Revelation," *Audience*, 7 (Summer 1960), 121-125.

Blackburn, Thomas. "Three American Poets," *Poetry Review*, 58 (Autumn 1967), 257-258.

Bogan, Louise. "Verse," *New Yorker*, 27 Apr. 1963, p. 175.

Boyers, Robert. "*Live or Die:* The Achievement of Anne Sexton," *Salmagundi*, no. 2 (Spring 1967), 61-71. Collected in McClatchy.

Brinnin, John Malcolm. "Offices (Boston University)," *American Poetry Review*, 4, no. 3 (1975), 15. Poem. Collected in McClatchy.

Carruth, Hayden. "In Spite of Artifice," *Hudson Review*, 19 (Winter 1966-1967), 698. Collected in McClatchy.

Conarroe, Joel O. "Five Poets," *Shenandoah*, 18 (Summer 1967), 84-91.

Demetrakopoulos, Stephanie. "The Nursing Mother and Feminine Metaphysics: An Essay on Embodiment," *Soundings*, 65 (Winter 1982), 430-443.

Dickey, James. "Five First Books," *Poetry*, 97 (Feb. 1961), 316-320. Excerpt collected in McClatchy. Reprinted in Dickey, *The Suspect in Poetry*. Madison, Minn.: Sixties Press, 1964. Reprinted in Dickey, *Babel to Byzantium: Poets & Poetry Now*. New York: Farrar, Straus & Giroux, 1968.

Dickey, William. "A Place in the Country," *Hudson Review*, 22 (Summer 1969), 347-352.

Fein, Richard J. "The Demon of Anne Sexton," *English Record*, 18 (Oct. 1967), 16-21.

Fields, Beverly. "The Poetry of Anne Sexton." In *Poets in Progress*, ed. Edward Hungerford. Evanston, Ill.: Northwestern University Press, 1967, 251-285.

Fraser, G. S. "Public Voices," *Partisan Review*, 37, no. 2 (1970), 299-300.

Gallagher, Brian. "The Expanded Use of Simile in Anne Sexton's *Transformations*," *Notes on Modern American Literature*, 3 (Summer 1979), Item 20.

George, Diana Hume. "Anne Sexton and The Awful Rowing," *Women's Voices*, 4 (Winter 1976), 12-13.

_____. "Anne Sexton's Suicide Poems," *Journal of Popular Culture*, 18 (Fall 1984), 17-31.

_____. "Beyond the Pleasure Principle: Anne Sexton's 'The Death Baby,'" *University of Hartford Studies in Literature*, 15, 2 (1983), 75-92.

_____. "How We Danced: Anne Sexton on Fathers and Daughters," *Women's Studies* (forthcoming).

_____. "Oedipus Iscariot: Anne Sexton's Judas," *Poesis: A Journal of Criticism* (forthcoming).

_____. "Two Immoderate Sisters: Kumin on Sexton, Kumin on Kumin," *Poesis: A Journal of Criticism* (forthcoming).

Gilbert, Sandra M. "Jubilate Anne," *Nation,* 14 Sept. 1974, pp. 214-216. Collected in McClatchy.

Gullans, Charles. "Poetry and Subject Matter: From Hart Crane to Turner Cassity," *Southern Review,* new series, 6 (Spring 1970), 497-498. Collected in McClatchy.

Gunn, Thom. "Poems and Books of Poems," *Yale Review,* 53 (Oct. 1963), 140-141. Excerpt collected in McClatchy.

Hartman, Geoffrey H. "Les Belles Dames Sans Merci," *Kenyon Review,* 22 (Autumn 1960), 696-700. Excerpt collected in McClatchy.

Hoffman, Nancy Jo. "Reading Women's Poetry: The Meaning and Our Lives," *College English,* 34 (Oct. 1972), 48-62.

Hoffman, Nancy Yanes. "A Special Language," *Southwest Review,* 64 (Summer 1979), 209-214.

Honton, Margaret. "The Double Image and the Division of Parts: A Study of Mother/Daughter Relationships in the Poetry of Anne Sexton," *Journal of Women's Studies in Literature,* 1 (1979), 33-50.

Howard, Richard. "Anne Sexton: 'Some Tribal Female Who Is Known but Forbidden.' " In his *Alone with America: Essays on the Art of Poetry in the United States Since 1950.* New York: Atheneum, 1969, 442-450. Collected in McClatchy.

_____. "Five Poets," *Poetry,* 101 (Mar. 1963), 413-414.

Hughes, Daniel. "American Poetry 1969: From B to Z," *Massachusetts Review,* 11 (Autumn 1970), 668-671.

Johnson, Greg. "The Achievement of Anne Sexton," *Hollins Critic,* 21 (June 1984), 1-13.

Johnson, Rosemary. "The Woman of Private (But Published) Hungers," *Parnassus: Poetry in Review,* 8 (Fall/Winter 1979), 92-107.

Jones, A. R. "Necessity and Freedom: The Poetry of Robert Lowell, Sylvia Plath and Anne Sexton," *Critical Quarterly,* 7 (Spring 1965), 11-30.

Jong, Erica. "Remembering Anne Sexton," *New York Times Book Review,* 27 Oct. 1974, p. 63.

Juhasz, Suzanne. " 'The Excitable Gift': The Poetry of Anne Sexton." In her *Naked and Fiery Forms: Modern American Poetry by Women, A New Tradition.* New York: Octagon, 1976, 117-143.

_____. "Seeking the Exit or the Home: Poetry and Salvation in the Career of Anne Sexton." In *Shakespeare's Sisters: Feminist Essays on Women Poets,* ed. Sandra M. Gilbert and Susan Gubar. Bloomington: Indiana University Press, 1979, 261-268.

Kammer, Jeanne H. "The Witch's Life: Confession and Control in the Early Poetry of Anne Sexton," *Language and Style,* 13 (Fall 1980), 29-35.

Kumin, Maxine. "A Friendship Remembered." Collected in McClatchy, 103-110. Reprinted in Kumin, *To Make a Prairie: Essays on Poets, Poetry, and Country Living.* Ann Arbor: University of Michigan Press, 1979.

_____. "How It Was: Maxine Kumin on Anne Sexton." In *The Complete Poems,* ed. Linda G. Sexton, xix-xxxiv.

_____. "Reminiscence Delivered at Memorial Service for Anne Sexton in Marsh Chapel, Boston University. October 15, 1974." In her *To Make a Prairie: Essays on Poets, Poetry, and Country Living,* 78-80.

_____. "Sexton's *The Awful Rowing Toward God.*" In her *To Make a Prairie: Essays on Poets, Poetry, and Country Living,* 81-82.

Lacey, Paul A. "The Sacrament of Confession." In his *The Inner War; Forms and Themes in Recent American Poetry.* Philadelphia: Fortress Press, 1972, 8-31.

Lant, Jeffrey L. "Another Entry in the Death Notebooks," *Southwest Review,* 64 (Summer 1979), 215-219.

Lauter, Estella. "Anne Sexton's 'Radical Discontent with the Awful Order of Things,'" *Spring: An Annual of Archetypal Psychology and Jungian Thought* (1979), 77-92. Reprinted in her *Women as Mythmakers.* Bloomington: Indiana University Press, 1984.

Legler, Philip. "O Yellow Eye," *Poetry,* 110 (May 1967), 125-127.

_____. "Reviews," *New Mexico Quarterly Review,* 37 (Spring 1967), 89-92.

Levertov, Denise. "Anne Sexton: Light Up the Cave," *Ramparts,* 13 (Jan. 1975), 61-63. Collected in McClatchy.

Lowell, Robert. "Anne Sexton." Collected in McClatchy, 71-73.

McCabe, Jane. " 'A Woman Who Writes': A Feminist Approach to the Early Poetry of Anne Sexton." Collected in McClatchy, 216-243.

McClatchy, J. D. "Anne Sexton: Somehow to Endure," *Centennial Review,* 19 (Spring 1975), 1-36. Expanded and collected in McClatchy.

McDonnell, Thomas P. "Light in a Dark Journey," *America,* 13 May 1967, pp. 729-731. Collected in McClatchy.

McGill, William J. "Anne Sexton and God," *Commonweal,* 13 May 1977, pp. 304-306.

Marras, Emma. "After a Conversation with Linda and Joy Sexton," *Paintbrush,* 6, no. 11 (1979), 34-38.

Maryan, Charles. "The Poet On Stage." Collected in McClatchy, 89-95.

Mazzocco, Robert. "Matters of Life and Death," *New York Review of Books,* 3 Apr. 1975, pp. 22-23. Excerpt collected in McClatchy.

Middlebrook, Diane. "Becoming Anne Sexton," *Denver Quarterly,* 18 (Winter 1984), 23-34.

_____. "Housewife Into Poet: The Apprenticeship of Anne Sexton," *New England Quarterly,* 56 (Dec. 1983), 483-503.

_____. "Poet of Weird Abundance: Anne Sexton: *The Complete Poems,*" *Parnassus: Poetry in Review* (forthcoming).

_____. "Three Mirrors Reflecting Women: Poetry of Sylvia Plath, Anne Sexton, and Adrienne Rich." In her *Worlds Into Words: Understanding Modern Poems.* New York: Norton, 1978, 65-96.

Mills, Ralph J., Jr. *Contemporary American Poetry.* New York: Random House, 1965, 218-234.

_____. "Four Voices in Recent American Poetry," *Christian Scholar,* 46 (Winter 1963), 327-332.

Mood, John J. " 'A Bird Full of Bones': Anne Sexton—A Visit and a Reading," *Chicago Review,* 23, no. 4; 24, no. 1 (1972), 107-123.

Morse, Samuel French. "Poetry 1966," *Contemporary Literature,* 9 (Winter 1968), 122-123.

Myers, Neil. "The Hungry Sheep Look Up," *Minnesota Review,* 1 (Oct. 1960), 99-104.

Nichols, Kathleen L. "The Hungry Beast Rowing Toward God: Anne Sexton's Later Religious Poetry," *Notes on Modern American Literature,* 3 (Summer 1979), Item 21.

Oates, Joyce Carol. "*The Awful Rowing Toward God,*" *New York Times Book Review,* 23 Mar. 1975, pp. 3-4. Collected in McClatchy.

_____. "The Rise and Fall of a Poet: *The Complete Poems* of Anne Sexton," *New York Times Book Review,* 18 Oct. 1981, pp. 3, 37.

Ostriker, Alicia. "That Story: Anne Sexton and Her Transformations," *American Poetry Review,* 11 (July/Aug. 1982), 11-16. Reprinted as "That Story: The Changes of Anne Sexton" in her *Writing Like a Woman.* Ann Arbor: University of Michigan, 1983.

Phillips, Robert. "Anne Sexton: The Blooming Mouth and the Bleeding Rose." In his *The Confessional Poets.* Carbondale: Southern Illinois University Press, 1973, 73-91.

Pinsky, Robert. "A Characteristic Figure," *New York Times Book Review,* 26 Nov. 1978, pp. 7, 90.

Pritchard, William H. "The Anne Sexton Show," *Hudson Review,* 31 (Summer 1978), 387-392.

Rosenthal, M. L. "Other Confessional Poets." In his *The New Poets: American and British Poetry Since World War II.* London: Oxford University Press, 1967, 131-138.

_____. "Seven Voices," *Reporter,* 28 (3 Jan. 1963), 47-48.

Rukeyser, Muriel. "Glitter and Wounds, Several Wildnesses," *Parnassus: Poetry in Review,* 2 (Fall/Winter 1973), 215-221. Collected in McClatchy.

Shurr, William H. "Anne Sexton's *Love Poems:* The Genre and the Differences," *Modern Poetry Studies,* 10, no. 1 (1980), 58-68.

_____. "Sexton's 'The Legend of the One-Eyed Man,' " *Explicator,* 39 (Spring 1981), 2-3.

Simpson, Louis. "New Books of Poems," *Harper's,* 235 (Aug. 1967), 90-91.

Smith, Hal. "Notes, Reviews and Speculations," *Epoch,* 10 (Fall 1960), 253-255.

_____. "Notes, Reviews and Speculations," *Epoch,* 12 (Fall 1962), 124-126.

Spacks, Patricia Meyer. "45 Mercy Street," *New York Times Book Review,* 30 May 1976, p. 6. Collected in McClatchy.

Spivak, Kathleen. "Sharers of the Heart: A Friend Remembers Anne Sexton," *Boston Globe Magazine,* 9 Aug. 1981, pp. 10-13, 35-42.

Swan, Barbara. "A Reminiscence." Collected in McClatchy, 81-88.

Swenson, May. "Poetry of Three Women," *Nation,* 23 Feb. 1963, pp. 164-166. Collected in McClatchy.

Tanenhaus, Beverly. "Politics of Suicide and Survival: The Poetry of Anne Sexton and Adrienne Rich," *Bucknell Review,* 24, no. 1 (1978), 106-118.

Tillinghast, Richard. "Five Poets," *Sewanee Review,* 72 (July-Sept. 1963), 510-513.

Wagner, Linda W. "45 Mercy Street and Other Vacant Houses." In *American Literature: The New England Heritage,* ed. James Nagel and Richard Astro. New York: Garland, 1981, 145-165.

White, William. "Lyrics Back to Sanity and Love," *Prairie Schooner,* 35 (Spring 1961), 3-4.

Williams, Polly C. "Sexton in the Classroom." Collected in McClatchy, 96-101.

Zollman, Sol. "Criticism, Self-Criticism, No Transformation: The Poetry of Robert Lowell and Anne Sexton," *Literature and Ideology,* 9 (1971), 29-36.

Zweig, Paul. "Making and Unmaking," *Partisan Review,* 40, no. 2 (1973), 277-279.

BIBLIOGRAPHICAL ESSAY

Bibliography

Cameron Northouse and Thomas P. Walsh have assembled the only substantial bibliography on Anne Sexton. Their *Sylvia Plath and Anne Sexton: A Reference Guide,* No. 1 of the "Reference Guides in American Literature" series under the general editorship of Joseph Katz, appeared in 1974 and attempts comprehensiveness for works by and on Anne Sexton through 1971. Thus it is of considerable use to those interested in places of original publication for Sexton's individual poems before their appearances in collections, for early reviews (through *Love Poems* and Sexton's unpublished play, *Mercy Street,* performed Off Broadway), and for a few of the major critical articles, most of which were written near the end of her career or after her death in 1974. The reference guide contains separate, chronologically arranged entries on each poet and includes an index. Each article and review is well and briefly annotated; the authors have attempted to examine all materials themselves. A final advantage of this bibliography is that it includes British reviews of Sexton's works, all of which were separately published in England. Although the Northouse and Walsh work remains useful, an update containing primary and secondary material published since 1971 is clearly needed.

Biographies

No book-length biography of Sexton has been published. However, the poet's literary executors have selected Diane Wood Middlebrook to write a critical biography, which is now in progress and which is expected to appear in 1987. Middlebrook plans to divide her book into three parts. "Part One: Apprenticeship" will deal with the years 1956-1962, from the date of Sexton's first poem, associated with her recovery from her first suicide attempt, through the publication of *All My Pretty Ones,* her second book. "Part Two: The Family and the Pathology" will contain chapters on Sexton's early life, her marriage, her psychiatric history, and an account of Sexton's suicide in the context of her illness. "Part Three: Famous Poet" will cover the on-going development of Sexton's mature poetry; the extended work on but brief production of her only play, *Mercy Street;* the evolution of her performance style as a popular reader on the poetry circuit; and her work as a teacher.

Selected Interviews

The most extensive and frequently quoted early interviews with Anne Sexton are by Patricia Marx in the Winter 1965-1966 *Hudson Review* and by Barbara Kevles in the Summer 1971 *Paris Review.* Both deal with Sexton's experiences as a poet during the first flush of both her popularity and her notoriety. Subsequent interviews often retrace the subjects covered in these early conversations and are therefore sometimes repetitious. Sexton's harsher critics frequently have assumed that, given the extremely personal nature of her poetry, interviews or letters could add little to readers' knowledge of the poet's life or work; however, the major interviews invariably show this view to be mistaken.

The Marx interview examines the genesis of Sexton's poetry as therapy after her first bout with mental illness. Sexton specifically addresses questions about the relationship between madness and creative genius, disclaiming any simple equations between the two and denying that mental instability was the cause of her poetry. She does subscribe, however, to the need for bringing order out of chaos that she believes is inherent in the writing process. The relationship between poetic and factual truth—a relationship central for all readers of Sexton, it seems—is defined by the writer with one of her most telling replies: "Behind everything that happens to you, every act, there is another truth, a secret life." Although Sexton and Marx discuss the connections between femininity and creativity, the poet clearly had not yet thought out this complex issue at the time of her conversation with Marx. The influences on her work of Robert Lowell and W. D. Snodgrass are also covered here, as they are in almost all subsequent interviews. The discussion of Sexton's use of form is very useful—"all form is a trick in order to get at the truth"—as is the summary of the development of her styles and themes.

In 1971 Kevles interview, actually conducted in 1968, clearly shows that Sexton suffered from Betty Friedan's "problem that has no name"—a sense that she had no identity beyond that prescribed by her role as housewife. With what was still essentially a prefeminist frame of reference, she says, "Until I was twenty-eight I had a kind of buried self who didn't know she could do anything but make white sauce and diaper babies. I didn't know I had any creative depths." Sexton repeats the story of her beginnings as a poet, and, providing new material about the relationship between her art and psychotherapy, she gives examples of how poetry "milks the unconscious." Sexton also describes the John Holmes workshop at the Adult Education Center of Boston University, the site of her initial meeting with Maxine Kumin, with whom she workshopped daily for more than fifteen years. In addition, she discusses the Robert Lowell workshop and comments on his teaching techniques and personality, on her well-known sessions with fellow workshop member Sylvia Plath at the Ritz in Boston, and on the influence of Snodgrass on her work. The relationship between her play and her poetry receives attention here, as do details of the writer's method of working, including her writing schedule, revision techniques, punctuation, and line lengths. A series of questions from Kevles about the nature of Sexton's "visions" produces replies useful to the critic, although Sexton eventually diverts that line of questioning into an illuminating discussion of religious quest as a subject in her poetry.

Two discussions focus on less personal issues. William Packard's "Craft Interview with Anne Sexton" (1974) addresses writing techniques, early workshops, the revision process, the influences of Lowell and others, rhyming, and the relationship between imagination and the unconscious. Readers interested in these subjects will find this interview most valuable. The 1968 *Talks With Authors* interview is clearly the transcript of a workshop session conducted under highly formal circumstances, and its tone is therefore somewhat stilted. It is nevertheless worthwhile for its close discussion of such texts as "Flight," "The Division of Parts," "I Remember," and "Young." Especially good is Sexton's lengthy explanation of the genesis of one poem, "All My Pretty Ones," including false starts, rejected lines, and progressive drafts.

The two late interviews—William Heyen's and Gregory Fitz Gerald's—are useful for entirely different reasons. "From 1928 to Whenever: A Conversation with Anne Sexton" is a transcript of a videotaped 1973 interview at SUNY/Brockport. A three-way conversation between Sexton, Heyen, and A. Poulin, the discussion is informal, almost breezy, but substantial; it thereby covers much of her usual interview territory in a new way. Sexton explains her commitment to the personal and discusses fictionalizing and the use of the persona in the confessional context: "If I did all the things I confess to, there would be no time to write a poem." New material here includes the story of writing *The Awful Rowing Toward God*, the production of the unpublished play *Mercy Street*, the genesis of *Transformations*, her response to hostile criticism, and the movement in her works away from madness and toward love and God.

The last major interview with Sexton, Fitz Gerald's "The Choir From the Soul," took place a few months before her death in 1974. Early sections of the interview cover the familiar terrain of all previous Sexton interviews, and do so well, with deepened perceptions on her part about, for instance, criticism and the creative process. At one point she declares, "I see everyone as writing the same poem, only with many voices. We're all writing the poem of our time, everyone differently." Material not available in other interviews includes Sexton's version of her relationship with a priest who told her that her typewriter was her altar and her poems her prayers. The amiable tension between Fitz Gerald and Sexton on the nature of her religious quest yields excellent data. She also discusses the conflicts between maternity and poetry in her first references to the feminist movement. Those seeking evidence of Sexton's emotional disintegration will unfortunately find it here; toward its end, the interview becomes disjointed, and Sexton's tone and manner verge briefly on the bizarre. Recovering her professional stance, however, she concludes with comments on teaching.

Critical Studies: Book

The only book-length study to date is Diana Hume George's *Oedipus Anne: The Poetry of Anne Sexton* (1986). Psychoanalytic in approach, it inverts the usual method of treating the writer as case study and instead claims for Sexton the status of mythopoeic analyst of her own, and her culture's, collective dilemmas. Feminist as well as psychoanalytic, *Oedipus Anne* maintains that Sexton was a female hero in the tradition of Oedipus, one who claimed for herself—on behalf of all women poets—the territory of the tragic quest, the "indefatigable inquiry" whose goal is to uncover deceptions in her search for the most complex forms of truth. Reading the Oedipus story through Freud and Bettelheim, George finds that Sexton takes on the power of the prophet, becoming not merely a tragic victim, but an embattled seer. Although Sexton claimed identification with Oedipus only once, in the Schopenhauer epigraph for *To Bedlam and Part Way Back*, its prefatory placement in her first volume of poetry constitutes, George believes, the poet's declaration of independence and bill of poetic rights. According to George, Sexton made good on her promise to American poetry to seek enlightenment concerning her own—and every woman's—fate. Although her private struggles sometimes caused her to capitulate to cultural patterns that demanded the ritual sacrifice of "all beautiful women," Sexton appropriated for her (and their) poetry a fiercely defended autonomy.

George contends that Sexton's poetic stories are of immense significance to mid-twentieth-century artistic and psychic life. Understanding her culture's malaise through her own, she deployed metaphorical structures at once synthetic and analytic. In other words, she assimilated the superficially opposing but deeply similar ways of thinking represented by poetry and psychoanalysis. Sexton explored the myths through which culture lives and dies: archetypal relationships among mothers and daughters, fathers and daughters, gods and humans, men and women. She perceived, and consistently patterned in the images of her poems, the paradoxes rooted in human motivation and behavior. George asserts that Sexton's poetry presents multiplicity and simplicity, duality and unity, the sacred and the profane, in ways that insist upon their similarities—even their identity. Thus the tension between life-embracing Eros and death-desiring Thanatos in her work allows her readers to imagine the ways in which life and death are as much intimates as opposites.

Oedipus Anne is divided into four parts that represent the major emphases of the study. Part I, "Mother, Father, I'm Made Of," concentrates on the achievement of Sexton's poetry in the familial and psychoanalytic mode, including an extensive meditation on the father-daughter relationship. Part II, "That Dear Body," explores Sexton's attitudes toward the dualities of the physical and the spiritual, and examines the relationships between feeding, feces, and creativity in Sexton's canon. Part III, "Person, Persona, Prophecy," examines the poetry in both traditional and feminist terms by placing Sexton's use of the persona both within and outside the confessional context, thereby moving toward a reading of the poems George calls "prophetic" and "visionary." Part IV, "Wanting to Die," which includes a discussion of contemporary attitudes toward suicide, treats Sexton's major works on death and suicide, advancing George's own conjectures on the connections between Sexton's poetry and her life. *Oedipus Anne* ends with a discussion of Sexton's "The Death Baby," which

George presents as Sexton's poetic version of Freud's controversial theory in *Beyond the Pleasure Principle.*

Critical Studies: Collection of Essays

J. D. McClatchy's *Anne Sexton: The Artist and Her Critics* is the single collection of criticism on Sexton. Published in 1978, the book was well reviewed and has held up under the scrutiny of later works on Sexton. Robert Pinsky, in a *New York Times Book Review* assessment of McClatchy's book and of Sexton's own posthumous *Words for Dr. Y.,* is patronizing toward the poet but has high praise for the level of criticism he finds in McClatchy's collection: the "quality of attention" throughout the anthology is, Pinsky declares, "grave and alert."

Anne Sexton is organized into five sections, collecting nearly all of the best work on Sexton through about 1976 in one readily available source. The interview section includes the Kevles, Marx, and Packard pieces (see above), which taken together supply the reader with all the major interviews available at the time of the collection's publication. A section on revisions supplies worksheets for "Elizabeth Gone," invaluable for a study of the poet's process and unavailable elsewhere for this poem. Only one other such extensive worksheet source is so far available to Sexton students: the "Suicide Note" worksheets published in the Fall 1970 issue of the *New York Quarterly* (see Worksheets in primary checklist above).

An extensive section of personal reflections on the poet includes pieces by Robert Lowell, Denise Levertov, Barbara Swan, Charles Maryan, Polly C. Williams, John Malcolm Brinnin, Maxine Kumin, and Lois Ames—a cross section that includes friends, collaborators, teachers, students, and fellow poets. Only Levertov's essay is more a lecture than a real reminiscence, but it is nevertheless valuable. Kumin's "A Friendship Remembered" is not only moving but genuinely useful for students of Sexton's work; and Barbara Swan's "A Reminiscence" is critically important because it sheds new light on the sources for some of Sexton's more obscure works, such as "To Lose the Earth." (Swan was Sexton's illustrator for several volumes of poetry.)

The reviews—over twenty are reprinted here—are a fair representation of the opinions (and sometimes the clear prejudices) that Sexton seemed to evoke in her critics. The well-known James Dickey review of *To Bedlam and Part Way Back,* included in his "Five First Books," is here, as indeed it should be, for it tells as much about

Dickey as about Sexton. McClatchy made an important decision in his selection of reviews: he reprints at least as many assessments bearing faint or cramped praise, even occasional attacks, as he does those expressing genuine admiration or respect. While he could certainly have altered the balance to serve his subject more generously, Mc-Clatchy has instead chosen to serve her in proportions that reflect her actual reception by the critics. Reviews end with *45 Mercy Street,* since *Words for Dr. Y.* and *The Complete Poems* had not yet been published when the collection appeared.

The final, overview section consists of four essays on the Sexton canon, some of which are of limited value in the wake of subsequent criticism that includes more about the later works. Following the critical wisdom that sees early Sexton as best Sexton, three of the four essays confine themselves to her first few volumes (only McClatchy's own article reaches toward statements that are more comprehensive); and three of the four—Richard Howard's, Robert Boyers's, and McClatchy's—are reprinted, sometimes in expanded form, from earlier sources.

Howard's "Anne Sexton: 'Some Tribal Female Who Is Known but Forbidden,'" which is somewhat thin, is the single essay of the four that might be called disappointing. Howard surveys the poetry through *Live or Die* without much of interest to say after the first few pages, which include some penetrating insights: here he calls Sexton a true Massachusetts heiress of Nathaniel Hawthorne's Pearl, who must be told by Hester Prynne that "we must not always talk in the marketplace of what happens to us in the forest." Howard's conclusion is that Sexton gains by virtue of her volume and kind of reportage the "sacerdotal stature" of a "priestess celebrating mysteries." Yet hers is the truth, says Howard, that cancels poetry.

Boyers's "*Live or Die:* The Achievement of Anne Sexton" is reprinted from *Salmagundi,* where its original publication in 1967 marked a high point in Sexton's rocky reputation among academic critics. Although it deals primarily with one volume, *Live or Die,* Boyers's essay makes large claims for the poet and her 1966 book: it is the "culmination, indeed the crowning achievement, of the confessional mode" since it reaches beyond literature to enlarge the possibilities of endurance for all human beings. Boyers mentions some of Sexton's defects (occasional crudities, imprecise similes, flatness of style in unexpected places) primarily to underscore his high praise of her as an "extraordinarily accomplished artist." He discusses the major thematic concerns of her poetry—victimization, entrapment, isolation, guilt, responsibility—as part of that poetry's ultimate "triumph of determination and insight" in the final decision to "Live" that frames the collection. The final statement might seem compromised by Sexton's suicide, since her personal and poetic survival seemed equally at issue in some respects; yet, as Boyers contends, her decision to live, with "the responsibility for human values planted firmly on her competent shoulders is a major statement of our poetry."

Jane McCabe's " 'A Woman Who Writes': A Feminist Approach to the Early Poetry of Anne Sexton" is the only piece here by a female critic and the only one that explores feminist approaches. McCabe begins from the sensible and easily forgotten premise that Sexton was not herself a feminist in the political or activist sense and that feminist criticism's appropriation of her has had to ignore some of her finest— and least "politically correct"—poetry. Yet although Sexton's poems do not offer women solutions, McCabe shows, many of them describe the difficulties of being a woman in contemporary society; Sexton, for example, defined her own alienation from her role of well-to-do suburban housewife as "witchery." McCabe discusses sexual difference and writing style in order to ask whether essential differences in gender and imagination exist. She finds politically feminist poetry less interesting and complex than Sexton's, which is far more ambiguous and resonant. Concentrating on the poet's early work, McCabe explores the mother-daughter poems in which Sexton gives her daughters the advice she tries to give herself and cannot ultimately accept: "love yourself 's self where it lives."

McClatchy's own "Anne Sexton: Somehow to Endure" takes seriously the psychoanalytic framework of Sexton's poetry. Identifying endurance as Sexton's original poetic impulse and her consistent concern, McClatchy examines the confessional context both through Theodor Reik's *The Compulsion to Confess* and through the theories of Freud and psychoanalytic theorist Ernst Kris. Confession is seen by Reik as the process of exorcism and the plea for absolution that temporarily halts disintegration of personality. While he examines the interrelationship between confessional poetry and psychoanalysis through characteristically Freudian epistemology, McClatchy does not reduce the poetry to symptom, but rather uses analytic theory as an illuminating subtext. The confessional poets, of whom McClatchy finds Sexton the most persistent and daring, function in poetry as survivors and as witnesses to the inner lives of large numbers of people. Applying this idea to a comprehensive survey of Sexton's works, McClatchy finds Sexton not only one of the more distinctive

voices of a generation of poets, but a figure of permanent importance
to the development of American poetry.

Critical Studies: Special Issue of Journal

Although no journal or newsletter is devoted to Anne Sexton,
the Summer 1979 *Notes on Modern American Literature* is a special number on Robert Lowell and Anne Sexton. Of the five essays included,
two are on Sexton. Critics interested in the well-established relationship between the two poets will find the journal number of interest,
even though the essays leave the connection between the two largely
implicit. The articles on Sexton are Brian Gallagher's "The Expanded
Use of Simile in Anne Sexton's *Transformations*" and Kathleen L. Nichols's "The Hungry Beast Rowing Toward God: Anne Sexton's Later
Religious Poetry."

Gallagher notes that Sexton depends heavily on simile and metaphor in all of her poetry but that in *Transformations* use of simile is
unusually pervasive. The critic contends that the volume's increased
reliance on simile results from the collection's special relationship to
another set of texts, in this case the fairy tales of the brothers Grimm.
Gallagher shows that Sexton uses simile to provide a running commentary on the story with three purposes and three corresponding
results: to give the stories contemporary application and reference;
to increase the scope of her retellings by reference to classical literature, thereby enlarging the mythopoeic context; and to expose the
latent sexual content of the fairy-tale genre. Although why simile is
employed instead of metaphor remains somewhat muddy, Gallagher
is otherwise clear, illuminating, and concise.

In "The Hungry Beast Rowing Toward God," Nichols examines
the compensatory function of religious myth in *The Death Notebooks*,
The Awful Rowing Toward God, and *45 Mercy Street*. Her Jungian approach emphasizes Sexton's need to find in death the ideal mother
and father, male and female archetypes of the unified self. Nichols
declares that Sexton's sea journey toward God becomes a regressive
one back to the mythic parents, and especially to the male principle
in which God is the lost and idealized father. The imaginative jour-
neying of the poet toward God is thus fetal in its return to primal
sources and undifferentiated preconsciousness. Two other points
touched on by Nichols could be developed far beyond their provocative mention here: Nichols discerns a Dantesque "divine comedy"
pattern informing the entire Sexton canon; and she compares Walt

Whitman to Sexton, whose anthems integrating hidden and conscious selves become a Whitmanesque "song of myself," even if such integrations are precarious and temporary. Nichols's short article is packed tightly with insights and is among the best of the criticism of the later poetry.

Critical Studies: Major Articles and Book Sections

Surveying the criticism of Anne Sexton before and after her death in 1974, one is inevitably struck by the intensely negative response she sometimes evoked in the critical community. James Dickey's 1961 *Poetry* review of her first volume, *To Bedlam and Part Way Back*, is representative: "One feels tempted to drop the poems furtively into the nearest ashcan, rather than be caught in the presence of such naked suffering." Paul Zweig in a 1973 *Partisan Review* assessment calls *Transformations* strong evidence for the death of storytelling and suggests "Reductions" as a more appropriate title. In what is ostensibly a review of *Anne Sexton: A Self-Portrait in Letters*, William H. Pritchard in "The Anne Sexton Show" (1978) is moved to genuine ill temper and perhaps even misogyny, summarizing only those selections of *Letters* that present Sexton at her smallest and most petty and announcing that she will be read less and less, "her main audience a few unhappy college students, probably female ones." While such diatribe is not frequent, it is equaled elsewhere in Sexton criticism: Jeffrey L. Lant's "Another Entry in The Death Notebooks" (1979), for example, goes through an oddly scrappy and irritable summary of her life, concentrating on the negative and self-aggrandizing and announcing firmly that "power corrupts" and that Sexton was an unfit mother whose professional accomplishments included "wheedling" her way into a Guggenheim Fellowship and "browbeating" her department chairman into a promotion. In at least some of these cases, it appears that the critics have a special axe to grind and that their vitriol should be automatically disqualified from serious consideration. Occasionally Sexton attracts the rabidly Marxist response that is more amusing than upsetting, as is the case with Sol Zollman's "Criticism, Self-Criticism, No Transformation" (1971), in which both Sexton and Lowell are found at fault for failing to "encourage rebellion" or to "carry on class struggle." Even some critics who were early well disposed toward Sexton, such as Louis Simpson, reach their limits; Simpson declares in his August 1967 *Harper*'s article that it was "a poem titled 'Menstruation at Forty' that broke this camel's back." That it is possible for a critic to find little to admire in Sexton's later work but to refrain from poisonous diatribe is illustrated by Robert Mazzocco's review of *The Awful Rowing Toward God* ("Matters of Life and Death," 1975). Although this critic characterizes her best work as "delicate, visceral, poignant," he can offer no other praise; Mazzocco is quite simply the best of the critical readers who come to this poetry with understanding, but who do not regard it as exceptionally worthy. Mazzocco never trivializes Sexton's work and never condemns her poetry or her person.

Erica Jong's 1974 assessment, "Remembering Anne Sexton," contrasts sharply with that of many male critics of Sexton. Jong declares, "Anne Sexton is one of the writers by whom our age will be known and understood in times to come—not as 'women's poetry' or 'confessional poetry'—but as myths that expand the human consciousness." Although it is tempting to conclude that Sexton's harshest critics are male and her most sympathetic ones female, this tendency is by no means a rule. The reader of Sexton criticism will find well-considered negative assessments of her work by women—for example, Rosemary Johnson's "The Woman of Private (But Published) Hungers" and Joyce Carol Oates's regretful, tough reviews of *The Complete Poems* and *Letters*—and this essay records many serious and admiring considerations of her work by men. Perhaps it is fair to say, however, that the personally disgruntled and ill-tempered critical responses tend to come from male reviewers. Conjectures on the reasons for this tendency are beyond the scope of this survey but not beyond the scope of some of the central pieces of Sexton criticism in recent years.

Alicia Ostriker's superb essay, originally published in 1982 as "That Story: Anne Sexton and Her Transformations" and reprinted the next year as "That Story: The Changes of Anne Sexton," focuses on the problematic relationship of Sexton to her critics. Ostriker suspects that the "sneer" toward Sexton derives from fear—"a fear of being stung into imaginative sympathy." The fear is threefold, Ostriker believes; Sexton's material is heavily female and biological; she is assertively emotional, and human nature responds to such vulnerability with cruelty, even contempt; and her quality of "unresignedness" is tiresome as well as frightening to readers who experience it as repetition instead of as creative tension between the contraries of Eros and Thanatos. Ostriker is critical of Sexton's shortcomings—repetition, sentimentality, flatness—but finds that the writing still "dazzles," especially the colloquial line that is vigorous, flexible, and earthy. Finding her subject's domestic imagery a genuinely new contribution to poetry, the critic claims that Sexton more keenly re-creates the child-self than does Roethke and defines inner demons more clearly than does Lowell. Ostriker's major discussion is of *Transformations* and *The Book of Folly*'s "Jesus Papers," in which, she declares, Sexton interprets prior, external, shared cultural traditions in a brilliant fusion of the public with the personal. Ostriker maintains that in *The Death Notebooks* and even beyond, Sexton tackles increasingly ambitious themes, with increasingly significant cultural implications. Like several others of Sexton's best critics, Ostriker also points to similarities between Sexton and Emily Dickinson. This essay is loaded with penetrating insights into large cultural concerns, intertwined with careful explications of the poetry.

Estella Lauter's "Anne Sexton's 'Radical Discontent with the Awful Order of Things'" (1979) deals with much the same material within a Jungian as well as a feminist framework. Lauter contends that between 1970 and 1974 Sexton created an extraordinary, "perhaps 'prophetic' body of poetry based upon images that have profound psychological and religious significance for our age." She calls Sexton's later poetry "stunning," especially in its alteration of the original terms of the writer's quest for a relationship with traditional Christianity, one which "broke open under the pressure of her imaginative scrutiny." The archetypal figures Lauter identifies in the later poetry are best understood, she believes, as part of Sexton's act of Jungian "soul-making"; unfortunately, however, Sexton was unable to name her own new (and often female) deities. Lauter places Sexton's discontent with a patriarchal God and her unnamed, alternative deities, in the contexts of archetypal psychology and feminist theology; among Sexton's achievements are revisions of the Christian parables and the Hebrew psalms, as well as both the creation and crucifixion stories. Her images of God range across boundaries dividing inside and outside, male and female, animal, spirit, and human forms, mythic and historical representations. To demonstrate her sense of Sexton's diverse heresies—which, whether or not one agrees with them, are nevertheless poetically and culturally daring—Lauter reads "The Jesus papers" as a "study of relationships between love and power."

In addition to her forthcoming biography, three of Diane Middlebrook's articles illuminate both Sexton's life and her poetry in unprecedented ways. "Becoming Anne Sexton" (1984) is indispensable for critics interested in the development of Sexton as poet. Taking up her subject's own statement that her poetic career had the shape of a story, Middlebrook's thesis is that Sexton's emphasis on suicide expresses an ambivalence she learned from her mother, a writer's daughter, regarding the roles of wife, mother, and writer. Sexton's version of her own development always began with her "break," a word Middlebrook says has a range of references in the story of Sexton's transformation from housewife into poet. A detailed discussion of the mother-daughter relationship in Sexton's life is enriched by previously unavailable, archival information that fills in the gaps in Sexton's story. Middlebrook declares that Sexton's understanding of her relationship to her mother leads her, in poems to daughters, to speak *as* a daughter *against* the domination of mothers. "The Double Image" is thus discussed in a new and illuminating context.

"Housewife Into Poet: The Apprenticeship of Anne Sexton" (1983) also explores Sexton's metamorphosis from suburban housewife into major poet who was handicapped by having had little formal education and by being, at intervals, "certifiably mad." The special contribution of this essay is Middlebrook's compelling account of the confrontational relationship between Sexton and her first workshop teacher, John Holmes, whose opposition to her sources and subject matter forced her, in reaction, to discover "her definitive strengths as a poet." Middlebrook ends with a graceful reading of "Somewhere in Africa," Sexton's elegy for Holmes.

Middlebrook's forthcoming review article on *The Complete Poems* ("Poet of Weird Abundance") demonstrates Sexton's increasing preoccupation with the "psychological consequences of inhabiting a female body." *The Complete Poems* yields most, says Middlebrook, when read as the narrative of a woman cursed with a desire to die. The story line of the canon plots a series of explanations—psychiatric, sociological, spiritual—for this desire; but the central problem, according to Middlebrook, lies in being female and therefore "defective." The critic identifies "Flee on Your Donkey" as a central departure point for Sexton in style and approach; thereafter she is no longer only the victim of her pathology, but its interrogator. This article's survey of the complete works—the most comprehensive one yet available in essay form—includes extensive discussion of Sexton's spiritual quest. Ending with the vexing question of merit, Middlebrook concludes that the type of poem Sexton evolved articulates the dilemma of the female recipient of ideas about social order and that Sexton is one of the genre's chief inventors and, at her best, "one of its masters."

Suzanne Juhasz's two essays on Sexton are both seminal, although "Seeking the Exit or the Home" (1979) has a tighter and narrower focus and might ultimately be the more valuable of the two for Sexton criticism. "The Excitable Gift" (1976) is based in part on a debatable contention that Juhasz does not qualify sufficiently: that Sexton's therapy, and thereby her poetry, was "occasioned by her womanhood itself." Juhasz's reading of "The Double Image" assumes this causal relationship and calls upon the poem for support through which not only Sexton's general illness, but specifically her suicidal impulses, are attributed to her "woman's situation." The critic balances this extreme statement with another one equally extreme, though more firmly founded in poetic fact: Sexton's affirmations of life through the acts of her poems also find their source in her womanhood. Because these are debatable propositions, one must read with care; but Juhasz presents her hypotheses convincingly enough to merit a hearing about the poetry, and perhaps even the life. As is usual for Sexton's critics, she locates a shift in development with *Transformations*, whose witch narrator is a "wisewoman, storyteller, seer" bridging the gap between the personal and the collective and between the child and the adult. A lengthy reading of "The Death Baby" sequence contends that Sexton's manic—or prophetic—language is used as a way to know her own death and to make powerful choices regarding it. Juhasz ends with a theoretical discussion of the poetry of Levertov, Plath, and Sexton on the issues of involvement, engagement, and commitment so often associated with contemporary women's poetry.

"Seeking the Exit or the Home" is a sober meditation on what poetry can—and cannot—do for a woman, for women, for writers, for readers. Juhasz examines the rat as Sexton's special animal, the alien aspect of the self that obstructs salvation and yet that is the source of creativity, vision, and poetry. The critic believes that becoming a poet was a move toward salvation for Sexton—"it gave her something to do with the knowledge that the rat possessed." But the rat is also death. The written poem turns the rat demon into an object separate and complete, once again alien. Thus the poems can never quite offer real salvation to their author; she "cannot kill the rat without killing the vision that is the source of her poetry." Juhasz ends on the hopeful note that such poetry does have different functions for its readers and its writers; yet after such eloquent, closely argued, clearly rendered pessimism, the conclusion is slight, perhaps even false, comfort. This short essay is among the most illuminating in Sexton scholarship.

Three of Diana Hume George's articles make major claims for

Sexton's poetry. "How We Danced: Anne Sexton on Fathers and Daughters" (forthcoming) is the only close reading of the father-daughter poems to balance the critical attention accorded the mother-daughter relationship. Even in the early poetry, George finds a structural outline for the psychic biography of gender, particularly for what Phyllis Chesler calls "woman's 'dependent' and 'incestuous' personality" in relation to her father; such a pattern has long been known to psychoanalysis—to the degree that therapeutic method colludes with patriarchy. Anne Sexton's was the first contemporary voice outside of the psychoanalytic community to describe from the daughter's point of view this normative relationship between father and daughter in American culture.

"Beyond the Pleasure Principle: Anne Sexton's 'The Death Baby' " (1983) presents Sexton's sequence of poems from *The Death Notebooks* as a poetic analogue to Freud's "death instinct," while drawing on Ernest Becker's *The Denial of Death* as the other analytic subtext for the essay. George also contends that in "The Death Baby" the wish for and the fear of death—representative of a psychic orientation to all primary oppositions—are functionally identical. The death-baby image is seen as the humanized, internalized metaphor for the repetition compulsion. (Estella Lauter reads this image similarly.) "Anne Sexton's Suicide Poems" (1984), another of George's essays, examines contemporary American approaches to death through the euthanasia and living will movements and then provides a detailed reading of Sexton's "Wanting to Die" and "Suicide Note."

Paul A. Lacey's fine reading of spirituality in Sexton, which was published in 1972, is the most remarkable of the early major essays on Sexton. "The Sacrament of Confession" begins with a lucid, greatly needed discussion of the confessional poem and its persona. Lacey uses Sexton's "Unknown Girl in the Maternity Ward" as an example of the pitfalls of criticism that assumes the identity of poet and speaker in confessional poetry. (This fault perhaps mars some of the best essays above, but most skirt the issue skillfully enough.) Reviewing the standard objections to Sexton's work—that it is raw, formless, technically out of control—Lacey shows that the poet's first four books are not lacking in forms and controls but rather are preoccupied with them. (Richard J. Fein's "The Demon of Anne Sexton," which appeared five years earlier than Lacey's essay, also argues effectively that art and form underlie the demonic power and tone of the poetry.) Lacey examines Sexton's uses of ritual, which are organized as rites of mastery, of initiation or cleansing, and of communion. Later critics, including feminist readers, seem to have overlooked this gracefully written, compelling essay. Jeanne H. Kammer's "The Witch's Life: Confession and Control in the Early Poetry of Anne Sexton" (1980) is also among the several strong essays countering the critical claim that Sexton writes "raw" instead of "cooked" verse; Kammer finds that the writer imposes on her chaotic experience "the boundary and counterpoint of intense poetic control." Sexton's use of language in the early work is direct, economical, even cryptic in Kammer's view.

Rise B. Axelrod's "The Transforming Art of Anne Sexton" (1974) is another early, short, and excellent article on Sexton. Axelrod finds that in her first three volumes, the poet explores the depths of her own consciousness, while in the later books she experiments with various mythopoeic possibilities of rebirth. Axelrod isolates two dual and opposing movements in the poetry: a "therapeutic" mode analyzes the cracked mirror of the self in search of the origins of its dissolution; a "visionary" mode allows resurrection of the self and reunification with others.

Linda W. Wagner's "45 Mercy Street and Other Vacant Houses" (1981) extends the comparison with Dickinson suggested by other critics: "From Dickinson's room in the family home in Amherst, Massachusetts, to Anne Sexton's lost family home on Mercy Street, is only a brief walk." Both Sexton and Dickinson speak of the need for an identity as a writer and of their search for a male authority figure to support the writing process, Wagner declares, and both poets were aware of the innovative and unconventional directions of their work. Their work shares exuberance, anger, guilt, frustration, and an uneasy but sometimes firm measure of self-acceptance. Dickinson also shares with both Sexton and Plath an alienation from the traditional world of poetry because of gender and from the traditional world of women because of poetry.

A. R. Jones's "Necessity and Freedom" (1965) contends that the work of Lowell, Plath, and Sexton constitutes a major breakthrough in the poetry of the 1960s. Jones thinks that American poetry, largely as a result of Lowell's example, has moved toward acceptance of the monologue as the predominant poetic mode, but one in which the persona is projected lyrically rather than treated dramatically. His view of Sexton is ambivalent: he finds her speaker essentially passive, a patient rather than an agent, and in Sexton, he believes, the quarrel between Eliot's "man who suffers" and "mind which creates" is nearly schizophrenic.

Nancy Yanes Hoffman's "A Special Language" (1979) finds that

Sexton searches not only for transformation but for transcendence of self. Desiring to be joined to another in love and each time ultimately disappointed, she is left near her life's end rowing toward God, who is "love imagined," in Hoffman's beautiful phrase. When vision turns into nightmare, love imagined turns into demons. The killer in her poetry's lovers speaks to another killer, the one in herself. The rowing of her last poetry is a metaphor for the striving of her life against that yearning for death. Margaret Honton's "The Double Image and the Division of Parts" (1979), a study of Sexton's mother-daughter relationships, shares some of the sympathies and insights of Hoffman's essay, although their thematic concerns are different. Like Middlebrook, Honton finds that Sexton's mother-daughter poetry exhibits a "terrible struggle against the Devouring Mother myth." In the poet's double image of that myth, the speaker accepts blame from her predecessor and guilt concerning her successor.

William H. Shurr discusses only "Anne Sexton's *Love Poems*" (1980), but he makes for this volume a sizable claim: the collection is not a series of occasional pieces on love, but the sustained account of one love affair in which Sexton searches for the essential contours and repeatable patterns of typical love affairs in countless human lives. Like Kathleen L. Nichols in her 1979 *Notes on Modern American Literature* piece, Shurr compares Sexton to Whitman, claiming for her a "female singer of the self to match his male persona." He points to Sexton's talent for "pseudobiography," and like many other critics, cautions that what appears as the intimate revelation of raw experience often turns out to be "intense fictional realism." Robert Phillips's "Anne Sexton: The Blooming Mouth and the Bleeding Rose" (1973) makes the same point: Sexton's work is populated by a "gallery of 'real' yet totally fictitious figures." Although he objects to the gimmicky quality of *Love Poems*, he finds that *Transformations* domesticates terrors with "outstanding artistic proficiency." His major discussion is of *Live or Die*, which marks Sexton's turning point from pessimism to optimism, in Phillips's view.

Ralph J. Mills, Jr., who calls Sexton "bold and impressive" in his 1965 essay, surveys the contents of *Bedlam* and *Pretty Ones* thoroughly and insightfully. Philip Legler's "O Yellow Eye" (1967) pronounces *Live or Die* a "brilliantly unified book." William J. McGill, in an exceptionally well-written essay titled "Anne Sexton and God" (1977), compares Sexton's religious poetry to the intense desire for God that characterizes religious literature of all ages. "Like Augustine, she roamed the fields and palaces of memory," McGill declares.

Both Beverly Tanenhaus and Rosemary Johnson are critical of Sexton's work for assorted failures of nerve, will, or imagination. In "Politics of Suicide and Survival" (1978), Tanenhaus unfavorably compares Sexton's poetry with Adrienne Rich's by distinguishing the suicidal female from the woman convinced that she deserves and is capable of liberation. Sexton's failure to understand her life in sufficiently political terms undermined her ability to negotiate and to make moral choices, says Tanenhaus—and also, implicitly, undermined her ability, in Tanenhaus's opinion, to write poetry of practical worth to women. Rosemary Johnson's "The Woman of Private (But Published) Hungers" (1979) is a review article of *Self-Portrait in Letters* and *Words for Dr. Y.* that is sometimes arch and patronizing, but also thoughtful.

Greg Johnson's "The Achievement of Anne Sexton" was published in 1984, but Johnson concentrates on poetry appearing in collections through *Live or Die* since he feels that from then on, Sexton stopped growing. The heart of her finest poetry, says Johnson, is a search for identity, and her infatuation with death has little to do with such a search. He contrasts her early work with Plath's, calling it a poetry of life in contrast to Plath's world of death, and labeling Sexton's poetry a record of her struggle against insuperable odds to remain in a world of health and wholeness. A pedagogical approach to Sexton's poems is found in Diana Hume George's 1984 article on the suicide poems; here George reveals that "Wanting to Die" has a strong impact on college students and is therefore an excellent choice for classroom use.

Several reminiscences (and other less classifiable pieces) not available in McClatchy's collection deserve mention here. Maxine Kumin's foreword to *The Complete Poems* is moving and critically useful, especially but not exclusively for those interested in influences of the two poet-friends on each other. (Her "A Friendship Remembered," available in McClatchy, is similarly helpful.) The Kumin review of *The Awful Rowing Toward God* both explains the circumstances of composition of this final book Sexton saw through press and discusses Sexton's need for spiritual absolution. John J. Mood's " 'A Bird Full of Bones': Anne Sexton—A Visit and a Reading" (1972) is a sentimental reminiscence of a reading. If one can make a path through the quite cloying soul-mate rhetoric, this odd essay includes interesting (if excruciating) details of Sexton's well-known fear of poetry readings. Kathleen Spivak's "Sharers of the Heart: A Friend Remembers Anne Sexton" (1981) moves from the early days of the Lowell workshop through Sexton's death. Both critical and generous, it includes some of the most acute perceptions available from either critics or friends. Her discussion of the relationship between Sexton and Plath and her conjectures on the common anger they shared are suggestive; and her memories of afternoons around Sexton's pool are deeply felt.

Although it is difficult to predict the future trends of scholarship on any contemporary poet, and perhaps especially on a poet as controversial as Anne Sexton, current patterns in existing criticism suggest several strong possibilities. First, it is obvious that because all or nearly all of Sexton's poems are now published, initial review articles will not continue to appear—unless, of course, new editions of poems are issued by her publishers. The disappearance of initial reviews will inevitably result in a decline in testy commentary of the kind examined above. Future criticism of Sexton is thus likely to be written by readers who find some degree of merit in her work, or who are interested in Sexton's place in American poetry. One might also expect that future criticism will focus on the larger, more inclusive patterns that should emerge from a consideration of the entire canon.

Second, current commentary suggests that the later works will be re-evaluated. Early criticism tended to concentrate on the achievements, for instance, of her first three or four volumes of poetry, and this focus seemed to prevail even after publication of the later works. Differences in style and subject matter between the early and late works, despite considerable commonality and continuity, have produced a critical trend in which early Sexton is perceived as best Sexton; works published after *Transformations* are frequently viewed as loose, uncontrolled, and sometimes unconsciously self-parodic. Criticism of the very late 1970s and early 1980s indicates that a re-assessment of the later works is indeed under way, qualifying if not reversing this earlier trend. While there is some biographical evidence to suggest that Sexton herself shared the concern of critics that her later work diminished in skill and control, recent criticism is less interested in hitting an admittedly easy target than in discovering the elements of the later work that might be worth attention by future readers. This shift in critical emphasis has thus far taken the form of broadening the contexts in which Sexton's work is viewed—of moving away from the necessary but narrowly circumscribed category of the confessional and toward the categories that are best described as mythopoeic, visionary, or prophetic.

Finally, it is still not possible to predict Sexton's ultimate place in American poetry, nor even to conjecture how she will be viewed during the remaining decades of this century. American poetry has thoroughly internalized and assimilated the narrative strategies represented by—and in part created anew by—Sexton; and these strategies, inadequately summarized by the term "confessional," were eschewed by our poetry a few short decades ago when they were mistakenly perceived as disjunctive rather than continuous with the larger poetic tradition. This internalization might speak well of the possibilities for Sexton's acceptance—and thereby her endurance and continuing availability to an increasing readership—as might new views of the shape and scope of her canon produced by feminist and other alternative critical trends.

Richard Wilbur

(1921-)

Bruce Michelson
University of Illinois

PRIMARY BIBLIOGRAPHY

Books

The Beautiful Changes and Other Poems. New York: Reynal & Hitchcock, 1947. Poems.
Ceremony and Other Poems. New York: Harcourt, Brace, 1950. Poems.
Things of This World, Poems by Richard Wilbur. New York: Harcourt, Brace, 1956. Poems.
Candide: A Comic Operetta Based on Voltaire's Satire, lyrics by Wilbur, book by Lillian Hellman, score by Leonard Bernstein; other lyrics by John Latouche and Dorothy Parker. New York: Random House, 1957. Operetta.
Poems 1943-56. London: Faber & Faber, 1957. Poems.
Advice to a Prophet and Other Poems. New York: Harcourt, Brace & World, 1961; London: Faber & Faber, 1962. Poems.
Loudmouse, illustrated by Don Almquist. New York: Crowell-Collier/ London: Collier-Macmillan, 1963. Children's poem.
The Poems of Richard Wilbur. New York: Harcourt, Brace & World, 1963.
Walking to Sleep, New Poems and Translations. New York: Harcourt, Brace & World, 1969; London: Faber & Faber, 1971. Poems, translations.
Opposites. New York: Harcourt Brace Jovanovich, 1973. Children's poems.
The Mind-Reader. New York & London: Harcourt Brace Jovanovich, 1976. Poems.
Responses, Prose Pieces: 1953-1976. New York: Harcourt Brace Jovanovich, 1976. Essays.

335

Selected Essays

"The Genie in the Bottle." In *Mid-Century American Poets*, ed. John Ciardi. New York: Twayne, 1950, 1-15.

"Poetry and the Landscape." In *The New Landscape in Art and Science*, ed. Gyorgy Kepes. Chicago: Paul Theobald, 1956, 86-90.

"The House of Poe." In *Anniversary Lectures 1959*. Washington, D.C.: Library of Congress, 1959.

Emily Dickinson: Three Views. Amherst, Mass.: Amherst College, 1960. Essays by Wilbur, Louise Bogan, and Archibald MacLeish.

Bynner, Witter. *Selected Poems*, introduction by Wilbur. New York: Farrar, Straus & Giroux, 1978.

Selected Story

"A Game of Catch," *New Yorker*, 18 July 1953, pp. 74-76. Reprinted in *American Accent*, ed. Elizabeth Abell. New York: Ballantine, 1954. Reprinted in *Prize Stories 1954: The O. Henry Awards*, ed. Paul Engle and Hansford Martin. New York: Doubleday, 1954. Reprinted in *Stories from The New Yorker, 1950-1960*. New York: Simon & Schuster, 1960.

Translations

Molière. *The Misanthrope*, translated with an introduction by Wilbur. New York: Harcourt, Brace, 1955; London: Faber & Faber, 1958.

_____. *Tartuffe*, translated with an introduction by Wilbur. New York: Harcourt, Brace & World, 1963; London: Faber & Faber, 1964.

_____. *The Misanthrope and Tartuffe*, translated with additional note by Wilbur. New York: Harcourt, Brace & World, 1965.

_____. *The School for Wives*, translated with an introduction by Wilbur. New York: Harcourt Brace Jovanovich, 1971.

_____. *The Learned Ladies*, translated with an introduction by Wilbur. New York: Dramatists' Play Service, 1977; New York: Harcourt Brace Jovanovich, 1978.

Racine. *Andromache*, translated with an introduction by Wilbur. New York: Harcourt Brace Jovanovich, 1982.

The Whale and Other Uncollected Translations, translated with an introduction by Wilbur. Brockport, N.Y.: Boa Editions, 1982.

Edited Books

A Bestiary, compiled by Wilbur, with illustrations by Alexander Calder. New York: Spiral Press for Pantheon, 1955. Children's poems.

Poe, Edgar Allan. *Poe: Complete Poems,* ed. with an introduction by Wilbur. New York: Dell, 1959.

Shakespeare, William. *Poems,* ed. Wilbur and Alfred Harbage, with an introduction by Wilbur. Baltimore: Penguin, 1966. Revised and republished as *Shakespeare, The Narrative Poems and Poems of Doubtful Authenticity.* Baltimore: Penguin, 1974.

Poe, Edgar Allan. *Poe, The Narrative of Arthur Gordon Pym,* ed. with an introduction by Wilbur. Boston: Godine, 1973.

Recordings

Poems. Spoken Arts, 1959.

Richard Wilbur Reading His Own Poems. Caedmon, n.d.

SECONDARY BIBLIOGRAPHY

Bibliographies and Checklists

Dinneen, Marcia B. "Richard Wilbur: A Bibliography of Secondary Sources," *Bulletin of Bibliography,* 37 (Jan.-Mar. 1980), 16-22. Secondary.

Field, John P. *Richard Wilbur: A Bibliographical Checklist.* Kent, Ohio: Kent State University Press, 1971. Primary and secondary.

Selected Interviews

Bogan, Christopher, and Carl Kaplan. "Interview with Richard Wilbur," *Amherst Student Review,* 16 Mar. 1975, pp. 4-5, 13-14.

Curry, David. "An Interview with Richard Wilbur," *Trinity Review,* 17 (Dec. 1962), 21-32.

Dillon, David. "The Image and the Object: An Interview with Richard Wilbur," *Southwest Review,* 58 (Summer 1973), 240-251.

Frank, Robert, and Stephen Mitchell. "Richard Wilbur: An Interview," *Amherst Literary Magazine,* 10 (Summer 1964), 54-72.

Graham, John. "Richard Wilbur." In *Craft So Hard to Learn: Conversations with Poets and Novelists about the Teaching of Writing,* ed.

George Garrett. New York: Morrow, 1972, 41-45.

_____. "Richard Wilbur." In *The Writer's Voice: Conversations with Contemporary Writers*, ed. George Garrett. New York: Morrow, 1973, 75-91.

High, Ellessa Clay, and Helen McCloy Ellison. "The Art of Poetry: Richard Wilbur," *Paris Review*, no. 72 (Winter 1977), 68-105.

Honig, Edwin. "Conversations with Translators, II: Octavio Paz and Richard Wilbur," *Modern Language Notes*, 91 (Oct. 1976), 1084-1098.

Hutton, Joan. "Richard Wilbur Talking to Joan Hutton," *Transatlantic Review*, no. 29 (Summer 1968), 58-67.

"An Interview with Richard Wilbur," *Crazy Horse*, no. 15 (Fall 1974), 37-44.

Packard, William, ed. *The Craft of Poetry: Interviews from the New York Quarterly*. New York: Doubleday, 1974, 177-194.

Pate, Willard. "Interview with Richard Wilbur," *South Carolina Review*, 3 (Nov. 1970), 5-23.

Critical Studies: Books

Cummins, Paul F. *Richard Wilbur*. Grand Rapids, Mich.: Eerdmans, 1971.

Hill, Donald L. *Richard Wilbur*. New York: Twayne, 1967.

Critical Studies: Collection of Essays

Salinger, Wendy, ed. *Richard Wilbur's Creation*. Ann Arbor: University of Michigan Press, 1983.

Critical Studies: Major Articles and Book Sections

Barksdale, Richard K. "Trends in Contemporary Poetry," *Phylon Quarterly*, 19 (Winter 1958), 408-416.

Benedikt, Michael. "Witty and Eerie," *Poetry*, 115 (Mar. 1970), 422-425. Revised and collected in Salinger.

Bly, Robert. "American Poetry: On the Way to the Hermetic," *Books Abroad*, 46 (Winter 1972), 17-24.

_____."The First Ten Issues of Kayak," *Kayak*, 12 (1967), 45-49.

Bosquet, Alain. "Preface" and "Richard Wilbur." In *Trente-Cinq Jeunes Poètes Américains*, ed. Bosquet. Paris: Gallimard, 1960, 9-37, 345-352.

Boyers, Robert. "On Richard Wilbur," *Salmagundi*, no. 12 (1970), 76-82.

_____."Richard Wilbur." In his *Contemporary Poetry*. London: St. James Press, 1975, 1676-1679.

Breslin, James E. "The New Rear Guard." In his *From Modern to Contemporary*. Chicago: University of Chicago Press, 1984, 23-52.

Brodsky, Joseph. "On Richard Wilbur," *American Poetry Review*, 2 (Jan.-Feb. 1972), 52. Collected in Salinger.

Cambon, Glauco. *Recent American Poetry*. University of Minnesota Pamphlets on American Writers, no. 16. Minneapolis: University of Minnesota Press, 1962, 8-16, 42.

Cargill, Oscar. "Poetry Since the Deluge," *English Journal*, 43 (Feb. 1954), 57-64.

Clough, Wilson O. "Poe's 'The City in the Sea' Revisited." In *Essays in American Literature in Honor of Jay B. Hubbell*, ed. Clarence Ghodes. Durham, N.C.: Duke University Press, 1967, 77-89.

Cooke, Michael G. "Book Reviews," *Georgia Review*, 31 (Fall 1977), 718-729. Review essay on *The Mind-Reader*.

Crowder, Richard. "Richard Wilbur and France," *Rives* (Paris), 25 (Spring 1964), 2-8.

Cummins, Paul. "Richard Wilbur's 'Ballade for the Duke of Orleans,' " *Concerning Poetry*, 1 (Fall 1968), 42-45.

_____. "*Walking to Sleep*, by Richard Wilbur," *Concerning Poetry*, 3 (Spring 1970), 72-76.

Daiches, David. "The Anglo-American Difference: Two Views." In *The Anchor Review*, no. 1, ed. Melvin J. Lasky. Garden City, N.Y.: Doubleday, 1955, 219-233.

Deutsch, Babette. *Poetry in Our Time*. Garden City: Doubleday/Anchor, 1963, 284, 347-348.

Duffy, Charles F. "Intricate Neural Grace: The Aesthetic of Richard Wilbur," *Concerning Poetry*, 4 (Spring 1971), 41-50. Collected in Salinger.

Eberhart, Richard. "On Richard Wilbur's 'Love Calls Us to Things of This World.' " In *The Contemporary Artist as Poet and Critic: Eight Symposia*, ed. Anthony Ostroff. Boston: Little, Brown, 1964, 4-5.

Farrell, John P. "The Beautiful Changes in Richard Wilbur's Poetry," *Contemporary Literature*, 12 (Winter 1971), 74-87. Collected in Salinger.

Faverty, Frederic Everett. "The Poetry of Richard Wilbur," *Tri-Quar-*

terly, 2 (Fall 1959), 26-30. Reprinted in *Poets in Progress,* ed. Edward Hungerford. Evanston, Ill.: Northwestern University Press, 1967.

Fiedler, Leslie A. "A Kind of Solution: The Situation of Poetry Now," *Kenyon Review,* 26 (Winter 1964), 54-79.

Fraser, G. S. "Some Younger American Poets, Art and Reality," *Commentary,* 23 (May 1957), 454-462.

Freed, Walter. "Richard Wilbur." In *Critical Survey of Poetry,* ed. Frank Magill. Englewood Cliffs, N.J.: Salem Press, 1982, 3091-3100.

Fussell, Paul, Jr. *Poetic Meter and Poetic Form.* New York: Random House, 1965, 78-79, 89, 103.

Garrett, George. "Against the Grain: Poets Writing Today." In *American Poetry,* ed. Irvin Ehrenpreis. Stratford-Upon-Avon Studies, 7. London: Arnold, 1965, 221-239.

_____. " 'Grace is Most of It': A Conversation with David Slavitt," *Georgia Review,* 26 (Winter 1972), 455-468.

Greene, George. "Four Campus Poets," *Thought,* 35 (Summer 1960), 223-246.

Gregory, Horace. "The Poetry of Suburbia," *Partisan Review,* 23 (Fall 1956), 545-553.

Hall, Donald. "The New Poetry: Notes on the Past Fifteen Years in America." In *New World Writing, Seventh Mentor Selection.* New York: New American Library, 1955, 231-247.

Hecht, Anthony. "The Motions of the Mind," *Times Literary Supplement,* 20 May 1977, p. 602. Review of *The Mind-Reader.* Collected in Salinger.

Heyen, William. "On Richard Wilbur," *Southern Review,* new series, 9 (Summer 1973), 617-634.

Holmes, John. "Surroundings and Illuminations." In *A Celebration of Poets,* ed. Don Cameron Allen. Baltimore: Johns Hopkins University Press, 1967, 108-130.

James, Clive. "As a Matter of Tact," *New Statesman,* 17 June 1977, pp. 815-816. Collected in Salinger.

_____. "When the Gloves are Off," *Review* (London), no. 26 (Summer 1971), 35-44. Collected in Salinger.

Jarrell, Randall. "Fifty Years of American Poetry," *Prairie Schooner,* 37 (Spring 1963), 1-27. Collected in excerpted form in Salinger.

_____. "A View of Three Poets," *Partisan Review,* 18 (Nov.-Dec. 1951), 691-700. Reprinted in his *Poetry and the Age.* New York: Vintage, 1953. Collected in excerpted form in Salinger.

Jensen, Ejner J. "Encounters with Experience: The Poems of Richard

Wilbur," *New England Review,* 2 (Summer 1980), 594-613. Collected in Salinger.

Jerome, Judson. *Poetry: Premeditated Art.* Boston: Houghton Mifflin, 1968, 168-169, 179-183, 348-349.

Johnson, Kenneth. "Virtues in Style, Defect in Content: The Poetry of Richard Wilbur." In *The Fifties: Fiction, Poetry, Drama,* ed. Warren French. De Land, Fla.: Everett/Edwards, 1970, 209-216.

Kinzie, Mary. "The Cheshire Smile: On Richard Wilbur," *American Poetry Review,* 6 (May-June 1977), 17-20.

Langbaum, Robert. "The New Nature Poetry," *American Scholar,* 28 (Summer 1959), 323-340.

Leithauser, Brad. "Reconsideration: Richard Wilbur—America's Master of Formal Verse," *New Republic,* 24 Mar. 1982, pp. 28-31. Revised and collected as "Richard Wilbur at Sixty" in Salinger.

Livey, Virginia. "The World of Objects in Richard Wilbur's Poetry," *Publications of the Arkansas Philological Association,* 7 (Spring 1981), 41-51.

McClatchy, J. D. "Dialects of the Tribe," *Poetry,* 130 (Apr. 1977), 41-53.

McConnell, Frank. "Reconsideration: The Poetry of Richard Wilbur," *New Republic,* 29 July 1978, pp. 37-39.

McGuinness, Arthur E. "A Question of Consciousness: Richard Wilbur's *Things of This World,*" *Arizona Quarterly,* 23 (Winter 1967), 313-326.

Mack, Perry. "Richard Wilbur's Three Treatments of Disintegrative and Metamorphic Change," *Innisfree,* 3 (1976), 37-44.

Mattfield, Mary S. "Some Poems of Richard Wilbur," *Ball State University Forum,* 11 (Summer 1970), 10-24.

Michelson, Bruce. "Richard Wilbur's *The Mind-Reader,*" *Southern Review,* new series, 15 (Summer 1979), 763-768. Collected in Salinger.

_____. "Richard Wilbur: The Quarrel with Poe," *Southern Review,* new series, 14 (Spring 1978), 245-261.

_____. "Wilbur's Words," *Massachusetts Review,* 23 (Spring 1982), 97-111. Collected in Salinger.

Miller, Stephen. "Poetry of Richard Wilbur," *Spirit,* 37, no. 3 (1970), 30-35.

Mills, Ralph J., Jr. "The Lyricism of Richard Wilbur," *Modern Age,* 6 (Fall 1962), 436-440. Expanded and reprinted in his *Contemporary American Poetry.* New York: Random House, 1965. Collected in original form in Salinger.

Montiero, George. "Redemption Through Nature: A Recurring Theme in Thoreau, Frost, and Richard Wilbur," *American Quarterly,* 20 (Winter 1968), 795-809.

Myers, John A., Jr. "Death in the Suburbs," *English Journal,* 52 (May 1963), 377-379.

Nejgebauer, Aleksandar. "Poetry 1945-1960: Self versus Culture." In *American Literature Since 1900,* ed. Marcus Cunliffe. London: Barrie & Jenkins, 1975, 145-149.

Nemerov, Howard. "What Was Modern Poetry: Three Lectures." In his *Figures of Thought: Speculations on the Meaning of Poetry and Other Essays.* Boston: Godine, 1978, 188-192. Collected in excerpted form in Salinger.

Nims, John Frederick, ed. *Poetry: A Critical Supplement,* 71 (Jan. 1948), 1-9.

Oliver, Raymond. "Verse Translations and Richard Wilbur," *Southern Review,* new series, 11 (Spring 1975), 318-330. Collected in Salinger.

Ostroff, Anthony, ed. *The Contemporary Poet as Artist and Critic: Eight Symposia.* Boston: Little, Brown, 1964, 1-21.

Plath, Sylvia. "Poets on Campus," *Mademoiselle,* 37 (Aug. 1953), 290-291.

Reedy, Gerard, S. J. "The Senses of Richard Wilbur," *Renascence,* 21 (Spring 1969), 145-150.

Reibetanz, John. "What Love Sees: Poetry and Vision in Richard Wilbur," *Modern Poetry Studies,* 11, nos. 1-2 (1982), 60-85.

Rosenthal, M. L. "Epilogue: American Continuities and Crosscurrents." In his *The New Poets: American and British Poetry Since World War II.* New York: Oxford University Press, 1967, 328-330.

_____. *The Modern Poets: A Critical Introduction.* New York: Oxford University Press, 1960, 8, 248, 253-255.

Sarton, May. "The School of Babylon." In *A Celebration of Poets,* ed. Don Cameron Allen. Baltimore: Johns Hopkins University Press, 1967, 131-151.

Sayre, Robert F. "A Case for Richard Wilbur as a Nature Poet," *Moderna Spraak* (Stockholm), 61 (1967), 114-122. Collected in Salinger.

Schulman, Grace. " 'To Shake Our Gravity Up': The Poetry of Richard Wilbur," *Nation,* 9 Oct. 1976, pp. 344-346.

Simon, John. "Translation or Adaptation." In *From Parnassus: Essays in Honor of Jacques Barzun,* ed. Dora Weiner and W. R. Keylor. New York: Harper & Row, 1976, 147-157.

Stepanchev, Stephen. *American Poetry Since 1945*. New York: Harper & Row, 1965, 93-106.

Sutton, Walter. "Criticism and Poetry." In *The Contemporary Poet as Artist and Critic*, ed. Ostroff, 174-195.

Swenson, May. "On Richard Wilbur's 'Love Calls Us to Things of This World.' " In *The Contemporary Poet as Artist and Critic*, ed. Ostroff, 12-16.

Taylor, Henry. "Cinematic Devices in Richard Wilbur's Poetry," *Rocky Mountain Modern Language Association Bulletin*, 28 (1974), 41-48.

_____. "Two Worlds Taken as They Come: Richard Wilbur's 'Walking to Sleep,' " *Hollins Critic*, 6 (July 1969), 1-12. Collected in Salinger.

Thurley, Geoffrey. "Benign Diaspora: The Landscape of Richard Wilbur." In his *The American Moment: American Poetry in the Mid-Century*. New York: St. Martin's Press, 1978, 35-50.

Torgerson, Eric. "Cold War in Poetry: Notes of a Conscientious Objector," *American Poetry Review*, 11 (July-Aug. 1982), 31-34.

Waggoner, Hyatt. *American Poets: From the Puritans to the Present*. Rev. ed. Baton Rouge: Louisiana State University Press, 1984, 591-600.

Weatherhead, A. K. "Richard Wilbur: Poetry of Things," *English Literary History*, 35 (Dec. 1968), 606-617.

Woodard, Charles R. "Richard Wilbur's Critical Condition," *Contemporary Poetry*, 2 (1977), 16-24. Collected in Salinger.

BIBLIOGRAPHICAL ESSAY

Bibliographies and Checklists

Two bibliographies on Wilbur have been published to date. One of these works appeared in 1971; the other, much more recent, is not designed to stand by itself. John P. Field's *Richard Wilbur: A Bibliographical Checklist* (1971), which scrupulously lists publications by and about Wilbur through the spring of 1969, can be trusted as a guide to the first twenty years of his career. For the January/March 1980 *Bulletin of Bibliography* Marcia B. Dinneen compiled and annotated a "continuation" of Field's bibliography, covering materials published through October of 1978. But Dinneen treats only secondary sources; in doing so she misses a few items of consequence—for example, Frank McConnell's excellent overview in the *New Republic* of 29 July 1978—and she also bypasses "some very short book reviews." However, her annotations are thoughtful and to the point. There has been a good deal written on Wilbur in the years since Dinneen's work appeared, and many of the important recent materials are gathered here; but no separate bibliography has kept up with Wilbur's small-scale work (reviews, speeches, recordings, and uncollected essays) since Field's.

Selected Interviews

Eloquent, learned, and unconventional in his ideas about poetry, Wilbur has been interviewed often in the past twenty years. The two-part interview in the Winter 1977 *Paris Review* is a good place to begin: Wilbur was questioned at his home in Cummington, Massachusetts, by Ellessa Clay High, and on the road in Louisville by Helen McCloy Ellison, and published together these encounters give a strong sense of not only the man's ideas but of the personality which lies behind them. Wilbur supplies much biographical information unavailable elsewhere in print, about, for example, his college days at Amherst and his first literary ventures, about World War II and the Italian Campaign of the 36th Division, and about his stint as a Junior Fellow at Harvard as American culture tried to reshape itself in the late 1940s. Wilbur also provides very important material on his relationship with Robert Frost, a discipleship which grew into an intense but touchy friendship as the younger writer went in his own directions. There is discussion here as well of Wilbur's amiable connections with Allen Ginsberg, Lawrence Ferlinghetti, and the City Lights poets of the middle 1950s. And through the conversation run affectionate but precise observations about D. H. Lawrence, Robert Lowell, Gary Snyder, Theodore Roethke, Stanley Kunitz, and many others, comments which help clarify both Wilbur's sense of his own place in his times and the spirit in which he reads the literature of this century. Edgar Allen Poe is mentioned too, of course—nearly every interviewer since the early 1960s has one way or another brought him up—but it is Wilbur's affection for Poe that dominates this discussion. Wilbur says, for example, that he first began reading Poe as an escape from reality during the battle of Monte Cassino, that at Harvard he began a book-length study of Poe's works, that in Wilbur's view "Modern studies of the dream-process are just catching up with some things that Poe noticed and, in his own way, set down," and that "there have been, good heavens, outcroppings of Poe, involuntary ones," in Wilbur's own poems. Beyond this material flows a tide of detail for anyone interested in the way one poet lives and writes: how he balances writing and living, what he does for recreation, what pressures and consolations he feels as he gets older, how he handles publishers, politicians, students, and his own other selves.

One of the most interesting interviews Wilbur has done appears in a hard-to-find journal, *Crazy Horse*. In "An Interview with Richard Wilbur" (Fall 1974), the poet talks in unprecedented detail about his upbringing, his Amherst education, his war experiences, his position as a Junior Fellow at Harvard, his first years as a poet, and the helter-skelter professional and personal life that followed. An excerpt will suggest the unusual openness and the interest of the whole:

> My Amherst class has always been very close-knit, partly because it lost so many in the Second World War. Even before our commencement, some had volunteered and had died in action. My own girding for war consisted in taking a Government correspondence-course in cryptography, barbarously practicing Morse Code transmission on my honeymoon, and joining the Enlisted Reserve Corps immediately thereafter. . . . Reporting for duty at Fort Dix, I was assigned to cryptographic training, and thereafter sent on to a secret cryptalytic camp in the woods of Virginia, where (as I later discovered) my progress into cryptanalysis was cut short by adverse security reports from the CIC and FBI. It was quite true that I held leftist views and had radical friends, and that I had been so stupid as to keep a volume of Marx in my foot-locker; but then as now I had an uncomplicated love of my country, and I was naively amazed to learn that my service record was stamped "Suspected of Disloyalty." For some reason, the Army then gave me a course in commando techniques after which I was sent overseas with a company of other undesirables, amiable bookies or bootleggers for the most part. Arriving, by way of Africa, in a replacement depot at Naples, I found myself profiting by another's ill-luck: a cryptographer in the 36 Infantry Division had just gone insane, and the divisional signal company was willing to overlook my disloyalty. I served with the 36th at Cassino and Anzio, in the Invasion of Southern France, and on through the Siegfried Line. . . .

Perhaps because the time of this interview is the early 1970s or because *Crazy Horse* provides an unusually relaxed forum, Wilbur speaks very much at his ease, offering good-natured pokes at some poetic fads of the time:

I should say that the world is ultimately good and every art an expression of hope and joy. But forced enthusiasm and an exclusive sunniness can put both of those propositions in doubt. What art needs to do, as Milton said, is to reflect how all things "Rising or falling still advance His praise," and in the process to make a full acknowledgement of the fallen-ness, doubt, and death. Not all art, of course, will accomplish these things on the scale of the Sistine Chapel; there is nothing wrong with modesty and homeliness. But there is something wrong with poems which lack all redeeming gaiety—and there may be gaiety in art which confronts the most desperate things. I do not enjoy poems which are mean, glum, artless and querulous. Isn't it odd that our American society, the most cosseted in human history, is now so given to petulance and dreary complaint, like the huge sad lady of Auden's "The Duet?" Grousing is not the mood or mode of any art which is doing its job.

The interview also includes essential information on the writing of some of Wilbur's later poems, including several from *Walking to Sleep*.

In a short conversation with Joan Hutton, published in 1968, Wilbur ventures into the realm of nature—as an influence upon the poetic consciousness, as a projection of the individual mind, as a teacher, as a repository of dark, even religious mysteries. His position on nature takes shape in fairly short responses to Hutton's well-aimed questions. Ralph Waldo Emerson in particular is treated by Wilbur as a point of both departure and comparison, and a sense of his own beliefs can be had from observing what he does and does not acquiesce to in Emerson's cosmology. Wilbur talks in some detail about his boyhood days on the farms and in the garden, and otherwise presents himself at his ease.

In the *New York Quarterly* interview (collected in William Packard's *The Craft of Poetry*, 1974) Wilbur seems less open and genial; his voice is that of a writer whose patience has been worn thin by an outbreak of silliness in art and politics. He explains why he has come back "only grudgingly" from a year's leave from the Board of Wesleyan University Press, having grown "sick of reading poetry" submitted for publication:

I don't feel able to distinguish between the better and the worse of it, because the fashionable aesthetics seem to me so distressing. I don't like, I can't adjust to, simplistic political poetry, the crowd-pleasing sort of anti-Vietnam poem. I can't adjust to the kind of Black poetry that simply cusses and hollers artlessly. And most of all I can't adjust to the sort of poem, which is mechanically, prosaically "irrational," which is often self-pitying, which starts all its sentences with "I", and which writes constantly out of a limply weird subjective world. There is an awful lot of that being produced. If you are given a box containing twenty manuscripts of verse, and eighteen of them are in that style, it's in the first place depressing, and in the second place you are unable for weariness to say that this is better than that. It's bad to be bored out of exerting one's critical faculty.

Balancing the swipes at current fashion are some disarming observations about himself as a mature poet whose own writing is coming more slowly. Wilbur talks about dry periods, what he does to fill up the time, the pleasure he finds in translating, and the lingering guilt about doing it, as a "way of distracting yourself from poems of your own which you might do if you left yourself exposed to the pain of your impotence."

Wilbur's answers here are generally briefer than in the *Paris Review* and *Crazy Horse* interviews, but when the questioner moves the conversation to the art of translation, the results are especially fine. Wilbur talks at some length about the special challenges of translating Racine, who presents "the finished and sonorous surface, and underneath that an awareness of violence, irrationality, disorder." Equally interesting are his reflections on how one can translate from a language one does not know: the long hours of having the original poem read over and over and of interrogating a native speaker about the nuances of particular words. And there are also thoughts on the liberating effect of working in traditional forms: "They are not simply a strait-jacket, they can also liberate you from whatever narrow track your own mind is running on, and prompt it to be loose and inventive, to entertain possibilities it hadn't foreseen."

Translation is also a subject in David Dillon's *Southwest Review* interview with Wilbur in 1973, but its most prevalent theme is the stages in the growth of the poet's mind. Dillon raises the issue and skillfully keeps it alive, and although Wilbur begins by saying, "I just don't want to have a critic's sense of my own concerns," he is eventually very analytical on the evolution of his thinking, of his process of self-renewal. Reviewing some of his own oft-quoted pronouncements made during the early 1950s, he reaffirms his ideas about prosody, but tries to correct notions that he is somehow dead-set against the style of the 1970s or that he scorns any idea that form should be self-generating:

> I wanted to say . . . that I never do set out to write within a stanza form. I think that I have always blundered into every form that I used. Even when I have written a ballade, it has always been a matter of discovering after four or five lines that I might just possibly have commenced a ballade—discovering that the material just wanted to take that form. . . . Generally speaking, unless one is writing a poem of enormous length, the repetition of a stanza pattern is not going to be confining, is not going to push the meaning or mood around. It is still, for me, a free verse poem. I'm thought to have a quarrel with free-verse poets; I really don't at all. I just choose to write free verse that happens to rhyme or to fall into a stanza pattern.

Wilbur also talks about his shift to longer, more dramatic poems, about the virtues of Ezra Pound, Robert Lowell, and Elizabeth Bishop as translators, about A. R. Ammons as "an extraordinary nature poet."

Fashion and style, poetry and politics, the poet and the audience, the fine arts and the postmodern mood—these are issues Wilbur deals with in his 1970 *South Carolina Review* interview with Willard Pate. The poet cautiously lays out his own position on the upheaval of those times and touches on everything from Vietnam War protests and pop art to Bob Dylan, Leonard Cohen, and the annual sales of the Wesleyan University Press. The mood is temperate and the method lucid, revealing a keen critical sense. Wilbur convincingly discusses, for example, the power of old rhetorical strategies and the reductiveness of ideologies that declare those strategies forever obsolete. Wilbur does pontificate a bit: he laments the demise of popular poetry of the sort Henry Wadsworth Longfellow wrote; he speculates that song lyricists of the present have begun to take up the slack; and he plays prophet by forecasting a division in American letters between "the poets who carry guitars and those poets who write for the printed page." There are plenty of quotable comments in the interview and a fine general look at Wilbur in his public guise—but not as much sense of the man behind the poetry and the pronouncements as other interviews have managed to flush out.

Critical Studies

Having won a wide following over the past three decades, Wilbur's poetry has sparked a lively, healthy, informative debate, causing readers to examine closely the problems and the assumptions behind contemporary poetics. Wilbur has taught many people to see both the world and poetry with fresh eyes; yet for all that, his work has frequently suffered unjust treatment; and not simply from his detractors but too often from well-intentioned admirers. As a writer, Wilbur has always gone his own way: in the early postwar years he won top prizes and became famous while still a young man; but in the mid-1950s, when American poets began clustering into hostile camps, Wilbur declined to join in. Instead, he continued to write verse unlike that produced by others of his own or younger generations, while he remained generous and undoctrinaire toward good poetry of any time, tribe, and political stripe and stayed wittily skeptical toward reductive thinking. In decades when aesthetics, philosophy, and politics have tended to merge, Wilbur has tried to keep each in its place; he has constantly affirmed the importance of reason, coherence, and sanity in poetry and in living. He has paid a price for his independence. Exploring for nearly forty years that "difficult balance" between rationality and mysticism, sanity and madness, faith and doubt, consolation and despair, Wilbur's poems are difficult, deceptive, vulnerable to every kind of misreading, from the condescending dismissal to the earnest, murderous dissection.

The essential problem for Wilbur may simply be this: in an age in which "serious" poetry is supposed to have a raw, offhand look, Wilbur's formal, intricately crafted works are out of step with fashion and liable to the charge of mannerism. William Meredith has nicely summed up the irony of his fellow-poet's predicament. For Meredith, the classic Wilbur poem

> invites careless reading: how genteel this all is, they think, how cheerful and Episcopalian, how very damned elegant. But these accusations, the ones that are actually derogatory, anyhow, are self-generated. The poems will not support them.

Meredith characterizes Wilbur's poetry in general as

> a kind of booby-trap that life itself mines our path with. A reticence is part of the riddle. We all ignore the world somewhat, each in his own dull way, but never except to our cost. These poems are the observations of a man who has a sharp eye and ear for moral order. You ask yourself whether some of the poets whose work proclaims that the universe has lately become un-

seemly are as observant as Wilbur, whether they have as much
regard for the riddle itself, the subject of our song.

There is a good chance, assert Meredith, Anthony Hecht, and others,
that Wilbur will prove one of the genuinely original voices of our
time: that he has brought poetry's traditional forms, powers, and
pleasures back to a valid new life and redeemed them as expressions
of a genuinely contemporary mind.

But from Wilbur's admirers there has also come trouble. The
poetry seems to tantalize New Critical instincts, the urge to analyze,
to parse, to talk about form and language as machines for the delivery
of major themes. A number of the longer and more enthusiastic
treatments of his work spend much more time scrutinizing the technical elements of the poems than in treating the shifting ideas and
the abiding mysteries behind the craftsmanship. They prove that Wilbur is a great technician; they do not prove that he matters. While a
great deal has been said about Wilbur as an inheritor and successor
to the Moderns, about his debt to Robert Frost and Wallace Stevens,
and about his often-misunderstood "quarrel" with Poe, there simply
is not a thorough, book-length discussion of Wilbur's work as a response to his own times, of the paradoxes implicit in his particular
vision and quest—about his attempt, in other words, to contend in
his own way with the spiritual and moral crises at the heart of the
"post modern" condition.

Critical Studies: Books

The most extensive study thus far of Wilbur's poetry was written
in 1967 and thus is not comprehensive in its treatment of the poet's
work. Donald L. Hill's Twayne book, *Richard Wilbur*, can offer nothing
about *Walking to Sleep, The Mind-Reader*, the translations, the many
later essays, interviews, and chapbooks Wilbur has produced since the
mid-1960s; neither can it say anything of the way his art has changed
over the last two decades. But Hill's book still has a number of special
strengths. Intended as a reader's guide, the volume treats Wilbur's
aesthetic and moral positions with the patience, the tentativeness, and
the sympathy they require. Hill is after what he calls the "logical
framework" of the poetry, and the bulk of his text, a sequence of
explications of many major poems, is chiefly about technique as a
working out of large-scale ideas. Hill was the first critic to make clear
that the "quarrel with Poe," as Wilbur has labeled much of his own

work, was not a matter of denying Romantic, Transcendental, or Symbolist impulses and of affirming a poetry of the mind; furthermore in one analysis after another, Hill manages to prove that his subject's form and flourish are not a refusal of chaos but a way of resisting it, even of expressing it. "Wilbur," says Hill, "begins and ends by cleaving to the things of this world. But, as I have often insisted, the spiritual state reflected in his poems is not so simple as that." Hill believes that "a good many of Wilbur's poems bear the marks, often 'lightly hid,' of a profound effort to resist the charm of some such ghostly siren as Poe's contempt for the world." In another passage Hill declares "we may understand his [Wilbur's] whole career as an uneasy oscillation between these grand opposites, orderly, witty wakefulness and destructive transcendence." Defining these paradoxes emphasizes the richness—but also the difficulty—of the poetry, and in discussing and interpreting the major poems Hill is cautious, perhaps at times too much so; one may grow impatient with his frequent confessions that he cannot quite make out the meaning of this or that crucial passage. But the overall effect is to the good, as Hill avoids making the poetry sound too "crackable," too doctrinaire. For example, "Caserta Garden," often presented as a demonstration that Wilbur affirms an excessively tidy artistic vision, is a poem Hill finds ultimately puzzling, as it includes within it, he ventures, an abiding suspicion of precisely those orderly, artificial beauties and contrivances that try to refuse the dust and the danger beyond the garden walls. This kind of hesitation is helpful rather than evasive, as it suggests the large and sometimes contradictory spirit behind the poetry.

Hill spends much time with poems he takes to be major expressions of Wilbur's cosmology, poems about the big questions; he is less patient with poems that seem to wrestle with something less than angels. Often he gets to the heart of the matter, as in his discussion of "A World Without Objects is a Sensible Emptiness." Sometimes the analysis is less satisfying: "Beowulf," one of Wilbur's most moving works on the imagination, is read inadequately here as little more than an odd experiment at recreating a Middle Ages atmosphere, and "Year's End," an important meditation about art, time, and the nature of the self, is passed by too hastily. These are minor objections; if there is a major weakness in Hill's early and therefore incomprehensive volume, it is that his third chapter, on *Things of This World,* is a falling off from the intensity that characterizes the rest of the book. The critic finds *Things of This World* marred by too much "ease and good humor," and his protracted and lukewarm response to the work seems to resist looking at the poems with the steadiness they require. For instance, in "Piazza de Spagna"—in many ways a dark poem about the illusions of life, about existence as a moment of beautiful ignorance before a plunge to oblivion—Hill can find only a stylistic exercise, an "adjustment of line movement and image to the actions described." "Marginalia," another unsettling poem about human life on the edge of the abyss, is also treated with fuzziness and uncertainty, and "Looking into History," a poem singled out often of late as a crucial one in the Wilbur canon, gets an early but unambitious reading. The famous title poem, which has since been recognized by many as an exceptionally moving and complex lyric, earns only condescension:

> It is good to follow this free and playful excursion of the mind, so unbound by anxiety, so unhurried, serene, and good-humored. Good humor—once again let it be said—is one of the primary aspects of Wilbur's charm. Yet all moods have their place in poetry. A bitter or anguished poet, if he is equally skillful and equally just in his response to his experience, may strike even more deeply into our feelings.

But Hill is the pioneer, and his book is remarkable for mustering and sustaining, through almost all of its 200 pages, a response as humane and variously sensitive as the poetry it treats. He fully comprehends that Wilbur is a poet who takes chances: he resists the claim of Rosenthal and others that these poems are wedded to the sunny side of life, and keeps as his object "to make clear that the surface composure of his poems is often but the rein of a strict control over genuine and disruptive tensions of the spirit." For recognizing that truth and demonstrating it so persuasively, Hill's book was, and remains, very valuable.

The danger of naming a critical series "Contemporary Poets from a Christian Perspective" is that the title might suggest, to readers trained in secular critical methods, some sort of evangelical tirade. Yet Paul F. Cummins's *Richard Wilbur* (1971), a pamphlet in this series, is neither naive, dogmatic, nor otherwise forced. Like Hill, Cummins perceptively addresses the implications of the "quarrel" with the irrational and transcendental impulses in the modern spirit and Wilbur's chosen position on the uncertain edges of the everyday world. The main axis of Cummins's discussion is the relationship of Wilbur's technique to his overall vision, the essence of that vision being that "It is both man's fate and his blessing that he must work out his destiny amid imperfection and ambiguity." Cummins briefly but effectively treats various features of Wilbur's technique—his imagery, wordplay, rhyme, and allusions. The critic skillfully discusses "The Pardon," "A World Without Objects," "Still, Citizen Sparrow," and "The Juggler" but examines intensely "Love Calls Us to Things of this World" as the most complete statement of Wilbur's themes, the clearest revelation of his ties with the Christian tradition. Wilbur believes, says Cummins, that the loss of innocence is fortunate, that life is a matter of keeping one's balance between opposing desires, that the struggle between the flesh and the spirit is somehow worthwhile and good. Cummins's study, in short, proves both reasonable and useful in its treatment of Wilbur's poetry.

Critical Studies: Collection of Essays

The list of good criticism on Richard Wilbur is not enormous; most of the best analyses, in fact, have been discerningly collected and intelligently introduced by Wendy Salinger in her 1983 volume, *Richard Wilbur's Creation*, part of the "Under Discussion" series begun at the University of Michigan under the general editorship of Donald Hall. Many of the articles and reviews discussed under Critical Studies: Major Articles and Book Sections in this essay are found in Salinger's volume, which is certainly the place to start in reviewing the Wilbur controversy and in locating the most provocative responses to his work.

Salinger's introduction sketches out the major events and issues in American poetry since World War II, correctly suggests Wilbur's relative position as the fray has shifted ground over the years, and gets to the gist of a dozen or so of the major pronouncements about him. About both Wilbur and the accretion of judgments about him, Salinger shows herself a critic of unusual skill in making sharp distinctions. Her discussion of a slippery and all-important matter in Wilbur's verse—the relationship of the self to the external world—is one of the best to date on the subject: it is precise, balanced, and fully aware of the problem's heritage since the Romantics and of the strong and weak spots in the contemporary argument. She acknowledges too Wilbur's awareness that there are many sides to the case and many impulses in the self other than to sanity and balance. Salinger makes a good case for a subtle but fundamental change, over the years, in the way Wilbur's poetry struggles with the world, and she offers passing observations on poetry's paradoxical condition since 1960—the division that headed off, in opposite directions at once, toward excesses that Wilbur is temperamentally and intellectually unwilling to embrace:

> It's even possible to see the confessional mode as a further development of the fifties privatism rather than as a counteraction. Some critics explained it as the response of the individual sensibility to a meaningless world: when the historical process begins to alienate the individual rather than enrich his life sense, he turns to what is local and intimate. Or one might see two roads diverging from the main thoroughfare, the thruway of the fifties: one leading deeper into a private sensibility, and one traveling outward to meet public event, war, and social revolution. And there were poets who worked both routes—Bly, Wright, Kinnell, and other so-called deep image poets, for example. Their form of privatism, however, was less confessional and personal than it was psychic and surreal—in fact, impersonal.

Readers who consult Salinger's collection would do very well to begin with her own discussion, for she shows a real expertise not only in Wilbur but also in Wilbur's time, and in a short space she brings perspective to the debate surrounding the poet.

Critical Studies: Major Articles and Book Sections

In reading the shorter criticism on Wilbur, it is best not to begin at random. As a complex artist who cannot be approached through the shortcut of a particular "school" or movement, Wilbur is very difficult to discuss in anything like a full and just way, and even his most enthusiastic interpreters can give incomplete, misleading impressions when they try to evaluate him. There has been an evolution in the way his work has been understood, a movement away from the notion that Wilbur's poems are treatises and toward the recognition that any ideas they suggest are a *poet's* ideas, full of reservations, anxieties, paradoxes. Because doggedly methodical approaches, however sympathetic, to his work can make Wilbur seem too much a riddler, a puzzle-buff like Wallace Stevens's Rose Rabbi, it is worth one's trouble to read a good impressionistic commentary to begin with. A splendid example is William Heyen's "On Richard Wilbur" (1973), which has no real point to prove yet comprehends the poetry brilliantly. Avoiding both the combative attacks and the dissection that often passes for sympathetic close reading of Wilbur, Heyen offers what he claims to be meandering thoughts, "with no program or outline in mind," set off into sections that indicate (he tells his readers) only when he stopped and went to bed. Although his tone may seem a bit precious, he provides a fresh approach to Wilbur, free of predisposition or reductive method. Heyen also avoids the commonplace mistake of trying to better one writer's name by beating down another's. He has friendly, admiring observations to make in passing about William Carlos Williams and even about Robert Bly (one of Wilbur's most persistent and petulant opponents): in the midst of the essay Heyen quotes some Bly verses and rhapsodizes their special powers. But the overall intent is to get past Wilbur's formal surfaces by the successful ruse of informality, not to treat Wilbur's as a sensibility that can be blueprinted. Heyen's assertions about the fullness of Wilbur's spirit, about the genuine "naturalness" of his vision, about the paradoxes that make him a human being stick in the mind: the mysteries that matter and endure are presented handsomely here. A representative passage shows the genuine magnanimity that suffuses the essay, a thoughtful delight not only in Wilbur but in the age he shares with his readers. After quoting Bly, Heyen states:

> If the busy man would only stand still, Bly says, miracles would happen again. I could talk about this fine poem for a long time. I think I know what is at stake. And I am moved by these four lines. At the same time, Richard Wilbur's voice strikes me as individual, powerful, undeniable, and in poem after poem he makes his taste and feeling for language mine. That taste is for raised, uncommon speech. Sophisticated, yes; fastidious, yes; occasionally even elegant, yes. Sophistication and fastidiousness and elegance are traditional virtues. I am not willing to throw them away in the name of some sort of truer truth. Formal, yes. . . . I believe Robert Kelley, writing in *A Controversy of Poets* (1965), when he says that "The only form possible is the form the poem spells itself out in. . . ." But I will not do away with the consciousness as the poem takes its shape. . . . I know what Kelley means; I know the world of awareness, peace, and love that a real poem or a poetry reading by a real poet can build. But belligerence and mind-lock when confronted with, say, a sonnet, or formal grammar, or iambic pentameter, is self-defeating, is as negative a contribution to anything as is a poem that relies on superficial, glittering constructs of some kind for its effect.

"The Wilbur I hear," says Heyen, "is not the mandarin poet he

355

is often considered to be," and the second half of the essay, insofar as it stays on course, is given over to showing us a Wilbur who takes chances and feels doubts and anxieties. In the process the critic discusses, quickly but trenchantly, "A Wood," "A Plain Song for Comadre," "The Undead," "An Event"—some of the less noticed poems. Heyen's final statement concludes nothing; he merely summarizes a feeling about Wilbur, a feeling that was (supposedly) inchoate when he began the essay, a feeling that many other critics have had less fortune in giving voice:

> There is for me in the poetry of Richard Wilbur something always just past the threshold of realization, something elusive, something toward which his formal structures edge and with which they bump shoulders, something that criticism can only hope to graze. This something, I think, is feeling, passion. It is a passion intricately involved with the tension that results from the clash between his language, his rage for the right word with the right sound, the right movement, and the knowledge manifested, embodied in those words and structures that the mind's graceful errors and the heart's unreasonable joys and sorrows and the losses that time has dealt us enable a man to go just so far. It is a passion involved with a poem's reaching for as much as possible while it knows that the distance between it and the stars is staggering. It is a passion of acceptance, and more: of a whole spirit's agonizing for something that will suffice, and of that spirit's joy in finding that in its world there is something that sometimes will.

Heyen's perceptions are eminently worth reading. Any good discussion of Richard Wilbur has to take into account the "something elusive," the poet's innate resistance to structure in the poetry and in the mind, that formal studies, however friendly, are likely to miss.

Another general essay of lasting importance suffers the disadvantage of having been published in an often inaccessible tabloid journal, the *American Poetry Review*. Mary Kinzie's "The Cheshire Smile: On Richard Wilbur" (1977) is perhaps as good a starting point in reading the criticism as Heyen's piece. Beginning as a review of "The Mind-Reader," the essay soon opens out into an ambitious discussion of the whole Wilbur canon, and in its course takes on four of Wilbur's toughest, most self-searching poems, "Walking to Sleep," "Castles and Distances," "The Fourth of July," and "The Mind-Reader." What Kinzie is after is the anti-Wilbur, the side of him that resists order and sunlight and actually yearns for the Poe-like escape from the real. Wilbur's art for Kinzie is very much the record of a soul in conflict with itself; what makes the orderly poems interesting is how they court their own destruction:

> Besides the formal grace which regulates the axial lines of his poetry, there is also in Wilbur's best verse a movement awry of the plane. Like the line of beauty for Hogarth or the clinamen of Lucretius, there is an implicit swerve of metaphor after the careful links and jumps have been established. The swerve in "The Mind-Reader" covers the distance between the unpleasant dramatic character and the blossoming of his vain heart and faculties at the point where, ironically, he cannot resist the comparison with God.

Kinzie's approach to Wilbur proves itself in the close readings she offers: her discussion of "The Fourth of July" is simply the best in print at the moment; she handles "Castles and Distances" with grace and depth; and she enters the monologues in a spirit that reveals their real intensity. Kinzie's essay should be read for its recognition that form and its undoing join in Wilbur's best work, and that this collision provides much of his energy and importance.

Clive James, an English critic, has taken on Wilbur's poetry and criticism on several occasions; and to read his articles in order is to see the education, over the years, of an insightful and influential reader. In the 1971 essay, "When the Gloves are Off " (reprinted in Salinger), James's patience with Wilbur is limited. His recent poems, James quips, are "the same old *acqua minerale* and either it or our liver has lost tone." Wilbur is an artisan past his prime, James declares: "While he was on balance, [he] wrote a good number of poised, civilized, and very beautiful poems. They'll be worth remembering when some of the rough, tough, gloves-off stuff we're lately supposed to admire starts looking thin." But six years later, in "As a Matter of Tact" (also in Salinger), James is less impressed by Wilbur's craft than he is by the poet's demonstrated and persistent courage of vision:

> The poems in *The Beautiful Changes, Ceremony,* and *Things of This World* sound better and better as time goes on. Where his coevals looked fecund, they now look slovenly; where he once seemed merely exquisite, he now seems a model of judicious strength; as was bound to happen, it was the artful contrivance which retained its spontaneity and the avowedly spontaneous which ended up looking contrived. There is no reason to be

ashamed at feeling charmed by Wilbur's poetry. The sanity of his level voice is a hard-won triumph of the contemplative intelligence.

Many of the other brief reviews reprinted in the Salinger collection serve a similar purpose: they offer less insight into Wilbur than they do into the sensibilities that have influenced poetry in the past four decades; they give a good idea of the political and aesthetic climate in which Wilbur's various collections have been published, and they suggest what luck his longstanding commitment to his art has had in shaping an audience.

An essay that transcends the limitations of the review form defined above is poet Anthony Hecht's "The Motions of the Mind" (1977). Reviewing *The Mind-Reader* for the *Times Literary Supplement,* Hecht makes his often-quoted declaration that Wilbur's "is the most kinetic poetry I know"; he studies and celebrates Wilbur's "pivotal and energetic verbs" and asserts that the mind which generates them is constantly in flux, anything but complacent. In his lucid enthusiasm, Hecht takes an amusing swipe at those readers who uncritically accept certain postmodern gospels:

> For those to whom formal poetry is itself unnatural, an embarrassed or twisted parlance of one who is self-consciously ill-at-ease holding the floor, any unusual feature of poetry, even its most towering graces, can be thought of as no more than the by-products, the industrial waste, entailed by meter and rhyme; and therefore (in the name of directness, of authenticity, of courage, of any number of Rousseauian virtues that belong exclusively to the noble savage) to be deplored as a victimization, as no grace at all but a crippled response to life and language. This sort of argument is marvellously self-serving, and based utterly on ignorance.

Hecht focuses his attention on an older poem and a new one: he finds in Tennyson's *Idylls* a convincing source for a crucial stanza of "Merlin Enthralled" and compares Tennyson's and Wilbur's virtuosity at dissolving "one realm of reality into another"; he shows how word choices in the first nineteen lines of "The Mind-Reader" suggest not only the "graceful motions of the mind" on its descent from conscious to unconscious life but also the peculiar mind of Wilbur's persona, the alcoholic Italian—part charlatan, part visionary—who is not "permitted to forget." Hecht closes with a prediction that "The Fourth of July" will be "the best thing to come out of the American

Bicentennial," and takes a parting shot at the age with which both he and Wilbur are out of step, "when great, shaggy herds of poets write only about themselves, or about the casual workings of their rather tedious minds." An informative review as well as an amusing polemic, Hecht's essay ought to figure into any further discussion of Wilbur's most recent collection.

Among recent, uncollected essays about Wilbur's overall achievement and importance, Frank McConnell's "Reconsideration: The Poetry of Richard Wilbur" (1978) in the *New Republic* is excellent as an attempt to penetrate the dark, disorderly depths behind the poet's sunlit facades, and to compare his boldness, favorably and contentiously, to that of some of the literary stars of the last decade. If Wilbur's assertions, says McConnell,

> "strike a comforting and . . . civilized balance between the omnivorous, self-consuming self of the confessional poets and the selfless, dizzily convex world of their anti-confessional colleagues, that does not mean that comfort is not, as all real comfort, all real sanity has to be, earned. To say that love calls us to the things of this world is *not* to say that love is easy, or that the things of this world are incapable of terror. Between the austere plane geometry of Lowell's vision and the topological catastrophe of Ashbery's, Wilbur's is indeed a calculus of delight. But a calculus is a way of describing limits you never reach, a science of possibilities intimated, not realized."

McConnell succinctly restates the parameters of Wilbur's ideas of poetry, of the imagination, of the connection of the self to the world, and he does it without reductiveness. As an attempt to place Wilbur at the center of important contemporary matters, McConnell's essay is well worth reading.

The *New Republic* also published an early version of Brad Leithauser's "Richard Wilbur at Sixty" (1982), which has been expanded into the closing essay in the Salinger collection. The article ranges widely, including a vignette of the way Wilbur presently lives, a description of the house and the grounds at Cummington, a history of his publications, and some insights into the differences among his various collections. Although Leithauser affirms that Wilbur confronts "absolutely enormous questions," he expresses some concern that he has, of late, shown "some loss in the capacity to surprise" and picked up a tendency "to be too articulate about what he confesses is ultimately ineffable." The essay offers a balanced, sympathetic overview of the achievement and a sense of the poet's life at present.

Salinger shows special diligence and judgment in collecting an important 1967 essay by Robert F. Sayre from the Swedish journal *Moderna Spraak.* Sayre takes issue with a "standard view" of Wilbur dignified in Randall Jarrell's influential *Poetry and the Age* (1953): this poet-critic's reviews began faulting Wilbur for safety and gentility in those days when Jarrell was promoting the careers of other poets more to his taste, first among them Robert Lowell. Sayre argues that Wilbur's poems actually reveal him to be "at present America's most profound moralist of man's relations with nature," and he advances the important thesis that the " 'New Formalism' is much more than a matter of return . . . to a more traditional verse. It is the poet's espousal of a formal relationship with his subject—particularly a formal relationship with nature." Discriminating in his choice of poems, Sayre faults "Speech for the Repeal of the McCarran Act" for a certain "dandyism" and favors instead those works which contend with an intractable universe. The critic's strongest discussion focuses on some of Wilbur's most difficult poems—on "Looking into History," for example, which ends with a mysterious melding of two opposed ideas of the imagination, as an ever-changing Proteus and as a "self-established" "live formality" (the language is Wilbur's). Readers who think of Wilbur's boxed and bounded "Caserta Garden" when they consider him as a nature poet would do well to consult Sayre's treatment of "Castles and Distances," a poem which, he convincingly argues, celebrates both the dark woods and the planned landscape, and the need humans have for "intimacy with both worlds."

Wilbur can have no more eloquent or enthusiastic defender at the moment than Ejner J. Jensen, whose "Encounters with Experience: The Poems of Richard Wilbur" originally appeared in the Summer 1980 *New England Review.* Like Sayre, McConnell, and Bruce Michelson, Jensen intends to show that Wilbur takes genuine risks, that his crafted verse is really a way of looking steadily and honestly into "the darker elements of human experience," that "the very beauty of [Wilbur's] designs may conceal from us the struggle and anguish of the experiences themselves." Jensen treats several of the poems in *Walking to Sleep,* including the title poem, as ventures into the "very homes of dread," and he sees both courage and genuine originality in the stand Wilbur, almost alone in his time, has taken up and defended.

In most of Western Literature, rational man is viewed approvingly and his triumphs celebrated. More recently, particularly in poets who reject modern society, the higher value attaches to instinctual man, to man in nature. In a way, each of these answers is false; certainly they are both too easy. The more daring vision is the one that maintains the paradox and confronts it with full awareness of its extremes.

The passage pays Wilbur a tribute and counters facile judgments that continue to be made of his work; but it also suggests the weak spots in Jensen's own discussion. The argument blunts itself by being too general, by talking too much about "modern society" and "Western literature" in sweeping ways, and by saying too little of substance about Wilbur's relationship to his contemporaries, about the poems with milder surfaces, or about any previous in-depth discussions of the poetry. The critic covers many of the poems that Hill treated a decade before, and does so without much variation or improvement, but says nothing about Hill's book; he digresses awkwardly to demonstrate—unconvincingly—that Wilbur responds to evil and to horror more deeply and self-consciously than did Robert Frost, whom Jarrell and Lionel Trilling admired as a suitably "terrifying" modern poet. And on Wilbur's short poem about the sculpture of Giacometti, Jensen overstates his case: "Rarely," he says, "has an artist in one medium drawn from a master working in another with so little sacrifice of power and truth. Verdi's levying on Shakespeare might be a comparable instance." Still, Jensen's enthusiasm seems refreshing, contagious, and for the most part persuasively supported.

A much more modest study, both in its aspirations and its accomplishments, is Charles F. Duffy's "Intricate Neural Grace: The Aesthetic of Richard Wilbur," which Salinger reprints from the Spring 1971 *Concerning Poetry*. Duffy limits his discussion to some poems of Wilbur's which are expressly about art or in which artists somehow are implicated. The selection seems a bit skewed—Duffy skips the cryptic, exciting "Museum Piece" but talks at length about "A Hole in the Floor" on the grounds that it is dedicated to Belgian painter René Magritte—and the theme Duffy finds everywhere is that Wilbur embraces wit and wakefulness, balance and control, "art as above all conscious form." "Giacometti," "L'Etoile," "A Dutch Courtyard," "Ceremony," and a few other poems are cursorily examined to reinforce the point. The critique is a little too tidy, both in choice and in interpretation: the "tigers in the wood" that haunt "Ceremony," the "fine El Greco" at the end of "Museum Piece" with French artist Edgar

Degas's pants hanging on it, the comedy at the close of "A Dutch Courtyard" are all passed over. Thus the true complexities of Wilbur's aesthetic, the darkness that haunts his most orderly Dutch courtyards, the doubt that mingles with his affirmations, the humor that challenges his sobriety, the comic and frightening disorder that his orderly poems do not stave off but engage with, or the way these ideas challenge contemporary intellectual fashion—none of these topics are addressed. Duffy breaks some ground, but there is plenty of work yet to do in exploring the role that the fine arts play in Wilbur's poetry.

Wilbur's famous declaration twenty years ago that much of his work could be taken as a "public quarrel with the aesthetics of Edgar Allan Poe" has been used and abused variously in criticism. John P. Farrell's essay, "The Beautiful Changes in Richard Wilbur's Poetry" (1971), gives a lesson in how to interpret the remark intelligently and how to make sense of Wilbur's abiding passionate interest in Poe and his works, the interest which has made Wilbur one of the most sympathetic and insightful students of the Poe canon. Farrell does not suppose that Wilbur's refusal of Poe's self-destroying transcendence makes the modern poet a "jejune optimist"; rather, he contends that Wilbur's stance, his "genuine reverence for life," comes of a "capacity to see beyond disintegrative change, into the metamorphic and regenerative life of the universe." Farrell is fond, however, of black-and-white oppositions: when he argues that Wilbur's understanding of beauty is "quite the contrary" of Poe's, that Poe's enchantment with the induced state of sleep is "altogether the opposite condition" from the spirit of Wilbur's poetry, he makes too schematic a case; he allows too little room to explain Wilbur's fascination with Poe, the Poe-part of Wilbur which Poe speaks to—the fact that Poe and Wilbur (perhaps like all fervent quarrelers) have something vital in common, a bond that makes for much of the tension and energy in Wilbur's poetry. Highlights of the essay include an analysis of "Looking into History," one of the most difficult poems in *Things of This World,* and discussions of the way that love and metamorphosis work as themes in "The Snow Man," "Advice to a Prophet," and "The Aspen and the Stream."

A strong sense of the precariousness of both the mind and the world in Wilbur's writing informs Charles R. Woodard's brief but pungent "Richard Wilbur's Critical Condition" (1977), which tries in the space of six pages to demonstrate the boldness of Wilbur's kind of vision and to attack the pretentious unpretentiousness of the "Williams school," the Confessional movement, "raw" poetry, and critics who have deteriorated into "emotional Jacksonians" (a clumsy way, perhaps, of suggesting how simple-mindedness gets confounded with honesty). Woodard discusses none of Wilbur's poems in any depth, but he does offer this kind of insight:

> Beneath the sensible surface of Wilbur's world another threatens, like the crack in Auden's teacup, to open into unspeakable voids— "the buried strangeness/Which nourishes the known." . . . His is a landscape of ephemera, of "opulent bric-a-brac," mined country, touched with a fatal "seeming" of the Edenic pear in "June Light," which constantly erodes the "truth and new delight" of the visible world. Each poem is a temporary victory over our knowledge of the nature of things; in each, like his juggler, he "has won for once over the world's weight," even as his prophet is being rehearsed to preach the "worldless rose" of an atomized earth. . . . In this connection, Wilbur's tendency to concentrate on things rather than on dramatic situations (people) is perhaps not without its own sinister implications.

And he does offer this tongue-in-cheek assessment of contemporary expectations for poets:

> We seem, in fact, to have arrived, in recent years, at a kind of unwritten contract with our poets. Were it formalized, it might read more or less as follows: "You may be a poet, and we will reward you with grants and fellowships and readings if you are fashionable, and publish your doings in the papers, like those of football players and television performers, but never forget that it is your suffering for which you are being paid. We will begin to take most interest in your work precisely when it shows clearest symptoms of your breaking down. We want to know of every visit to a sanitarium, every cut, cuddled, and sucked thumb, your bouts with alcohol and depression, your flirtations with suicide. And then, to prove your seriousness you must write a final poem, in the form of a leap from a bridge or a pulled trigger. Then we will believe. Then we will establish a cult and proclaim you unreservedly a poet."

Readers should consult this essay for a discussion not only of Wilbur's complexity and modernity, but also of the chances he takes.

Wilbur's achievements as a translator—an art that he is practicing increasingly of late—have received surprisingly little critical attention. Showing much more than finesse, precision, or a "good ear," Wilbur has set new standards, has established principles as radical in their

way as those that Pound provided three generations ago. For the first
time in our history Wilbur has made Molière really accessible to readers of English; having had similar fortune with Old English, Old
French, and modern Russian, he has lately taken on the "untranslat-
able" Racine—relying on the demanding rigors of rhymed couplets
to convey the original's tension between tight form and violent, passionate subject matter. In every major translation Wilbur takes risks
and succeeds; but as yet there is only one article comparing his technique to others practiced in our time. Luckily, the article is especially
fine. Raymond Oliver's "Verse Translations and Richard Wilbur"
(1975), reprinted in Salinger, considers first the basic, enduring idea
behind translation—starting at the beginning with the etymology of
the word. Oliver discusses translation's history as an art form in its
own right and the important redefinitions of the art by French and
American poets of the past century. Taking very little for granted,
he builds a strong case for the virtues of translation over "imitation,"
arguing that the latter shows a lack of understanding for formal devices and deprives readers "of all but the most limited, self-centered
relations with other cultures and the past." The second half of the
essay closely examines Wilbur's achievements in translating French,
compares his rendering of Valéry's "Hélène" to Lowell's treatment of
the same poem, and finds Wilbur's superior, both as a rendition of
the original and as a poem with its own merits. Wilbur's performance
ranges, for Oliver, "from reasonably good to superlative," and he
ends the essay by considering the work with Russian writers, with
medieval Latin and Old English, and especially with French verse
plays:

> Wilbur's rhyming is consistently brilliant; he keeps the para-
> phrasable content of Molière to a remarkable degree; he preserves
> the meter and closed couplets of the originals; he is sometimes
> more colloquial, succinct, and vivid than Molière, sometimes
> less—on balance, I suppose the French and English are about
> equal as verse.

Readers interested in translation should also consult John Simon's
1976 essay in the festschrift *From Parnassus,* a collection honoring
Jacques Barzun. "Translation or Adaptation" compares Wilbur's *Tartuffe* to Tony Harrison's freewheeling rendition of the same play.
Simon poses the crucial questions: which translation works better,
which demonstrates more genuine fidelity not only to the letter but

to the spirit of the original text, which version is, finally, in its own right a better piece of stagecraft. In Simon's carefully defended judgment, Wilbur resoundingly wins.

James E. Breslin's book *From Modern to Contemporary* (1984) includes an extensive, informed discussion of Wilbur as an influential figure in the decade after World War II, but the study is marred. Designed to praise Frank O'Hara, John Ashbery, Denise Levertov, Allen Ginsberg, and the later Robert Lowell not merely as poets but also as cultural heroes, bold revolutionaries, and champions of freedom and truth in poetry, Breslin's history needs villains; he accordingly sets Wilbur up as a usurping King Log whose regime slipped into authority in a postwar artistic vacuum, and who, with his complacent comrades, had to be overthrown for the common good. Despite the general tendency of literary history to embue each new literary generation with Oedipal anxieties, Breslin truly oversteps the mark; and Wilbur is indicted in distinguished company: Jacques Barzun, R. P. Blackmur, Leslie Fiedler, Louise Bogan, and even the young Adrienne Rich are named as reactionary coconspirators. But the charge reserved for Wilbur is "revisionism." In pressing his case Breslin raids Wilbur's poetry rather than reads it, bolstering his belabored accusation that Wilbur conspired to thwart Modernism and disinherit its offspring, that behind Wilbur's mild and courteous and reasonable facade there always lurked the insidious enemy of the revolution:

> Wilbur's own more modest and nonprogrammatic stance can reduce in its own quiet ways. Here, it sounds as if he were offering a balanced critique of the excesses of a revolutionary movement, a sensible gesture that few would debate at least until they saw it applied. In fact, the theories that Wilbur does cite as reductive— the attempts to "purify poetry of all but organic rhythms," "the Imagist insistence that ideas be implicit in description," and the efforts to "abandon logical progression, and to write in quasi-musical form"—were not the extreme and extravagant edges of modernism; they were all serious attempts to find ways of organizing experience that were subversive of those very procedures validated and established by both the culture and the literary tradition. Wilbur actually questions modernism at its core. Like his concern to reconcile "experimental gains" with traditional forms, his revisionist account of modernism, which may strike us at first as an all-too-minimal shift, actually causes a tremor along the foundations which shatters the entire modernist enterprise.

Breslin's argument must be examined through a series of factors. First, he looks through the distortions of current feuds and politics back to a brief, good-natured interlude in American poetry before the battle lines were drawn by Charles Olson, Lawrence Ferlinghetti, the Beats, and the Black Mountaineers. Second, Wilbur's attitude toward his contemporaries and juniors has been to allow them their own artistic and critical development rather than to evangelize or engage in literary quarrels. Wilbur has in fact proved a friend and a helper to poets that Breslin counts among Wilbur's opponents; he has shown remarkably little interest in taking sides or attacking different views. Third, there is a limit to what bearing the debates of the 1950s should have on evaluating anyone's work from the perspective of the 1980s. The time cannot be far off when the who-opposed-whom of a few years ago will wane into a matter of minor interest, and when the canon of any writer will have to stand on something other than which side he or she played for in the modern-postmodern political-poetic game.

Hyatt Waggoner's revised *American Poets: From the Puritans to the Present* (1984) provides insights one might not expect from so wide-ranging a volume. Short as it is, Waggoner's overview of Wilbur sees its way past early professions of an impersonal poetry and of loyalty to modernist thinking and thus points out poems "often closer in theme, and occasionally even in style, to that of Romantic and vision-ary poets of the past than is true of any of the others [of Wilbur's generation] . . . except Roethke." Asserting Wilbur's affinity to Hart Crane, E. E. Cummings, and Emerson, Waggoner discusses "A World Without Objects" and "The Beautiful Changes," generally demon-strating that even an entry in a large-scale literary history can have something new and important to offer. Walter Freed's approach in the 1982 *Critical Survey of Poetry* is also insightful if less surprising: asserting that Wilbur's strength lies in "capturing what is abstract in a mesh of concrete imagery" and that the most powerful sense one gets from reading Wilbur is of the "deep humanity which runs through his work," Freed discusses "The Pardon," "A Hole in the Floor," the three "Running" poems, and "Lamarck Elaborated" as works which convey an "ordinary understanding of life in an extraor-dinary and uncompromising way."

A longer piece, included in Warren French's collection *The Fif-ties: Fiction, Poetry, Drama* (1970), is more interesting now as an out-moded expression of puzzlement than as a lasting contribution to the criticism of Wilbur's poetry. Kenneth Johnson's "Virtues in Style, Defect in Content: The Poetry of Richard Wilbur" reads Wilbur reductively and faults him for being reductive. Johnson asks, "if Wilbur so highly values and is enamoured by this tangible world, why is he so often—and so easily and gladly—lured away from it?" This is a rich question, not an enigma; but Johnson is stumped by it because he cannot see the poet's ideas of the imagination and the real world in any but either-or terms: "the imagination, for Wilbur, does become a 'refuge'—not an expedition moving toward the hidden treasure of richer levels of reality, but a citadel where one can find protection from reality. . . . Wilbur almost never sees objects in the tangible world as valid messages of the ideal world." Critics of the 1970s and later have done their job in demonstrating that Wilbur is not nearly that simple, that in the paradoxes lie the richness and the fun—but Johnson can be profitably read as a stage in Wilbur criticism and as an impasse that some readers still hit in reading the poems.

Three essays by Bruce Michelson treat subjects that have consistently engaged Wilbur's critics: his relationship with Poe, his definition as a constrained or visionary poet, and his extraordinary handling of language. Michelson's earliest piece on Wilbur, in the Spring 1978 *Southern Review,* looks closely at the impact of Poe upon Wilbur. Holding that a "quarrel between artists, especially one that a living man picks with a dead one, can never be assumed a clash of opposites," Michelson shows "how very *un*opposite these poets are" and focuses on Wilbur's adaptation of some of Poe's most powerful symbols: the abyss, the whirlpool, the dream landscape. The critic discusses "Marginalia," "For the New Railway Station in Rome," "The Undead," "Merlin," and "Beowulf " in some detail and concludes that "Wilbur strives to be an artist of both intense imagination and wakeful skepticism. He is a poet struggling to speak . . . to a world which as either despaired of the power of imaginative flight or given itself excessively to hopeless and solipsistic fantasy." In a follow-up piece in a 1979 *Southern Review* Michelson discusses *The Mind-Reader* in some depth, focusing on Wilbur's shift toward a "new roughness," wildness, and defiance in voice. The critic discusses "Cottage Street, 1953," "Children of Darkness," "What's Good for the Soul is Good for Sales," "Sleepless at Crown Point," and the title poem. The narrator of "The Mind-Reader," the critic contends, is an exploration, for Wilbur, of a quite personal concern: "for this mind worn down with detail and misfortune and all those perceptions which can break anyone who seeks the 'resonance in all their fretting' *is* Wilbur, the other side of the man—not simply the visionary that he struggles against becoming, but the visionary that, for all controlled surfaces, he always is." In his 1982 *Massachusetts Review* essay, Michelson argues that Wilbur's extraordinary use of language, particularly his many puns and spreads of meaning, "is an attempt to use magical, incantatory, creative forces. His famous wordplay is in fact the very essence of his imaginative transcendence of the world, as well as his reconciliation *with* the world." The discussion of wordplay's "serious" side in "The Regatta," "Year's End," "Love Calls Us to Things of the World," "In a Church-yard," and "The Mind-Reader" illustrates the variations and enrichments which Richard Wilbur's strategy—something more than a strategy—has undergone in the past thirty years.

Cumulative Indexes

Cumulative Index to Authors

Cumulative Index to Critics

Critic Index

Critic Index   *Contemporary Authors*

Hoag, Gerald   1:289
Hochman, Baruch   2:200
Hoffa, William   1:255
Hoffman, Daniel   2:200
Hoffman, Frederick J.   1:329; 2:146, 300
Hoffman, Michael J.   1:139
Hoffman, Nancy Yanes   2:330, 331
Hoffman, Steven K.   2:199
Hogan, Robert E.   1:381
Holder, Alan   1:73; 2:194, 197, 202
Hollahan, Eugene   1:154
Hollenberg, Susan W.   2:285
Holley, Linda Tarte   2:94, 104
Hollowell, John   1:258
Holmes, John   2:296, 302
Honton, Margaret   2:331
Horn, Bernard   1:259
Howard, Jane   1:20, 359; 2:21
Howard, Maureen   1:315
Howard, Peter   1:243
Howard, Richard   2:97, 321
Howard, Zelma Turner   1:401
Howe, Irving   1:32, 36, 141
Howell, Elmo   1:419
Hughes, Daniel J.   1:137
Hughes, Langston   1:29
Hugo, Richard   2:287
Hummer, T. R.   2:93
Humphrey, Robert   2:141
Hungerford, Edward   2:154
Hunt, George   1:172, 173, 174, 192, 369, 370, 377, 381
Hunt, John W.   1:207
Hutchinson, George   2:262
Hutton, Joan   2:346
Hux, Samuel   1:153
Hyde, Lewis   2:21
Hyman, Stanley Edgar   1:286, 374
Ilson, Robert   2:200
Inge, M. Thomas   1:33, 286
Irving, John   1:186
Isaac, Harold B.   1:30
Isaacs, Neil D.   1:400
Isaacs, Stan   1:242
Italia, Paul G.   2:104
Jacobson, Daniel   1:31
James, Clive   2:357
Jameson, Fredric   1:257

Janeway, Elizabeth   1:169
Janoff, Bruce   1:69, 211
Jarrell, Mary   2:142, 144, 146, 148, 149, 152, 157, 158, 160
Jarrell, Randall   2:22, 59, 194, 195, 197
Jefchak, Andrew   1:134
Jensen, Ejner J.   2:360, 361
Johnson, Glen M.   1:190, 191
Johnson, Greg   2:332
Johnson, James William   1:318, 320
Johnson, Kenneth   2:366, 367
Johnson, Rosemary   2:325, 332
Johnson, Tom   2:231
Jolly, John   2:104, 105
Jones, A. R.   2:330
Jones, Alun R.   1:411, 413
Jones, Harry L.   1:34
Jones, John Griffin   1:397
Jones, Mary E.   1:19
Jones, Peter   2:161
Jones, Peter G.   1:212
Jones, Roger   1:142
Jones, William M.   1:412
Jong, Erica   2:325
Jordan, Enoch P.   1:72
Joseph, Gerhard   1:65
Juhasz, Suzanne   2:327, 328
Kael, Pauline   1:332
Kahane, Claire   1:345
Kahn, E. J., Jr.   1:168
Kakutani, Michiko   1:184, 362
Kalstone, David   2:46, 47, 52, 53, 55, 61, 67, 68, 69
Kammer, Jeanne H.   2:330
Kapp, Isa   1:186
Karl, Frederick R.   1:175, 205, 213, 215
Katz, Joseph   2:315
Kaufmann, Donald L.   1:243, 244
Kazin, Alfred   1:149, 173, 180, 254, 281, 286, 333; 2:156, 157
Keegan, Brenda M.   1:203
Keen, William P.   1:189
Kehler, Joel R.   1:137
Keller, Lynn   2:46, 65, 66
Kellman, Steven G.   1:289
Kelly, Frank K.   1:310
Kelly, Richard J.   2:19

381

Critic Index